KEN SARO-WIWA

A Three Continents Book

KEN SARO-WIWA

Writer and Political Activist

edited by
Craig W. McLuckie
Aubrey McPhail

LYNNE
RIENNER
PUBLISHERS

BOULDER
LONDON

Published in the United States of America in 2000 by
Lynne Rienner Publishers, Inc.
1800 30th Street, Boulder, Colorado 80301
www.rienner.com

and in the United Kingdom by
Lynne Rienner Publishers, Inc.
3 Henrietta Street, Covent Garden, London WC2E 8LU

Library of Congress Cataloging-in-Publication Data
Ken Saro-Wiwa : writer and political activist / edited by Craig W.
  McLuckie and Aubrey McPhail.
     p.   cm.
  "A three continents book."
  Includes bibliographical references and index.
  ISBN 0-89410-883-2 (hc : alk. paper)
  1. Saro-Wiwa, Ken, 1941–   2. Authors, Nigerian—20th century—
Biography. 3. Political activists—Nigeria—Biography.
I. McLuckie, Craig W. II. McPhail, Aubrey, 1956–   .
PR9387.9.S27Z74   1999
823—dc21   99-31267
                                                                CIP

British Cataloguing in Publication Data
A Cataloguing in Publication record for this book
is available from the British Library.

Printed and bound in the United States of America

The paper used in this publication meets the requirements
of the American National Standard for Permanence of
Paper for Printed Library Materials Z39.48-1984.

5 4 3 2 1

This volume is dedicated to the activists,
and to Jeanne Boekelheide,
and George and Ferne Boekelheide

Contents

Acknowledgments   ix

PART 1   THE CONTEXT

1   Ken Saro-Wiwa, or "The Pacification of the Primitive
    Tribes of the Lower Niger"
    Charles Lock   3

2   A Political Assessment: *Genocide in Nigeria:*
    The Ogoni Tragedy
    Joseph McLaren   17

PART 2   THE LITERARY EXPERIMENTS

3   Literary Memoirs and Diaries: Soyinka, Amadi,
    and Saro-Wiwa
    Craig W. McLuckie   29

4   The Poetry: *Songs in a Time of War*
    Tanure Ojaide   53

5   The Short Fiction: *A Forest of Flowers* and *Adaku and*
    Other Stories
    Aubrey McPhail   69

6   The Novel: *Sozaboy: A Novel in Rotten English*
    Maureen N. Eke   87

PART 3   THE PUBLIC MAN

7   Pipe Dreams: Ken Saro-Wiwa, Environmental Justice, and
     Microminority Rights
     Rob Nixon   109

8   "Buried Beneath Six Feet of Crude Oil": State-Sponsored
     Death and the Absent Body of Ken Saro-Wiwa
     Misty L. Bastian   127

9   Saro-Wiwa the Publisher
     Laura Neame   153

PART 4   POPULAR MEDIA

10   The Children's Series
     John LeBlanc   177

11   *Dream of Sologa, Eneka,* and *The Supreme Commander:*
     The Theater of Ken Saro-Wiwa
     Chris Dunton   201

PART 5   EPILOGUE

12   "From This Hurt to the Unquestioning World":
     Seven Poems from *Delta Blues*
     Tanure Ojaide, with an Introduction by John Lent   215

APPENDIXES

Appendix 1: Chronology of Ken Saro-Wiwa's Life
     Laura Neame   233
Appendix 2: Chronology of the Nigerian Civil War
     Ross Tyner   237
Appendix 3: An Annotated Bibliography
     Craig W. McLuckie and James Gibbs   245

The Contributors   285
Index   287
About the Book   291

Acknowledgments

I am pleased to acknowledge the assistance and cooperation of the following people and institutions: Ross Tyner and Laura Neame, librarians, Okanagan University College; Faith Peyton, Inter-Library Loans, Okanagan University College; Jake Block and Steve Rosco, Computing Services, Okanagan University College; the OUCFA Professional Development Fund; the library staff at the Universities of Washington (Seattle), Alberta (Edmonton), Stirling, and Calgary.

Jean Hay, Lesli Brooks Athanasoulis, Beth Partin, and Sally Glover of Lynne Rienner Publishers have been key figures in this project. Their advice, industry, and encouragement permit us to acknowledge them as de facto coeditors. Angela Smith, director of the Centre for Commonwealth Studies, University of Stirling, offered a list of potential contributors; our discussions and correspondence on matters postcolonial formed a backdrop to this project.

I have had the opportunity of exploring the relationship between political commitment and the literary arts with numerous classes; particular appreciation is extended to seminar participants in "Literature of Africa and the Caribbean": Dave, Cait, Mike, Ginger, Shannon, April, Maria, and Kathleen.

Michelle McLuckie held the line for seventy-five days in frigid (political, economic, meteorological) conditions; her example and commitment are exemplary. Work of this nature requires the forbearance of a great many people: thanks go to Ronald and Doreen; Peter Murray; John and Shirley Murphy; B. J. Tyner; Francis Aleba; and especially to Emily, Nathan, Jessica, Anna, Callum, Tia, and Max.

Ronald Ayling, professor emeritus, University of Alberta, has assisted this project in a variety of ways—from making materials available to reading each chapter. His advice, his attention here and in his own work to an elegant prose style that communicates effectively, and his commitment as a human being are all deeply appreciated.

To risk a Kelmanesque phrase: thank Christ they're still around.

* * *

The editors gratefully acknowledge Ken Wiwa, son of the late Ken Saro-Wiwa, and the Maggie Noach Literary Agency, literary executor of the Estate of Ken Saro-Wiwa, for their kind permission to quote from the works of Ken Saro-Wiwa in this volume.

The editors also acknowledge Indiana University Press and *Research in African Literatures* for permission to reprint Chris Dunton's essay.

Craig W. McLuckie

Myth draws selectively from the past, but its key purpose is to provide a contemporary reservoir of legitimation for belief and action. The . . . myth lends itself to two main interpretations, an activist one which seeks the resolution of the apparent contradiction between real social inequality and an egalitarian ideology in favour of the latter. However, there is also a second, more conservative interpretation of the myth, that if man is primordially equal, then social structural inequalities do not matter, and nothing needs to be done. It is sufficient that "we're a' Jock Tamson's bairns."

—*David McCrone*

PART 1

The Context

1

Ken Saro-Wiwa, or "The Pacification of the Primitive Tribes of the Lower Niger"

Charles Lock

Nigerian literature first came to international attention forty years ago. An initiating and defining moment of anglophone writing in Africa—Chinua Achebe's *Things Fall Apart* (1958)—has found its gruesome prolepsis fulfilled. That short novel concludes with the district commissioner—the servant of empire—planning to write a book:

> Every day brought him some new material. The story of this man who had killed a messenger and hanged himself would make interesting reading. One could almost write a whole chapter on him. Perhaps not a whole chapter but a reasonable paragraph, at any rate. . . . He had already chosen the title of the book, after much thought: *The Pacification of the Primitive Tribes of the Lower Niger.* (Achebe, pp. 147–148)

That title—parodic of colonial discourse, of its customary euphemisms, of its presentation of autobiography and memoir in the guise of history and anthropology—could well serve as a summary of the fate of the Ogoni. In 1958, African literature discovered a voice, and the Shell Petroleum Development Corporation discovered oil in Rivers State, in the Niger Delta of southeastern Nigeria: river and nation fortuitously named for the black gold that would bring prosperity to many, and misery to a few (Vidal, pp. 20).[1]

SARO-WIWA, THE OGONI, AND SHELL

Ogoni! Ogoni!

Ogoni is the land
The people, Ogoni
The agony of trees dying

3

In ancestral farmlands
Streams polluted weeping
Filth into murky rivers
It is the poisoned air
Coursing the luckless lungs
Of dying children
Ogoni is the dream
Breaking the looping chain
Around the drooping neck
of a shell-shocked land.[2]

"Shell-shocked" is a two-faced homophone. We hear oil, and we see Ogoni divided by trenches, another Flanders Fields; and what links oil and trenches is gas: gas-flaring, poison gas. The simple chiasmus of the poem's opening: "Ogoni is the land / The people, Ogoni"—writes the inseparability of the Ogoni, the people, from Ogoni the land, a people doomed by their tree-like immobility, their rootedness: not just an indigenous people but an ecosystem, almost an ecosyntax. "To the Ogoni, the land and the people are one and are expressed as such in our local languages" (Saro-Wiwa, *A Month,* p. 2), wrote Ken Saro-Wiwa in July 1994. And the repetition of Ogoni makes its "agony" as inevitable as an echo. It was this poem, written in prison, that gave rise to the slogans of the Greenpeace protest against the environmental despoliation of Ogoni—"A Shell-shocked land" and "Get the (S)hell out of Nigeria"—slogans that were then taken up around the world by those protesting against the imprisonment and trial of Ken Saro-Wiwa.

One cannot write about Saro-Wiwa without writing about the Ogoni, whose symbol he remains and whose unofficial leader he was, as head of the Movement for the Survival of the Ogoni People (MOSOP). Nor can the name of Saro-Wiwa be mentioned without invoking that of Shell. One still lacks the evidence to blame Shell directly for the execution at about 11:30 A.M. Friday, 10 November 1995, of Saro-Wiwa and eight other leaders of MOSOP. Saro-Wiwa was not alone, either in his struggle or in his death.

It has been alleged—in *The Drilling Fields,* the Channel 4 documentary first broadcast in Britain in May 1995—that at a top-level meeting of Shell executives in London, a decision was taken to impede the work of MOSOP, and to put Saro-Wiwa under surveillance. This is sketched by Saro-Wiwa himself: "Shell had been working extraordinarily hard to destroy all my efforts. Now, do not ask me for hard evidence. These things are never done in writing" (Saro-Wiwa, *A Month,* pp. 146, 160). Shortly before his arrest, when he first heard rumor of the allegations that would be brought against him and eight other Ogoni leaders, Saro-Wiwa declared: "They are going to arrest us all and execute us. All for Shell"

(Greenpeace pamphlet, summer 1995). Most damning of all, one of the prosecution witnesses confessed during the trial in October 1995-that he, like other witnesses, had been offered bribes of £300 (300 pounds, a very large sum in the Nigerian economy) by Shell to make statements incriminating Saro-Wiwa.[3] Furthermore, Saro-Wiwa's brother, Dr. Owens Wiwa, alleged (after the execution) that Shell had some months earlier offered to negotiate a deal whereby Shell would arrange for Saro-Wiwa to be released without his case going to trial—if Saro-Wiwa would promise to make no further criticisms of Shell. Owens Wiwa refused to negotiate under such conditions (Cooly, pp. 18–20).

By a process of no little irregularity, Saro-Wiwa and his associates were tried by a special tribunal in Port Harcourt, the capital of Rivers State. They were charged with the murder of four Ogoni chiefs, who had disagreed with Saro-Wiwa and the MOSOP leadership and had advocated support for the federal government of Gen. Sani Abacha. The murders took place on 21 May 1994. The defendants were not allowed to select their own defense lawyers. It was not necessary even to establish that Saro-Wiwa (or any of the eight codefendants) was at the scene of the crime. They were judged to have abetted and incited, even in and by their absence from the scene of the crime, and were sentenced to death on 31 October. Eight days later the sentence was confirmed by the Nigerian government. The Heads of Commonwealth States were meeting in Auckland, and hope appeared to rest on their collective protest and especially on the personal authority of Nelson Mandela.

The South African president did nothing dramatic and spoke, somewhat mysteriously, of the value of quiet diplomacy. The cynical reaction of the day was that Mandela did not want to endanger Shell's involvement in the fragile economy of his own country. Mandela's failure of both tact and judgment forms a melancholy sideshow. (Let it be said that within days of the executions, Mandela promised to work for a complete oil embargo against Nigeria; more significantly, he threatened to suspend Shell's operations in South Africa if Shell failed to cooperate.) (Let it also be said, in a separate parenthesis, that Saro-Wiwa's son, Ken Wiwa, flew to Auckland to make his appeal and was prevented, by the organizers of the Commonwealth Conference, from meeting Mandela. Not until after the conference, and long after it was too late, did Mandela learn that Ken Wiwa had been in Auckland.)

Shell's response statement (undated) "to the allegations put forward in *Delta Force* asserts that Shell Nigeria has never been approached or pressured 'by the military to provide input.'. . . Nor would Shell Nigeria do so if it had been approached." This is strictly true: Shell's dealings were not with the military but with the police. Thanks to a dispute between Shell and XM Federal Limited (and its Nigerian subsidiary Humanitex Government Licensed Dealers on Fire-Arms) that came to the Federal High Court in Lagos in July 1995, an incriminating array of documents was brought into the public domain. A letter, for example, from Shell Nigeria, dated 19 January 1994, to the inspector general of police in Lagos, asked for 150,000 rounds of 9 mm ammunition and 130 semiautomatic rifles, only six of which were to be used in Lagos: sixty-four were for Warri and sixty for Port Harcourt, both in Rivers State.

The accusations that Saro-Wiwa made, in various speeches and writings, about the "genocide" and "environmental devastation" being perpetrated in and on the Ogoni by collusion between Shell and the Nigerian government are hardly refuted by such evidence:

> Shell . . . having successfully waged an ecological war against the Ogoni people since 1958, has been giving protection money to the Nigerian security agencies to complete the genocide which it began. Of the 126 Ogoni villages, the military regime have burned around 30. (Saro-Wiwa, quoted in Gerner, *Index,* pp. 4–5, 219)

Saro-Wiwa was an exceptionally energetic writer, publicist, and activist, who used hyperbole to publicize the sufferings of the Ogoni, appealing to such dissenting factions and sequestered outposts of conscience and good faith as have survived the global commodification of behavior, the market valuation of values. At first Saro-Wiwa's outrage was pitched at a political level—the corruption of Nigerian society—and then at an economic level, with accusations against multinational interference in local communities. As Saro-Wiwa became more attuned to the lobbying procedure and the arcane hierarchy of grievance that pertains at the United Nations and other international bodies, he focused on two issues: the environment and the rights of indigenous peoples (see Saro-Wiwa, *A Month,* pp. 93–101).

Through shrewdness and determination, Saro-Wiwa managed to articulate the plight of the Ogoni in the terms of almost all the good causes of our day: he could appeal to the ideals of both Greenpeace and Amnesty International, to International PEN and the UN Working Group on Indigenous Populations. Such unlikely and even unholy alliances drove capitalism and its governments into disgraceful, shameful collusion in the executions. Most shockingly, it can be said that no judicial murder has been carried out in such a brazen absence of secrecy. Without even waiting for the dispersal of the Commonwealth Heads of State, the military government of Nigeria had the executions carried out. Ideals have seldom appeared quite so powerless, almost contemptibly feeble.

SARO-WIWA AND LANGUAGE

The novel has been characterized as the literary genre in which linguistic deviation has been tolerated. It is worth noting that poetry and drama, as oral forms, seldom trouble with deviant orthography. Tonal variation need not be signaled at the orthographic level for it to be realized in enunciation. By contrast, in M. M. Bakhtin's words, the novel "alone is receptive to new forms of mute perception" (Bakhtin, p. 3). The occurrence of orthographic irregularities in fiction is thus closely involved with the "muteness" of the genre. Characters in fiction are represented orthographically as speaking in ways that reveal their identity, their difference from the standard. This differs markedly from the occurrences of nonstandard orthography in poetry and drama, which almost always serves a comic purpose. Actually to hear deviant speech is, it seems, necessarily comic. That is the difference between Shakespearean "Mummerset" and the somber irregularities of the unheard speech in *Wuthering Heights* or *Tess of the d'Urbervilles*.

Until quite recently, however, orthographic deviation in fiction was confined to direct speech. Orthographic standardization and stylistic purity are instruments of a central authority. Deviation and even stylistic opacity can be seen in terms of resistance. Each instance of linguistic resistance is a mark of the regional or peripheral and a constitution of the localized particular voice against, or merely outside, the general chorus, the symphony of accordant voices. For Bakhtin, the history of the novel is the history of resistance to the homogenizing discourses of modernity. In view of the metaphorical gathering of discourse, currency, and purity—a clustering that runs through and can be traced back to the sources of Western literature—it is fitting that the first novel in which orthographic deviance spills over the banks of its quotation marks should have been a novel about the Mississippi. Mark Twain's *Huckleberry Finn* (1884) muddies the waters of English. T. S. Eliot writes of the Mississippi: "I think that the river is / A strong brown god—sullen, untamed, and intractable"[4] and thus figures that river in contrast to the Spenserian well of "English undefiled" and the river as figure of poetry in "Prothalamion": "Sweet Thames, run softly, till I end my song" (Spencer, p. 760).

The River Niger is of course our clue, a river named for blackness, yet a river and a delta not so black as to be beyond pollution by the spilling and overflowing of oil. One hundred years after the publication of *Huckleberry Finn,* Ken Saro-Wiwa issued *Sozaboy* (1985) with that most remarkable, defiant subtitle: *A Novel in Rotten English*. The putrid corruption and the shameless deeds of commercial exploitation and degradation are both to be opposed by a novel whose language seeks to be anything but clear, limpid, or transparent, to break every rule of *Modern English Usage* as propounded by the happily-named Fowler. The "Author's Note" to *Sozaboy* explains:

> Sozaboy's language is what I call "rotten English," a mixture of Nigerian pidgin English, broken English and occasional flashes of good, even

idiomatic English. This language is disordered and disorderly. Born of a mediocre education and severely limited opportunities, it borrows words, patterns and images freely from the mother-tongue and finds expression in a very limited English vocabulary. To its speakers, it has the advantage of having no rules and no syntax. It thrives on lawlessness, and is part of the dislocated and discordant society in which Sozaboy must live, move, and have not his being. (Saro-Wiwa, *Sozaboy,* p. xi)

We find examples in Saro-Wiwa's earliest writings, such as "High Life," a story first published in 1969:

All I was thinking was how I will get one portable damsel to deposit in my room for that night. I was near the market place when I saw one. That damsel was a bundle of sophistication I tell you. And she was perambulating lackadaisically along the road. (Saro-Wiwa, *A Forest,* p. 70)

That sort of lexical and idiomatic incongruity appears stylistically absurd and politically inauthentic. It does not represent any one of the numerous Englishes now spoken in the nations of the Commonwealth. In making a plural of English, one makes of each variety a self-sufficient and self-validating language; one no longer speaks in terms of dialect and degrees of deviation.[5] The claim of Ebonics is not that there is such a way of speaking, but that it has the order and rationality that we ascribe to *language.* The latter assumption is the greatest fallacy of all, the one that we have lived with and within since discourse and reason were comprised within the one word *logos.*

Instances of modified and internally consistent Englishes have been represented by various postcolonial writers. With few exceptions, by using deviant orthography and syntax, such writers aim to represent consistently the deviations of a particular group of speakers. They remain attached to the logocentric assumption that writing represents speech. Bakhtin insists that novels are "mute," and a few linguists have explored the ways in which novelistic discourse resists or dispenses with utterance.[6] Saro-Wiwa's originality lies precisely here, in the understanding that a novel is not obliged to represent a voice, and therefore that its language is free to be deviant without being consistently so. Furthermore, the representation of deviation as consistent may well be a falsification and one that serves the homogenizing imperative to equate language with rationality.

By mixing the discourses, one creates an impossible language, according to those linguists who would maintain that a language must have rules and syntax. "Rotten English" is a rottenness not of speaking (for which of us speaks grammatically? Whose accent gives voice to standard orthography?) but of writing. *Sozaboy* is intensely, almost hypnotically readable—and unspeakably so.

SARO-WIWA AND LITERATURE

Saro-Wiwa makes a distinction between the rotten English that forms and informs the entire text of *Sozaboy,* and that which represents the speech of Nigerians, such as Madam in *Basi and Company:*

> Madam spoke different Englishes according to her mood. [This sentence is in the idiom not of rotten English, but of postcolonial academic jargon.] Sometimes she spoke standard English, at other times pidgin English, and she had an English reserved for the most vicious moments—rotten English which was a mixture of all types of English, her mother-tongue which she hardly ever spoke, and the predominant Yoruba of Adetola Street. (Saro-Wiwa, *Basi,* p. 30)

It should be said that there is very little dialect in *Basi and Company:* the speeches are written in standard English, obviously to be enunciated by Nigerian actors, for whom standard orthography—also used in the connecting narratives—is the normative representation of the way Nigerians speak.

Sozaboy is even less protected from spillage than *Huckleberry Finn* is: the latter book is at least structured in an orderly fashion. In *Sozaboy* the rottenness spreads even into the structure of the book, the paratextual elements.[7] The chapters are not called chapters but "lombers," that is, numbers. This is how Lomber One begins:

> Although, everybody in Dukana was happy at first. All the nine villages were dancing and we were eating plenty maize with pear and knacking tory [gossiping] under the moon. Because the work on the farm have finished and the yams were growing well well. And because the old, bad government have dead, and the new government of soza and police have come.

Two pages later we read the first sentence again, this time with its grammar somewhat amended:

> So, although everyone was happy at first, after some time, everything begin to spoil small by small and they were saying that trouble have started. People were not happy to hear that there is trouble everywhere. . . . Radio begin dey hala as 'e never hala before. Big big grammar. Long long words. Every time.
>
> Before before, the grammar was not plenty and everybody was happy. But now grammar begin to plenty and people were not happy. As grammar plenty, na so trouble plenty. And as trouble plenty, na so plenty people were dying. (p. 3)

Rather than claim the dignity of a language for each variety of English, the eponymous narrator of *Sozaboy* associates war with grammar and peace with the agrammatical. The dislocated and discordant language fits and even honors a society for whom order is exclusively regimented, military.

The biafran war has begun by Lomber Five (Saro-Wiwa insisted on spelling "biafra" without an upper-case initial, so strong was his distaste for separatist movements within Nigeria):

> The man with fine shirt stood up. And begin to talk in English. Fine fine English. Big big words. Grammar. Fantastic. Overwhelming. Generally. In particular and in general. Haba, God no go vex. But he did not stop there. The big grammar continued. Odious. Destruction. Fighting. I understand that one. Henceforth. General mobilisation. All citizens. Able-bodied. Join the military. His Excellency. Powers conferred on us. Volunteers. Conscription. Big big words. Long long grammar. (pp. 46–47)

And so our nameless narrator, our eponymous anonymous is conscripted and becomes a reluctant Sozaboy. This pronunciation of "Soldier-boy" is, we learn from *Basi and Company* (p. 19), distinctive to the Niger Delta, the River States, including Ogoni. Their "jays" becomes "zees," and Dandy has special difficulty with the word "exchange" (p. 127).[8] "Sozaboy" is a name given to our hero by others. Though we have no direct indication, it may be that his trouble is partly because he is called "Sozaboy"—not "Sojaboy." The deviation from deviation contrasts obviously with the regular orthographics of the Latinate "big big words." We may note that the reading of the above passage is amusing when muted; when voiced, we must say such phrases as "Powers conferred on us" in a voice that is not Sozaboy's. "Rotten English" takes advantage of the muteness of the two-voiced or unvoiced dialogical text.

SARO-WIWA, WEALTH, AND SOCIETY

The ambiguity of the voice or tone in the dialogical text is matched by Saro-Wiwa's own conflicting voices and contrasting loyalties. Let us read "About the Author" on the back of one of his (self-published) books:

> Ken Saro-Wiwa was born in Bori, Rivers State of Nigeria on 10th October, 1941. He took a scholarship to the prestigious [variant: elitist] Government College, Umuahia, and studied at the University of Ibadan. He has taught in Nigeria's universities, served in government at Cabinet level and is an established businessman [his business organization is Saros International Limited]. [In 1967, during the Nigerian civil war, he was pressed into public life as Administrator of the war-ravaged oil port of Bonny. He held the portfolios of Education and Information in the government of Rivers State from 1968 to 1973. In the latter year, he

turned to business, establishing his own trading firm. He has continued to play a role in Nigerian public life and was recently appointed to Nigeria's National Directorate for Social Mobilisation.] He has travelled extensively worldwide. He is married with children.

Such a profile is rather different from that presented by the aggrieved indignation of the media, of an Ogoni "pure and simple," an oppressed representative of an oppressed tribe. Different, also, from that presented by Shell and the Nigerian government, for whom Saro-Wiwa was a dangerous and irresponsible terrorist. Saro-Wiwa was successful in a variety of activities, political, financial, and literary. He attended the most prestigious school in Nigeria, Government College, Umuahia, and thus grew up with the future military, political, and business leaders of the independent nation. He was no outsider, no stranger to power and its corridors: "Indeed," writes Saro-Wiwa in *A Month and a Day,* "most of the top Nigerian employees of Shell happen to have been my contemporaries at school and university" (p. 167). In *On a Darkling Plain,* his account of the biafran war, Saro-Wiwa explains how he maintained relationships with Ibos: "Ordinary Ibos, of course, found a ready welcome in the homes of their friends and associates. Like others, I played host to a number of Old Boys of Government College, Umuahia. No war, however acrimonious, could ever separate Umuahians" (Saro-Wiwa, *Darkling,* p. 236). The only thing that could separate Umuahians from one another was an individual act of "retribalization"—the rejection of one's achieved "detribalization." Saro-Wiwa himself was accused of fermenting strife between tribes even though it seemed clear that the political future of Nigeria had to lie in detribalization. Yet he always insisted that he was not a separatist, that he was a Nigerian patriot, and that any other position could lead only to another civil war.

Not for Saro-Wiwa the political gambit of "going native," of renouncing European dress and disdaining his educational and social privileges. Saro-Wiwa's contempt for Lt. Col. Chukwuemeka Odumegwu Ojukwu, the culprit of the biafran war, reaches its magnificent crescendo when Ojukwu—who was educated not at Umuahia but at a leading public school in Britain—is invested as a "chief":

> In his village of Nnewi, there are people waiting to make him a "chief." Iboland has been remarkably void of "chiefs" in the past. These days, honorific chiefs are two a penny. . . . But Ojukwu is named "The Ikemba of Nnewi," whatever that means. The bush has reclaimed its own. Goodbye, Epsom College! Goodbye Oxford! (Saro-Wiwa, *Darkling,* p. 255)

Ojukwu (but not Saro-Wiwa) attended Oxford; Idi Amin, Sandhurst; Pol Pot, the Sorbonne: the elite academies of the West have nurtured serpents.

But, we might ask, have these men really been traitors to the West or its most subtle, devious allies?

There was little self-evidently virtuous or noble in the career of Saro-Wiwa. He had many opportunities to advance or to enrich himself, and he took them. As a businessman, he was extremely successful and enjoyed considerable wealth, sufficient to pay for his children to be educated at the most expensive English boarding schools. Whatever the nature of the business, there is no escaping Saro-Wiwa's involvement in the very same sources of greed and corruption that filled the foreign bank accounts of the late General Abacha's military regime. Above all, necessarily, from oil revenues, for there can be no wealth in Nigeria that is not immediately dependent on oil: oil accounts for 96 percent of Nigeria's gross national product (GNP).

It may be embarrassing to mention that one of the groups actively protesting the imprisonment and trial of Saro-Wiwa was made up of the fellow parents of Etonian pupils, among them Lady Antonia Pinter (see the *Weekly Telegraph,* 1 March 1995). This is not a plausible postcolonial scenario. Or perhaps it is. At any rate, those parents included some influential figures on the *Times* newspaper, and the *Times* has consistently served as a prominent advocate for and source of information about Saro-Wiwa and the Ogoni. Oddly, the influential group of Etonian parents did not significantly overlap with the equally or even more powerful group of Shell's major shareholders. One might say that the fate of Saro-Wiwa was decided less by a special tribunal in Port Harcourt than in the British establishment, through a sort of civil war between the City and the Old School Tie. Yet in comparison with the retribalization of Ojukwu or Pol Pot, such middle-class aspirations seem distinctly unharmful.

One should not skirt the issue of Saro-Wiwa's wealth. That he knew all facets of Nigerian society explains his power as a satirist: as an Ogoni he knew what it was to be exploited, and as a successful businessman he must have known something of the joys and rewards of exploitation. In Nigeria he was best known neither as an Ogoni activist, nor as a politician, nor as a businessman, but as the author and producer of the television serial *Basi and Company,* watched weekly by 30 million Nigerians. The satire is directed against those who are constantly dreaming of scams to make a million without doing any work. If the satire has the force of precision, it may be because the author knew all the secrets of which his characters were shown to be so foolishly dreaming.

Oil pollutes, and when it so dominates an economy as it does Nigeria's, its corrupting influence cannot be contained. Nobody can be untouched or claim to be pure. In a speech that he was not allowed to make at his trial but that was smuggled out of prison (by whose connivance?), Saro-Wiwa claims that not only he and his fellow defendants are on trial but also Shell, and the military regime. And he continues:

> On trial also is the Nigerian nation, its present rulers and all those who assist them. . . . The military do not act alone. They are supported by a gaggle of politicians, lawyers, judges, academics and businessmen, all of them hiding under the claim that they are only doing their duty. . . . We all stand on trial, my lord, for by our actions we have denigrated our country. . . . As we subscribe to the subnormal and accept double standards, as we lie and cheat openly, as we protect injustice and oppression. . . .

And the speech concludes with a plea not of righteous innocence but a denial of wrongdoing in a restricted instance: "In my innocence of the false charges I face here . . . " (Saro-Wiwa, quoted in Gerner, *Index,* pp. 6, 166).

Ken Saro-Wiwa was deeply implicated in his country's corruption: there lies his power as a satirist. He did not claim spotless innocence, and that is his attraction. Yet it has made his case difficult to advocate for those who like their good causes to be shining white and crystal clear. It is this ethical "confusion" or "pollution" that accounts for and is reflected by the unprecedented qualities of his prose.

In playing such a variety of roles, Saro-Wiwa also commanded a variety of languages—including four of those spoken by the Ogoni—and, most important, a range of Englishes. "Rotten English" can be seen as a tribute to both the sad necessity and the cheerful possibility of using so many dialects, so many variants, so many registers. Only novelistic discourse can hope to represent the linguistic situation of a society as linguistically complex as Nigeria.

There could have been no clearer evidence of the link between the writer and the activist—nor that such a link must be established at the discursive level—than a piece of prose that was issued eleven days after the execution of Saro-Wiwa. The following appeared in most of the major newspapers in the English-speaking world on 21 November 1995: "The following is a message from Shell International Petroleum Company Limited, London, England. Clear Thinking in Troubled Times."

CONCLUSION

Shell's defiance and transparent hypocrisy (what was that appeal—"The Chairman of the Shell Group of Companies sent a personal letter appealing to the Nigerian Head of State to show clemency on humanitarian grounds" (Cooly, "Shell's Secret Dealings," p. 18)—if not intervention?) is not motivated, we should understand, by crude greed and profit. There is money in goodwill, and Shell's reputation has suffered drastically. What is at stake is black as oil: if Shell had not signed the $4 billion deal (for a liquefied natural gas plant on Bonny Island; completion in 1999), as it did just five days after the executions, the Nigerian government would presumably have leaked to the press some of its correspondence with Shell

(Bates and Bowcott, "Shell Undeterred," p. 1). Shell—and the British and Dutch governments seem to be deeply implicated also—is at the mercy of the pollution controls of the Nigerian government.

Yet these pollutions, rebellious in nature, threaten both. The confusion of Englishes is more than the literary excitements of postcolonialism or fashionable dialogism. The Austrian satirist Karl Kraus declared that the fate of civilization hung on the right placement of a comma: Saro-Wiwa remarked that "proofreading has become the most interesting part of publishing for me. Will I ever publish an error-free book?" (Saro-Wiwa, *A Month*, p. 59). When the British had an empire, there was one English, and the myth of the language and its right usage was bound up with myths of transcendental order and purpose. The Shell advertisement unnervingly pays tribute to Sozaboy in its very unspeakability: it can be read aloud only as a parody.

Also in that week after the executions, as Shell was directing its powers of pollution against the English language, General Abacha launched "a campaign to clean up [sic] his image abroad and a financial appeal for the Sani Abacha Foundation to Promote Peace, Unity and the Brotherhood of Man" (Vidal, p. 4). Such a complicit disorderliness, a coalition of linguistic chaoses (if one may make a plural of chaos), might make one nostalgic for the days when hypocrisy was well ordered and elegantly phrased.

What fascinates us in language and prompts us to wonder is not only how it conceals, but that it conceals: "style" can be an index of shame. Saro-Wiwa is the victim, among much else, of the linguistic shamelessness—the worldwide shamelessness of all the Englishes—that he deployed so cunningly: perambulating lackadaisically. What might he have made of Shell's determination to *bestow* on the *public* the *right* to clear *thinking?*

It is truly cleansing to return to the linguistic impurities of Sozaboy who, at the end of the novel, returns to Dukana from the biafran war and learns that his mother and wife have both been killed and that, because he is himself presumed dead, he will be taken for a ghost. As his friend Duzia tells him, the villagers like to kill ghosts:

> So I said to myself that if I did not die for Iwoama and I did not die in refugee camp and I did not die that time that Manmuswak took me from prison to shoot me and the other prisoners, God forbid that I will die when the war have already finish. And even if I will die sef, I cannot just stay in that Dukana and allow people to come and kill me like goat or rat or ant when I am Sozaboy. So now I just think to myself that as Duzia is cripple man, he cannot follow me and if I run away the only thing he can do is to hala and call people and since they are all fearing and sitting in their rotten house with every door closed, they will not hear him. And even sef, I do not think that Duzia will shout because if he shout and the people come out and they do not see me, they will say Duzia is talking with ghost therefore he is very bad man and they can even kill him one time.

So now I just get up from where I was sitting. I did not say one word to Duzia again. I just get up and begin to go. As I was going, I looked at the place where my mama house used to stand. And tears began to drop like rain from my eyes. I walked quickly from my own town Dukana and in fact I did not know where I was going.

And as I was going, I was just thinking how the war have spoiled my town Dukana, uselessed many people, killed many others, killed my mama and my wife, Agnes, my beautiful young wife with J.J.C. and now it have made me like porson wey get leprosy because I have no town again.

And I was thinking how I was prouding before to go to soza and call myself Sozaboy. But now if anybody say anything about war or even fight, I will just run and run and run and run and run. Believe me yours sincerely. (p. 181)

The *Lagos Times* reported that as the noose was fitted around his neck, Saro-Wiwa articulated a prayer: "Lord, take my soul, but may the struggle continue." The struggle of the Ogoni people leaves no part of the global economy unimplicated. And it is a struggle in which we participate whenever we compose a sentence in the language of Shakespeare, which is also the language of international capitalism: a struggle between *Sozaboy*'s "rotten English" and the gas flaring of the Shell advertisement.

An aesthetics of linguistic and stylistic purity has always served a technology of pollution. A view of language, which takes the literal meaning as normative and identifies meaning with rationality, treats figures and tropes as mere oddities and inconveniences. *Sozaboy* prompts the converse reflection: that language itself, oozing and spilling from trope to trope, is no more rational or straightforward than the Niger Delta and that if we could acknowledge language as inherently "rotten," there might be less pollution of whatever is outside the text. One novel in "rotten English"— issued from the Lower Niger, delta of English most defiled—may yet cleanse a Shell-shocked land and a Shell-shocked language.

NOTES

I am greatly indebted to my relative, F. D. B. Somerset, district officer of Ogoni in 1955–1956, for first drawing my attention to Ken Saro-Wiwa.

1. At the Bomu oilfield. See "The Ogoni Bill of Rights," §7, in Saro-Wiwa, *A Month and a Day,* p. 67.

2. By Ken Saro-Wiwa, written in prison and first published in Gerner, *Index on Censorship*, 1994: 4, 5, 219.

3. Paul Lewis, "In Nigeria's Oil Wars, Shell Denies It Had a Role," *New York Times*, 13 February 1996. Two of the prosecution witnesses later retracted evidence and said they had been bribed by the government.

4. T. S. Eliot, "The Dry Salvages," *Four Quartets* (1944).

5. John Platt, Heidi Weber, and Ho Mian Lian, *The New Englishes* (New York: Routledge, 1984).

6. Ann Banfield, *Unspeakable Sentences: Narration and Representation in the Language of Fiction* (London: Routledge, 1982).

7. See Gérard Genette, *Paratexts: Thresholds of Interpretation.* Trans. J. E. Lewin (Cambridge: Cambridge University Press, 1997).

8. Also of interest is the explanation in *Basi* (Saro-Wiwa, *Basi and Company,* pp. 19, 22) of the name Saro: it denotes a Nigerian whose origins are in Sierra Leone. Elsewhere, however, Saro- (used as a prefix) is said to be an Ogoni term to designate the eldest son.

WORKS CITED

Achebe, Chinua. *Things Fall Apart.* London: Heinemann, 1958.

Bakhtin, M. M. "Epic and Novel." In *The Dialogic Imagination.* Ed. M. Holquist and C. Emerson. Austin: University of Texas Press, 1981.

Banfield, Ann. *Unspeakable Sentences: Narration and Representation in the Language of Fiction.* London: Routledge, 1982.

Bates, Stephen, and Owen Bowcott. "Shell Undeterred by Nigeria Hangings." *Manchester Guardian Weekly* 153, no. 21 (19 November 1995): 1.

Cooly, Glen. "Shell's Secret Dealings: Did Shell Promise to Intervene for Ken Saro-Wiwa in Return for His Silence?" *Now* (Toronto), 7–13 December 1995: 18–20.

Genette, Gérard. *Paratexts: Thresholds of Interpretation.* Trans. J. E. Lewin. Cambridge: Cambridge University Press, 1997.

Gerner, Jason. "The New Beggers." *Index on Censorship* 75, no. 6 (1995): 79–86.

———. "No Minor Matter." *Index on Censorship* 23, nos. 4 and 5 (1994).

Lewis, Paul. "In Nigeria's Oil Wars, Shell Denies It Had a Role," *New York Times,* 13 February 1996.

Saro-Wiwa, Ken. *Basi and Company: A Modern African Fable.* Port Harcourt: Saros International, 1987.

———. *A Forest of Flowers.* Port Harcourt: Saros International, 1986.

———. *A Month and a Day: A Detention Diary.* Harmondsworth: Penguin, 1995.

———. *On a Darkling Plain: An Account of the Nigerian Civil War.* Port Harcourt: Saros International, 1989.

———. *Sozaboy: A Novel in Rotten English.* London: Longman, 1994.

Spenser, Edmund. "Prothalamion." In *The Complete Poetical Works of Spenser.* Ed. R. E. Neil Dodge. Boston: Houghton Mifflin, 1908.

Vidal, John. "Black Gold Claims a Higher Price." *Manchester Guardian Weekly,* 15 January 1995.

2

A Political Assessment: *Genocide in Nigeria: The Ogoni Tragedy*

Joseph McLaren

Ken Saro-Wiwa's advocacy of the Ogoni cause was achieved through writings that directly address the relationship between the Ogoni and the Nigerian state. These works show his skills as a pamphleteer in support of environmental and human rights issues. Published in 1992, the year Saro-Wiwa was first detained by the Nigerian government, *Genocide in Nigeria: The Ogoni Tragedy* is similar to Saro-Wiwa's *The Ogoni Nation Today and Tomorrow* (1968; reissued 1993); both works were brought out by Saro-Wiwa's press, Saros International.

The Ogoni Nation Today and Tomorrow is an instructional work directed to an internal audience. *Genocide in Nigeria,* however, appeals to national and international readers by expanding on the ideas presented in *The Ogoni Nation Today and Tomorrow,* which was reissued because Saro-Wiwa wanted to make it available to the "young Ogoni men and women who could not have had access to it when it was first published" (Saro-Wiwa, *The Ogoni Nation,* p. 4). These "young Ogoni" were probably members of the Movement for the Survival of the Ogoni People (MOSOP). Another pamphlet publication, *Nigeria: The Brink of Disaster* (1991), contains articles written by Saro-Wiwa for various newspapers from 1970 to 1989 and several unpublished essays, but it does not specifically focus on the Ogoni question.

Genocide in Nigeria functions as an ethnography of the Ogoni, a discussion of the colonial experience, a commentary on the Ogoni status in the transition to Nigerian independence, an overview of the Nigerian Civil War, and, most important, a criticism of the role of the Shell Petroleum Development Corporation–British Petroleum (Shell-BP) and the Nigerian government in the pollution of the Niger Delta region. The pamphlet emphasizes genocide and appeals especially to an international audience. Saro-Wiwa had stressed the genocidal argument in one of his final interviews, which reiterated his support of the Ogoni and presented the case squarely in ethnic terms, accusing the "ethnic majority who run Nigeria of practicing genocide against the Ogoni people" (quoted in Bates and Bowcott, p. 11).

Structured chronologically, *Genocide in Nigeria* is a logical argument for autonomy and economic rectification. The arguments, issues, and evidence supplied in the pamphlet became repeated motifs expressed in later documents concerning the military government and supporting the Ogoni cause. By 1994, with the arrest of Saro-Wiwa, the Ogoni crisis had been examined by such organizations as Human Rights Watch, which echoed the main points in his 1992 document that blamed Shell and the Nigerian government. They "ravaged their [Ogoni] land and contaminated their rivers, while providing little, if any, tangible benefit in return" (Human Rights Watch, "The Ogoni Crisis," p. 2).

The articulation of these issues in the 1992 pamphlet was one of the first comprehensive historical statements concerning the Ogoni, giving an extended and detailed treatment of the issues. Furthermore, by bringing the "plight of the Ogoni people to the attention of the international community," *Genocide in Nigeria* contributed to spurring interest in the cause by Greenpeace, the Body Shop, and the UK's Channel 4 television (Zell, p. 4).

The focus on Ogoni ethnicity in *Genocide in Nigeria,* though apparently ethnocentric, is not presented as a negative or narrowed interest but rather as a democratic concern linked to the fear of genocide. Saro-Wiwa had addressed similar interests in a 1980 newspaper article, "A Recipe for Ethnic Peace," in which he suggested cautionary ideas for the creation of states in Nigeria so as to balance the relationship between majority and minority ethnic groups *(*Saro-Wiwa, *Nigeria,* pp. 24–26).

Genocide in Nigeria first presents the social structure and origins of the Ogoni to establish the group's unique presence in Nigeria; the purpose is to define the Ogoni as a "distinct ethnic group within the Federal Republic of Nigeria" (Saro-Wiwa, *Genocide,* p. 11). In order to accomplish this, Saro-Wiwa assumes the roles of geographer, anthropologist, social historian, and cultural expert, designating the spatial parameters of the Ogoni in the Niger Delta to the extent that he includes latitude and longitude markers. Designating the 404-square-mile territory of the Ogoni, who numbered approximately 500,000, establishes the group as a legitimate entity in its own right. The ethnographic background of the Ogoni is supported by two theories, one suggesting migration across the Imo River, another arguing an origin in Ghana, which is supported by the linguistic similarity between the word *Khana*, used by many Ogoni to designate their identity, and the word *Ghana (*Saro-Wiwa, *Genocide,* p. 11). The fifteenth-century origins of the Ogoni and the establishment of the six kingdoms—

Babbe, Eleme, Gokana, Nyo-Khana, Ken-Khana and Tai—give further credence to their individuality and distinctness (Saro-Wiwa, *Genocide,* p. 11).

The underlying issue in presenting the origins of the Ogoni is clearly political, in that the region to which they attribute their ancient rights is the delta, which was not only agriculturally blessed but also provided ample food resources through fishing. Saro-Wiwa emphasizes the legacy of land preservation and the historically militant defense of these territories by the Ogoni. However, the connection to the land is also defined in spiritual and ritualistic terms, where earth, soil, and water are considered sacred possessions. In his interpretation of Ogoni belief systems, he turns to the spiritual concept of human souls inhabiting the bodies of forest animals. These issues are relevant to the environmental questions that were part of the MOSOP campaign of the 1990s (Saro-Wiwa, *Genocide,* p. 12). By linking land and environment to traditional sources, Saro-Wiwa strengthens the legitimacy of the Ogoni claims for self-determination.

The background of the Ogoni also includes the Atlantic slave trade and the Ogoni's unique history; although Ogoni land was directly en route to the coast, "no Ogoni man or woman was taken as a slave" (Saro-Wiwa, *Genocide,* p. 14). To support this assertion, Saro-Wiwa uses the *Polyglotta Africana,* in which there is no indication of Ogoni languages. In other words, had there been European contact, Ogoni language would have likely been included in that work. Furthermore, among the Ogoni there was an abhorrence of slavery, a fact indicated by the oral tradition and a proverb that refers to the slave markets of Bonny.

In detailing the history of the Ogoni to 1900, Saro-Wiwa stages the entrance of British colonialism, introducing a discussion of how British rule was initiated by forceful incursions that resulted in resistance by the Ogoni, though they were ultimately defeated in 1914. Ogoniland, like other British colonial possessions, was subject to taxation, court systems, and missionaries such as the Methodists and the Anglicans. One form of resistance was the participation of Ogoni women in the 1929 Women's Tax Riot; other results of colonialism were the building of roads and, by the advent of World War II, the enlistment of Ogoni men in the British Army (Saro-Wiwa, *Genocide,* pp. 16–17).

Important for Saro-Wiwa's argument is that by the end of World War II, the Ogoni had pressed for a "separate administrative division" based on their being a "distinct ethnic group with its own language and culture" as well as their having a population of sufficient size to warrant such a designation (Saro-Wiwa, *Genocide,* p. 17). As a consequence of their efforts, in 1946, through the Constitutional Amendment Orders-in-Council, the Ogoni Division was established within the Rivers Province. These developments pointed toward the Ogoni's establishing a separate status and returning to the kind of self-rule of the precolonial era. The creation of the

Ogoni Native Authority in 1947 marked an attempt at self-rule under the guidance of T. N. Paul Birabi. The course of self-determination would include establishment of representative bodies as well as organs to promote Ogoni authority. Such groups as the Ogoni Central Union and later the Ogoni State Representative Assembly (OSRA) augured autonomy and ethnic continuity.

Despite the apparent levels of autonomy reached by the Ogoni by 1950, the underlying reality was that Nigeria in its move toward independence was a precarious federation for "minority" ethnic groups such as the Ogoni, which had not had prolonged contact with the British and were in a less advantageous position in comparison to the Yoruba, Igbo, and Hausa-Fulani. Saro-Wiwa's recounting of this period includes the details of the pre-independence constitution especially relevant to the oil resources of Ogoniland.

It was the failure to adhere to the 1960 Constitution that led to economic subjugation and genocide issues. According to the constitution,

> [t]here shall be paid by the Federation to each Region a sum equal to fifty percent of (a) the proceeds of any royalty received by the Federation in respect of any minerals extracted in that Region; and (b) any mining rents derived by the Federation within that Region. (Saro-Wiwa, *Genocide,* p. 21)

The situation of the Ogoni was complicated by the structure of the federation; those smaller ethnic groups in the self-governing Eastern Region, such as the Ogoni, feared domination by an Igbo majority. At that time, the failure to establish a Rivers State comprising the "minority" ethnic groups such as the Ogoni contributed to this sense of domination. Underlying Nigerian independence in 1960 were the "competitive" nature of the federation and the imminence of civil war (Saro-Wiwa, *Genocide,* p. 23). The oil workers' discovery in 1958 in Dere, in Gokana, Ogoniland, reflected these realities. The principal issue was an equitable federation versus ethnic self-determination, the underrepresentation of 300 minority ethnic groups in contrast to the prominent status of the three larger groups.

According to Saro-Wiwa's argument, the minority situation had been articulated in Obafemi Awolowo's *Path to Nigerian Freedom* (1947), which called for a balance within the federal concept so as not to create a disequilibrium of power. An ideal or "true Federal Constitution" would support self-determination and certain political and economic entitlements: "Opportunity must be afforded to each to evolve its own peculiar institution" (Saro-Wiwa, *Genocide,* p. 26).

Although Saro-Wiwa is obviously arguing against the kind of federalism that developed in Nigeria, he was, nevertheless, federal administrator for the oil port of Bonny in the period of the Nigerian Civil War. He documented the situation of the Ogoni during the civil war in *On a Darkling Plain: An Account of the Nigerian Civil War* (1989), which addresses the evacuation of the Ogoni to Igboland as a result of federal interests in the oil-rich Ogoni territory. It is ironic "[t]hat twenty-five years after the Biafran revolution a one-hundredth part of that nation known as the Ogoni thought of another rebellion" (Ezenwa-Ohaeto, p. 2). Saro-Wiwa's discussion of Ogoni refugees and the death of some 30,000 Ogoni during the civil war forms a prelude to the explanation of "the Shell-B.P. role" (Saro-Wiwa, *Genocide,* pp. 43–44).

Saro-Wiwa's position is boldly anti–federal government/Shell-BP, pointing to the government's need to raise funds during the final phases of the civil war when "every encouragement was given to Shell-B.P. to continue its genocidal plans against the Ogoni people" (Saro-Wiwa, *Genocide,* p. 44). The Ogoni were unable to withstand the incursions of modern industrial activity, a process that, after twelve years, resulted in the memorandum-petition of 25 April 1970 sent to the military governor of Rivers State. In order to provide documentary evidence, *Genocide in Nigeria* cites the memorandum and the response of Shell-BP.

Containing twenty-one issues, the petition is an overview of the effects of oil production in Ogoniland; environmental issues are primary, but the petition also requests solutions, essentially asking the military governor to act on behalf of the Ogoni. Though the approach of the petition is environmental, it is equally political and economic, reinforcing the connection between federal revenues and a disregard for the environmental effects of oil drilling and refining. Oil drilling devastated the land and, consequently, the "entire economy" of the Ogoni. "So long as the nation gets her royalties, nobody bothers what happens to the poor rural farmer whose land has been expropriated" (Saro-Wiwa, *Genocide,* pp. 45–46). From an economic perspective, oil production meant the loss of agricultural earnings in the fertile delta territory. According to the memorandum, an acre at that time yielded £1,000 to £2,000 during a farming season. The plight of the farmer is also linked to the future prosperity of family members, especially the educational pursuits of children.

In the Bomu (Dere) location, the plowing under of a variety of agricultural cash crops, including maize, pepper, cassava, yams, and melons, is a specific environmental-economic example. Most important, the "peasant" farmer is portrayed as unable to launch opposition to the "flagrant violation" of the Petroleum Regulations of 1969. Other environmental issues are the pollution of water supplies, the devastation of the mangrove swamps, and the destruction of oysters, fish, and crabs, thus affecting another economic resource for the Ogoni population. Furthermore, the petition describes the destruction of roads as a result of the transportation of heavy machinery. The counterargument of Shell-BP was that the state government was responsible for the maintenance of the roads. Related concerns in the petition were the avoidance of hiring Ogoni, the absence of educational scholarships, and the limited presence of Ogoni in the administrative class of the state government (Saro-Wiwa, *Genocide,* pp. 46–47).

The 1970 memorandum appeals to the Rivers State government for economic and judicial recourse, arguing that the state government should become an "arbitrator" in relationships between the landowners and the petroleum company. The fundamental economic point is that the "nation has been collecting her fabulous oil royalties on the ruin and destitution of a section of her population" (Saro-Wiwa, *Genocide,* p. 48). This appeal to a national interest and to the Rivers State government appears in hindsight to have been absolutely futile. The reality of ethnic privilege is in direct contrast to the appeal of the memorandum, which is hopefully nationalistic perhaps only for rhetorical purposes.

The response of Shell-BP was a denial of the points of the memorandum, as might be expected. Its reply to the specific paragraphs was considered by Saro-Wiwa as a form of "Shellspeak"—with broader continental and racial implications—in which such phrases as "Efficiency in finding and producing hydrocarbons" could be translated as "speedy extermination of human beings and their environment, particularly if these happen to be in Africa" (Saro-Wiwa, *Genocide*, p. 56). The environmental havoc was especially dramatized by the major oil blowout that occurred in July 1970, resulting in the declaration of a state of emergency on 28 July 1970 by the young people of Dere. Saro-Wiwa provides photographic evidence to document the destruction of the environment; these images include polluted water sources, oil pipeline routings, ecological changes, and flaring gas pipes.

The accusation of genocide is supported by letters from the "Youths of Dere," which address the failure of Shell-BP to "control the present catastrophe" related to the oil blowout. The letters show the involvement of the younger generation, their commitment to environmental reclamation, and their recollections of hoped-for prosperity when Shell-BP initially began oil explorations in Dere. This misnaming of Dere as Bomu was considered an "injustice" and a mark against those who sought employment by the company (Saro-Wiwa, *Genocide,* pp. 65–66).

The series of letters by Dere youth, which included references to Chevron as well as Shell-BP, bolster the environmental argument of the pamphlet by offering a preponderance of evidence reassessing the results of the oil blowout. The genocide accusation is reaffirmed by Saro-Wiwa in poetic language evoking the oral tradition. "I hear in my heart the howls of death in the polluted air of my beloved home-land; I sing a dirge for my children, my compatriots and their progeny" (Saro-Wiwa, *Genocide,* p. 83). Having demonstrated the complicity of Shell-BP in environmental contamination, Saro-Wiwa considers the subsequent actions of the federal government as "The Nail in the Ogoni Coffin." Domination by the majority ethnic group is linked to the prospects of profits from oil revenues under the Yakubu Gowon government, and various administrations after 1972 are implicated in the expropriation of oil revenues at the expense of the Ogoni. The 1979 Constitution contributed to the usurpation of Ogoni rights under the military rule of Olusegun Obasanjo because it revised previous provisions that secured certain economic rights for the Ogoni. Another example of constitutional revision is the Land Use Decree, which also granted ownership of "all land" to the federal government. The Obasanjo regime and the succeeding Shehu Shagari government are viewed by Saro-Wiwa as having limited the economic rights of the Ogoni to 2 percent of their property through revisions by the Revenue Allocation Commission (Saro-Wiwa, *Genocide,* pp. 85–86).

Just as Shell-BP had been accused of genocide, Saro-Wiwa similarly links the "ethnic majority" to Ogoni decimation. "The refusal of the ethnic majority to pay mining rents and royalties to the Ogoni and other delta minorities confirms their genocidal intentions" (Saro-Wiwa, *Genocide,* p. 86). Moreover, expressed in "the language of colonialism," a 1980 pronouncement by Chevron director Philip Asiodu is viewed—perhaps out of frustration—as more objectionable than the European colonial actions: "Even the Europeans did not treat the colonized with such open contempt" (Saro-Wiwa, *Genocide,* p. 87).

Saro-Wiwa's overview of Nigerian regimes and their links to oil revenues denied the Ogoni includes the overthrow of Shagari in 1983, the effects of the Mohammadu Buhari regime, and, finally, the takeover by Ibrahim Babangida in 1985, which "sealed the fate of the Ogoni" (Saro-Wiwa *Genocide,* p. 88). Similar to constitutional revisions in earlier years, the changes under Babangida also hampered the interests of the Ogoni, especially in the increase in the number of states in 1991 and the continuation of ethnic majority privilege. The issue at this juncture is the reliance of non-oil-producing states on those of the delta. The unviable multiethnic Rivers State, in which the Ijaws are dominant, represents a "microcosm of Nigeria in which the majority ethnic groups triumph while the minorities gnash their teeth in agony" (Saro-Wiwa, *Genocide,* p. 89). Here the question of ethnic dominance in local states is compared to the same dilemma at the national level. Furthermore, the differing situations of states is exemplified by Borno State in the North, where there is "free education" at various levels, in contrast to the Ogoni area, where the children are "out of school" (Saro-Wiwa, *Genocide,* p. 89). Saro-Wiwa considers as well the larger national dilemma and the inefficacy of the nation-state in light of ethnic affiliation and conflict, which contribute to problems within the banking and university systems.

The solution offered by Saro-Wiwa is "the Autonomy Option," in which "each ethnic group would have autonomy and be directly responsible for its own salvation" (Saro-Wiwa, *Genocide,* p. 93). The *Ogoni Bill of Rights* of 1990 is attached to the pamphlet; it is a summary of historical issues contained in the pamphlet and includes an addendum, all of which restate the principal environmental, economic, and ethnic arguments forwarded by Saro-Wiwa.

The final plea, however, is presented by Saro-Wiwa as writer to the international community. Not only does he challenge the silence of Nigerian writers, singling out Kole Omotoso for his review of *On a Darkling Plain,* but urges the international community to act jointly to prevent "twenty-first century genocide" (Saro-Wiwa, *Genocide,* pp. 100–102). In the closing appeal, Saro-Wiwa presents his own "ten-point" plan, a summary of the major points of the pamphlet with the addition of certain proposals, most notably, the appeal to the United States to discontinue its purchase of Nigerian oil. The World Bank and the International Monetary Fund (IMF) are urged to cease loan payments to the federal government. The international approach is also suggested in pleas to the United Nations, the Organization of African Unity (OAU), and the Commonwealth of Nations to impose sanctions in response to human rights violations. The West should curtail aid, suspend credit, and grant refugee status to Ogonis who seek it. Compensation should be paid by Shell and Chevron (Saro-Wiwa, *Genocide,* p. 103).

Because *Genocide in Nigeria* is a clear plea for the Ogoni, in many respects it is also a challenge to the concept of Nigeria as a nation, similar in certain respects to Wole Soyinka's complaints in *The Open Sore of a Continent* (1996). Soyinka warned that "[i]f Ken Saro-Wiwa's death-cry does prove, in the end, to have sounded the death-knell of that nation, it would be an act of divine justice richly deserved" (p. 153).[1] Saro-Wiwa's attempt to secure for the Ogoni both economic and environmental justice was inseparable from a reevaluation of the imbalance of ethnic power within Nigeria, the inability of the nation "to cohere, 35 years after independence" (Gates, p. 4). Although Saro-Wiwa's support of the Ogoni could be perceived as ethnocentric in its own right because it is unabashedly about self-determination for the Ogoni, his advocacy goes beyond Ogoni interests because it is concerned with the domination of minority ethnic groups other than his own: "Ethnocentrism blinds even the best men to injustice, discrimination, even genocide perpetrated against those who are not of their own ethnic groups" (Saro-Wiwa, *Genocide,* p. 101). Saro-Wiwa's vision, though focused on the Ogoni, also encompassed, in a pan-African manner, "other indigenous peoples and national minorities on the African continent" (Saro-Wiwa, "Acceptance Speech," p. 17).

Beyond Ogoni advocacy, Saro-Wiwa's legacy is that of human rights advocate and especially environmentalist, as reflected in a memorial tribute poem by Dennis Brutus, which referred to "the factor / of polluted lands /

over-run by sludge" (Brutus, p. 35). However, three years prior to Saro-Wiwa's execution in 1995, the appeal in *Genocide in Nigeria* to the international community, though impassioned, fully documented, and logically argued, had little effect on reversing the policies of the Nigerian government. Nevertheless, the pamphlet did contribute to increased international awareness of the Ogoni dilemma. The broader issue of international human rights is inevitably connected to political interests such as those of the Unrepresented Nations and Peoples Organization (UNPO). In a 1992 address to the Working Group on Indigenous Populations of the UNPO, Saro-Wiwa referred to *Genocide in Nigeria,* presented to the secretariat of the Working Group, as a work that "explains the Ogoni case fully" *(*Saro-Wiwa, *Month,* p. 97); but to what extent did the international community respond to Saro-Wiwa's urging in 1992?

The dilemma is that "an international human rights system" is "severely and intolerably constrained by the material interests of great powers" (Okafor, pp. 31–32). Saro-Wiwa's plea in his "ten-point course of action," his asking the international community to "[p]revail on the American Government to stop buying Nigerian oil . . . [because] . . . [i]t is stolen property" is politically relevant to "material interests" (Saro-Wiwa, *Genocide,* p. 102). Such political-economic pressures are reminiscent of the international antiapartheid movement. *Genocide in Nigeria* not only proposes these kinds of solutions but sets forth a platform for internal and international initiatives to resolve the Ogoni dilemma and those of other ethnic minorities caught between global oil interests and state power.

NOTE

1. Though Soyinka was sympathetic to Saro-Wiwa's fate in 1996, Saro-Wiwa had offered a satirical critique of Soyinka in "Open Letter to Wole Soyinka," 1989, in which he challenged Soyinka's motives in connection with a fund-raising event for a foundation (Saro-Wiwa, *Nigeria,* pp. 86–88).

WORKS CITED

Bates, Stephen, and Owen Bowcott. "Shell Undeterred by Nigeria Hangings." *Manchester Guardian Weekly* 153, no. 21 (19 November 1995): 1.

Brutus, Dennis. "Poem by Dennis Brutus for Ken Saro-Wiwa, 5/30/96." *African Literature Association Bulletin* 22, no. 2 (Spring 1996): 35.

Ezenwa-Ohaeto. "Ken Saro-Wiwa: A Death Not in Our Stars." *African Literature Association Bulletin* 22, no. 1 (Winter 1996): 2.

Gates, Henry Louis, Jr. "Is There a Spark of Hope in Nigeria's Darkest Hour?" *Globe and Mail,* 16 December 1995: D4.

"Hanged Writer's Final Words of Hope." *Guardian* (Manchester), 14 November 1995: 11.

Human Rights Watch Africa. "The Ogoni Crisis: A Case Study of Military Repression in Southeastern Nigeria." *Human Rights Watch/Africa* 7, no. 5 (July 1995): 1–44.

Okafor, Obiora Chinedu. "In Spite of the Crucifix? International Law, Human Rights, and the Allegory of the Ogoni Question." African Studies Association Conference, Hyatt Embarcadero Center, San Francisco, 23 November 1996.

Saro-Wiwa, Ken. "Acceptance Speech by Ken Saro-Wiwa: 1994 Fonlon-Nichols Laureate." *African Literature Association Bulletin* 20, no. 2 (Spring 1994): 17–21.

———. *Genocide in Nigeria: The Ogoni Tragedy.* Port Harcourt: Saros International, 1992.

———. *A Month and a Day: A Detention Diary.* New York: Penguin, 1995.

———. *Nigeria: The Brink of Disaster.* Port Harcourt: Saros International, 1991.

———. *The Ogoni Nation Today and Tomorrow.* 2nd ed. Port Harcourt: Saros International, 1993.

———. *On a Darkling Plain: An Account of the Nigerian Civil War.* Port Harcourt: Saros International, 1989.

Soyinka, Wole. *The Open Sore of a Continent: A Personal Narrative of the Nigerian Crisis.* New York: Oxford, 1996.

Zell, Hans. "Tribute to Ken Saro-Wiwa." *African Book Publishing Record* 21, no. 4 (1995). Reprinted in *African Literature Association Bulletin* 22, no. 1 (Winter 1996): 4.

PART 2

The Literary Experiments

3

Literary Memoirs and Diaries: Soyinka, Amadi, and Saro-Wiwa

Craig W. McLuckie

I begin this chapter with a brief quotation from William McIlvanney's *Surviving the Shipwreck,* for it encapsulates the social forces that, in their widely differing ways, Elechi Amadi, Wole Soyinka, and Ken Saro-Wiwa rebel against. Their rebellion is both practical, in that their memoirs of the events involve some shaping and reconsideration of the effects of history upon themselves and their humanity. McIlvanney writes: "The opting out of society is the ultimate surrender to society just as to disown history is to give history total authority over you" (McIlvanney, p. 131). Happily not content to opt out or to accept "official" history, these writers, in *Sunset in Biafra* (1973), *The Man Died: Prison Notes of Wole Soyinka* (1972), and *On a Darkling Plain: An Account of the Nigerian Civil War* (1989), respectively, offer subaltern histories, cases of opting in and frequently challenging received notions of what occurred, depicting the effect it had in real terms, human and subjective. This chapter will concentrate on these memoirs and will then offer a postscript on Saro-Wiwa's last book.

DEFINITIONS

It is apposite at the outset to offer some sense of the distinction between literary and political memoirs because the idea of self and communal invention is very much at the root of the distinction. The *Oxford English Dictionary* (*OED*) offers a note of caution in its definition of memoir: "A record of events, not purporting to be a complete history, but treating such matters as come within the personal knowledge of the writer." The question may be posed as to the difference between a memoir and an autobiography.

To a limited extent, this is answered as follows: "Memoirs differ from autobiography proper in that they are usually concerned with personalities and actions other than those of the writer, whereas autobiography stresses the inner and private life of its subject" (Holman and Harmon, p. 285). In the memoir, then, the private is subjugated to a more general, communal narrative. R. Pascal writes well on the nature of the genre, though, at points, there is an unquestioned agreement with assumptions that contemporary critical theory has brought into question:

> Memoirs proper may be defined as the more personal and private aspect of public affairs. Since political decisions are of so complex and so far-reaching an importance, the memoirs of statesmen, high officials, generals, etc. are an almost obligatory complement to their office and an important source for the historian. Memoirs, limited by personal experience and coloured by temperament, are not reliable as history. (Pascal, vol. 1, p. 76)

The assumption that only those in high office need write memoirs is an antiquated one. If for no other reason than that the people's voice be heard, memoirs should be seen as a more egalitarian form. Of course, the writers of the memoirs under review are privileged to a certain extent, as writers, but none of the three sees his role ending at the desk. More apt are Pascal's further comments:

> [Y]et a peculiar truth arises from restriction and bias. . . . Without aiming at a self-portrait the memoirist gives an account of both circumstances and himself, thus enriching as well as distorting the historical situation. . . . Partisanship, bias, may be not only an attractive feature of the memoir, but also a greater help than too strenuous a straining after objectivity, since the truth of what is written may be better assessed if the predilections and prejudices of the author are patent. (p. 76)

In the three works, there is no question about each writer's perspective on the war, nor about his sense of how things could or should have been. The partisanship, the taking of sides, is what gives each work a human value. This is what differentiates their work from that of the politicians; a little unreason creeps in, a sense of the self. Shaping the experience undergone anew, stylizing it, but retaining the human touch is to offer an aesthetic of being that can be challenged, reviewed, and adapted. But, without the voice and the courage to articulate it, artists will leave us with the official story; without these voices complexity will be diminished, multifarious perspectives will die, and the classroom, the village square, the local pub will become dominated by the view that currently prevails in mass media television and radio: simplify, nullify, deaden. Heralding event, community, and character over date and campaign, the memoirist often-times comes across more forcefully than the historian because minutiae and anecdote are a metalanguage:

> That was where . . . those other fine intelligences—great minds ab-stracted from their bodies and floating loose in a formaldehyde of the-ory—came to grief. . . . They all tried to invent human nature [and human history] instead of discovering it. (McIlvanney, p. 124)

THE PRISONER: THE POSSIBILITY OF COMMUNAL PRAXIS IN *THE MAN DIED*

The closest of the three writers under examination to McIlvanney's concerns is Wole Soyinka.[1] He is, like McIlvanney, an outspoken adherent of social-ist and humanist concerns. Also like McIlvanney, Soyinka has concerns about the artist/intellectual in society. He believes that African artists, over-taken by modernist artistic notions, produced "a magnitude of unfelt ab-stractions" (Soyinka, "The Failure," pp. 137–138) in their early postinde-pendence work. Such abstractions were due in part to the writer's isolated position in society, where literacy rates were extremely low and the writer's sense of an international audience detached him or her from the community. Soyinka saw Nigeria as a country where some communal involvement re-mained. Indeed, Soyinka's work, no matter how linguistically dense, has al-ways revealed a close association with communal values and progress. Soyinka's journalistic piece, "Let's Think Again About the Aftermath of This War" (p. 8), stresses the active nature of his involvement—if time is too short for a more thorough literary contemplation of the issues, then direct appeal is used, boldly speaking not only to Nigeria's divided leadership but also to the populace at large, in hopes that if motivation is not apparent in the powers-that-be, then perhaps the people can make them change.

As the narrative of *The Man Died* attests, the response of the military leadership to Soyinka's plea for contemplation of the nation's issues was a long and cruel incarceration. The bile that Soyinka directs at the military is apparent in his poetry and plays of the period; in *The Man Died*, how-ever, Soyinka reveals that there was more to his actions than a general ap-peal. He recapitulates thus:

> [M]y denunciation of the war in the Nigerian papers; my visit to the East; my attempt to recruit the country's intellectuals within and outside the coun-try for a pressure group which would work for a total ban on the supply of arms to all parts of Nigeria; creating a third force which would utilize the ensuing military stalemate to repudiate and end both the secession of Biafra,

and the genocide-consolidated dictatorship of the Army which made both
the secession and war inevitable. (Soyinka, *The Man,* p. 19)

Obviously, Soyinka is not for secession; he sees that act as symptomatic of
a larger evil within the country. The fact that Soyinka attempted to see
commanders of both sides is a clear indication of this broader and deeper
perspective. The "third force" is perhaps the most interesting point because it underscores a larger political action that Soyinka was engaged in.
The word "creating" suggests a leading role in the "third force." Thus
Soyinka declares his commitment to "all feasible acts which would
demonstrate an ethical absolute" (p. 2), an absolute that exhibits itself in
an uncompromising justice and an independent judiciary, that makes it a
crime for one man to interfere with another "for reasons of tribe" (p. 22).
Such a force, Soyinka argues, presented the only "truly national, moral
and revolutionary alternative" (p. 95); what is more, it was in operation in
the Mid-West, as "Victor Banjo's Third Force" (p. 95). As we shall see,
Amadi has no such plan or alliance in mind, whereas Saro-Wiwa's group-
ing is tribe-specific. Antitribal, justice-oriented, with a military wing of its
own, but what more? Indeed, how would it go about effecting change in
accordance with its abiding principles?

The third force appears to consist of Christopher Okigbo, Lt. Col.
Adekunle Fajuyi and Lt. Col. Victor Banjo, the Marxist, Major Philip
Alale, and perhaps Chinua Achebe, whom Soyinka had worked with on "a
new front" (p. 155) in 1967. At Fajuyi's request, Soyinka planned trips to
the North and the East as well as potential talks with Lt. Col. Chukwuemeka Odumegwu Ojukwu and Lt. Col. Yakubu Gowon (Obasanjo, p. 31).
Such activities represent one possibility for the recentering of the nation, a
bringing together of the factional forces. Rather than a barbaric destruction
and weakening of one element within the nation, Soyinka's route sought a
new birth. However, the trips and discussions had only limited success because Gowon would not grant him an interview. Nevertheless, the idealism
of Soyinka and his friends should be acknowledged, for the third force
thought "in terms of a common denominator for the people" (Soyinka, *The
Man,* p. 178), of "building a [humanistic] socialist state" (p. 177): "It is
better to believe in people than in nations. In moments of grave doubts it
is essential to cling to the reality of peoples; these cannot vanish, they
have no questionable *a priori*—they exist" (p. 175).

Unsuccessful in the public arena, incarcerated for his efforts, Soyinka
was driven to introspection—*A Shuttle in the Crypt* is a painful and
poignant rendition of that experience. *The Man Died* is no less poignant
in its recreation of the prison experience, but it is more of a political act.
Soyinka makes it consciously so and heightens our awareness in "The

Unacknowledged" section: "[b]ooks and all forms of writing have always been objects of terror to those who seek to suppress the truth" (p. 9). What makes this all the more truthful about *The Man Died* (than *A Shuttle*) is that the experience remains linguistically and experientially accessible and human to the greatest number of people, as the memoir form should in its service to the community. The opening out of his prison notes from the personal to the public also underscores the validity of his statement. Intense subjectivity (as in the poems of *A Shuttle*) can obscure and defer the empathic nature of the reading.

Reviews of *The Man Died* in Nigeria's press reveal the precision of Soyinka's words, for the response they evoke is invariably ad hominem: "Wole Soyinka reveals himself as nothing but a narrow Yoruba jingoist. . . . Soyinka had Fajuyi firmly under his spell and . . . acted as Fajuyi's intellectual storm trooper and snooper."[2] A common denominator of the people hardly comes out as tribalism, and if Soyinka has Fajuyi under his spell, then why is he working for him? These early reactions, contradictory as they are, consistently fail to acknowledge the conditions in which Soyinka was kept and the statements others were making about him when he was not in a position to respond, but most important, they do not engage the arguments he puts forth. Out of prison, Soyinka remains consistent to his populist aims: he does not wish to intellectualize the experience out of the people's reach; rather, he wishes to depict it in such a way that they might share and empathize with it: "this language was not simply the language of one 'aggrieved writer'; it is the hidden language of an oppressed populace—the writer does no more than expose it, reappropriating it for the commencement of liberation therapy" (Harrison, p. 105).[3] The individual experience is a reflection of the communal one; the two are inextricably bound, serving and enlarging the vision and wisdom of each other.

Given this purpose, it is no surprise that in the original text Soyinka went one stage further in the individual's identification with community to pose *The Man Died* along with George Mangakis's testimonial as political tools in the service of the international community, "a kind of chain-letter hung permanently on the leaden conscience of the world" (Soyinka, *The Man*, p. 11). This expression of intent echoes Soyinka's aesthetics, where the individual acts in order to alert the greater society to the need for change. Soyinka's aesthetics draw art and society together in an aesthetic of being. But, is Soyinka truly alerting anyone? A closer examination of the isolated prison experience allows an answer to the question.

The Man Died is a "first step" (p. 15) toward revolutionary change, and so we cannot expect more than the first stage of communal reorientation. Soyinka's position toward his incarceration quickly becomes clear: he will not "keep silent in the face of tyranny" (p. 13); even small examples, for instance, Mallam D's (the interrogator's) use of manacles, invite a response: in this case, a hunger strike. In addition, Soyinka writes an essay rather than a confession, which is designed to have his captors try him publicly. But why a trial? The "communal" judiciary has gone awry; so an appeal through it would be dangerous. Quickly, he sees that the idea of a trial was a "stupid moment," one in which his consciousness is working with legal ideals rather than the legal reality. He has been responding as if society were where it should be.

Nonetheless, society and social consciousness do get transformed. An Igbo woman is mistakenly placed in Soyinka's cell (p. 42), and upon seeing someone of Soyinka's stature (in the popular consciousness) imprisoned, she breaks into tears. Her hopes and remaining faith in the ideal of a just society have been vanquished. Yet there is room to envision a more enlightened society because prison has become an equalizer, and prisoners soon draw support and comfort from one another across the boundary (in the politicians' consciousness) of tribe. Their gestures to one another embolden them in their future isolation, where though physically alone, a spiritual communion remains. Thus, at a base level there is communal continuity; it embodies Soyinka's sense of society in its purest form. It is a telling aesthetic moment, when artistry in the form of symbolic value is introduced as an element in the memoir.

Underscoring the need for the individual to retain his or her strength as a building block for a more humane community, Soyinka's first act on entering prison was "to be alone with [his] thoughts" (p. 46), to face his environment and to understand it, lest unpreparedness or perceived weakness infect others: "doubts are created, even in one solitary example . . . then you have established your race of serfs whose docility will be justified forever by 'if he could break, then who are we to struggle?'" (p. 96). The concern expressed is for the largest social construct—humanity—to be improved through the individual's efforts. During his incarceration, Soyinka's social vision remains unimpaired, reliant upon "necessary social egalitarian agreements as the norm for any community of human beings" (p. 237), that is, a socialist state, humanist in nature.

In the realm of political activism, Wole Soyinka presents a surprisingly consistent position. It is challenging because of his inherent belief in the beneficial nature of adapting, extending, and changing "traditions" and "mores" to accommodate historical circumstances. It is a less clearly defined vision in that we perceive where we have come from, capture the present moment, but know little of how change can be effected communally. Rooted in the individual, Soyinka's praxis lacks clarity in the means to an ambiguously defined social end, yet it enforces vigilance, participation, and the quest for understanding in and from others.

THE "SOLDIER":
INDIVIDUAL STASIS IN *SUNSET IN BIAFRA*

Elechi Amadi's *Ethics in Nigerian Culture* (1982) offers an apparently
straightforward, if brief, summation of the civil war:

> The civil war . . . had tribal overtones, but it was not simply a fight be-
> tween the Hausa and the Igbo; other tribes joined in order to secure eco-
> nomic and political advantages. However, the concept of national unity
> finally eclipsed all other considerations. (Amadi, *Ethics,* p. 39)

Caution is needed here, however, because although Amadi is fairly consistent in *Ethics,* a very general and personal overview, his perspective in
his novel of the war, *Estrangement,* and to a lesser extent in *Sunset in
Biafra* places greater emphasis on economics and on received history than
it does on human waste and suffering. It is depersonalized in many areas
and is less subjective and human than *The Man Died* as a result.

Little has been set down about Amadi's life prior to the Nigerian Civil
War, other than the facts to be gleaned from the biographical blurb reproduced on the covers of his novels. Amadi obtained a degree in physics and
mathematics, worked as a land surveyor and teacher, and then joined the
Nigerian military. The last point is the most interesting and least explica-
ble, given that Amadi resigned his commission in the army "at a time
when he was needed most" (Amadi, *Sunset,* p. 2), in November 1965—just
over a month before the January 1966 coup—amid social upheaval.
Nowhere in *Sunset* do we receive a clue toward explaining the motive for
this decision; tentatively, we must assume that Amadi was strongly con-
vinced that his contribution to society lay elsewhere.

Thus Amadi returns to a lower-paying teaching position in Rivers, his
home area, and the coup of January 1966, which toppled the civilian administration of Prime Minister Alhaji Abubakar Tafawa Balewa, quickly
follows. Amadi does not rejoin the army. Maj. Gen. Ironsi assumes leadership of the country after defeating the "rebels"; Amadi works on.
Gowon's countercoup is successful; Amadi works on. Amadi remains un-
involved. *Sunset* provides virtually nothing in the way of reasons for
Amadi's chosen path; it is like *Ethics* in that it describes but does not define. It is full of descriptions governed by the voice of the subject, not
quite an objective, distanced observer but also not an engaged participant
in events. Even the emotion is undramatized, the participation noted in
passing—reflections upon events are kept, consciously or not, to an absolute minimum. Consequently, Amadi's descriptions must be carefully examined to yield his perspective. His attitude toward a possible military

takeover, for instance, aligns him with proponents of a civil democracy, one that permits continuity in traditions; the military represents "orders barked out at gunpoint; drastic cuts in some of our cherished traditions . . . perhaps arbitrary arrests . . . and a host of other inconveniences" (p. 6).

It is not surprising, therefore, that Amadi negatively portrays the January 1966 coup leaders as "rebel officers," akin to thieves in that they were holding out in Kaduna (p. 6). These pejorative remarks come after, not during, the event, at a time when Amadi implicitly suggests that a united Nigeria, in the short term at least, must dissuade further coups and the promotion of the ideals behind the events of January 1966 until such time as a social foundation, national in scope, is laid. Nevertheless, the position smacks of the status quo.

Amadi writes perceptively of the best means to gauge the health of a nation: "It is the people's day-to-day reactions to the strains of living that provide a . . . basis of judgement" (p. 9). And under the brief tenure of Maj. C. N. Nzeogwu's 1966 revolutionary council, Amadi could whistle in the bath, argue with his wife (p. 9), or adjust "to civilian life" (p. 11). For Amadi, the social upheavals in 1966 meant little because his life went on normally. The majority of the book's first half, in fact, centers on Amadi's return to civilian life. There are periodic interruptions where he "describes" what is taking place elsewhere in the country, but these often dissolve into rhetorical outbursts reliant upon newspapers and other media, not personal involvement. A contentious point, which reveals shades of bias, arises from his discussion of the Biafran leader Ojukwu: "In all his [i.e., Ojukwu's] lamentations, what irritated me most was that he could never concede as some honest Ibos did, that his people had, even if unwittingly, struck first, on 15 January 1966" (p. 19). The parenthetical insertion of "honest" is disconcerting, especially when combined with the slightly more objective assessment of an apparently unconscious tribalism in the coup. To disagree with Amadi is to lay oneself open to the charge of dishonesty, for honest people presumably admitted Amadi's "fact." As to the interpretation of unwitting tribalism, none of the perpetrators of the 1966 coup were Ojukwu's men; in fact, Ojukwu briefly remained as one of Gowon's regional governors in the federation, until their conceptions of how to maintain national unity caused a split: "the central issue of the war was essentially the same as that of pre- and post-colonial politics: national cohesion. The war was fought largely to determine whether or not Nigeria would continue as a federation according to Gowon's twelve-State scheme, or would split into its component parts in a confederal system, as Ojukwu wanted" (Graf, p. 43). Siding Ojukwu and the leaders of the 1966 coup together by tribe is a shallow and dishonest strategy; there is little concrete evidence to suggest that as early as January 1966, a conscious Igbo plot to take control of Nigeria was afoot.

Dishonest, perhaps, but such unsubstantiated speculations allow Amadi to move into the federalist camp against Ojukwu. This parallels the movement in books by another minority tribesman, Ken Saro-Wiwa, who sees the federation, at this point at least, as the lesser of two evils with respect to minority rights. Amadi discusses Ojukwu's rhetoric and summarizes as follows: "This method of argument—saying yes and no simultaneously—ran through all of his speeches. General Gowon, a straightforward military man, found this type of talk very trying indeed" (Amadi, *Sunset,* p. 19).[4] One need hardly be reminded that Gowon was the military ruler at the time of writing and of publication. So, Gowon's side, indeed his mind and personality, is entered into through weak ad hominem attacks on Ojukwu. The reasons for Amadi's method of "argument" and political alignment are summarized neatly by Dieter Riemenschneider. In *Sunset in Biafra,* Riemenschneider writes, "we encounter a book in which the author does not hide his aversion to Biafra and the Ibos; but the one-sidedness which results from such an attitude, affects the objectivity and meaning of this autobiographical account, especially of its first part" (Riemenschneider, p. 83). The reasons are political and tribal: Amadi, a member of the minority Ikwerre tribe, feared for the safety of his people and the continuity of their traditions. Where the Igbos sought an independent state because of the northerners' political control of Nigeria, the Ikwerre feared an independent Biafra that "never took into consideration the will of its minorities" (p. 41) who wished to remain part of Nigeria, but in charge of their own region as a defense against the cultural extinction they would face under the Igbos. Concerns of internal colonization in Amadi's book predate similar concerns in Saro-Wiwa's. Soyinka offers some support for Amadi's immediate reactions but places them within a larger historical context:

> The madness of power, unchecked, is there for the world to see. And yet, the note is one of optimism. Why? Simply because the note of ethnic opportunism of 1965 and 1966 cannot be repeated. I believe that the stage of ethnic opportunism and therefore, of ethnic battlelines has been surpassed. There is a nationwide recognition of the deprived and their exploiters, of the oppressed and their oppressors, of the cynical and the derided.[5]

Amadi serves the Rivers people at discussions with Ojukwu on the status of minority tribes but contributes nothing (Amadi, *Sunset,* p. 17); an indication that his mind is made up against Biafra and Ojukwu, for he apparently does not even test the waters with some of his own ideas. He assists his tribal union (p. 24) and is detained for two weeks as a result; he evades demonstrations in support of Biafra (p. 38), thus reemphasizing his profederalist (for Amadi, this equates to a traditionalist) stance; he protects his family and his land against confiscation by the Igbos (p. 53). In all, he remains true to his people (in this limited sense) and his convictions in these areas—a display of integrity. He could affirm his federalism by joining its army against Biafra, but he worries about the safety of his family and realizes that he still serves a useful function within the community: "I knew what [the Biafran soldiers'] limitations were and would not let them exploit the local people" (p. 63). Again, a specific tribe comes before the larger communal group. John Povey usefully comments that "Amadi at least had the comfort of believing that there was a sense of propriety and order in things" (Povey, p. 359), which purportedly is society's true nature. However, a "temporary and intermittent lapse in the moral order" (Povey, p. 359) had taken place. It is this sense of belief that a concrete moral world exists, although there has been a temporary collapse of it, that supports Amadi through a second, lengthier period of detention and separation from his family.

Release from detention at the time of Port Harcourt's fall to the federal side brings about Amadi's constructive rather than isolationist and survivalist tendencies. He is involved in an ad hoc committee to mediate between soldiers and civilians (Amadi, *Sunset*, p. 144); he rejoins the federal army (p. 149), now the power broker, and actively fights to reunite Nigeria; he helps to revivify Port Harcourt (p. 151), thus demonstrating a life-affirming role. For Amadi construction begins from what exists—people and facilities—and grows from there. Although he is in the army once more, Amadi's desire for a return to civilian life, to a state of normalcy, is reflected in his repeated efforts to recruit and pay civilians for their labor in the reconstructive process (p. 164).

Accomplishing a great deal for others takes its toll because their reunions, their rebuilding of homes and lives, remind Amadi of his missing family. He quits the army again (p. 169) because of such familial concerns but disconcertingly goes to Lagos (he even worries over the style of a suit!) rather than in search of his family (p. 170), joins the Rivers State Government Service (p. 171), and runs a rehabilitation service for refugees (p. 175) and a recruitment service to provide guides for the federal army (p. 180). Shortly after he assumes the ministerial role for Local Government and Information (p. 182), Amadi's family returns to him. Luck, fate, or a preordained plan have accomplished this return; Amadi, in *Sunset*, reveals that his contribution moved from passive to active only after the political tides had changed.

The conclusion of civil strife, detention, imprisonment, and destruction with his participatory role in the military and then civilian reconstruction is metaphorically projected in the reunion: the family unit, now together, invites comparison with the later reunion of Nigeria when Biafra falls. Amadi's belief in traditional values finds some reinforcement in this return to normalcy. His belated involvement in the larger national community underscores the desire for a return to prewar life: reconstruction, renewal, reunion. Consequently, political activity for Amadi is the reaffirmation of the old; his family has come together one and the same as before; there is no indication of change, of new roles and alignments adapted from the old ways in light of recent travails. In short, Amadi's social commitment is reflected in his relatively neutral political activities: conservatism in the sense that one acts to maintain the known social order.

In terms of Amadi's technique, Hugh Webb summarizes the less artistic nature of Amadi's achievement concisely:

> There is no significant attempt, within the narrative, to project or examine any possible coherence that may be inherent in the experience (apart from some general comments on the nature of war and suffering). Amadi's personal experiences are always in the foreground. The particular interest is always tied to the question: what happens next? *Sunset in Biafra* carries the sub-title of "A Civil War Diary," while the author writes of "an intimate, personal story, told for its own sake." The stress on a story told for its own sake sharply differentiates Amadi's work from *The Man Died.* (Webb, p. 12)

There is within Amadi's arguments and rendition of events a sense that the status quo is propagated, artistically and socially, and that tradition and received values are everything; if so, then the work of the artist becomes socially impotent, a passive chronicle of received history rather than an active ingredient in it.

Ethics in Nigerian Culture underscores my assessment of Amadi's worldview as a traditional received one, but the morality that Amadi views as central to art is more fully described there. Amadi strives for the perfection (not the adaptation) of his received ethical base in the face of social schisms. Rather than see the reality within such schisms as that of a system or social ordering that can no longer work, Amadi seeks "moral instruction" (Amadi, *Ethics,* p. 105) to promote a national egalitarianism, where "the universal brotherhood of man [will be] the basis of a Nigerian ideology" (p. 106). The position might be more laudable if the old system had not disintegrated; reinventing the past—stasis—is no substitute for a rigorous reappraisal of the system of communal interaction, as Soyinka's work has shown.

THE ADMINISTRATOR: MINORITY AND ETHICAL ISSUES IN *ON A DARKLING PLAIN*

Ken Saro-Wiwa's memoir appears, at first glance, to be a hybrid of Amadi's apparent lack of involvement and Soyinka's active role and developed vision. It is not. Although Saro-Wiwa provides more character sketches of participants and a fuller sense of some of the events, his "position" is contradictory at times, and the "vision" of communal order has serious ethical problems at its base:

> Controversy still rages over Saro-Wiwa's highly personalized view of recent history. . . . In accord with the dictum that history is written by the victorious, Saro-Wiwa presents his war experiences from the perspective of a Nigerian federalist. *On a Darkling Plain* therefore must be understood as an indictment of Biafran military leadership, but it goes well beyond criticism of Igbo motives and actions on the battlefield. Saro-Wiwa sees premeditated antiminority signs in every Biafran policy and action. . . . In the process he appears to gloss over incidents in his personal life that do not present a positive image of his own motives and that might lead to very different interpretations of the events he describes. (Ezenwa-Ohaeto, pp. 336–337)

Much of *On a Darkling Plain* is told in an archaic language and an at times pompous, if not ludicrous, style that inhibits the reader's attempts to garner a sense of Saro-Wiwa's contribution and vision of a communal future. The "Author's Note" helps, as Saro-Wiwa states fairly directly where he wants to go: "My account shows [what] the world and posterity have to know—the real victims of that war were the Eastern minorities who were in a no-win situation. They are the oppressed in Nigeria" (Saro-Wiwa, *On a Darkling Plain,* p. 10). That statement is fairly direct, but it is not long before the reader encounters overwritten passages like the following: "A conference of all chiefs in the Federation was scheduled [by Ironsi] for Ibadan in July of 1966. From North, East, South, and West they came, chiefs in regalia and out of regalia, chiefs with thrones and chiefs without thrones, chiefs with subjects and chiefs without subjects, natural chiefs, social chiefs, they all were there" (p. 36). The passage is a catalogue that fills up space; there is little descriptive value to it; there is little if any significance in the content, except, perhaps, a satiric comment on the proliferation of chieftaincy titles. Worse is the following mixture of "high" and guttural English, where pomposity meets cliché. Reacting to the idea of secession, either northern or eastern, Saro-Wiwa writes: "But it caused me considerable pangs of pain. The idea was anathema, for I did not see how the country could be allowed to go to the dogs. The judgement of history would be too severe on the generation that had allowed that to happen" (p. 39). Although the style in this passage is cumbersome and at times an annoying distraction, there is at least a sense of a desired communal order, however hazy. Not all passages are this badly written; at times, Saro-Wiwa uses metaphor with a degree of effect:

> The heat evaporated the seas and rivers and the sky grew thick with ominous clouds. Thunder clouds presaging the coming of the rains hung threateningly in the sky. And some people prayed for the thunderstorm. For a storm might scour the earth, thunder might break, but the desiccated earth stood to benefit afterwards, for when the storm ceased, the earth might be blessed with freshness. (p. 76)

It is a fairly common metaphor in writings about war, where weather is used as a harbinger of change. What is different here is the introduction of a conflict in the people—some pray for it; others, presumably, do not or pray against it.

The content of passages becomes problematic for the reader when he or she encounters the likes of the following, which refers to Gowon's assumption of command: "Those who had lived in trepidation and fear lest the country should break heaved a sigh of relief. At least it would not happen without some form and order" (p. 39). It is nice to know that, minimally, the destruction of one's country will take place in an orderly fashion. The tenor of approximately one-third of the information Saro-Wiwa conveys with more "grace" as the book progresses is rumor, hearsay, and secondhand opinion. This may well be the communications circuit in a time of war, but the author held back on the publication of *On a Darkling Plain* for twenty years, "in deference to the process of reconciliation in Eastern Nigeria, it being strong in certain of its views" (p. 9). There is nothing wrong with taking a strong stand; however, arguments, supporting points, and background documentation need to be marshaled carefully so that the stand shows itself to be exacting and rigorous in its construction and delivery. Rumor will not do the job. A sense of the period is conveyed, certainly, but when the book's second objective is to expose an upcoming generation "to as many facets of the war as possible" (p. 9), then greater care needs to be taken. A chapter on the deleterious effects of rumor would have been a useful addition, so that unproven ideas about the wartime situation are put in their proper context. Comparatively, Elechi Amadi's hesitancy about putting too much information into *Sunset in Biafra* is an appropriate response in this context.

Stylistic matters aside for the moment, what was Saro-Wiwa's contribution? Where did he see the Nigerian community (or the parts thereof) going? As the statement of intent in the "Author's Note" stresses, Saro-Wiwa is very much with the minority tribes and their desire for some form of "self-determination" (Saro-Wiwa, *On a Darkling Plain*, p. 12) within the Eastern Region. It takes some time before he becomes involved in an official capacity, but the story that leads up to his role as administrator allows a sense of the man's immediate reactions to the war and of what he can accomplish outside official circles.

At Ibadan, when the January 1966 coup occurs, Saro-Wiwa's reaction is a combination of disbelief and Amadi-like practicality: "A coup? Impossible! I did not believe it. I walked in to the dining hall and had lunch in silence" (p. 17). The response, in its mixture of historical events and the mundane, borders on the absurd; yet what response to war that does not evoke the absurd is worthwhile? During the second coup d'état, which topples Ironsi's governing council, Saro-Wiwa "went to lunch" (p. 37) on hearing the news. A repetition of the reaction suggests the habitual nature of the loss of government; surprise at events is gone; the drama of the situation and its human effect is lost. There is, then, a sense of Saro-Wiwa's deadpan humor, as in *Basi and Company,* at work here.

There is also a sense of sympathy for the coup makers: "In the five years of national independence, no change had come to the generality of the people. If the purpose of independence was ever to improve the lot of a people, Nigerian independence had failed woefully" (p. 24). The position expressed is that of a populist. There is no action taken to meet this laudable end, though; when Gowon assumes command and the situation becomes tense, Saro-Wiwa, like the easterners he criticizes, moves back to the East: "in Ibadan and Lagos, the weak minded needed only a word of encouragement and they were instantly on the move back home. . . . I travelled . . . the following day back to Port Harcourt" (p. 40). There is no sense of irony here. The intent seems to be to separate himself from the "weak minded," but the proximity of the two ideas places him in their midst. Irony would have allowed a fuller sense of the man, indicated some of his fears, and provided a more dramatic means of conveying the self. Soyinka's *The Man Died* contrasts sharply because he weds the event and its drama in a masterful way. In Saro-Wiwa, the impression created is of one who is unreflective in both life and art. Yet the direction of the book moves back to one of populist concern for the nation's minorities:

> [Ibadan] showed me how deep the ethnic grain runs in Nigerian society and how important it is to take cognizance of it in any Nigerian settlement. Additionally, I began to see the need for creating a proper identity for the small ethnic groups who . . . were wont to be lumped together with the major groups. (p. 47)

The concern is real, and Saro-Wiwa acts on it through his association with the Rivers Leaders of Thought, a minority group who lobbied Gowon's Ad Hoc Conference on Constitutional Proposals for self-determination: the constituting of a Rivers State within the federation. He also races back to Bori to be present at the Eastern Nigerian Consultative Assembly's meeting to vote on "a more democratic outlook" for the assembly, but because members were handpicked, his hopes of gaining power for his people were not fulfilled this way. He returns to the East again after people are brutalized in the intertribal violence that preceded the war. His intent, however, was not to serve his people but rather to wait until arrangements with the University of California at Berkeley were complete, so he could leave Nigeria to undertake doctoral studies in theater (p. 58). Commitment seems to have gone by the wayside.

During his wait, Saro-Wiwa stays at Nsukka, where he has a good vantage point to see what is happening in the East. His descriptions of Ojukwu's actions are fairly good, and he does, at least, provide a sense of that leader's apparent duplicity to substantiate his dislike for Ojukwu (p. 84ff.), whereas Amadi does not. There is even an instance of an alternative path not taken by Ojukwu, which lends credibility to Saro-Wiwa's views: "If Ojukwu had said in clear terms that he wanted to unite the progressives in Nigeria against reaction, he would have won support from several parts of Nigeria, in all of which both progressives and reactionaries are to be found. But Ojukwu was fired by no such vision" (pp. 84–85). Ultimately, Saro-Wiwa finds "nothing new" (p. 86) in the newly formed Biafra: "[i]t was Nigeria in a different name" (p. 88). His dissatisfaction is increased when Gowon puts forth a proposal for the creation of twelve states, which "offered a glimmer of hope" (p. 88) to minorities, a possibility of greater self-determination and fair treatment. Perhaps because of this allegiance with the federal side, Saro-Wiwa throws what compassion he has to the wind and hopes that Nsukka "would receive a deserving baptism of fire" (p. 94) when the war accelerated. That the people of Nsukka seemed keen on the idea of war is no reason for such a nasty invocation; it does even less for the case of the minorities if the potential leadership is shown to be petulant and small-minded rather than compassionate. Logic goes by the wayside when such attitudes are adopted; unreason becomes contagious.

Time passes, with Saro-Wiwa adopting a passive attitude, where "there was not much [he] could do, except sit at home, [his] ears glued to the radio, sometimes looking for something to read, at other times attempting to write" (p. 111). Examples of the "poetry" are sprinkled throughout the narrative. "Thoughts in Time of War" is typical of them. It is a rewrite of Wilfred Owen's "Dulce et Decorum est . . . ," lacking in Owen's rhythm and precision in the choice of image: "But there is nothing / Save the monotonous rhythm of rain / The bumping thud of bombs." The alliteration only serves to underscore the silliness of the piece. And so, time passes. Saro-Wiwa does reflect on events and possible roles for himself. Here his actions are a little more advanced than those of Amadi: "Gradually, however, it dawned on me that silence would be no answer to the problem, and I had begun to speak to friends and to stir up resistance [to Biafra] wherever I could. I cannot say that I was particularly successful, for people were generally frightened" (p. 114). Here he is candid and to the point. The lack of success soon leads to plans to escape and thus oppose Biafra from the outside, maintaining a sense of his goals for the minorities, at least for a brief time. Disconcertingly, though, Saro-Wiwa soon changes his tack and his reasoning:

> It did not seem right . . . that I should be pottering around doing nothing while my friends were making progress in their studies and in their careers. The way the war was dragging on, it might take a long time before it would end. And if it ended in three or four years, no matter in what way, I would be no better off than I was in that year, 1967. I proposed to leave to seek my fortunes in the wider world. I might return to Ibadan to complete my second degree or go abroad. (p. 117)

Here, quite obviously, the sentiment is one of self-advancement, not communal improvement. The ethic is purely economic in nature. Escape from Biafra follows, with his wife, although he expresses disappointment at her desire to leave with him. It is a chauvinistic response, especially given the role of a woman, his mother, in the organization of his escape (p. 117).[6] Although that interpretation is qualified by the book's dedication to his wife, "For Maria, my companion on this journey," what chance is there for communal change and betterment given such views? And, if the reader finds them unproblematic, the drama of the escape is destroyed by circuitous and deadening passages such as the following: "The tide was in our favour—that was the reason we set off at that time of day"(p. 128) or "[Emmanuel Isukul], too, was a man of few words, and on that occasion he did not speak much. My wife was not in the best of health; soon after the rain stopped, she busied herself preparing our brunch" (p. 131). Through an unwitting contrast, Saro-Wiwa declares sense and communal nurturing to be the properties of women; statements of the obvious are the province of men.

Once in Lagos, Saro-Wiwa contacts "the Rivers State elements" there; apparently the University of California, the University of Ibadan, and other goals he has had for himself have been supplanted by a renewed sense of community. Opportunism (governmental rather than academic advancement) is the motivator this time. Appointed the "administrator of Bonny," he sets about assisting civilians on the island and refugees from the East with rebuilding their lives. However, it is as an administrator that Saro-Wiwa commits an abomination—neglecting, brushing aside the needs of an individual and of justice. An officer in the Nigerian army rapes a female secretary in his office. Saro-Wiwa reports the incident but backs away from further involvement when the commanding officer decrees the charge to be a lie. Saro-Wiwa summarizes: "I have been witness several times to this type of brutalization of civilians by the military. It was tolerable in wartime (I had not pursued the Bonny affair any further—what's a rape in wartime?)" (p. 165). Put simply, a rape is a violent nullification of another's human rights. Less simply stated but from a comparable, recent context: "Rape is systematically being used by Burma's military as part of a policy of 'ethnic cleansing.' . . . Many ethnic leaders and pro-democracy activists claim that the violence against women is directly related to the military's goal of wiping out all ethnic resistance" (Bernstein and Kean, p. D4). Although there is no documentary evidence to support the presence of a similar "program" in Nigeria during the civil war, Saro-Wiwa's concern in various pamphlets, essays, and books with respect to "ethnic genocide" draws our attention to its potential presence; it also suggests his early complicity. One act of barbarity, if allowed to stand unchallenged, will lead to further acts. If decency and humanity cannot be maintained at the level of one individual toward another, then any community built on that absence will be rotten, an abomination of greater or lesser degree, but an abomination nonetheless. When accountability is lost, justice is too. Ezenwa-Ohaeto makes this point when he writes that "Saro-Wiwa believes that there can never be peace in his society without justice and that there can never be justice without a settlement of the minority question" (Ezenwa-Ohaeto, p. 339). The issues that remain are what sort of justice and for whom and who will act as an example of the type of action sought for a just society.

In the end, Saro-Wiwa's memoir is more like Obasanjo's *My Command* or Ademoyega's *Why We Struck*, for it lacks fine writing, a literary sensibility that places events in a humanistic context. The book is an account, not as immediate and personal as Amadi's or Soyinka's, because it draws on recently published analyses and memoirs of the war, in addition to the personal experiences of Saro-Wiwa himself. In this sense, it is an attempt to produce an official, comprehensive history. His "revolt" is tailored to giving the Biafrans their comeuppance, but what he achieves is a badly rendered, biased, and in areas a repugnant memoir of an individual who only seems sure when and how to act if the action directly affects himself.

> Those of us who had placed so much hope on the emergence of a new society were to feel a great sense of betrayal in the years after the war. That betrayal started as soon as the war ended. We were to know that, far from being a war of unity, the war was being fought by the three old adversaries for the oil wealth of our areas and that we were to be bruised, battered and bloodied and left to flounder helplessly on a darkling plain in an uncaring, ignorant country. (Saro-Wiwa, *On a Darkling Plain,* p. 238)

Although the minority position receives eloquent expression as well as the majority of critical attention in *On a Darkling Plain,* the perspective I have taken is to highlight marginalized and problematic areas of the story as literature and as a testament to human fallibility.

POSTSCRIPT ON *A MONTH AND A DAY*

> Make a careful study of people under a dictatorship, and invariably you
> will observe that it marks a period of internal retreat into cultural identities.
> —Soyinka, *The Open Sore*, p. 139

Soyinka's words are apposite as a transition between the concerns Saro-
Wiwa expresses in *On a Darkling Plain* and those he espouses in *A Month
and a Day*. *A Month and a Day* carries the subtitle "*A Detention Diary*." In
that subtitle resides the general form of this assemblage of thoughts, daily
records, polemic, and pamphlets. The *OED* offers a sixteenth-century use
of *diary* that is in keeping with Saro-Wiwa and by extension MOSOP's
goal: "kepe a diary memoreall of all the places of our marchinge." Next is
an author's "Preface," wherein Saro-Wiwa notes that he completed the
first draft in mid-1994 and that "two of the men to whom I give a lot of attention, Mr. Albert Badey and Chief Edward Kobani, were cruelly murdered along with two other Ogoni men at Giokoo in Ogoni. That gruesome
and sad event altered my original story somewhat but has not made material difference to it" (Saro-Wiwa, *A Month*, p. 1). Wole Soyinka puts the
situation into perspective as follows:

> Four prominent sons of Ogoni had been hacked to death, creating a per-
> manent breach within the Ogoni movement, MOSOP.
>   Now, there had been serious moves to heal the breach, with limited
> glimmerings of hope. I know this firsthand, because I was contacted by
> both the relations of the murder victims and the peace brokers. Such a
> process could only have been initiated as a result of the mounting suspi-
> cion that the bloodguilt lay outside of the Ogoni community . . . the per-
> manent agents provocateurs in the pay of Abacha's regime. (Soyinka, *The
> Open Sore*, pp. 151–152)

A Month and a Day is Saro-Wiwa's memorial, but one that leans heavily
on the Ogoni people's lengthy marching for greater autonomy:

> However, given the fact that I am not certain what the immediate future
> will bring, I have thought it wise to get my original draft published and
> have therefore smuggled it into my detention cell and am correcting and
> redrafting in very difficult circumstances. This may affect its quality
> somewhat, but should also not make material difference to it. (Saro-
> Wiwa, *A Month*, p. 1)

Authorial reservation to the side, *A Month and a Day* is more accomplished literature than *On a Darkling Plain*. Although an obvious conceit,
the building of immediate, concretely realized physical surroundings into
a metaphor for the state of the nation is well done: "the scrappy offices of
the State Security Service," "the crummy stairs," the "generally run-down

and definitely grubby" place (Saro-Wiwa, *A Month*, pp. 3–4). The theme of a general decrepitude that permeates the country is intermingled with a promotion of Saro-Wiwa's thesis of "indigenous colonization" (p. 7), "internal colonialism" (p. 18), "indigenous colonialism" (p. 63), and the effects of this process on "minorities" (p. 67). The need of sustenance for the fight is explicitly repeated (pp. 6, 7, 8, 12, 13, 14). These references, added to those about the nation's decrepitude, are refrains for the state of the nation and the state of the self—how each is being treated. They do, also, suggest a certain degree of fussiness, especially given that he's taken into police custody, in spite of "my security guards" (p. 8) for protection. Saro-Wiwa casually mentions what might appear to other prisoners or to his reader as a fairly privileged status in jail.[7] For example, he notes:

> When I began to whine about breakfast Mr. Ogbeifun stopped the vehicle beside a roadside stall, where he bought me corn and coconut. Ordinarily I would not have touched it for reasons of hygiene, but my standards were now being lowered, and I even found it tasty. By Jove! . . . When you are on your way to becoming a beast, courtesy of the Nigerian security system, a wretched meal becomes a feast. It is a part of the dehumanization process. (p. 35)

"You can tell the state of a nation by the way it keeps its prisons, prisoners being mostly out of sight. Going by this criteria, Nigeria was in a parlous state indeed" (Saro-Wiwa, *A Month,* p. 224). Saro-Wiwa has already made his point in the early going of *A Month,* but this repetition and explicit statement reminds us of his desire for full comprehension by the greatest number of people he could reach.

Chapter 4 (pp. 49–117) provides considerable information on the Ogoni movement Saro-Wiwa spearheaded. Looking at the numerous documents that fill *A Month and a Day*, it is obvious that Saro-Wiwa is using every opportunity from book readings to speeches to advance the Ogoni cause. Some of the texts included are a piece from *The Ogoni Nation Today and Tomorrow* (pp. 52–54), *The Ogoni Bill of Rights* (pp. 67–70), and *Addendum to the Ogoni Bill of Rights* (pp. 89–92). *A Month and a Day* ends with moral advice in a language that is presumably designed to delight and to instruct the masses:

> [General Babangida's] touted transition truck is completely rusty, without a roadworthiness certificate or an insurance policy; its licence has expired. Yet its driver insists on taking it on an endless journey. The driver's licence needs renewal, but he insists on proceeding without it, depending on his ability to bribe the traffic policemen along the way. Loaded with touts, the truck stops at odd places to pick up stranded passengers. . . . The touts, dependent on the driver for their "chop" money, chant his praise even as he drives recklessly without a spare tyre or headlamps towards the

precipice. I fear for the truck, the driver and the touts, and I fear for the passengers. God grant that they do not involve innocent bystanders in an accident. I advise everyone to stand far away from the possible paths of the deadly truck. (Saro-Wiwa, *A Month,* pp. 112–113)

If Nigeria is the truck, and Babangida is the driver and he has no democratic mandate (a license), who are the traffic policemen? What sort of advice is that apparent stoicism: "stand far away from" the truck's path? How does one get involved to effect change? The allegorical reading does not seem to work consistently. Yet in its confusion it is an effective and abridged comment on the state of the nation. In these literary strategies, Saro-Wiwa fulfills what Edward Said deems the task of the intellectual in society:

> The intellectual's representations—what he or she represents and how those ideas are represented to an audience—are always and ought to remain an organic part of an ongoing experience in society: of the poor, the disadvantaged, the voiceless, the unrepresented, the powerless. These are equally concrete and ongoing; they cannot survive being transformed and then frozen into creeds, religious declarations, professional methods. (Said, p. 84)

Where creeds seem to be established is in the unchanging nature of Saro-Wiwa's beliefs and the social science documents at their root. For example, much has been written on the nature of imperialism since Robert Heilbroner's *The Future as History* (1960), yet Saro-Wiwa, perhaps because of his various business concerns, his writing, and his social and environmental activism, is unable to update his theorizing of the Ogoni condition.

Saro-Wiwa's anthem for the Ogoni, a poem in Khana ("Yoor Zaansin Ogoni") and English (Saro-Wiwa, *A Month,* p. 207), suggests new directions for the writer, an Ngugi-like return to the primary audience—his own ethnic group. In all of these senses, then, Saro-Wiwa's diary more closely approximates historical examples of the genre, which C. Hugh Holman and William Harmon note meant the maintenance while writing of "a possible audience," though they "are not extended, organized narratives prepared for the public eye" (Holman and Harmon, p. 142). The fragmented nature of *A Month and a Day,* largely due to the insertion of other forms of discourse, approximates the *OED* definition of *memoir*—"a record of events, not purporting to be a complete history, but treating such matters as come within the personal knowledge of the writer." The more mundane calendrical ordering of Saro-Wiwa's text pulls it back to the diary genre. Indeed, if J. A. Cuddon's fracturing of the diary into two subgenres is a means to greater clarity—the *intimate* recording, interpreting, and filtering of emotions and events by the diarist and the *anecdotal* chronicle of events witnessed (Cuddon, p. 42)—then Ken Saro-Wiwa's *A Month and a Day: A Detention Diary* is a re-fusion of the subgenres, as his mixture of the personal (daily ablutions) and the public (his participation in rallies) attests. "Notebook" might have been a more apt generic classification, but this form lacks the coherent shape and greater sense of audience implicit in the first two forms. As the word itself suggests and as the *OED* concurs, a notebook is closer to "memoranda" and to the drafting process. Overall, the three genres are linked by their necessarily personal and private nature. Their purpose in that field is to be a "literature of personal revelation" (Shipley, p. 32), wherein the writer is the first student and beneficiary. The memoir is intended for publication, the diary occasionally so, the notebook rarely. Conditions forced Saro-Wiwa into early publication of his material, but even so, *A Month and a Day: A Detention Diary,* in its conflation of discursive types (the historical impact found in the memoir, the personal involvement found in the diary, the incomplete notes for future action/aspirations), suggests the heterogeneous nature of all literature and thus disavows generic classification as purposeful in any but the most limited fashion: as a loosely descriptive label. It is precisely that effect that makes Saro-Wiwa's book a worldly text, dramatizing as it does the disparate strains and contestation of forces—literary and political and personal. An unfinished, unpolished text is a testament finally to the greater work *in process.*

CONCLUSION

Any disquiet that a reader feels with respect to some of Saro-Wiwa's problematic phraseology and opinion must be tempered by knowledge of the country in which he lived. Wole Soyinka's summation of the execution puts it into brutal, inhuman perspective:

> An executioner was dispatched from the north to Port Harcourt, but the levers of death had lain unused for far too long and repeatedly thwarted the hangman, prolonging the agony of the condemned men in a scene of shabby cruelty, an unspeakably inhuman drama. Ken Saro-Wiwa was the first among the nine, and it took five attempts to hang him. On November 10, as he was led away from the scaffold the third or fourth time, Ken Saro-Wiwa cried out, "Why are you people doing this to me? What sort of a nation is this?" (Soyinka, *The Open Sore,* pp. 148–149)

Like Studs Terkel's "talking book," *The Great Divide* (1988), Saro-Wiwa's two books, in addition to Soyinka's and Amadi's memoirs, add to a cross-section of opinions and beliefs about the Nigerian community and its future, even though the cross-section is a privileged one and lacks the perspective of women. Nevertheless, the contributions are noteworthy, in that although official history continues to record the achievements of the victors and in spite of General Gowon's comment about "No Victors, No Vanquished," Saro-Wiwa emphasizes the need for new efforts toward the building of a national consensus. Wole Soyinka's memoir, *The Man Died: Prison Notes of Wole Soyinka,* comes across as accessible to all. Yet, as several commentators have suggested, Soyinka, too, needs to draw voices dissident to his own into the debate and to apply the formidable intellectual gifts he has to find an equitable and honorable role for each voice. Elechi Amadi's perspective, in *Sunset in Biafra,* deserves support for its appeal to tradition and traditional values, but this does not mean that mere legislation will bring it into being. If tradition is to have a role in any new nation, then it must be worked for vigorously, and its attendant benefits must be shown, not simply asserted. Even then, the past cannot be returned to; it must be molded into and become part of the future. Ken Saro-Wiwa offers a perspective on the situation that minorities find themselves in. As a spokesperson, Saro-Wiwa is truthful in his conveyance of his contradictory role and attitudes; it is just that the personal truth he lays bare emphasizes the need for much more care and attention to the socialization of the people, to their education, and to their compassion. Elechi Amadi and Ken Saro-Wiwa produce limited memoirs, in that they are personal histories; these revolts against received history expanding out from the individual to the community are weak and devoid of serious reappraisals of the nation's sense of itself and its structures. *A Month and a Day,* too, has some shortcomings, but there is an attempt within its pages to consolidate the discourse of minority rights with the discourse on internal colonialism and the discourse on self. Its lesson to us, like the lesson Soyinka draws from Saro-Wiwa's death, is that Nigerians "have warned and pleaded. Now [Nigerians] are paying yet another heavy price for the comatose nature of global conscience" (Soyinka, *The Open Sore,* p. 152) and their own failures within the nation.

Saro-Wiwa's literary legacy will reside with *Sozaboy* and a handful of the poems and short stories, but his political legacy will remain in these broken texts: purposeful, raw, and explosive—there is something we, irrespective of culture and ethnicity, can learn about the world from them.

NOTES

1. This material on Soyinka has undergone a previous incarnation in my *Nigerian Civil War Literature* (1990).

2. Adamu Ciroma, "Review—*The Man Died,*" in *When the Man Died—Views, Reviews and Interviews,* ed. John Agetua (Benin City: John Agetua, 1975). It is a representative example of the "positions" taken on the book.

3. Wole Soyinka, "Ten Years After," in *The Man Died: Prison Notes of Wole Soyinka* (London: Arrow Books, 1985: xvi).

4. The "facts" of the Aburi Accord would seem to undermine Amadi's point, given that Ojukwu took the issues seriously and was thoroughly prepared, whereas Gowon's approach was more lax.

5. Wole Soyinka, "Ten Years After."

6. See also *A Month and a Day* for various statements that objectify women, such as, "I have to confess that between herself and the meal she served, I might have preferred her if she had been equally available" (p. 29).

7. Compare his circumstances, for example, with what Soyinka outlines in *The Man Died* or the situation of Ngugi wa Thiongó in *Detained.*

WORKS CITED

Ademoyega, Adewale. *Why We Struck: The Story of the First Nigerian Coup.* Ibadan: Evans Brothers, 1981.

Amadi, Elechi. *Ethics in Nigerian Culture.* London: Heinemann, 1982.

———. *Sunset in Biafra.* London: Heinemann, 1973, 1978.

———. *Estrangement.* London: Heinemann, 1986.

Bakhtin, Mikhail. *Speech Genres and Other Essays.* Trans. Caryl Emerson and Michael Holquist. Austin: University of Texas Press, 1986.

Bernstein, Dennis, and Leslie Kean. "War Crime: Rape of Ethnic Women Just Another Strategy for Burmese Army." *The Globe and Mail* (Toronto), 4 July, 1998: D4.

Cuddon, J. A. *A Dictionary of Literary Terms and Literary Theory.* 3rd. ed. London: Blackwell, 1991.

Ezenwa-Ohaeto. "Ken Saro-Wiwa." *Twentieth Century Caribbean and Black African Writers.* Dictionary of Literary Biography 157: 3rd series. Ed. Bernth Lindfors and Reinhard Sander. Detroit: Gale, 1996: 331–339.

Graf, William D. *The Nigerian State: Political Economy, State Class and Political System in the Post-Colonial Era.* London: James Currey, 1988.

Harrison, Tony. "Speaking for the Inarticulate." *Index on Censorship 2*, no. 4 (Winter 1973).

Holman, C. Hugh, and William Harmon. "Diary, Memoir." In *A Handbook to Literature.* 5th ed. New York: Macmillan, 1986.

McIlvanney, William. "The Shallowing of Scotland." In his *Surviving the Shipwreck.* Edinburgh: Mainstream, 1991.

Obasanjo, Olusegun. *My Command: An Account of the Nigerian Civil War.* London: Heinemann, 1981.

Oxford English Dictionary. Oxford: Oxford University Press, 1961.

Pascal, R. "Biography." In *Cassell's Encyclopedia of World Literature.* 3 vols. Ed. J. Buchanan-Brown. New York: William Morrow, 1973, vol. 1: 76.

Povey, John F. "The Nigerian War: The Writer's Eye." *Journal of African Studies* (Fall 1974) 1.

Riemenschneider, Dieter. "Biafra War in Nigerian Literature." In *Jaw Bones and Umbilical Cords.* Ed. Ulla Schild. Berlin: D. Reimer Verlag, 1984.

Said, Edward W. *Representations of the Intellectual.* London: Vintage, 1994.

Saro-Wiwa, Ken. *On a Darkling Plain: An Account of the Nigerian Civil War.* London, Lagos, and Port Harcourt: Saros International Publishers, 1989.

————. *A Month and a Day: A Detention Diary*. Harmondsworth: Penguin, 1995.
Shipley, Joseph T., ed. *Dictionary of World Literature*. New Jersey: Littlefield, Adams, 1968.
Soyinka, Wole. "The Writer in a Modern African State." In *The Writer in Modern Africa*. Ed. Per Wastberg. New York: Africana Publishing Corp., 1969.
————. "The Failure of the Writer in Africa." In *The Africa Reader: Independent Africa*. Ed. Wilfred Cartey and Martin Kilson. New York: Random House, 1970.
————. "Let's Think About the Aftermath of This War." *Nigerian Daily Sketch,* 4 August 1967.
————. *The Man Died: Prison Notes of Wole Soyinka*. Harmondsworth: Penguin, 1979; London: Arrow Books, 1985.
————. *The Open Sore of a Continent: A Personal Narrative of the Nigerian Crisis*. New York: Oxford University Press, 1996.
————. *A Shuttle in the Crypt*. London: Collings/Eyre Methuen, 1972.
Webb, Hugh. "Soyinka's Novelistic Autobiography." *New Literature Review* 5: 11–21.

4

The Poetry:
Songs in a Time of War

Tanure Ojaide

Ken Saro-Wiwa as a writer is so well known for his hilarious television series, *Basi and Company,* and for his novel *Sozaboy* and short stories *A Forest of Flowers,* that many people do not seem to be aware that he is an accomplished poet too. Though not well known, his poetry ironically synthesizes many of the subjects, themes, and techniques of his drama, fiction, and nonfiction (see Appendixes 1 and 2). His perception of the Nigerian-Biafran conflict, his closeness to the terrain of the Niger Delta for which he fought both the Nigerian military dictatorship and the Shell Petroleum Development Corporation–British Petroleum (Shell-BP) and got hanged, his passion for life and his beliefs, his sensitivity, and his serious yet humorous dimensions are some of the characteristics that poetry, by its very lyrical nature, has enabled him to realize succinctly in *Songs in a Time of War.* Though he wrote a prose account of the civil war, *On A Darkling Plain: An Account of the Nigerian Civil War,* it is his poetry that best captures the mood and temperament of the crisis and his personal response to it. The relationship between Saro-Wiwa's prose account of the civil war and his poetry about it is comparable to the relationship between Wole Soyinka's book *The Man Died,* his prison notes, and *A Shuttle in the Crypt,* which expresses his mistreatment by the federal authorities for his involvement in the national crisis. Saro-Wiwa's *Songs in a Time of War* is poetry based on a specific issue at a particular place and time. The historical context makes the poetry more relevant because the poet is documenting history from an artist's perspective, not that of the professional historian. Writing the history of the Nigerian Civil War has largely been controversial because those from each side of the war tend to contradict those from the other side. In his poetry, Saro-Wiwa strikes a balance: the emphasis is more on humanity than on taking sides.

Though Saro-Wiwa belongs to a minority group that was marginalized in what was then Eastern Nigeria, his poems still show abhorrence for the Nigerian Civil War and the preceding civil disturbances. He begins from a rather alienated position and moves to a more activist role as the war progresses. In fact, the civil war period can be said to be the beginning of his self-awareness and minority group awareness, which was to be followed by a radical activism that would lead to his judicial murder by the Nigerian military government. Saro-Wiwa exposes the lies behind the war on both sides and, despite his supporting the federal forces against secessionist Biafra, stands above the fray to cast a cold eye on man's inhumanity to man. The poet uses different techniques to portray the sociopolitical situation and his predicament of loving and hating Nigeria and, in so doing, expresses many ironies and contrasts.

Saro-Wiwa's poetry can also be seen in relation to other Nigerian poets who wrote on the national crisis that resulted in a civil war from 1967 to 1970. Like Christopher Okigbo in his poems prophesying war, Saro-Wiwa's desire for justice in the treatment of his minority Niger Delta people made him support the federal government at that time to throw off Igbo hegemony. He is also like J. P. Clark-Bekederemo, Wole Soyinka, and Chinua Achebe in his moral outrage against the savagery of war. Furthermore, he is a minority person from the Niger Delta, whose riverine and oil-rich landscape and minority status in a federal but centralized Nigerian government have become poetic metaphors for marginalization, neglect, and exploitation.

As Kobena Eyi-Acquah, a young Ghanaian poet, puts it in his *Music for a Dream Dance:* "there are some things / Which can only be said in song" (Eyi-Acquah, *Music,* p. 3). Whether in the form of a mask, persona, or direct voice, the poetic voice carries the writer's sensitivity, passion, and viewpoint, or lack thereof. The totality of the poet's sensibility appears in the poetry in the forms of emotions and ideas, which involve affairs of the heart, brain, and soul. Being an integrative medium, poetry appears to have been an appropriate forum for Saro-Wiwa (like many of his fellow Nigerian writers of the troubled period) to capture not only the mood and atmosphere of, but also his individual response to, the national crisis. Theo Vincent, in his introduction to the poems, finds that Saro-Wiwa's "concern for style and the need to capture his intense feelings and emotions about Nigerian society and humanity in general, lead him, inevitably to poetry. . . . The trauma of war, the unspeakable horrendous bestialities of war are not material for expansive prose" (Saro-Wiwa, *Songs,* p. 9). As Saro-Wiwa himself admits, "My forte, if there was such a thing, was, I always thought, either short-story writing or the drama. But at that time, my thoughts only came down in verse" (Saro-Wiwa, *On a Darkling Plain,* p. 111). In a war, poetry that comes out in inspirational outbursts is a ready medium of expression.

Belonging to a minority group in the Igbo-dominated Eastern Region that Lt. Col. Chukwuemeka Odumegwu Ojukwu declared the Republic of Biafra, Saro-Wiwa felt that his people did not belong to Biafra. After all, the government in Enugu neglected the non-Igbo areas that became the South-eastern and Rivers States and that today are Cross River, Akwa Ibom, Rivers, and Bayelsa States. When Lt. Col. Yakubu Gowon tried to preempt the declaration of the Eastern Region as Biafra with the creation of East Central, South-eastern, and Rivers States on 27 May 1967, he was, for strategic reasons, separating the minorities from the majority Igbo group whose dominance had marginalized others.

The Niger Delta gives identity to its indigenous peoples. The inhabitants of this watery land of lush vegetation on both sides of the Niger River have always been minorities in either the Eastern or Western Regions or the Nigerian nation. Their status is that of an exploited and neglected people. In *On a Darkling Plain,* Saro-Wiwa says that

> competition between the three majority ethnic groups in Nigeria brought about the civil war and continues to threaten to destroy the country. This unhealthy competition has done grave injury to the minority ethnic groups who are continually marginalized, thus making Nigeria one of the most unjust societies in the world. (p. 11)

For this reason, one of the Niger Delta writer's orientations is to signify the Delta, showing its paradox of sitting on oil and gas wealth and yet remaining impoverished. The Yoruba, Hausa-Fulani, and Igbo are the "three overlords" who take their turn to ride their Delta victim in my book, *Labyrinths of the Delta.* This neglect is reflected in "Ughelli":

> To see her dry-skinned when her oil rejuvenates hags
> to leave her in darkness when her fuel lights the universe
> to starve her despite all her produce
> to let her dehydrate before wells bored into her heart
> to have her naked despite her innate industry
> to keep her without roads when her sweat tars the outside world
> to make her homeless when her idle neighbours inhabit skyscrapers . . .
> It is a big shame. (Ojaide, *Labyrinths,* p. 74)

Ughelli, located in the Delta area, is an oil- and gas-producing center. At the time I wrote the poem in the early 1970s, Ughelli had no electricity or running water. This total neglect is similar to what Saro-Wiwa writes of the Ogoni experience:

> [I]t is no wonder that thirty years after Shell-BP discovered oil in commercial quantity in Ogoni country, on perfectly arable land, in one of the most densely-populated areas in Africa, the Ogoni people remain one of

the most destitute in the world. Every oil well drilled by Shell has enough water to drown the entire Ogoni people. Thirty or forty wells later, the Ogoni still drink water from guinea worm–infested streams. Shell flares all its gas and has destroyed the Ogoni environment in the process. No Ogoni village has electricity. . . . Thus the ugly face of international capitalism joining the hideous nature of majority ethnic colonialism in Nigeria have reduced the Ogoni and other minorities in the delta to beggardom. (Saro-Wiwa, *On a Darkling Plain,* p. 12)

Many Niger Delta people feel cheated by the regional and federal governments' neglecting development in the Delta, despite the wealth its people give to the country.

Neither the Nigerian nor the Biafran parties to the conflict owned up to its motives for the civil war, but it was generally believed by the Niger Delta people that the war was fought for the soul of the Niger Delta because of its huge oil reserves. The neglect and marginalization of the Niger Delta minorities led Isaac Adaka Boro (a former policeman and university student who declared the Niger Delta Repubic) to revolt against the Aguiyi-Ironsi regime. The plight of the people would be made worse by the alliance of multinational corporations and military dictatorship that Saro-Wiwa would fight against.

Saro-Wiwa was "one of the very few Nigerians who were privileged to be close to the crisis in its various theatres" (Saro-Wiwa, *On a Darkling Plain,* p. 10). Though at the University of Nigeria at Nsukka when Biafra was proclaimed and the civil war broke out, Saro-Wiwa soon escaped into his Rivers State to be on the federal side. He was so much a nationalist, as "Dis Nigeria Sef" shows, that much as he condemned the organized killings of Igbos in the north of the country, he would not condone a divided Nigeria. He saw the great strength and benefits that size and diversity brought, and for so much love of Nigeria he would not support any efforts to bring about the disintegration of his country.

It is from this background that one can better appreciate Saro-Wiwa's war position as expressed in *Songs in a Time of War*—that though the federal army was liberating his Ogoni people from Igbo domination, he still condemned war as needless violence that lays waste human and natural bounties and results in loss of lives and property and also in the dissipation of energy that would have been used in nation building. Clark-Bekederemo and others like me found ourselves in this same dilemma during the civil war. Mid-west State (today's Delta and Edo States) was, as the war progressed, occupied by the Biafran army in a so-called liberation exercise. The Biafrans renamed Mid-west State the Republic of Benin and named Lt. Col. Victor Banjo as its head of state. This affront made many of us from the Delta area who were ardent supporters of Biafra and the Igbo people question our attitudes. How could the Biafrans be "liberating" us by "conquering" and making our state a colony of Biafra? Were Biafra and the federal government not both just interested in our oil reserves rather than in us as human beings? Rumor already had it then that the Biafrans had pledged the oil reserves to the French for military assistance. Later the federal side would successfully liberate Rivers and Bendel, the Delta states that produce about 95 percent of all Nigeria's national revenue. To Saro-Wiwa,

> there was neither intellectual rationalization nor social for me in biafra. I abhorred the senseless killings in the North; I detested the perpetrators of these acts. But I perceived that these were but the results of the struggle for power between the three major ethnic groups, a struggle in which the minorities were mere pawns. (Saro-Wiwa, *On a Darkling Plain*, p. 88)

But still, every sensitive heart went to the Igbo people, who had suffered the pogrom before the war and were still being harassed elsewhere in the federation. The tales of fleeing Igbo people from the North touched every heart. In many cases, those not identified as Yoruba were declared "nyam miri," Igbo. Both Biafran and federal sides claimed provocation for dastardly acts that offended the human spirit. Reflecting on the war, I wrote "War Games," in which I said: "if you saw through masks of liberators / to thieving armies bolstering faith in blood relations / you would pull down Heroes' Arcade." No one was fooled by the claims of both sides not to see their brutality. As Wole Soyinka, who tried in vain to diffuse the crisis, puts it, "The man dies in all who keep silent in the face of tyranny" (Soyinka, *The Man Died*, p. 23). Saro-Wiwa's *Songs in a Time of War* is a product of both the Nigerian Civil War and the minority status of the Niger Delta people.

Songs in a Time of War is Saro-Wiwa's individual response to the history of Nigeria at a critical period. The context of the poems is public, but his response is private. The poet uses his "song" to record, as a witness, the events of the civil war period and how they affected him and his people. He condemns the conspiracy of Nigeria's major ethnic groups by writing: "The world and posterity have to know that the real victims of that war were the Eastern minorities who were in a no-win situation. They are the oppressed in Nigeria" (Saro-Wiwa, *On a Darkling Plain*, p. 10). In these poems, the poet comes across as committed to justice and fairness. He is not only the conscience of his people but also the one who will rouse them from lethargy.

Songs in a Time of War opens with "Voices," which conveys the poet's position at the outbreak of the war. He is alienated from the rest of society because he is not concerned with what engages others:

> They speak of taxes
> Of oil and power

> They speak of honour
> And pride of tribe
>
> They speak of war
> Of bows and arrows
>
> They speak of tanks
> And putrid human flesh
>
> I sing my love
> For Maria
> (Saro-Wiwa, *Songs,* p. 13)

In much of his war poetry, Saro-Wiwa highlights paradoxes. A bright young man of twenty-six in 1967 when the war broke out, the poet was more consumed by his love for Maria than arguing about petty, divisive, and violent issues of taxation, oil, power, and war. He thus "sings" as they "speak." At this time the poet appears detached from societal and national issues in his immersion in love. But he is soon drawn out of the private domain into the public. War is too serious not to affect everybody in its path. Ken Saro-Wiwa was in the war's path, not just as a Nigerian but as a Niger Delta person whose land held the prize of petroleum. He soon realized the moral depravity that war brings about. War drums are beaten, a "lie" to lure unknowing troops to "die" for what they think is a worthy cause. There is propaganda on both sides: "the loud resonance / Of an empty lie" (p. 14). Of course, Saro-Wiwa, like many of us at the time, listened to the broadcasts of Radio Biafra and Radio Kaduna, both parties saturating the airwaves with "lies." Okon Ndem, who read news for Radio Biafra, became a household name because of his uncanny ability to transfer suffering to assault his listeners. Nigerian Radio opened every news broadcast with jingles such as "To keep Nigeria one is a task that must be done." In such a period of inflammatory heart-melting broadcasts, it was extremely difficult to have "Objective detachment / Sound judgement" (p. 15).

The poet paints a devastating picture of war—even when it is "civil" war or a "police action," like the Biafra-Nigeria one—in both "Corpses Have Grown" and "Ogale—An Evacuated Town." In the latter poem, there is this ugly picture:

> Cars cannibalized
> Amputated
> Lie by the road side
> Abandoned
> Forgotten

A lone lean dog
Scrounging for food
Reaps human skulls
In a shallow gutter.

Broken houses roofless
Gape forlorn
At wet angry skies

Ogale lies in broken images. (p. 29)

War wreaks material and spiritual desolation. There is no shelter, no food, and no family. The physical destruction translates into spiritual hollowness:

The xylophone of the deceased chief
Is still, has forgot the past.
Ancestral spirits driven from home
Walk tearful abroad
The orphaned land weeps. (p. 18)

In times of war, life is even more uncertain than in normal times. In "Night Encounter," a gun-carrying soldier smiles one moment and in another gets killed.

With regard to the savagery of war, there is a difference in perception between those at the front who experience its ugly truth and the propagandists who fictionalize events for specific political and strategic goals. Clark-Bekederemo, an Ijo of the Niger Delta area, writes about those outside the war front in "The Casualties," ironically dedicated to Chinua Achebe:

The casualties are many, and a good number well
Outside the scenes of ravage and wreck;
They are emissaries of rift,
So smug in the smoke-rooms they haunt abroad,
They do not see the funeral piles
At home eating up the forests.
They are wandering minstrels who, beating on
The drums of the human heart, draw the world
Into a dance with rites it does not know.
(Clark[-Bekederemo], *Casualties,* p. 37)

In *Songs in a Time of War,* Saro–Wiwa condemns those who lie to make war look glorious, the sort Clark-Bekederemo criticizes and Chinua

Achebe calls "war drummers." The honor and pride associated with war are a ruse meant to deceive and lure the unwary and inexperienced into disaster. Thus it is a "lie" to make people "die." The poet strongly condemns the civil war and the two opposing sides, even though he is a minority Rivers person supposedly being liberated by the federal forces that the secessionists—the same Biafrans the poet's people consider to be occupiers of their land—see as aggressors.

Saro-Wiwa goes beyond the easily visible physical devastation and the physical hurt and losses. These are seen as the outer manifestations of some inner spiritual malaise. He tackles the moral, ethical, emotional, and psychological levels of dysfunction that lead to and get exacerbated by a senseless war. It is the inhumanity of the war drummers and political leaders on the one hand and the dehumanization of the victims—the fighters on both sides—on the other hand that break the poet's heart. As Clark-Bekederemo puts it in the title poem of his book *Casualties*, "We fall, / All casualties of the war" (p. 38). Similarly, Saro-Wiwa sees as victims those who are directly involved and those who are inexorably drawn into the war. The inhabitants of Ogale, both humans and animals, are innocent victims. And beyond these, the war exacted emotional and spiritual tolls on every Nigerian.

A constant theme in *Songs in a Time of War* is the sharp contrast the poet delineates between the noise, destruction, and discomfort of the human war machine and the peacefulness of nature. The poet seems to be suggesting that war results in unnatural happenings. In "Near the Front," it is "hot and stifling / With metal doors banging / Harsh boots on stones grating" at "hush of night when the world / Is still" (Saro-Wiwa, *Songs*, p. 17). War becomes "the curse of doom / On man" (p. 17). In many of these poems, there is the stable sempiternal background of nature with its peace, quiet, and assumed innocence. In contrast, war is a temporary, destructive phenomenon preying on nature and humans.

Saro-Wiwa relates war to nature in a complex way. On the surface, war is the opposite of what nature stands for, but war's disruption is symbolically conveyed through the use of pathetic fallacy. Nature is presented on occasion as reflecting the human dimensions of war. Clouds and rain symbolize war that destroys the peace and happiness that the sun and moon connote. Thus, "Prayer on a Moonlight Night," informed by traditional folklore, becomes an allegorical statement:

> The woman who sits in the moon
> Breaking wood
> Watching the earth
> Is hard at work tonight.

> Clouds, do not stop her view
> Into our nuptial chamber
> Where sweet deeds leave us
> Withered and strong
> In the tender arms of gentle sleep. (p. 28)

Of course, the clouds could prevent the moon from shining into the "nuptial chamber," just as war already has destroyed the happiness of the Nigerian people. The moon is associated with blissful love, and the poet would rather be involved in a love that would drain him physically and still strengthen him emotionally than experience war, which only destroys. In "To Sarogua, Rain Maker," there is the "Thunderstorm / Raining blood" (Saro-Wiwa, *Songs*, p. 30).

However, the same nature that reflects the sociopolitical condition of the land during the war also becomes the source of redemption. That is why the poet invites the rain maker to "Receive us, mighty one / With a cleansing shower" (p. 30). Subsequently, in "The Escape," the poet flees from "the stink of war." He travels through Delta rivers and creeks, the only safe travel-ways then, to Lagos for peace. In Bane,

> after the storm become brilliance
> As we rowed down miles of calm
> On the Andoni river,
> Swimming on beyond the canoe
> A lone fish dived and resurfaced
> Leading on, so it seemed
> To the realms of peace. (p. 19)

This is the familiar Niger Delta of the poet, and he moves easefully out of war. Ironically, the Lagos he arrives in may not hold the peace he seeks: the Biafrans soon after bomb Lagos with a B-52 aircraft. Delta, being home, is the only safe place for the poet, even though the war has already touched it in Bonny, where federal naval guns boom, apparently in defense. The Delta terrain is so natural and peaceful, whereas the war is an unnatural intrusion brought about by greed and bitterness. The poems give the impression of a Niger Delta that is despoiled and desecrated because of the civil war. This physical and spiritual damage will proceed after the civil war in the aggressive oil exploitation of the area by Shell-BP.

The use of nature in *Songs in a Time of War* can be compared to Soyinka's use of nature in his Nigerian crisis poems, *A Shuttle in the Crypt*. "Flowers for My Land" mythologizes the national tragedy as a garden "furrowed still and bare" (p. 62). The land has been laid waste by the savagery, and in place of the life, youth, and beauty that flowers connote, there is death. The flowers also symbolize humans—the good who are dead and the evil ones alive. The country is turned into a wasteland of corpses. The wasteland motif is reinforced by the echo of T. S. Eliot's poetry in "I do not / Dare to think these bones will bloom tomorrow" (Soyinka, *A Shuttle,* p. 64). In addition to the pervasive decay, tares occupy the land. The allusion to Christ's parable of good crops choked by bad weeds brings a moral dimension to the poet's perspective.

A slight difference exists between Saro-Wiwa's and Soyinka's perception of nature during the crisis. Soyinka seems to see nature having both good and bad aspects like human beings. In fact, in "Background and Friezes," he perceives nature as colluding with a bloody tyrant: "Our hands are clean / The rains have fallen twice and earth is deep" (Soyinka, *A Shuttle,* p. 74). Saro-Wiwa sees nature as an extension of the Niger Delta terrain—as a refuge—and its creeks, rivers, flora, and fauna as manifestations of a pristine environment that the civil war and later the oil corporations have polluted with impunity.

Saro-Wiwa presents war as an ironic phenomenon that through violence and disruption brings out the humanity, sensitivity, and tenderness in humankind. Love in a time of war is not a contradiction or a weakness on the part of the lovers but an affirmation of faith in both life and love as the ultimate salvation of humankind. As already mentioned with regard to "Voices," the poet in the midst of national wrangles sings of his love for Maria. Saro-Wiwa also dedicates *On a Darkling Plain: An Account of the Nigerian Civil War* to "Maria, my companion on this journey." The poet's love poems, "For Maria" and "For Her," convey his humanity even in a period of depravation. For these moments the poet shuts off the national tragedy of war to reminisce about his love for Maria. Unlike the depravity that causes and fights wars, the tender heart in love connotes peace and happiness.

In both poems, Saro-Wiwa invokes memories of his love to contrast the present imbroglio with the past idyll. He remembers days when he was much younger, "Fresh as a cob of maize in May" (Saro-Wiwa, *Songs,* p. 26); again, a nature image conveys a positive image of the vitality, gusto, and beauty of youth. In a time of crisis, memories of youth and love help to assuage the present pain:

> When clouds invade my sky
> And stars cannot peep out of doors . . .
> Be the moon and the stars
> And let me play still
> In the softness you shed. (p. 26)

War has not only broken the ecstatic life he used to live with his love but has separated them.

> And do you remember that day
> When the dying sun shot gold-tinted arms
> And we swam the river from shore to shore?
> Do you remember the words I said to you?

Intense love metaphorically becomes a kind of storm or war of passion. The poet's tenderness contrasts sharply with the hate and bitterness in wars. The love poems also make one better appreciate the peace, tranquillity, and happiness of normal times. These love poems also indirectly decry the savagery of war and the physical and emotional loss associated with fighting.

It is important to emphasize that this note of love in a time of war is absent from the war poems of Clark-Bekederemo, Soyinka, and Achebe, who are consumed by their respective positions of condemning those they feel are responsible for the crisis. Saro-Wiwa instead situates the civil war in his life—as the abrogation of his youth, lovers, and humanity. He pleads in "To Palm Wine" that "In this frothing sweetness / Be my name recorded" and acknowledges the "wild thrill of piping passion" and his sensuality (Saro-Wiwa, *Songs*, p. 31).

"To Palm Wine" and "Courtesan" appear to be occasional poems in the sense that they are not directly related to the civil war. The poet seems to be saying that despite war, in some ways life goes on as it used to. Human passions are aroused and need to be filled. Soldiers from both the Nigerian and Biafran armies were notorious during the war in their sexual escapades, which involved rape and kidnapping of women. Thus, the speaker of "Courtesan" is even more refined than the typical Nigerian or Biafran soldier who would rape rather than go to a prostitute, a "late bird." He is drunk too. Apparently human drives persist in a time of war, which sometimes exacerbates some of them such as sex and drinking.

Perhaps the most controversial poem in *Songs in a Time of War* is "Epitaph for Biafra." Critics of the poet might pick on this poem as proof of his taking sides during the civil war. Of course, he took sides—he was against the dismemberment of the Nigerian nation, and he did not want the Niger Delta to be forced into a Biafra whose antecedent Eastern Region had marginalized his minority people. After talking about the plight of those in Biafra after its surrender to federal troops, he rhetorically asks about the consequences of decisions and actions:

> Didn't they know that bones are brittle
> The matchet swing a bloody path?
>
> Didn't they test the hardness of the egg
> On the skin of their teeth
> Before dashing it against the rocks?

>Didn't they know that water turned wine
>But once in days of yore? (p. 34)

In other words, people should accept the consequences of their actions. Ken Saro-Wiwa was no lover of Biafra, and personal sentiments no doubt make him appear to gloat over the collapse of the secessionist enclave. Maybe the Biafrans should have learned a lesson from the tale of the tiger and the tortoise. But the poet has consistently separated the Igbo people from their leadership, which he blames here for the catastrophe of Biafra. For example, in *On a Darkling Plain,* after a glowing tribute to the Igbo as a group, he castigates their leadership:

>I am fully convinced that were Ibo LEADERS of a different persuasion in their attitude and in the objective analysis of the situation before and during the war, the Ibos as a people would have behaved differently. Hence I accuse Ibo leaders, and particularly Ojukwu, of exploiting Ibo suffering for their private purposes and of destroying the community that was Eastern Nigeria. (Saro-Wiwa, *On a Darkling Plain,* p. 10)

If Saro-Wiwa is seen as anti-Biafra in "Epitaph for Biafra," the poet is also ambivalent about Nigeria. He expresses the agony, dilemma, and irony (in the questioning that lives side-by-side with the patriotism) of the Nigerian patriot in "Dis Nigeria Sef." Here the poet, a concerned nationalist and patriot, agonizes over the contradictions of his homeland. He is angry because "For yonder soza dey shoot him enemy / Nigeria soza de shoot him brother" (Saro-Wiwa, *Songs,* p. 38); that is, the civil war is a war against his own brothers and sisters: the Biafrans. The poet's "confusion" comes out in the line, "I-love-I-no-love Nigeria" (p. 44). His partisanship during the war does not blunt his critical blade from hacking what is evil or antisocial. His ability to criticize the land he so loves redeems him from any criticism of being both ethnocentric and anti-Biafra. And when we consider the latter part of Saro-Wiwa's life and his conflicts with Gen. Sani Abacha's regime, this poem turns out to have been prophetic. He writes: "Small time now you fit send your picking / Weder soza police or kotuma ash bottom / Make dem wahala my life" (p. 41).

In this "grey season," it is significant that the poet is able to use humor, wit, puns, and other techniques to lighten the tedium of war atrocities. In "Thoughts in Time of War," he plays with "lie" in a direct allusion to Wilfred Owen's "Dulce et decorum est":

>Perhaps they must die
>So we live for ever.
>For this have we told the lie
>The famous lie about the sweet and honour
>That lie in dying for one's country. (p. 24)

In "Dis Nigeria Sef," there is copious humor as the poet satirizes his country and its people. On the predilection of his compatriots to give their children borrowed names, he writes:

> Name sef you no get, Peter, Paul
> Nicodemus Isaac John Joshua Saul
> Nincompoop Appolos Fred George Victoria
> Sabina Pepper Excreta Letitia Maria
> Abdullahi Hussein Muhammadu Haba! (p. 39)

The litany of names is made ludicrous by the use of juxtaposition. For instance, placing Excreta beside other names shows how disgusting the poet finds these imported European, Christian, and Muslim appellations.

According to Theo Vincent, Saro-Wiwa is a consummate stylist and experimenter with form and language (Saro-Wiwa, *Songs,* p. 9). There are rhymes and wit in most of the poems, but these qualities are best displayed in "Dis Nigeria Sef," a poem in pidgin English. In this poem, the speaker is a Nigerian Everyman who talks to his people about their condition in an accessible medium. For here he is not just a nationalist and a patriot but also a teacher and a priest admonishing his people to do good while exalting the land. (It is worth noting that the FM radio station in Port Harcourt, Rivers State, and Delta State Television in Warri frequently use pidgin English, the lingua franca of the Delta, in their news and entertainment broadcasts.) The poet operates on the same wavelength as his people, some 80 percent of whom are illiterate but speak and understand "rotten English."

The Niger Delta area signifies minority status and oil exploration. As a result of the people's exploitation and marginalization, there is a history of struggle for a fair share of resources and for survival in the federation of Nigeria. The people of the Niger Delta felt the civil war was fought for the soul of the Delta because of the oil reserves. The problems in Saro-Wiwa's time during the civil war had to do with neglect by the regional government and the then distant Lagos administration. In the 1990s these problems have been made worse because of the alliance between multinational oil corporations and the military dictatorship. Saro-Wiwa's early struggle, recorded in *Songs in a Time of War,* has to do with the freeing of his minority people from the Eastern Region dominated by an Igbo hegemony. Ironically, after the war, the subsequent military dictatorships soon strengthened the federal government, giving it overall control of the revenues accruing from oil. Saro-Wiwa called for investment in the area to correct the ecological destruction suffered over decades of oil exploration.

The Movement for the Survival of the Ogoni People (MOSOP) embodies the temperament of the Niger Delta people. The Niger Delta means much to its inhabitants. In addition to providing refuge, defense, and sustenance, it gives the people a unique identity. In *Songs in a Time of War,* Saro-Wiwa reflects the dilemma of the Delta native, loving Nigeria and wanting to be freed from Eastern or Western regional hegemonies and being neglected by the federal government to the extent that the creeks, rivers, and waterways are polluted, the soil damaged, and the air poisoned by oil spills and gas flares.

This poetry represents the beginning of Saro-Wiwa's self- and group realization. He is awakened from the anomie that has kept his people marginalized. Here begins his politicization, his stand for his minority people. This positioning is not parochial but a struggle against neglect, marginalization, and exploitation of minority groups, a stand against injustice, inequality, and lack of fairness. This phase in Saro-Wiwa's life will be followed by a more radical one in the 1980s and 1990s. But already the poet speaks out. His strong voice reinforces the condemnation of war and its attendant immoralities and inhumanity, which others like Achebe, Clark-Bekederemo, and Soyinka, from their own individual perspectives and for different reasons, have also expressed.

In only one collection, Saro-Wiwa established himself as a strong poetic voice that has ennobled different traditions of Nigerian poetry. He reinforced some aspects and differed in his own personal way from others. But his position seems to have been conditioned by his minority status in a Niger Delta that has suffered marginalization. *Songs in a Time of War* is a testament to the minority and environmental activist's beginning the fight for his people and their formerly pristine Niger Delta environment. In this collection, he bears witness on behalf of himself and his people to the Nigerian Civil War. His poetry output may be small, but the voice herein is strong, passionate, and mature.

WORKS CITED

Achebe, Chinua. *Beware Soul Brother.* Enugu: Fourth Dimensions, 1971.
Clark[-Bekederemo], J. P. *Casualties.* London: Longman, 1970.
Clark-Bekederemo, J. P. *A Decade of Tongues.* London: Longman, 1981.
———. *A Reed in the Tide.* London: Longman, 1965.
Eyi-Acquah, Kobena. *Music for a Dream Dance.* Accra: Asempa, 1989.
Okigbo, Christopher. *Labyrinths.* London: Heinemann, 1971.
Ojaide, Tanure. *Labyrinths of the Delta.* Greenfield Center, N.Y.: Greenfield Review Press, 1986.
———. "Nativity and the Creative Process: The Niger Delta in My Poetry." Paper presented at the Conference on Space, Culture, and Society in Africa at the Center for African Studies, University of Illinois at Urbana-Champaign, 28–30 March 1996.
———. *The Poetry of Wole Soyinka.* Lagos: Malthouse, 1994.

————. "War Games." In *Cannons for the Brave*. Lagos: Malthouse Press, forthcoming.

Saro-Wiwa, Ken. *On a Darkling Plain: An Account of the Nigerian Civil War*. Port Harcourt: Saros, 1989.

————. *Songs in a Time of War*. Port Harcourt: Saros, 1985.

————. *Sozaboy*. Burnt Mill, Harlow: Longman, 1994.

Soyinka, Wole. *Idanre and Other Poems*. London: Eyre Methuen, 1967.

————. *The Man Died*. Harmondsworth, Middlesex, UK: Penguin, 1972.

————. *A Shuttle in the Crypt*. London: Rex Collings/Methuen, 1972.

5

The Short Fiction:
A Forest of Flowers and
Adaku and Other Stories

Aubrey McPhail

It is, or at least it ought to be, with a measure of trepidation that a critic
embarks on the delicate task of exposition. The more so in tackling two
collections in which thirty-seven stories so varied in theme, tone, character, and plot are represented as in Ken Saro-Wiwa's *A Forest of Flowers*
(1986) and *Adaku and Other Stories* (1989). But the task of exposition becomes less daunting if one keeps in mind the premise that every serious
writer is, on some fundamental level, a moral writer. And indeed, Ken
Saro-Wiwa is no exception. As Rose Ure Mezu rightly notes:

> Ken Saro-Wiwa was a committed writer. His was a belief in the func-
> tionalism of art without excluding embellishing tropes and other re-
> sources of the imagination. Not for him the theory of art for art's sake.
> Misguided or not, he embraces with fervor diverse issues ranging from
> the socio-political, economic, cultural to feminism, themes of friendship,
> conflict between the individual conscience and society. (Mezu, p. 113)

First I need to provide the important caveat that Mezu's comments are
much more accurate apropos of *A Forest of Flowers* than of *Adaku and
Other Stories*. Of Saro-Wiwa's two volumes, *A Forest of Flowers* is
markedly superior both in structure and in content. It is also clearer and
more compelling in its handling of the various moral issues that it raises.

Although *A Forest of Flowers* received relatively sparse critical attention, this should in no way serve to diminish its appeal among sensitive
readers of the genre; its being short-listed for the prestigious Commonwealth Writers Prize in 1987 would otherwise attest to its value. In the preceding year, critic Graham Hough bestowed abundant praise on the collection in the *London Review of Books*:

> Saro-Wiwa's extremely accomplished collection of short stories stands to
> Nigeria in something of the same relation as Joyce's *Dubliners* to Ireland.
> They are brief epiphanies, each crystallising a moment, a way of living,
> the whole course of life. . . . There is immense satisfaction in the adroit-
> ness and variety of presentation . . . the parts where the narrator speaks in
> his own person have a straightforward elegance that is extremely attrac-
> tive. (Hough, pp. 22–23)

Although the interesting comparison to *Dubliners* may be a little hyper-
bolic, nevertheless, there is much in Hough's comments that rings true of
the collection taken as a whole. Suggestive of the forethought and attention of an accomplished writer and editor, Saro-Wiwa's *A Forest of Flowers* is divided effectively into two distinct but intricately connected parts.
The first part contains eight stories; the second part, the bulk of the collection, contains eleven stories. Setting, it seems, is crucial to the entire
volume, for it functions both as an organizational principle as well as an
indication of thematic orientation. Each story in the first part of the collection is set in Dukana, a small, rural town surrounded by the forest. The
stories in the second part of the collection move to urban settings such as
Aba, Port Harcourt, Lagos, and Kano.

Dukana, of course, is the home of Mene, the fatherless, poorly educated narrator of *Sozaboy*. And although equated metaphorically with the
world of the "forest," the Dukana from which Mene comes is predomi-
nantly a place of squalor, ignorance, superstition, fear, and intolerance. No
unadulterated Romantic visions of benevolent nature here; no Rousseauian
"noble savage" here; rather, the narrator of the first story alludes to a nasty
Hobbesian world, both "brutish and short" (Saro-Wiwa, *Forest,* p. 3). As
N. F. Inyama so cogently puts it:

> The first section deals with the "forest"—a metaphor for the rural, forest-
> bound world of Dukana. . . . The flowers that bloom in the forest village
> are *fleurs de mal,* of ignorance, superstition, filth, stagnation. . . . Saro-
> Wiwa refuses to shield these negative elements under a fake, romanti-
> cized, rural innocence. The much vaunted African rural world of peace
> and harmony is revealed to harbour the most bizarre and pernicious
> vices: greed, envy, and sheer cruelty. (Inyama, p. 46)

"Time does not matter in Dukana," the narrator of the first story in the
collection tells us (Saro-Wiwa, *Forest,* p. 5). Indeed, that "Time does not
matter in Dukana" is a kind of implicit refrain for the first part of the collection, a subtle but almost audible leitmotif informing each of the stories.
Essentially, time does not matter to the community of Dukana because it is
steeped in its own primordial ignorance, ignoring, as it were, the modern
world. In a similar sense, time does not matter to the community of
Dukana because of the overwhelming weight of its own past, its own

traditions—the overwhelming weight of the dead on the affairs of its living.

The first story, ironically entitled "Home, Sweet Home," is also the titular heading for the first part of the collection. The story affirms the preponderance of the deadening weight of Dukana's uncritical adherence to tradition and convention, even on the sensitive consciousness of a young girl who has had the enlightening privileges of education and travel. Initially, the young college girl "felt then that excruciating pain which knowledge confers on those who can discern the gulf which divides what is and what could be" (p. 4), but her own insights will fall prey to the "communal wisdom" that maintains "Dukana is home, and as everyone will proudly tell you in these parts, 'home is home'" (p. 2). The following passage encapsulates the backwardness of Dukana, reaffirms the theme of willful blindness, and reveals the flavor of Saro-Wiwa's sparse, measured, ironic, and evocative style:

> Of course I knew Dukana as well as any young girl who had been born there might be expected to know it. But as I grew older and traveled, its delights had diminished in my eyes and comparison had dimmed its supposed qualities. Some, taking a cursory look at it, would have considered Dukana a clearing in the tropical rain forest peopled by three or four thousand men, women and children living in rickety mud huts and making a miserable living from small farmlands in the forest or from fishing in the steamy creeks around the village. Some such, not being of Dukana origin, would hold that the absence of a health clinic, of a good school, of pipe-borne water, of electricity, was a blight on the town, and would think it primeval. Such ill-informed, malicious people might look at its emaciated, illiterate population and assert that there was malnutrition, that disease was rampant, that life for its inhabitants was brutish and short. And they would dismiss it as doomed in a modern world where man was headed for space and science had transformed man's ability to control his environment. (pp. 2–3)

If the young narrator's explicit attitudes suggest detached emancipation from the overwhelming weight of the past, the conclusion of the story undermines this useful fiction by revealing that the narrator's childhood friend, Sira, has been exiled from Dukana and by intimating that Sira's twins have been destroyed—the deadly legacy of archaic customs unassailable by "a modern world where man was headed for space":

> "I won't go until you tell me what's happened to my friend."
> Mama saw that I was determined to know; then she said, enjoining to secrecy. "Well, you remember her last pregnancy? She [Sira] had twins. She could not stay in town anymore. She went away across the river."
> I looked at Mama very closely. She averted her eyes from mine.

> "She's not dead?" I inquired.
> "Oh no, she's not dead."
> "And the twins?"
> "I believe they died. And don't ask me any more questions." (p. 9)

The narrator's response to her mother's fearful injunction of silence reveals her hesitant but de facto complicity in the cabal of communal secrecy; hence the narrator is, willing or not, crushed by the deadening weight of bitter reality in Dukana. Her diction is telling: "The words I wanted to say came flooding into my lips, but died there. I got up and walked heavily to my room and lay down" (pp. 9–10). Although the idealistic narrator had looked forward to returning to Dukana with life-affirming intentions, "to give something back to [her] home" and to "be part of the community" (p. 2), nevertheless, it is the deadening weight of the "spirits" that haunt her community that emerges victorious. The bitter irony of the final paragraph is all the more poignant for its rueful, melodious understatement:

> And out of the bowels of the night came the rhythm of drums in the distance, the hooting of owls, the swooping and beeping of bats, the burping of toads, the humming of night birds and the words of a mournful song welcoming me to the embrace of the spirits of my home, my sweet home. (p. 10)

Finally, emerging from the cosmic tragedy of Sira and the resigned complicity of the narrator, the question of communal cohesion arises. As "Home, Sweet Home" suggests, it is not simply a matter of "them and us," of Dukana versus the outside world. Dukana does, however, exhibit remarkable cohesion on the level of traditional mores and united action. When the need arises, as in "The Inspector Calls," the people of Dukana— including its most impoverished—join forces to thwart outside interference such as the visit of a government "Sanitary Inspector." Hence, when threatened by "them," the people of Dukana,

> quite independently of each other, weighed the matter carefully, consulted the wisdom of the ages and come to the conclusion that the Sanitary Inspector was an unnecessary intrusion on the privacy of the town, and as such had to be ejected before he, or his principals, could do the town harm, any harm whatsoever. (p. 13)

And all this even though the narrator admits that the visit is a "great idea" since there is "overgrown grass everywhere, food crops among the houses, excrement from dogs and children liberally spread on the footpaths, and the only road leading into town suffering from neglect, required the services of the Inspector" (p. 13). Chief Birabee manages to bilk the people of money and goods, and when the inspector arrives he

> and his assembled assistants fed him the good things of life and gave him a good, fat envelope containing you know what, and made sure he drank alcohol to his heart's delight, and led him out again, on the same path by which he had come. . . . And once again, Dukana returned to his accustomed peace, somnolence, tranquillity, dirt and happiness. (pp. 17–18)

Dukana's excrement, dirt, and stagnation are secured, unscathed by outside forces, and the reader's reaction tends to be mildly sardonic amusement rather than any sense of moral outrage. Here, something akin to Bakhtinian carnival laughter seems to be the authorial intent and the appropriate response. But as we have seen, the communal values and the cohesion they generate are also shown to have a darker, more sinister underbelly. There are deadly consequences when they intersect with anomalous individuals. Under the right circumstances, Dukana can eat its own young. We see this dynamic played out in both "A Family Affair" and "The Bonfire."

It is a commonplace that a society's level of moral civilization may be measured by how it treats its most vulnerable members. In "A Family Affair," this general premise is tested and further refined down to the level of family. And here, Dukana's own are found wanting. Once again, the overwhelming weight of mortality—this time in the form of communal loathing and of familial shame—impinges on the land of the living. The ubiquity of the town's presence is immediately felt in the opening of the story:

> When one morning Dabo, one of Dukana's most successful fishermen, instead of heading for the creeks, suddenly burst out in song, there was consternation in town. . . . That morning, Dukana was not amused. Ripples of worry gradually spread around town and drew everyone to Dabo's house. (p. 27)

Subsequently, much time and money is spent trying to cure Dabo of his madness, and "everyone," it seems, voices an opinion about the fallen fisherman, since "[t]he news ran through Dukana like fire in a dry wind, leaving everyone who heard it dumbstruck" (p. 28). The narrative voice builds this sense of a spreading moral conflagration by moving from the particular comments of familiar individuals such as Duzia and Terr Kole to a general crescendo of communal frenzy: "The story was told"; "Some said he should be taken to a church"; "Others said Oyeoku the powerful Juju should be consulted"; "Some in the sanctuary of their living rooms, said they were not surprised"; "It began to be said that Dabo had even murdered a young girl years back and offered her as a sacrifice"; "So the whispers went" (pp. 28–29). The attempts at a "cure" are continued, but when, after escaping being beaten "night and day with a big leather belt" (p. 30), Dabo becomes "the town's only beggar," we read that "he was a shame to his family, [and a] walking scandal" to the community's sensibilities. Dukana will not tolerate the revealing insights of the likes of a mad Nietzschean Zarathustra who constantly cries out, "'You are all liars, all'" (p. 30). Collapsing under the weight of shame, the most communal manifestation of human disgrace, Dabo's family finally comes to "an unspoken and menacing agreement: 'One day shall be one day'" (p. 30).

The day comes when Dabo succumbs to a deep, deathlike sleep. Thinking him dead, Dabo's family members prepare him for burial, but "in the midst of noise and fuss the beggar woke up from sleep" (p. 31). With masterful economy and restrained pathos, Saro-Wiwa renders one of Dukana's sleeping-dead trying to reenter the waking world of his family:

> The beggar was confounded to find himself the centre of attention. Never since he could remember had so many of his relatives taken an interest in him. He threw them a weak greeting. No one answered him. He repeated the greeting. Again, no one answered him. He repeated the greeting a second time. (p. 31)

But significantly, Dabo is now only "the beggar," and his faint supplications for confirmation as a living human being meet with deadening negation:

> "You are dead, so shut up," one of the relatives whispered hoarsely.
> "I'm not dead," the beggar replied. "I was only sleeping."
> "Sleeping, Huh! What's the difference between sleep and death? You are dead."
> "I'm not dead," the beggar said weakly, beginning to whimper.
> "You are dead. Brothers help me carry him away."
> "But I'm not dead yet."
> "You will die today. You died this afternoon."
> "God, I'm not dead. I'm not dead yet. I don't want to die," the beggar whined like a dog. (p. 32)

No longer useful to his family or to Dukana, a blight on the landscape of collective consciousness, Dabo is denied his humanity, and then he is stripped of his life. The family abandons its most fundamental role as collective guardian and becomes the unified instrument of death. (Inyama makes a similar point in "Ken Saro-Wiwa," p. 47.) They wrap Dabo in a raffia mat and drag him into the forest:

> The relatives dug a hasty grave, not deep, very narrow. From within the bundle a voice could be heard.
> "I am not yet dead, oh God."

"Then you must die today, you eyesore, you disgrace of the family.
You must die today."
"I'm not dead yet, oh God, I'm not dead yet." (p. 32)

But, of course, to his family Dabo is dead, for he is an aberration, a dangerous deviation from the accustomed norms of Dukana. And the overwhelming weight of these norms is no trifling matter. It brings with it both familial betrayal and heartless murder, and perhaps even more chilling, it brings with it abeyance of individual compassion—a willing suspension of common decency and human sympathy. The weight of communal convention bears down on personal responsibility, finally squeezing it out of the individual, even in the face of another's humanity and one's own questioning conscience:

> The relatives were surprised at the amazing clarity of the man. Was he not mad? How was he able to distinguish between life and death? Could even madness know the difference between these two? Each asked himself the question. Each resolved within himself to bury the answer with the mad beggar. (p. 32)

Ultimately then, the greatest betrayal in the story is the conscious decision—the resolve—to betray one's own conscience by burying it.

The overwhelming weight of death is also felt in "The Bonfire." And again, death comes to an anomalous individual, but this time its source and the target of Saro-Wiwa's critique is ignorance, superstition, and communal scapegoating. As Willfried F. Feuser notes, "'The Bonfire,' a story of masterful economy, takes us into the darkest recesses of Dukana's collective consciousness, or collective frenzy; its theme of death-centered scapegoatism foreshadows the novel *Sozaboy*" (Feuser, p. 56). This is true, but in another sense the story takes us into Dukana's collective unconsciousness, into its willful ignorance and stubborn superstition: scapegoating is simply an inevitable consequence of these dark forces, one physical manifestation of a deeper social pathology.[1]

Much of the story, like the title itself, is ironic. A number of people die in Dukana "in quick succession" but,

> No one bothered to find out how each person died. Heart attacks, ruptured kidneys and livers, pneumonia, senility; these noted killers of man are happily unknown in Dukana. All the deaths within a short period of time were attributable to a culprit who had to be identified. (Saro-Wiwa, *Forest*, pp. 34–35)

After one of Dukana's "shining lights," Alee, dies in a far-off town, the people decide some evil, envious person must have magically killed him, even though they learn the autopsy "spoke of diabetes" (p. 38). A young man called Nedam is singled out as the source of this and the other deaths, and he is summarily burned to death in his hut on the day of Alee's funeral.

Nedam's sins are twofold. He was "born with two teeth in his infant mouth" (p. 35), and he spends his time working in the forest on his progressive palm plantation rather than lazing about in Dukana.[2] Ironically, Nedam had been a friend of Alee's and was himself one of Dukana's unrecognized but real hopes for the future. He is a hard-working, intelligent, progressive young man who "loved to see things grow" and who grows cash crops in the forest "where no one dared to go because it was supposed to hold wicked terrors by day and night" (p. 35). Unsatisfied with mere subsistence farming, Nedam "had often wondered," the narrator tells us, "why the people of Dukana left the task of farming to women and children." The narrator congratulates Nedam "on his hard work and sound common sense" (p. 37), but in Dukana, it seems, common sense is the least common of all senses. Nedam was different—nor did he participate in the "system of co-operative labor which was practiced in Dukana"—and individualism and difference amid ignorance breed fear and contempt; thus Dukana's judgment on Nedam is as harsh as it is foolish: "He was to be feared and dreaded. . . . He was an evil man" (p. 35). Nedam himself thought the people of Dukana "were a superstitious, rumour-mongering lot who truly did not understand much" (p. 36), but even he could not have imagined to what depths of depravity collective fear and superstition would take his fellow youth. Soon, however, he comes to a brief and terrible knowledge; he is swiftly silenced and burned alive, his screams are the only defense he is afforded:

> It was over in a flash. They seized him by the throat so that he could utter neither word nor cry, and dragged him away towards his house. They threw him in a heap into the house and locked shut the door in his face. They struck a match and set the house ablaze. . . . Soon a whirlwind of fire raced upwards and rose into the sky like the tongue of a huge torch. . . . And now came a horrendous clamour of human screams, a shriek of anguish and terror which rose above the bonfire. As the house burned, the youth of Dukana formed themselves into a ring round it to ensure their victim did not escape. (p. 39)

Once again, Saro-Wiwa reveals the awful cohesion of a community unified by the shared experience of ignorance and superstition. But it is an immoral cohesion, bereft of compassion and deadly in practice. The macabre irony is that the bonfire is not one of communal celebration at the "burial carnival" (p. 39) but of killing solidarity toward the misunderstood.

In "The Divorcee," Saro-Wiwa turns his attention to marriage customs and, in particular, to the treatment of women. Much of the power of the story resides in how the issues are treated; the narrative tone is objective, dispassionate, and matter-of-fact. Lebia, a young girl, returns to her mother's hut early one morning, sent away by her husband of three years. The marriage has produced no offspring, and although she has been a good wife in all other respects, predictably, the full weight of blame for barrenness is borne by the woman, Lebia:

> She cooked his meals, washed his clothes and swept their one room apartment. And at night, when he had had his meal and his bath, she did her duty. Faithfully. Loyally. Every day. The months passed by. He expected she would bear children. It was for that primarily that he had married her. For every man has reason to expect that he would be a father some day. Every man was capable of being a father. If he did not become a father, there was something wrong with his wife. (p. 51)

Here, the deeply entrenched inequity between the sexes is rendered in an almost perfunctory manner—no fanfare and no vitriol. Lebia "was family property" of her husband, but "Lebia's mother was happy. Her daughter had found a good husband and she had some spending money" (pp. 50–51). And earlier, we read that her mother's hut "bore the happiest memories of her life; memories which had now dimmed beside the nightmare of those three years whose brutality she would have given the world to forget" (p. 47), but neither is there jubilation at her return home. For mother and daughter alike, the marriage was economically advantageous, "not a bad bargain" (p. 51), and Lebia's emancipation from marriage offers little more than a change in venue and a return to other sorts of bondage that typified her life at home:

> This sameness, this monotony was the hallmark of their life. . . . She had fetched water, helped on the farm during the planting season, weeded with her mother when the rains made the weeds explode on the farm, harvested with her during the dry season. And she had learnt to cook the meagre meals they ate . . . it was always with a great sense of dissatisfaction that she returned home to the hard discomfort of the mound of mud in the outer room and the monotony of life with her mother. (pp. 48–49)

The alliteration of the last sentence helps emphasize the repetitive tedium that her life will become once more.

But, of course, it is not just tedium that is at issue. Saro-Wiwa is perceptive enough to recognize that the hardships facing the young women of Dukana are part of a larger complex of forces. Like the narrator in Jane Austen's *Pride and Prejudice*, who understands that marriage is often a woman's best "preservative from want" (Austen, *Pride and Prejudice,* p. 111), Saro-Wiwa realizes the unfortunate fact that economic necessity is very often the sole impetus for marriage: "But surely she would find a man who would take care of her. For that was the ultimate aim of a Dukana woman. To be the only wife of a poor man. Or one of the many wives of a rich man" (Saro-Wiwa, *Forest*, p. 49).

But the problem is not even that simple. The view of marriage is but one manifestation of an ingrained moral tunnel vision. Options are not seen in Dukana; rather, the notion of marriage as young women's only "preservative from want" is passed down from generation to generation: "So every mother had told her daughter. So all daughters believed. They in turn, would have to tell their daughters who would have to believe" (p. 49). Socialization is yet one more manifestation of the overwhelming weight of the dead.

I have emphasized the dark side of Dukana found in Part One, but there is also a gentler side, a potentiality for compassion and humanity marked by the word *community*. Indeed, the final story in Part One, "A Death in Town," offers no sinister underbelly, but rather suggests the potential for positive solidarity and communal compassion. Many of the other stories' notable characters are gathered at Adda's wake. They criticize the interference in their lives by government and church alike, and they reaffirm their own values. Like the life-affirming Dionysian dance at the end of Nikos Kazantzakis's *Zorba the Greek* (1946), their communal solidarity in the face of life's hardships and inevitable death is poignantly rendered in Duzia's funeral speech:

> "Lie there, brave hunter. Lie there, poor man, far from the tax gatherers, the big liars. You have paid the final tax to Oyeoku and your god. Lie there and watch us slowly live this death in life, our life a burden and a terror. But see us smile like sunshine, sing like the cricket through it all. And join us at the feast of new yam; celebrate with us, brave ancestor, the feast of the maidens fresh from the fatting rooms. Then watch us succumb at the touch of nature, watch us die a happy death, the final death. Farewell . . . What else is there to say?" (Saro-Wiwa, *Forest*, p. 62)

Part Two of *A Forest of Flowers* takes the reader into the urban environment. Overall, the stories in the second part have more the flavor of Bakhtinian carnival than Sophoclean tragedy. They reveal the astonishing lightness of the living—the incredible lack of moral density and communal commitment found in the cosmopolitan landscape. In one sense, the urban context is Dukana writ large. Many of the same moral flaws, as well some new additions, are to be found in the cities, but without the grounding cohesion of a shared communal experience.

But, except for the last story, "A Legend on Our Street," no such solidarity and no such community is to be found in Part Two. There is no shared moral sensibility or collective experience that can offer the faint hope of individual and communal redemption. What we find is a world without a moral center, a world where the most objectionable features of Dukana's communal crimes find culpable expression and deviant variation in individual conduct.

The first story, "High Life," sets the tone for much of the remainder of the volume. Written in the "rotten English" of *Sozaboy*, the language reflects the "disordered and disorderly" world that is urban Nigeria.[3] There is both fascination and bewilderment at the pace and complexity of modern urban life. The narrator of the story is enticed by the "high life" to be found in the city. A carnival atmosphere pervades its streets; on the surface, it seems a place of immense possibility and happy equality, and almost anything, it seems, is for sale:

> Christ Jesus! I have not seen one town in this country where everybody is equal. . . . Then if you go to the hotel, you will see a young man who will come and buy beer, beer not tombo, for everybody in the hotel. Wonderful. And then when you think of fine babies, you can't beat Aba. If you want high society one, you will get it; if you want proper teenager who sells in the chemist shop, you will get it. And sometimes you will get them cheap, because everything in Aba is cheap. (p. 65)

Seeking the full pleasures offered by Aba, the narrator drinks beer, smokes opium, and looks for a woman to take home. He finds one, but when he begins "to make romantica with the woman" (p. 71), he meets with a shocking discovery:

> Then I began to remove the woman's loin cloth. . . . All this time, the woman said nothing at all. . . . I started to remove her knicker . . . slowly . . . very slowly. . . . God Almighty! the women was a man! A proper man. I was flabbergasted. I shouted "Help! help! help!!!" Then the woman-man picked up all his-her things and gave me three sound slaps of the face and ran away. (p. 71)

The response of the crowd now around him is that it was a "spirit," or a "fairy," or a "ghost." And a policeman among them asks for money to look for the woman-man, but "When the police saw that I had no money for him, he said: 'My friend, you are victimised by a magnanimous hallucination.' All the people who were in that house laughed; and then he went out and all the other people followed him one by one" (pp. 71–72). The story, of course, is meant to be humorous, and it is, but it also conveys something of the illusory world that is Aba. Aba is a superficial "masquerade" (p. 66), where surface appearances mask a deeper moral malaise. Teenagers can be bought for sex; policemen need to be bought to do their jobs; drugs are readily available; crass hedonism and foolish superstitions thrive. The moral "lightness of the living" is rendered with mildly sardonic humor, but it is there, under the surface of things, palpable enough for those who can notice it. Saro-Wiwa is no bombastic evangelical preacher; but although unobtrusive, his moral concerns are discernible. Indeed, the humorous and carnivalesque quality of much of the second part of the collection reflects Mikhail Bakhtin's conception of the moral function of carnival. In the vulgar, bawdy, excremental world of carnival, laughter can be instructive. As Bakhtin points out in *Rabelais and His World*, carnival "[l]aughter purifies from dogmatism, from the intolerant and the petrified; it liberates from fanaticism and pedantry, from fear and intimidation, from didacticism, naivete and illusion" (p. 123).[4]

"Case No. 100" further illustrates some of the social ills of urban life. And here, the excremental vision is made explicit in a police station. The prisoners are objectified, dehumanized.[5] Punctuating the snoring of the policemen, the prisoners variously cry out, sometimes "almost tearfully," sometimes "prayerfully and insistently," "I wan piss" or "I wan shit." They are met with callous replies of the policemen, "'Awright, you can fit to piss dere. . . . Awright, you can fit to shit dere'" (p. 75). Here, of course, the excrement and stench symbolize the moral corruption of society.[6]

But it is not only a matter of dehumanization and callous disregard for the feelings of others. The police get a call from a citizen whose house has been the object of an attempted armed burglary, but the response is a lackadaisical one. Furthermore, since "[n]o brandy was forthcoming [and the policeman] was being exhorted to do his duty without encouragement, without hope of a reward" (p. 81), "he remembered nothing of the facts of the case; he had taken no notes, inspected nothing, done nothing" (p. 81). The police do not respect each other, and they certainly care little for the citizens they are charged to protect. The moral malaise that is expressed as a lack of humanity and compassion in the jail is shown to be even more dangerous when it is expressed as a practical failure of the agents of the government to serve and protect its citizens. This becomes painfully obvious as Sergeant Ikeme peruses his notebook:

> Case No 25: Housebreaking, 50 Aba Road: Investigation instituted.
>   Case No. 50: Murder on the road; dead body found; no traces of blood. Investigation continues. . . . "Stupid Nigerians," Ikeme mused, "always expecting something for nothing." . . . Case No 100: Attempted burglary, 3 Abeokuta Street. Investigation continues. (pp. 83–84)

It becomes clear that the astonishing moral lightness of those in positions of power and trust can have dire consequences for the proper functioning of civil society. In Saro-Wiwa's urban landscape, moral corruption is endemic, and it finds new and insidious ways to manifest itself, depending on the vocation of those involved.

"Acapulco Motel" considers corruption in the business world and hints at the ineffectuality of the government and the courts to deal with that corruption. The narrator describes a trip with his aunt to see Alhaji, the crooked but apparently successful "man of business" (p. 87), who the narrator's aunt fears "had duped her of land and money" (p. 88). The crass materialism of the likes of Alhaji and the moral decay that it stands for is represented by the trophies of conspicuous consumption that he so proudly displays—by the teeth he had capped with gold, ironically, during his first pilgrimage to Mecca, and by the vulgar breach of good taste that is his car:

> [A] brand new Mercedes-Benz car. Underneath the plate was a title. The owner of the car wanted it known that he was some sort of chief. Everyone in the country was either a chief or about to be one . . . the inside of the Mercedes was completely covered by some white fluffy material. A cow's tail dangled prominently from the roof of the car. My aunt whispered that it would have to be Alhaji's car. We walked past this glorious show of wealth and power into the Acapulco. (p. 89)

Again, the discrepancy between reality and illusion—between superficial appearance and underlying reality—comes to the fore. Alhaji has the outer trappings of a "chief," but he is really just a thief, a confidence man, who sells the same piece of land to "three or four unsuspecting individuals" and who "also ensured that each buyer had his piece of land properly registered at the Government Land Registry" (p. 86). Similarly,

> the likes of Alhaji made sure that when the buyers all went to court to sort out the tangle, the case was so complicated and went on so long that either all four contestants despaired or died, or the judge who sat on the bench got transferred to a different corner of the earth. (pp. 86–87)

Unable to depend on the government or the courts, the narrator and his aunt can look only to themselves to try to get back her land. But, of course, they get nothing but laughable "promises" from Alhaji, and when they return to the Acapulco some time later, the motel is closed down, and there is no sign of the swindler.

In "Robert and the Dog," Saro-Wiwa refines his general social critique down to the level of the individual. The story is one of authentic pathos, as the effects of poverty and dehumanization are revealed in the life of an honest, hardworking man who has been "accustomed to moving from household to household" (p. 105), from one harsh and insensitive employer to the next. He finally finds an employer, a young doctor, who treats him with kindness and respect. Later, when the doctor's European wife arrives with a dog, Robert is worried she may be an "ogre," but "the young lady extended every consideration to him. Robert began to feel like a human being" (p. 106).

The dog is very well treated by the doctor and his wife, and Robert becomes resentful:

> [T]he lady spoke tenderly to the dog. As she ensured that he was well fed
> with tinned food and milk and meat and bones. And she held the dog lov-
> ingly in her arms, brushed his hair and tended him carefully. . . . Robert
> thought, in the order of things, the dog was more important than himself.
> Try as hard as he could, he could not dismiss from his mind that the dog
> was doing better than himself. (pp. 106–107)

When the dog is taken to a doctor, it is "the straw that broke the
camel's back" (p. 107). When Robert compares the life of the dog to that
of his own children with their "distended stomachs gambolling in the filth
which simmered in a swollen stream at his door, and watched them hungrily swallow small balls of 'eba,' he asked himself, 'Who born dog?'" (p.
107). Finally, when Robert's employers take an extended vacation, he is
left to care for the dog. But on the third day, "watching the dog lap his
milk from the plate" the question again comes into his mind, "'Who born
dog?'"(p. 108). Robert can only answer "Dog," whereupon he "gathered
up all the tins of dog food, all the tins of milk, tethered the dog to the set-
tee and walked off, out of the house and the job he had loved to do. . . .
And the dog died" (p. 108). Here, the pathos is genuine, not because of the
perfunctory announcement of the dog's death, but because of the bitter social conditions that force an individual to feel dehumanized and to leave a
job where he finally "began to feel like a human being."

Social ills are also explored in a number of the other stories in Part
Two. In "Garga," we see the results of oppression and tribal hostilities as
senseless violence erupts in the city. In "Love Song of a Housewife" and
"A Caring Man," we see the mistrust and betrayal between the sexes, the
damage to interpersonal relations caused by the lack of moral density and
human commitment. In "The Stars Below" and "Night Ride," we see
something of the inability of individuals to make a positive difference
amid the corruption, confusion, and apathy that is post–civil war Nigeria.

The last story in Part Two, like the last story in Part One, does offer
some hope for the future. Ironically enough, this hope is to be found in
"Papa," a man who is a "great-great-grandfather" (p. 143). Papa is a man
who has traveled widely and experienced life:

> Papa was born in colonialism, saw the Great Depression, could have
> fought in the Second World War, fought colonialism, welcomed the na-
> tion's independence, went along the way of neo-colonialism, became a
> republican and was now busy watching us make a mess of independence
> and gravitate back to colonialism. (p. 144)

Papa is very old, but it is his active engagement with life and his moral
fiber that is important. He is an honest man, a man who reads and who has
learned important lessons from the various positions he has held during his
long life. He is a man who is self-reliant and dedicated to his family and

community. Papa's robust physical health is a symbol of his spiritual health, and although he falls ill, as men and nations are apt to do, he recovers and gets on with the business of his life. As a symbol of Nigeria's potential, Papa's picture offers a hopeful moral vision, a practical antidote to the astonishing lightness of the living.

POSTSCRIPT: *ADAKU AND OTHER STORIES*

Although critics agree that *A Forest of Flowers* showed significant accomplishment and immense promise for Saro-Wiwa as a short story writer, the promise is not fully met in *Adaku and Other Stories*. The collection contains eighteen stories, seemingly arranged at random. The stories continue Saro-Wiwa's capable rendering of the vagaries of human existence, and with clarity of detail, they do capture the flavor of Nigerian life. And as Inyama notes:

> *Adaku and Other Stories* gives the reader a mixed perspective on life and society. Two things are notable, however: the historical range is broadened to reveal the well-spring of the author's creativity. Events range from the pre-colonial to the colonial and the immediate post-colonial era. . . . The second and the more important fact is that the author concentrates extensively on the fate of women in their relationships with men. (Inyama, p. 48)

Many of the stories also continue to explore themes found in *A Forest of Flowers,* but the moral vision in *Adaku and Other Stories* is, by and large, less focused, less clear. Although about half the stories in the collection raise issues about the relationship between the sexes and the treatment of women, the narrative tone is often disconcertingly vague, and thus, the moral vision is blurred. For example, in "The Empire Builders," a young woman is rented out to the "Native Authority Treasurer" as sexual payment for the tax collection money her husband has spent in order to marry her. The woman is eventually returned to her husband, a washerman, and the story ends as follows:

> In later years, whenever the subject arose, the washerman was heard to say, "I only lent her to the Treasurer for some time. He refused to return her to me after three weeks."
> To which the young woman, now a mother of three, would add, laughing, "Better to stay at the Treasurer's than have your dear husband go to jail for misappropriating tax money." (Saro-Wiwa, *Adaku*, p. 24)

How are we to react to this? Should we admire the woman's sexual sacrifice? Was it a sacrifice or just lusty complicity in the objectification of women? Are we meant to make any judgment here? Or are we meant to laugh along with the wife? If so, precisely what are we meant to laugh at? The story is funny at times, as when the Treasurer first comes to collect the overdue tax money. The washerman's wife is in the room "lightly dressed, barely covering her breasts with a loose loin-cloth." The Treasurer stares from the man to the woman, and we read:

> "You should have paid the breasts a month ago," he said.
> "I don't understand," replied the washerman.
> "I mean the tax. You should have paid your collection to the Treasury a month ago."
> "I know that."
> "Why haven't you paid?" . . .
> "I will pay," the washerman said after a while, a forlorn look in his eyes.
> "You have to pay the breasts . . . I mean, tax . . . immediately. It's urgent." (p. 14)

One cannot help but be amused at the Treasurer's blunder, but at the same time, one need not be a prig to catch oneself in that amusement, to wonder for a moment about the deeper implication of what is going on here.

A similar problem in tone is to be found in "A Message from Adama." Adama, a divorced man who laments having never been able to please his wife, wants to put a stop to West's beating his wife, since "she filled the night with her howls and yelps" (p. 32). But later, after Mrs. West has left, declaring of her husband, "'He's not a bad man!'" the narrator asks him, "'Did it ever strike you that in spite of all those nightly howls and yelps, Mrs. West never spotted a black eye, nor any laceration of the skin?'" (p. 32). Adama responds, "'Well, now that you mention it, it's quite true. A man of West's build pounding away nightly at the slim, fragile woman should have left her in bits and pieces. What are you suggesting, ole boy?'" (p. 33). The narrator replies, "'That if you had given your wife what West gave his, you would have ended up with not two or three books of vice, but with a testimonial like Mrs. West's. A simple, one-sentence, incontrovertible testimonial.'"

Again, the reader is left wondering just how to react. The misunderstanding of Adama is mildly amusing, but what precisely are we being told here? That rough, satisfying sex is the answer to marital problems? Unlike much of the moral critique in *A Forest of Flowers,* the handling of the issues raised in some of the stories in *Adaku and Other Stories* seems unsure, unclear, and sometimes morally suspect. There is a carnival flavor here, but often without the clear moral impulse that gives the earlier volume its consistency and power. Unlike the clear moral vision one is left with in the earlier volume, in *Adaku and Other Stories,* the reader is often left in a state of moral vertigo.

There are also a number of stylistic shortcomings in this collection. For example, clichés are numerous, and there are also a number of references that have no discernible function in the story. These references, like the one to John Milton in "The Empire Builders," often seem heavy-handed and obtrusive; they may reveal the writer's knowledge, but invariably they distract from the story. Similarly, some of the writing does not meet the high standards set in *A Forest of Flowers*. Admittedly, sex is probably one of the most difficult experiences to render well, but consider the description in the following passage from "Adaku":

> She was not a child; she was a woman experienced in the ways and desires of boys. Seeing that his body was strong with desire, she drew him to herself and took his being in her mouth. Instantly, the gates of heaven opened to the Christian judge and he saw Saint Peter open the gate of Paradise to let him in. He walked in and the sight of it engineered in him a feeling of wonderment, a wonderous, immeasurable sensation which made him shut his eyes and fall instantly into a bed of roses [and so on, and so forth!]. (p. 54)

Here, the metaphors are mixed and the diction poor, clichéd and repetitive, and the overall effect is one of excess and confusion. In all fairness, there is still much fine writing in *Adaku and Other Stories,* but as a whole the volume shows far less technical expertise and clarity of vision than *A Forest of Flowers*. For this reason, I must disagree with Abiola Irele's assertion that "the second series of short stories can be seen as a necessary complement to the first" (Irele, p. 104). What the collection does do, however, is reveal Saro-Wiwa's immense imagination, his creativity, and his willingness to explore a broad vista of human experience.

NOTES

1. Rose Ure Mezu notes the story's theme precisely: "'Bonfire' records the tragic consequences that can result from ignorance and superstition" (p. 98).

2. As Mezu points out, "Malformations like twins are considered abominable. For Nedam to be born with two front teeth was the mark of the devil" (pp. 98–99).

3. In the "Author's Note" to *Sozaboy,* Saro-Wiwa refers to "High-Life," which he wrote as a student at Ibadan University. He comments that "[b]oth 'High-Life' and *Sozaboy* are the result of my fascination with the adaptability of the English language and of my closely observing the speech and writings of a certain segment of Nigerian society." The language of "Rotten English," he adds, "is disordered and disorderly. . . . It thrives on lawlessness."

4. See also where Bakhtin's moral tone is clear in repeatedly referring to aspects of carnival as "false seriousness" and "preparing a new sober seriousness" (pp. 376, 380, 426, 439, 448, 453, and 454).

5. Mezu rightly comments that "cruel indifference with which the needs of the detained suspects is treated makes them anonymous 'cases' rather than living entities" (p. 104).

6. Again, Mezu makes this point.

WORKS CITED

Austen, Jane. *Pride and Prejudice.* New York: Norton, 1993.

Bakhtin, Mikhail. *Rabelais and His World.* Trans. Helene Iswolsky. Bloomington: Indiana University Press, 1984.

Feuser, Willfried F. "The Voice from Dukana: Ken Saro-Wiwa." *Matatu* 1, no. 2 (1987): 52–66.

Hough, Graham. "Afro-Fictions." Review of *A Forest of Flowers,* by Ken Saro-Wiwa. *London Review of Books,* 3 July 1986: 22–23.

Inyama, N. F. "Ken Saro-Wiwa: Maverick Iconoclast of the Nigerian Literary Scene." *African Literature Today* 20 (1996): 35–49.

Irele, Abiola. "Ken Saro-Wiwa." In *Perspectives on Nigerian Literature: 1700 to the Present.* Vol. 2. Ed. Yemi Ogunbiyi. Lagos: Guardian Books Nigeria Limited, 1988: 333–344.

Mezu, Rose Ure. "Ken Saro-Wiwa and *A Forest of Flowers.*" In *Ken Saro-Wiwa: The Life and Times.* Ed. S. Okechukwa Mezu. Randallstown, Md.: Black Academy Press, 1986: 91–114.

Saro-Wiwa, Ken. *Adaku and Other Stories.* London: Saros International Publishers, 1989.

———. "Author's Note." In *Sozaboy: A Novel in Rotten English.* Port Harcourt: Saros International Publishers, 1986.

———. *A Forest of Flowers.* Port Harcourt: Saros International Publishers, 1986.

6

The Novel:
Sozaboy: A Novel in Rotten English

Maureen N. Eke

Before his untimely death, Ken Saro-Wiwa was still relatively unknown to many scholars in the field of African literature, especially those located outside Nigeria. It is safe to state, however, that his environmental activism drew even more international attention to his literary creativity. Since his death on 10 November 1995, at the hands of the Nigerian military government, many discussion sessions at academic conferences have been devoted to his works. These sessions often cite his death as epitomizing the repression of democratic processes in Nigeria. His unjust trial and execution have also galvanized international support from a diverse group of organizations and scholars for pro-democracy and environmental activism in Nigeria.

One of his often cited works is *Sozaboy,* his novel in "rotten" English, which allegorizes the Nigerian/Biafran Civil War as indicative of the social malaise in Nigerian society. The critical attention that has often been devoted to this novel explores Saro-Wiwa's use of language. For instance, most of the essays in the collection on *Sozaboy* edited by Charles Nnolim are devoted to discussions of language. Although I also very briefly explore the use of language in *Sozaboy*, my emphasis will be on the sociopolitical awakening of Mene, alias Sozaboy, and how that becomes an indication of Saro-Wiwa's own politicization. Language use in this novel can be seen as an extension of this politicization of both the protagonist and novelist.

At the end of his adventure narrative, Sozaboy expresses his disillusionment with war and underscores the havoc that it has wreaked on his life and his people. This disillusionment with war and society in general becomes a central theme in Saro-Wiwa's narrative about a "naive young boy who joins the army out of romantic idealism" (Chukwuma, p. 45). In this chapter, I attempt to read Saro-Wiwa's text through postcolonial theory, including essays by Chinua Achebe, Frantz Fanon, and Saro-Wiwa himself; to discuss Saro-Wiwa's political and social criticism of his society through the seemingly naive but emerging sociopolitical consciousness of his protagonist, Sozaboy; and to examine, very briefly, the use of language, what Saro-Wiwa describes as "rotten English," as a trope and a deliberately masked weapon for rendering social criticisms.

In his essay, "The Novelist as Teacher," Achebe states that "The writer cannot expect to be excused from the task of re-education and regeneration that must be done" (Achebe, *Hopes and Impediments,* p. 45). He adds, "he should march right in front. For he is, after all—as Ezekiel Mphahlele says in his *African Image*—the sensitive point of his community" (p. 45). Saro-Wiwa seems to agree with Achebe's vision of a writer's commitment to his society. In a letter to William Boyd written from jail, Saro-Wiwa asserts that his art is functional, particularly as a tool for addressing the social ills in his society. "I'm in good spirits. . . . There's no doubt that my idea will succeed in time, but I'll have to bear the pain of the moment" (Boyd, p. xv), he writes. Then he adds:

> the most important thing for me is that I've used my talent as a writer to enable the Ogoni people to confront their tormentors. I was not able to do it as a politician or a businessman. My writing did it. It makes me feel good! I'm mentally prepared for the worst, but hopeful for the best. I think I have the moral victory. (p. xv)

As is suggested in his letter, one of the primary goals for his art is to raise the social and political consciousness of his readers, especially of those marginalized by the dominant, elite Nigerian culture; Saro-Wiwa pursues that purpose in *Sozaboy*. Through the transformation of his protagonist, Mene, from a seemingly naive character who is unaware of the implications of the social upheaval about to engulf his people, to a disillusioned and embittered but socially conscious character, Saro-Wiwa comments on the social and political decay of Nigeria. The "rottenness" the protagonist perceives in Dukana is symptomatic of the problem with contemporary Nigeria. As Achebe has noted, "the trouble with Nigeria is simply and squarely a failure of leadership" (Achebe, *Trouble with Nigeria,* p. 1). "The Nigerian problem," he continues, "is the unwillingness or the inability of its leaders to rise to the responsibility, to the challenge of personal example which are the hallmarks of true leadership" (p. 1). In his observations about the society, Sozaboy underscores Achebe's criticism that the national leadership has lost its focus and functionality. As Fanon would claim, the nation is experiencing the throes of a "failed national consciousness" (Fanon, "The Pitfalls," pp. 156–157) stemming from the inept leadership of a middle class in its infancy.

WRITING NATIONAL DISMEMBERMENT AND VIOLENCE

When the novel opens, Sozaboy hints that it is the end of an era of hard labor: "All nine villages were dancing and we were eating plenty maize with pear and knacking tory under the moon. Because the work on the farm have finished and the yams were growing well well. And because the old, bad government have dead, and the new government of soza and police have come" (Saro-Wiwa, *Sozaboy,* p. 1). But of greater significance than the end of the planting season is the death of the decadent politics and social irresponsibility of the former government. Sozaboy describes the euphoria of the people of Dukana:

> Everybody was saying that everything will be good in Dukana because of the new government. They were saying that *kotuma ashbottom* from Bori cannot take bribe from people in Dukana again. They were saying too that all those policemen who used to chop big big bribe from people who get case will not chop again. Everybody was happy because from that time, even magistrate in the court at Bori will begin to give better judgement. And traffic police will do his work well well. (p. 1)

Saro-Wiwa cannot resist a critique of the moral perversion he observes in the old government. The audience is told that the new era marks the death of the "old" and "corrupt" ruler; it is a new beginning whose promise of change is underscored by the seeming tranquillity of the community. Communicating the people's dreams and excitement, Sozaboy adds, "Even one woman was talking that the sun will shine proper proper and people will not die again because there will be medicine in the hospital and the doctor will not charge money for operation. Yes, everybody in Dukana was happy. And they were all singing" (p. 1). Yes, this is the beginning of a fairytale era, marked by a new consciousness and a new spirit of optimism.

Even Nature is expected to behave accordingly because of the change. In fact, the political and social renaissance coincides with a period of sufficiency that evokes the vegetation myth's archetypal cycle of life and rebirth. In the novel, Saro-Wiwa marks the end of a period of both social and agrarian famine/need (death) with the dying of the old government and the beginning of a period of sufficiency (rebirth) with the emergence of the new government. Social anguish and nightmare are replaced by hope and excitement. In addition to the agrarian imagery, Saro-Wiwa provides a food metaphor. Corruption is represented as something edible as Sozaboy informs us that with the new era, "all those policemen who used to chop big big bribe from people who get case will not chop again" (p. 1). Implied in his statement is the assumption that as in eating, those corrupt government officials will eventually become content and desist or refuse to "chop" the people's wealth anymore. But like people, who often overeat because of their greed, the government is no exception, Sozaboy suggests.

Consequently, Saro-Wiwa denies his audience any glimmer of hope in the declared honesty of government of "soza," because the professed change is only illusory, a falsehood suggested by the modified opening statement of the novel: "Although, everybody in Dukana was happy at first" (p. 1). The statement interrogates itself, demanding to know what followed the now destroyed happiness. Saro-Wiwa, however, suspends giving an explanation for the next two pages. According to Sozaboy, the "old" government, which is a masked reference to Nigeria's "First Republic," reeked of corruption at all levels, affecting the politicians, the judicial system, and even the medical services. In fact, to survive under the First Republic's civilian government meant participating in upholding the rottenness that Saro-Wiwa can adequately describe only in "rotten English."

Sozaboy's comments and Saro-Wiwa's criticism of the government echo the words of Nzeogwu's Radio Kaduna message to Nigerians after the 15 January 1966, coup; the idealistic military leader criticized the corruption of the deposed civilian leaders and promised to restore the honor of the nation. But like the new regime in 1966, the new government in Saro-Wiwa's novel, which Sozaboy sees as the salvation for his people, metamorphoses into a new nightmare as suggested in his comments:

> Anyway, to talk true, there was no bribe for some time. But after some time they begin again. The traffic begin with small small bribe. Then they increased it by small. Until they begin to take bigger bigger bribe than before. Then the people begin to say that now wey soza and police be government, nobody can be able to arrest traffic when they chop bribe. Because government cannot arrest government. So therefore, everything will be okay for the big big people who are chopping the bribe. (pp. 2–3)

Certainly, as Sozaboy points out, the new leadership has also imbibed the values of its predecessor, and the people's excitement about a new sense of social justice transforms into bitterness and disillusionment with the new government of soza.

The social malaise that Sozaboy sees in the society is communicated through the image of a people held hostage by the deceptive and incomprehensible rhetoric of its leadership, a language that he describes metaphorically as "big big grammar." This "big big grammar" is used constantly to confuse or dumbfound the people. In fact, that theme of bewilderment is echoed several times in Sozaboy's refrain: "these things were confusing me" (p. 2). Like Sozaboy, the people of Dukana are confused. They can neither trust their government nor escape it. They are caught in a dilemma in which total submission to the whims of dominant institutions seems to be their only survival. Faced with Chief Birabee's betrayal and abdication of power to the soldiers, the community loses its cohesion and sacrifices itself to the soldiers. Many people, including "all the big big men in Dukana begin to bring goat, yam, chicken and plantain. They full the motor of the soza people" (p. 39). But those individuals who cannot offer their belongings and food as appeasement to the new "gods" of power offer their children, as in the case of one man who "bring him daughter to give the soza captain. But the sozaman do not want the girl so she went away crying" (p. 39).

Although the incident Sozaboy describes is a commentary on the disempowerment of the people of Dukana, it also reveals the acute marginalization of women, especially, daughters, for in the absence of money, food, and animals to donate to the soldiers, daughters are offered as pawns in this game of power. Here, women are objectified, and their lives are subsumed under the category of merchandise for barter, to be exchanged for the lives or freedom of the men. Certainly, the interrelationship between power and female sexuality in this case cannot be missed. The father's offer is informed by his multiple readings of female sexuality and its relation to power. On the one hand, female sexuality is seen as a potential means of disempowering a man, even if only briefly. In other words, the father's offer evokes the Samson-Delilah binary wherein Delilah (the daughter) through her sexuality, will gain the father's freedom from Samson (the soldier captain) by metaphorically "killing" the latter, that is, distracting him. On the other hand, offering the daughter as a gift, slave, prostitute, or mistress to the captain becomes an affirmation of his status as the possessor of power; the ownership of another person signifies the ultimate assertion of domination.

In this representation, Saro-Wiwa, either wittingly or by accident, allegorizes the occupation of Dukana as a form of prostitution. Indeed, this reading is not unlike similar readings of colonization as a form of prostitution in certain nationalist discourses. Besides, the prostitution of young women was not unfamiliar among many "occupied" communities during the Nigerian/Biafran Civil War. In fact, many young women were abducted by occupying Nigerian or Biafran soldiers at different times. Other women were often "married" off to these soldiers by their families in order to secure the safety and survival of family members. Still other women ran off with occupying soldiers who were seen as representing an opportunity for a better life. The significance of the father's offer in *Sozaboy* also addresses the relations of power between the occupying soldiers and the occupied. Although Saro-Wiwa does not elaborate on the meaning of the act, to both the father and the soldier, the daughter is utterly powerless because of her gender. She is an object that can be bartered freely. Like the women of her society, she must obey the men's orders without protest. Besides, as Sozaboy tells us, "Dukana people say woman does not get mouth. And it is true" (p. 8) because "Women do not talk in Dukana meeting. . . . Anything the men talk, the women must do" (p. 8). But when Birabee levies a tax on the men and women, the men protest that the women are paying too little. The contradiction in the perception of the relations of power is clear.

As Sozaboy notes, the new government, like its predecessor, takes delight in impoverishing its own citizens. It is a government that is no longer accountable to its people because, as Sozaboy says, "government cannot arrest government. So therefore, everything will be okay for the big big people who are chopping the bribe" (p. 3). Again, Sozaboy reemphasizes the image of the new government as a kleptocracy. As he observes, power is located in the hands of the "big big people," or those with guns. Thus, he sees the soldiers who occupy Dukana as locusts, harbingers of the terror that soon sweeps through Dukana, destroying everything in its path. His observation, however, undermines Chief Birabee's representation of the soldiers to his people. According to Birabee, who defines himself as "the friend of the government," the soldiers are protectors. Scolding his people, he says, "Government have sent soza here to come and see you people, protect you, love your sons and your daughters" (pp. 39–40). But these soldiers do not bring love; they are interested neither in protecting the community nor in respecting the lives of its inhabitants. Like Birabee, the soldiers are preoccupied with their own self-gratification. And like Birabee, they terrorize Dukana people into submission.

Their presence in Dukana also signifies the collision of distinct private interests (one of which invokes the national interest as a justification) because the soldiers' presence in the village represents an encroachment into the lives and spaces of Dukana people. Following their arrival in the village, they begin to demand donations of food from the village and slowly deplete the people's food resources. But when the villagers can no longer sustain the soldiers' craving for more food, the latter begin to use coercion to obtain more food. They intrude further into the private spaces of the people. Sozaboy informs us that "[s]ome time sef they will enter person house begin to ask for chop. And if the person do not give them chop, they will hala and hala and then begin to beat the women" (p. 40). Consequently, the soldiers violate both the human and individual rights of the villagers. Subsequently, the soldiers, who signified safety earlier, gradually become sources of terror and threaten both communal cohesion and personal peace.

The emerging national chaos, where the local and the national interests of the people collide, can be described as symptomatic of what Fanon has termed a "failed national consciousness." In "The Pitfalls of National Consciousness," Fanon warns against the misuse of national consciousness by the middle class of "young and independent nations." According to Fanon, the danger in such abuse would lead to a "process of retrogression, that is so harmful and prejudicial to national effort and national unity" (Fanon, "The Pitfalls," p. 156) because "the nation is passed over for the race, and the tribe is preferred to state" (p. 156). Indeed, as predicted by Fanon, the Nigerian/Biafran Civil War, which Saro-Wiwa uses as the historical backdrop for his novel, epitomizes such "retrogression." In the novel, the new government of soza engages in the dismembering of the nation into fragmented entities. Sozaboy constantly refers to this fragmentation and potential national anguish when he indicates: "People were not happy to hear that there is trouble everywhere. Everywhere the people were talking about it. In Pitakwa. In Bori. And in Dukana" (Saro-Wiwa, *Sozaboy*, p. 3). National dismemberment becomes a refrain of the novel. The dismemberment is later symbolically articulated through the environmental devastation that the land experiences as a result of bombardments and the digging of trenches or pits during the war.

Paradoxically, what is wrong with the new government of soza is also wrong with Dukana and its people. Like the characters in Saro-Wiwa's "sitcom," *Basi and Company,* neither the government officials and soldiers nor the citizens of Dukana want to work. Although the soldiers terrorize the community in general, some Dukana citizens, either out of fear or greed, collude with the soldiers to tyrannize other citizens, especially those in debt. Protected by the soldiers who collaborate with them, some seemingly wealthy or moneylending people of Dukana transform themselves into a mafia. According to Sozaboy, the soldiers "begin to make debt collector in Dukana" (p. 40) and lose sight of their role as leaders. Sozaboy elaborates on this reversal of the soldiers' role and the attendant violence they wreak on the citizens:

> If I owe you money and I cannot pay, then you will call soza for me. The soza will come and begin to bully on me until I give you the money. Then you and sozaman will share the money. But if after he have bullied on me I still cannot pay, then they will beat me proper proper till blood commot from my mouth and body and they will take me away to the soza people camp and prison me there. (p. 40)

In the emerging chaos, the community is powerless. Communal loyalty and cohesion are lost, and the people neither complain about their dilemma nor think of ways to collectively resist the terrorism of the soldiers and a few greedy individuals. Even the local leader (Chief Birabee) has been co-opted and collaborates with the soldiers against his own people.

The national government, which sees itself as the representative national "middle class," and local leaders, represented by Birabee, suffer from the "underdevelopment" that Fanon describes as characteristic of the emergent national middle class of postcolonial states immediately following independence. Fanon points out: "The national middle class which takes over power at the end of the colonial regime is an underdeveloped middle class. It has practically no economic power, and in any case it is in no way commensurate with the bourgeoisie of the mother country which it hopes to replace" (Fanon, "The Pitfalls," p. 156). Like the middle class Fanon describes, the leadership of both the civilian and military governments in Saro-Wiwa's *Sozaboy* epitomizes the decadence and weakness of the emergent middle class of postcolonial states. But unlike the colonial middle class that had both capital and experience to maintain power, the national middle class of the postcolonial state immediately after independence has neither capital nor experience.

In fact, the often dictatorial, repressive, and militaristic nature of the governments of many of these postcolonial states is testimony to the youth of the national bourgeoisie and its desperate attempt to maintain power. The oppressive tactics of the soldiers who visit Dukana in Saro-Wiwa's novel have an uncanny similarity to the abuse of power that Fanon associates with the inexperience of the new middle class. Locally, Chief Birabee also embodies the negative qualities of the underdeveloped middle class, whose aspiration is to attain the economic status of its colonial predecessor. Chief Birabee, Sozaboy informs us, is a weak leader who feels empowered only in the presence of the soldiers. His economic self-interest and power-mongering are exposed in his unabashed and frequent evoking of his liaison with the soldiers to silence his people. Sozaboy informs us that "when any sozas come [to Dukana] it is to his [Birabee's] house they will first go. Then he will give them drink and chop" (Saro-Wiwa, *Sozaboy,* pp. 40–41). Although Chief Birabee is the leader of the community and the soldiers who seem to be abiding by expected norms of social behavior within the culture must have his permission to enter the village, Sozaboy sees Birabee's relationship with the soldiers as perverted:

> Chief Birabee like to do all this because when the sozas are there, he can have power more than in Dukana. By the time nobody can disobey what him talk like before. Yes, before before, this Chief Birabee is chief but he is not very important. He cannot prison anybody if you like, you can refuse to go and judge your case in his house. After all he have no police or kotuma, so if you disobey him what can he do to you? (p. 40)

Although the soldiers may have initiated the visit, Birabee exploits it for financial and political empowerment. Like his people, he recognizes the power of the gun and its usefulness as a tool of terror. Hence, Sozaboy explains that "Chief is no chief nowadays. Only to tief, chopping money from poor woman plus money wey dem collect for village" (p. 41).

Clearly, Chief Birabee's quest for more power has alienated him from his people. Fanon points out that a leader such as Birabee sees his people as ungrateful and judges their ingratitude harshly. Consequently, Fanon adds, "every day that passes [such a leader] ranges himself a little more resolutely on the side of the exploiters. He, therefore, knowingly becomes the aider and abettor of the young bourgeoisie which is plunging into the mire of corruption and pleasure" (Fanon, "The Pitfalls," p. 157). Indeed, Birabee is aware of his estrangement from his people, for he tells them, "I am a friend of the government now, you see. You stupid people of Dukana" (Saro-Wiwa, *Sozaboy*, p. 39). Then, admonishing them, he adds, "When I tell you to do what I say, you cannot understand" (p. 39). And, as if to reassert his importance, he claims, "Government have sent soza here to come and see you people, protect you people, love your sons and your daughters. All because Chief Birabee is here. You see now?" (pp. 39–40). In this relationship between the people and their new government, the people are like the colonized, and Birabee represents the "middle man," a collaborator. As in the cases of the colonial encounter and the enslavement of Africans, the freedom and national rights of the African people are being trampled by a few greedy individuals, even if they are Africans. Saro-Wiwa, therefore, presents Dukana as the site for playing out, at a microcosmic level, the political and social chaos that has engulfed the nation, a situation that also threatens the idea of a nation, regional security, and individual peace.

Although the soldiers are not colonizers, their brutality against their own people places them in a similar position to an occupying force. Indeed, Sozaboy and the Dukana people see the soldiers not as protectors or allies in a national struggle, but as terrorists. This imaging of the soldiers as harbingers of communal fracturing underscores Saro-Wiwa's attempt to re-unify his people, the Ogonis, whose lands were occupied by both Biafran and Nigerian federal troops at various times during the civil war. Like the Dukana people, located at the crossroads of the national crisis, the Ogonis were also located at the site of contestation of rights in the national conflict.

Saro-Wiwa has stated that *Sozaboy* was the product of a "very impressionable time in [his life], a time of great drama and even greater challenge" (Saro-Wiwa, *A Month and a Day,* p. 59). To the people of Dukana, as seen through Sozaboy's point of view, the war is about control, especially of wealth and lands. Likewise, Saro-Wiwa, the author, insists that "the war was mostly about the control of the oil resources of the Ogoni and other ethnic groups in the Niger River Delta" (pp. 49–50). Although he limits the motives of the war to the control of Ogoniland and neighboring ethnic groups in the Niger River Delta, it would be much more accurate to argue that the war, in fact, was about the control of most of the lands in the South-eastern Region of Nigeria—oil-producing and non-oil-producing areas. Certainly, although the control of the oil resources, as Saro-Wiwa has suggested, seems to be the impetus for the encroachment into Ogoniland, the crisis was also about the mapping out and reclaiming of national boundaries. In other words, the war is a nation's attempt to re-assert its integrity and sovereignty, even if it means forcibly enclosing or incorporating "errant" regions into the national boundaries. The soldiers in Dukana, therefore, are engaged in acts of national preservation, albeit through force.

THE POLITICAL AWAKENING OF SOZABOY

In narrating the story of a nation experiencing fragmentation, Saro-Wiwa emphasizes the survivalist tendencies that inform Sozaboy's choices, and perhaps, Saro-Wiwa's own pledge of loyalty to the Nigerian federal government instead of Biafra during the civil war. To Saro-Wiwa, Ogoni people's preservation as a united group within the larger national body called Nigeria superseded the desires of any other regional underprivileged group to secede from the nation. Consequently, he implies that the nation's desire to safeguard its boundaries must be privileged over the rebellious competing interests of another regional minority group. Addressing his people as the commissioner of the Rivers State cabinet in his pamphlet "The Ogoni Nation Today and Tomorrow," Saro-Wiwa highlights the importance of securing Ogoni interests as part of a larger nation, Nigeria. He states:

> We have now been given an opportunity to reassert ourselves side by side with all other nationalities in the Nigerian Federation. We cannot let this opportunity slip past us. If we do, posterity shall not forgive us, and we shall disappear as a people from the face of the earth. This must not happen. (Saro-Wiwa, "The Ogoni Nation," p. 52)

As is evident in this statement, Saro-Wiwa privileges the preservation of his people in the collectivity of the nation, although the group's survival is presented as a facet of the construction of national unity. He sanctions the federal military government, appealing to it or "whatever government succeeds it to continue to show concern for small nationalities such as ours— especially in constitution making" (p. 54). In so doing, he hopes to liberate the Ogonis from those "neighbours who have vowed to keep [them] as slaves for all time" (p. 53).

Like his author, Sozaboy also privileges the survival of Dukana people over national unity. Although he is unaware of the origins of the crisis that threatens his community and the nation, he joins the army, informed by a romantic desire to preserve the safety and cohesion of his family and community against external threats and, more immediately, against the brutality of the soldiers. In fact, Saro-Wiwa's novel fits into the category that Simon Gikandi has described as the modernist novel, or "fiction of crisis" in African literature. According to Gikandi, "the modernist novelist is not overtly concerned with specific social modes; he is concerned more with the symptoms rather than the socio-historical dynamics of our experience" (Gikandi, p. 112). Certainly, Saro-Wiwa's concern in his novel is not to provide answers but to expose the symptoms of the social cancer from which his society suffers. Therefore, through Sozaboy, Saro-Wiwa interrogates "historical reality." Like the character in the "fiction of crisis," who according to Gikandi "lives on the periphery of a society he would like to negate in its entirety" (p. 112) and through whose perception the author renders reality, the protagonist of Saro-Wiwa's novel is a fringe dweller, an outsider. At the beginning of the novel, a seemingly naive and disengaged Sozaboy attempts to reintroduce himself to his community (Dukana) by returning home. But his growing awareness of the moral laxity, or "rottenness," of the soldiers, of people in his community, particularly elders such as the "quartet" (Duzia, Zaza, Bom, and Terr Kole), and of community moral leaders such as Pastor Barika and Chief Birabee, force Sozaboy to begin to reevaluate his relationship with his society and to reject the worldview these people articulate. At the end of the novel, Sozaboy rejects his society "in its entirety."

Sozaboy's emerging rejection of the rules of his society and its new government of soza is articulated strongly and clearly on the road from Pitakwa after being "body-searched" by the women militia. In his frustration during what appears as a brief moment of introspection, he states: "As we got nearer Dukana, I begin to vex when I think how those girls were giving me orders. I vex bad bad. I think I cannot have that nonsense again. I must go join the army immediately" (Saro-Wiwa, *Sozaboy,* p. 54). Like the men in his patriarchal society, Sozaboy is unable to perceive women in leadership positions as equals or even as his superiors. According to him, women do not have power in Dukana. For instance, he casts Agnes, his future wife, and his mother in gendered roles as wife and mother, respectively. In order to garner their support for his desire to join the soldiers, he cunningly manipulates their "gendered" desires and perceptions of his duty as a man. His mother wants him to get married and produce an heir. Fearing that he might die in the war, she opposes his joining the army. Agnes, however, wants a husband who could protect her; therefore, she wants him to become a soldier to prove his manhood. Although the immediate interests of these two women contradict each other, Sozaboy skillfully exploits the tension between their desires to attain his goal. Like a trickster and playing one woman against the other, he sets his plan in motion and informs us, his unwitting accomplices, that Agnes "likes me to be soza. So she will tell my mother that unless I am soza, she will not marry me. Then my mother because she wants this picken [a grandchild], she must allow me to go to soza after I marry Agnes" (p. 57). His conclusion is informed by his assumption that the women's gendered expectations and perceptions of his role as a man will influence their decisions.

Sozaboy also sees being a soza as an opportunity to "wear uniform like those boys . . . sing those fine songs. Begin to march up and down, chop better chop" (p. 54). In other words, joining the soza will enable him to attain power like the soldiers in Dukana and the new recruits he saw marching in Pitakwa. In addition, because of his new status, "Zaza cannot make *yanga* for [him] again" (p. 54). Ironically, like Birabee, Sozaboy perceives going to war to become a soza as an opportunity to "fatten" himself either physiologically by "chopping" "better chop" or psychologically by acquiring power through the gun. Also, being a soza provides him with a chance to reinvent himself socially and to assert his masculinity. He concludes, rather romantically, that while he is "marching with gun and singing, prouding, all the people will come and look at [him]. They will say how [he is] brave man. Very brave man" (p. 54). "And no woman," he adds, "whether Simple Defence or no Simple Defence cannot begin to give me order on the road like say I no sabi anything" (p. 54). His naive perceptions, however, undermine his patriotism, as it becomes obvious that he is seduced by externalities such as the army uniform, the facade of power, and the marching groups of young army recruits. Besides, he cannot resist the captivating power of the soldiers' songs, which continually emphasize patriotic devotion to one's country, calling out to the individual, "Why do you delay / Come and save the nation . . . There is danger / Why do you delay?" (pp. 48–49).

Saro-Wiwa, however, lampoons Sozaboy's naiveté about war and, perhaps, that of the younger generation by presenting another perspective through Zaza, the World War II soldier. Although Zaza's story is renarrated by Sozaboy as a romance, highlighting the young and naive Zaza's exploits in Burma during World War II, the mature Zaza abhors war. Hence, when asked if he would go to war again, he refuses, describing the current war as "like children playing." Commenting on his war experience, Zaza cautions Sozaboy as well as both his immediate and imagined audiences against the dehumanizing effect of war, stating, "What man picken have seen only God can know" (p. 30). To further emphasize the psychic violence caused by war, Zaza adds, "some time . . . no food, some time, no water. Even sef you have to put your urine inside water bottle and after some time you will drink the urine because of no water" (p. 30). This narration foreshadows Sozaboy's experience on the battlefield, especially Bullet's consumption of the Captain's urine. Because Bullet does not drink the urine out of a desperate need to quench his thirst but as punishment for raiding the Captain's quarters for beer, the psychological effect is significant. After the incident, Sozaboy informs us that Bullet is transformed; he is stripped of his titles; he silences himself, an act that Sozaboy reads as "wickedness" entering Bullet's body. In both Bullet's and Zaza's stories, the individuals are bestialized and, consequently, fractured psychically. Bullet is driven to "temporary insanity" and later kills his Captain, whereas Zaza returns from war unable to take care of himself or anyone. In fact, Sozaboy describes him as "useless" and "no better man"; he is often seen half-clad and carries a picture of his lost mistress hidden in his loincloth.

In narrating Zaza's story, Saro-Wiwa also foreshadows Sozaboy's experience because the latter character undergoes a similar transformation from naiveté to experience. Like Zaza, who went to fight in an earlier war guided by his romantic heroism to kill "Hitla" so as to enable ships to bring salt to Dukana, Sozaboy also wants to protect Dukana from destruction. In fact, Helen Chukwuma describes Zaza as "an antecedent of Mene [Sozaboy]" (Chukwuma, p. 49). Zaza's narrative, therefore, can be perceived as a cautionary tale about the horrors of war; Sozaboy, however, misreads the narrative. In addition to Zaza's voice, Saro-Wiwa incorporates other voices such as those of the boys who denounce war and militarization and tell Sozaboy that "going to soza is not good thing" (Saro-Wiwa, *Sozaboy,* p. 43), because, they argue, "soza is stupid useless animal who will just shoot and kill and then he can also be shoot and kill" (p. 43). Clearly, through these voices, Saro-Wiwa renders a harsh social commentary on war, reasserting his opposition to it. But whereas Saro-Wiwa's authorial consciousness, like Zaza, has hindsight and is aware of the violence associated with war, Sozaboy's consciousness is still too naive to understand the implications of war. Consequently, Sozaboy's sojourn in the military can only be seen as a necessary stage in his social awakening. Like the hero of a romance, whose persona Sozaboy seems to have appropriated, he believes he must undertake a quest to conquer or slay the "dragon" that threatens his damsel in distress (Agnes), save the land (Dukana) from starvation, and return a hero. In fact, Sozaboy's thoughts, like those of the naive Zaza before his World War II experiences in Burma, seem to reinscribe the pattern of the romance narrative. In addition, by sending Sozaboy to war and narrating the experience through Sozaboy's perspective, Saro-Wiwa forces his audience to undertake a similar journey of discovery to uncover the horrors that his protagonist observes. As an allegory of the Nigerian/Biafran conflict, then, Sozaboy's narrative about his experience on the war front becomes, for Saro-Wiwa's audience, a reinscription and social criticism of the destructiveness of the historical Nigerian Civil War.

For Saro-Wiwa, however, the war is only a manifestation of what is wrong with the country and its leadership. Like the old government—rotten, corrupt, and inept—the new government has betrayed its citizens. Both Saro-Wiwa and Sozaboy see the new government and its leaders undermining the citizens' perceptions of the responsibility of any national government or leadership to its people. The new government fails to protect its people. The crisis that escalates into a war activates the latent violence that both Saro-Wiwa and Sozaboy associate with the leadership and corrupt body politic of the nation. But the violence is also an indication of a nation at war with itself, a society where both the leaders and citizens are committed to self-gratification and appropriation of power. This is a society where both the leaders and citizens believe in the ideology of "man-must-wak" or "chop," but where only a few powerful individuals consume the national wealth and brutalize the marginalized "common" people into further submission. It is also a society where, in desperation, the powerless collaborate with the powerful to further disenfranchise others, including friends, family members, and neighbors.

It is not surprising then that Manmuswak, the mercenary who criss-crosses the war front providing information to all the fighting groups, epitomizes the ills of the society. Like "Eshu Elegbara," the Yoruba trickster god or figure, who mediates through tricks, Manmuswak is a trickster.[1] Like Eshu, he is Janus-faced; he is friend and foe simultaneously. In fact, an important stage in Sozaboy's epiphany is his realization that "Man-muswak is proper cunny man" (p. 113). Consequently, Sozaboy attributes the devastation caused by the war and the death of his colleagues to Man-muswak's machinations: "Na him come confuse all of us. Na him come spoil the war. And now all my friends don die or sometimes Manmuswak don take some of them make prisoner of war" (p. 113). With this new consciousness comes one of Sozaboy's harshest criticisms of war. Battered, emotionally drained, and alone because his camp has been destroyed by the bombing that killed Bullet and the other men, Sozaboy is disillusioned and comes to the conclusion that

> war is a very bad thing. War is to drink urine, to die and all that uniform that they are giving us to wear is just to deceive us. And anybody who think that uniform is fine thing is stupid man who does not know what is good or bad or not good at all or very bad at all. All those things that they have been telling us before is just stupid lie. (pp. 113–114)

In this brief moment, alone and surrounded by death and the environmental destruction of war, Sozaboy criticizes both war and its rhetoric. He challenges all the symbols that have been used to make war appealing, including the uniforms, those seductive patriotic songs, and Agnes's romantic imaging of soldiers. Interestingly, Sozaboy also rereads Zaza's narrative and interrogates his earlier sense of its glorification of war. "All that one that Zaza is talking about is not true at all" (p. 114), he says. Then adds, "Zaza have not gone to any Burma to fight any Hitla. He have not married any white woman at all" (p. 114). In addition, Sozaboy embraces Zaza as a kindred spirit, acknowledging that "[s]ometime Zaza is just like myself wey dem drive to the war front like *mumu* goat who does not know where he is going. Sometimes he is just like myself who will only obey and do anything that he is told" (p. 114). In acknowledging this similarity between himself and Zaza as mere pawns in the war, Sozaboy destroys his earlier depiction of himself as heroic and attributes his enlistment in the soza to confusion caused by Zaza's story. We could claim here that Sozaboy has finally "heard" and read Zaza's narrative correctly. Rather, it is a naive Sozaboy who failed to heed the caution or the moral of Zaza's story because of his zeal to become a soldier.

Sozaboy's introspection culminates in his proclamation of the unarticulated "truth" about the war propaganda, which is that the soldiers do not know why or whom they are fighting. Sozaboy comments:

> Even, I no understand what I was doing until now. I come begin see as I dey think for that swamp that day that true true I do not know why we are fighting the war. The Chief Commander General have not told us why we are fighting. No Tan Papa did not tell us why we are fighting. The soza captain did not tell us why we must go inside the pit. I just carry gun, fight, go inside pit because they tell me to carry gun, fight, go inside pit; right turn, left turn, about turn, udad arms, run, no run, stand still, chop, piss, shit. Every thing they tell me, I must do, no questions. (p. 114)

Sozaboy's dilemma, however, is one shared even by those in authority. The Chief Commander General and Tan Papa cannot provide reasons for the war to Sozaboy and the other soldiers because they too do not know but are carrying out instructions given by their superiors. This observation underscores the alienation of the leaders from those whom they govern. It also highlights Sozaboy's own growing alienation from his society because the war has changed his worldview and has made him more critical of his society. Consequently, he is no longer at ease in his society or among his own people. This alienation from his society is even more acutely pronounced upon his return to Dukana from war. He notes that not only has the war destroyed his village by changing its landscape, but also that it has destroyed a sense of communality among his people. Like Manmuswak, they have become mercenaries who willingly betray family members and friends in order to survive. Even Sozaboy, who went to fight for their safety, left his family endangered. Disillusioned and with no family or home to return to, Sozaboy embarks on voluntary exile, declaring:

> And as I was going, I was just thinking how the war have spoiled my town Dukana, uselessed many people, killed many others, killed my mama and my wife, Agnes, my beautiful young wife with J.J.C. and now it have made me like porson wey get leprosy because I have no town again. (p. 181)

In his closing remarks, he states, "And I was thinking how I was prouding before to go to soza and call myself Sozaboy. But now if anybody say anything about war or even fight, I will just run and run and run and run and run Believe me sincerely" (p. 181).

"KNACKING TORY" IN ROTTEN ENGLISH

What makes Sozaboy believable as a naive protagonist who eventually matures into a socially conscious persona is his use of language. Saro-Wiwa has stated that the social malaise and chaotic condition he perceives in his society can only be inscribed effectively through "rotten" English. According to him, this "language is disordered and disorderly. . . . It thrives on lawlessness, and is part of the dislocated and discordant society in which Sozaboy must live, move and have not his being" (Saro-Wiwa, *Sozaboy,* "Author's Note"). From the very beginning of the novel, Sozaboy highlights the acute corruption of the society and its government by evoking linguistically the image of greed. He uses the metaphor "chop" to signify the leadership's consumption of the national wealth as well as to suggest the consumptive nature of the social degeneration. For instance, Sozaboy exposes the warped logic in Inspector Okonkwo's discontent with his promotion from sergeant, because the rank of inspector, although a higher rank than sergeant, would earn less money. As inspector, Okonkwo announces, "dis promotion na demotion" because, we are told, when the inspector was sergeant, he "chopped bribe from drivers until he can be able to marry four wives and build better house for his town" (p. 2). In a society where things have fallen apart and the government is run by a pack of rogues, only a warped moral code makes sense. Inspector Okonkwo's protest against his promotion can only be rationalized from the perspective of the rogue culture or the lawlessness that informs it. It is no wonder that the young and innocent Sozaboy finds Okonkwo's logic confusing.

Through language, Sozaboy also successfully undermines the hypocrisy of the government's official rhetoric of responsible and curative governance. The language uncovers the rottenness of a government that manipulates "big big grammar" and "long long words" to camouflage its rancid ideas and empty promises. As we discover, the effect of this "grammar" is chaotic, for Sozaboy informs us that as "grammar plenty, na so trouble plenty. And as trouble plenty, na so plenty people were dying" (p. 3). According to Asomwan S. Adagboyin, "The stylistic beauty of *Sozaboy* may be said to rest in the hero-narrator's attempt to express a reality he is passing through in a language form he has fashioned entirely for himself. This language form is personal, unorthodox and quite rebellious" (Adagboyin, p. 31). Sozaboy is able to utilize this language effectively because like him, the language belongs to the fringes of society. Whereas many members of the Nigerian elite may understand pidgin or "rotten" English, they refuse to use it because to them, it signifies powerlessness, very little education, lower-class values, lawlessness, and the disorder that Saro-Wiwa also has mentioned. Consequently, only those characters located at the margins of society or the underprivileged employ this "rotten" or pidgin English.

But this use of language in *Sozaboy* can also be described as Saro-Wiwa's personal rebellion against a society whose elitism is only a facade because this elite is even more perverted than the underprivileged masses whom it disdains. Seen from this perspective, Saro-Wiwa's use of language affirms Achebe's comment on the African writer's use of English. Reflecting on his own use of English in his essay, "The Role of the Writer in a New Nation," Achebe suggests that an African writer can manipulate or reconstruct English to reflect his or her own experience. Thus, he states:

> The African writer should aim to use English in a way that brings out his message best without altering the language to the extent that its value as a medium of international exchange will be lost. He should aim at fashioning out an English which is at once universal and able to carry his peculiar experience. (Achebe, "The Role of the Writer," p. 16)

As Achebe puts it, the question of language use is a "grave issue." It is also an issue that is continually being addressed by African writers from Ngugi wa Thiongó to Wole Soyinka.

In another essay, Achebe returns to this issue of the function of English, asking, "If I write novels in a country in which most citizens are illiterate, who is my community? If I write in English in a country in which English may still be called a foreign language, or in any case is spoken only by a minority, what use is my writing?" (Achebe, *Hopes and Impediments,* pp. 59–60). For Achebe, obviously, it becomes necessary for the artist to find an appropriate language through which to communicate to the large majority of his readership. In *Sozaboy,* Saro-Wiwa attempts to expose the ills of the society through the eyes of a semiliterate protagonist and to reveal these ills, especially to the marginalized masses, through a language often associated with the fringes of Nigerian society. By employing "rotten" English, Saro-Wiwa, according to William Boyd, hijacks English as "a perfect vehicle for the story" (Boyd, p. ix). But this "hijacking" of English involves a reconstitution or remolding of the language, destabilizing its use and meaning as the discourse of the dominant group and making it function anew. In fact, like many postcolonialist writers, Saro-Wiwa indigenizes English in his novel, giving it a uniquely Nigerian flavor and transforming its functionality. By using this "rotten" or pidgin English, a melange of indigenous linguistic forms and English, Saro-Wiwa is able to deliver what George Lipsitz refers to as "heavily coded covert messages about the past" (Lipsitz, p. 4), the Nigerian/Biafran Civil War, and the present social and political environment in Nigeria. For instance, although the dominant culture or power that associates pidgin English with subdominant groups—that is, the poor, illiterate masses—may perceive Saro-Wiwa's narrative as "not serious" work, the writer is able to call the attention of the so-called masses to the "rottenness" of its leadership.

Thus, Saro-Wiwa can deliver his criticism behind the mask of a naive protagonist whose use of language is seen as ludicrous and disorderly.

Saro-Wiwa's use of language is representative of the malleability of language in many postcolonial narratives. According to Bill Ashcroft, Gareth Griffiths, and Helen Tiffin in their book, *The Empire Writes Back*, "The crucial function of language as a medium of power in post-colonial writing defines itself by seizing the language of the center and replacing it in discourse fully adapted to the colonized place" (Ashcroft et al., p. 38). Although the center in Saro-Wiwa's novel is no longer the imperial metropolis, it has appropriated the discourse and power position of the colonial metropolis. Adagboyin, a Nigerian critic of Saro-Wiwa's novel, succinctly summarizes the relationship among language, the narrative of *Sozaboy,* and the social criticism that is Saro-Wiwa's goal:

> In *Sozaboy,* Saro-Wiwa has, indeed, created an Africanized English. He has created an authentic hero-narrator, too, who narrates his disgust for the Nigerian civil war in a form that explicates and, in fact, does reflect the dislocated, fragmented and atomistic society that serves as the back-cloth of the narrative. (Adagboyin, p. 37)

CONCLUSION

Boyd has described *Sozaboy* as "not simply a great African novel but also a great antiwar novel—among the very best of the twentieth century" (Boyd, "Introduction," p. ix). Saro-Wiwa would agree, pointing out that the novel fulfills his dictum and that of several African writers that the artist in Africa must be, to use Saro-Wiwa's term, *"l'homme engagé."* Achebe, for instance, believes that the writer must be a leader, a teacher, who marches "in front" of his community. During his short life, Saro-Wiwa responded to the call that the writer "march in front" of his people through his political and environmental activism. As he has stated in what he calls his "credo":

> [L]iterature in a critical situation such as Nigeria's cannot be divorced from politics. Indeed, literature must serve society by steeping itself in politics, by intervention, and writers must not merely write to amuse or to take a bemused, critical look at society. They must play an interventionist role. (Saro-Wiwa, *A Month and a Day,* p. 81)

As a writer, Saro-Wiwa's numerous TV dramas, essays, and fictional works function as a continuous social commentary on Nigerian society. Through humor and effective manipulation of language, he lampooned both the leadership and disengaged masses of Nigerian society. But his literary life was only a facet of a larger interest—the struggle for social and political equity among all Nigerians. He combined his literary and political interests in his role as the leader of the Movement for the Survival of Ogoni People (MOSOP) in order to fight, locally and internationally, for Ogoni rights and their protection against environmental death (see Appendix 1). In this role, Saro-Wiwa epitomizes his ideal writer, *"l'homme engagé:* the intellectual of action." According to him, such a writer

> must take part in mass organizations. He must establish direct contact with the people and resort to the strength of African literature—oratory in the tongue. For the word is power and more powerful is it when expressed in common currency. That is why the writer who takes part in mass organizations will deliver his message more effectively than one who only writes waiting for time to work its literary wonders. (Saro-Wiwa, *A Month and a Day,* p. 81)

Certainly, Saro-Wiwa did not believe in such waiting. His activism is a testimony to his relationship with his people—the Ogoni—and to his commitment to his call for action. But for many, their only contact with him was through his literary works. And one of these works, *Sozaboy*, attests both to his critical insight into Nigerian society and to his commitment to awakening the social consciousness of all Nigerians about the past and the present through what he perceives as a powerful weapon: language—words "expressed in common currency," namely, "rotten" English.

NOTE

1. Eshu-Elegbara, or Esu, is the Yoruba trickster god or figure of signification and confusion. He figures in the oral narratives and mythology of many African diaspora cultures, especially those with a strong Yoruba presence. For a detailed discussion, see Henry Louis Gates, Jr., *The Signifying Monkey: A Theory of African-American Literary Criticism.* A corresponding trickster figure among the Igbos is *mbe,* the tortoise.

WORKS CITED

Achebe, Chinua. *Hopes and Impediments: Selected Essays.* New York: Doubleday, 1989.
———. "The Role of the Writer in a New Nation." *Nigeria Magazine,* 18 June 1964.
———. *The Trouble with Nigeria.* London: Heinemann, 1983.
Adagboyin, Asomwan. "The Language of Ken Saro-Wiwa's Sozaboy." In *Critical Essays on Ken Saro-Wiwa's* Sozaboy: A Novel in Rotten English. Ed. Charles Nnolim. London: Saros International Publishers, 1992: 30–38.
Ashcroft, Bill, Gareth Griffiths, and Helen Tiffin, eds. *The Empire Writes Back: Theory and Practice in Post-Colonial Literatures.* New York: Routledge, 1991.

Boyd, William. "Introduction." In *A Month and A Day* by Ken Saro-Wiwa. Harmondsworth: Penguin, 1995.

Chukwuma, Helen. "Characterization and Meaning in *Sozaboy.*" In *Critical Essays on Ken Saro-Wiwa's* Sozaboy: A Novel in Rotten English. Ed. Charles Nnolim. London: Saros International Publishers, 1992: 39–52.

Fanon, Frantz. "The Pitfalls of National Consciousness." In *The Post-Colonial Studies Reader.* Ed. Bill Ashcroft, Gareth Griffiths, and Helen Tiffin. New York: Routledge, 1994: 156–157.

———. *The Wretched of the Earth.* 1977. Trans. Constance Farrington. New York: Penguin, 1961.

Gates, Henry Louis, Jr. *The Signifying Monkey: A Theory of African-American Literary Criticism.* New York: Oxford University Press, 1988.

Gikandi, Simon. *Reading the African Novel.* Portsmouth, N.H.: Heinemann, 1987.

Lipsitz, George. *Time Passages: Collective Memory and American Popular Culture.* Minneapolis: University of Minnesota Press, 1990.

Ngugi wa Thiongó. *Decolonising the Mind: The Politics of Language in African Literature.* Portsmouth, N.H.: Heinemann, 1987.

Nnolim, Charles, ed. *Critical Essays on Ken Saro-Wiwa's* Sozaboy: A Novel in Rotten English. Port Harcourt: Saros International Publishers, 1992.

Saro-Wiwa, Ken. *Basi and Company: A Modern African Folktale.* Port Harcourt: Saros International Publishers, 1987.

———. *A Month and a Day: A Detention Diary.* New York: Penguin, 1995.

———. *Sozaboy: A Novel in Rotten English.* Port Harcourt: Saros International Publishers, 1985; reprint 1986.

PART 3

The Public Man

7

Pipe Dreams: Ken Saro-Wiwa, Environmental Justice, and Microminority Rights

Rob Nixon

Shell operations still impossible unless ruthless military operations are undertaken for smooth economic activities to commence.
—Nigerian government memo, 5 December 1994

Ken Saro-Wiwa squints at us from the cover of his Nigerian detention diary, the posthumously published *A Month and a Day*. His mustache looks precise and trim; his eyes are alight; a gash scrawls across his temple. But it's his pipe that governs the picture. It's an intellectual's accessory, a good pipe to suck and clench, to spew from and lecture with. Saro-Wiwa had expected tobacco to kill him: "I know that I am a mortuary candidate. But I intend to head for the mortuary with my pipe smoking" (*The Independent,* 11 November 1995). In the end, it was the other pipes that got him, the Shell and Chevron pipes that poured poison into the land, streams, and bodies of Saro-Wiwa's Ogoni people, provoking him to take up the life of protest that was to be his triumph and his undoing (see Appendixes 1 and 2).

Saro-Wiwa believed to the last that his writing would return to haunt his tormentors. Shortly before his execution in 1995 in the Nigerian coastal city of Port Harcourt on trumped-up charges of murder, he declared: "The men who ordained and supervised this show of shame, this

A shorter version of this essay first appeared in *The London Review of Books* 18, no. 7 (April 1996). The current version was published in the inaugural issue of *Black Renaissance* (Fall 1996).

tragic charade, are frightened by the word, the power of ideas, the power of the pen. . . . They are so scared of the word that they do not read. And that will be their funeral" (*Mail and Guardian,* 11 November 1995). Saro-Wiwa's conviction that the pen is mightier than the goon squad may well sound, to European and North American ears, like an echo from another age. But across much of Africa, the certainty persists that writing can make things happen.

In one of his final letters from detention, Saro-Wiwa assured his friend, the novelist William Boyd:

> There's no doubt that my idea will succeed in time, but I'll have to bear the pain of the moment—the most important thing for me is that I've used my talents as a writer to enable the Ogoni people to confront their tormentors. I was not able to do it as a politician or a businessman. My writing did it. . . . I think that I have the moral victory. (*The New Yorker,* 27 November 1995)

Elsewhere, he prayed that his work would have as visceral an impact as André Gide's 1927 journal, *Voyage au Congo,* which prompted an outcry against Belgian atrocities and helped to secure their cessation (Saro-Wiwa, *Genocide in Nigeria,* p. 9). Saro-Wiwa saw himself as part of that testimonial tradition, a witness to what he called the "recolonization" of Ogoni land by the joint forces of the oil companies and the Abacha regime, which together had transformed the Niger Delta into a Bermuda triangle for human rights.[1]

Saro-Wiwa wrote as a member of a microminority: one of 500,000 Ogoni in a nation of 100 million, composed of nearly 300 ethnic groups. He produced tireless testimonies of the devastation of his culture by the oil-driven avarice of vast forces beyond its control. He recognized, however, that the justice of a cause—particularly an African cause—is no reason to believe that it will gain the international attention it merits. As a writer and campaigner, he saw the strategic necessity of analogizing, of turning what he called the "deadly ecological war against the Ogoni" into a struggle emblematic of our times (Saro-Wiwa, *A Month and a Day,* p. 131). His profuse writings thus laid the groundwork for a broader estimation of the global cost, above all to microminorities, of the ongoing romance between unanswerable corporations and unspeakable regimes.

The problem of competitive ethnicity is widespread in Africa, but it is particularly acute in Nigeria. The roots of the problem derive from the British invention of Nigeria in 1914. The British historian Lord Malcolm Hailey once described Nigeria as "the most artificial of the many administrative units created in the course of European occupation of Africa" (quoted in Saro-Wiwa, *Genocide in Nigeria,* p. 19; see also Saro-Wiwa, *Nigeria: The Brink of Disaster,* pp. 45–46). When Nigeria gained independence in 1960, it kept its improbable borders with the result that almost 300 ethnic groups were clustered under the umbrella of one nation-state. For all but ten of the thirty-six years since independence, this formidably diverse society has suffered under military rule. Unelected officials from the three largest ethnic groups—the Yoruba, the Igbo, and the Hausa-Fulani—have totally dominated national politics.

The Ogoni constitute approximately 0.5 percent of the Nigerian population. Thus, like the other sixteen microminorities who dwell in the oil-rich delta, the Ogoni lack the political leverage and the constitutional protection to lay claim to the wealth that has been taken from their land. Nigeria's independence initially promised a measure of economic justice for microminorities: the 1960 Constitution required that the government return 50 percent of any mining revenues to the region of extraction.[2] But instead of the 50 percent constitutionally due to them, the Ogoni have been awarded a mere 1.5 percent and, in effect, not even that.[3]

As a rule of thumb, the greater a nation's reliance on a single product for its economic survival, the higher the chances that the society is riddled with corruption. Nigeria's dependence on oil is absolute. It constitutes 90 percent of all exports, half of it going to the United States (*New Statesman and Society*, 17 November 1995), and generates 80 percent of government revenue. Thus, oil has become a precondition of and a byword for military power.

Shell Petroleum Development Corporation is by far the largest stakeholder in the Nigerian economy, owning 47 percent of the oil industry. Its joint venture partner in the petroleum business was the Abacha regime. Yet Shell representatives repeatedly declare that they exercise no influence over Nigeria's rulers. This allows the world's largest oil company to continue to duck behind the brutalities of its militaristic financial partners. It also enables the corporation to ignore appeals by the Ogoni and neighboring minorities for a share of oil revenues, a measure of environmental self-determination, and economic redress for their devastated environment. These, in Shell's terms, are internal Nigerian matters, belonging to a realm inaccessible to corporate influence.

By the time Saro-Wiwa was executed, the Nigerian military and Mobile Police Force had killed 2,000 Ogoni through direct murder and the burning of villages.[4] Ogoni air had been fouled by the flaring of natural gas; Ogoni croplands scarred by oil spills; Ogoni drinking and fishing waters poisoned. Although Shell was driven out of Ogoniland in 1993, it simply moved on to other parts of Nigeria's once lush delta, now a delta of death. Meanwhile, the Shell legacy continues to seep into the environment and into the bodies of the people of the local farming communities, which, unlike the international corporation, have nowhere else to go.

One witness described the aftermath of an oilfield explosion near the Ogoni village of Dere as

an ocean of crude oil moving swiftly like a great river in flood, successfully swallowing up anything that comes its way. Cassava farms, yams,
palms, streams, and animals for miles on end. There is no pipeborne
water and yet the streams, the only source of drinking water, are coated
with oil. You cannot collect a bucket of rain water for the roofs, trees and
grass are all covered with oil. . . . Men and women forced by hunger have
to dive deep in oil to uproot already rotten yams and cassava.

In the words of a second witness: "We can no longer breathe natural oxy-
gen; rather we inhale lethal and ghastly gases. Our water can no longer be
drunk unless one wants to test the effect of crude oil on the body." The
flaring of vast volumes of gas meant that villagers spent their night beneath an artificial sun:

> The people were used to having 12 hours of day and 12 hours of night.
> But now their position is worse than that of the Eskimos in the North
> Pole. For while nature gives the Eskimos six months of daylight followed
> by six months of night, Shell-BP has given the Dere people about ten
> years of continuous daylight. (Witnesses quoted in Saro-Wiwa, *Genocide
> in Nigeria,* pp. 58, 66, 79)

Subsistence farming and fishing are the mainstays of these Ogoni communities, yet they have received no compensation for the devastation of resources on which they utterly depend.

The half-million Ogoni retain nominal ownership of most of their
densely populated territory. But since oil extraction began forty years ago,
they have suffered massive subterranean dispossession. Shell, Chevron,
and successive Nigerian regimes have siphoned $30 billion of oil from be-
neath Ogoni earth (*New Statesman and Society,* 17 November 95). Yet the
locals still find themselves lacking a hospital, electricity, piped water, and
basic roads, housing, and schools. The community has found itself, in the
fullest sense of the word, thoroughly undermined.

Faced with the neocolonial politics of mineral rights in the Niger
Delta, Saro-Wiwa continued to believe that written testimony, backed by
activism, could make a difference. Like many African authors before him,
he recognized that in a society with frail democratic forces and a thin intellectual elite, interventionist writing required versatility and cunning
(Saro-Wiwa, *A Month and a Day,* p. 81). His life as a public intellectual
was distinguished by his astute sense of strategy. Saro-Wiwa was alert to
shifts in audience and occasion, locally and internationally; he would adjust his register and focus accordingly. He produced more than twenty
books across an ambitious spread of genres: novels, plays, short stories,
children's tales, poetry, histories, political tracts, diaries, satires, and newspaper columns. *Sozaboy: A Novel in Rotten English,* a witty and wrenching
book about life in the Nigerian Civil War, is an iconoclastic work in patois,

daring and brimful of fine writing.[5] But across anglophone West Africa, Saro-Wiwa achieved his greatest renown as the creator of the TV comedy hit, *Basi and Company:* 30 million Nigerians tuned into it primetime on Wednesdays. Saro-Wiwa wrote 150 episodes of *Basi*, a robust satire with a moralistic edge. The series pokes fun at the street scammers and wide-boys who are such a feature of the Lagos life Saro-Wiwa loved and loathed. ("Living in Lagos," Saro-Wiwa wrote, "is an invention in itself and no one, I repeat, no one who lives in it can fail to be touched by its phoniness" [Saro-Wiwa, *Nigeria: The Brink of Disaster,* p. 118].) But after the death of his son in 1992, Saro-Wiwa cut back on his TV and literary activities. He devoted himself single-mindedly to the Ogoni cause, becoming the chronicler of his people's genocide and, finally, a death-row diarist.

Saro-Wiwa's generic versatility, his belief in an instrumental aesthetics, and his obsession with land rights place him in an established tradition of African writing. Yet there the similarities end. For in East and Southern Africa, such tendencies have been routinely associated with writers whose anticolonialism—or anti-neocolonialism—has been inseparable from their socialism.[6] One thinks, for instance, of Ngugi wa Thiongó's *Barrel of a Pen* and Mafika Gwala's essay, "Writing as a Cultural Weapon" (which became the credo for a generation of South African writers). Saro-Wiwa, by contrast, cultivated a deeply international sensibility while standing outside any lineage of African socialism. He was the first African writer to articulate the literature of commitment in expressly environmental terms. And as a successful small businessman—successful enough to send a son to Eton—he was never anticapitalist per se. But he did find himself painfully well placed to protest one of the signal developments of the 1980s and 1990s: the consolidation and increasingly unregulated mobility of transnational corporations. Five hundred corporations, Shell among them, now control 70 percent of global trade (Korten, p. 124).

As a microminority intellectual in a poor African country, Saro-Wiwa viewed deregulation as a synonym for corporate lawlessness of the kind that had ruined Ogoniland. But it is a testament to Saro-Wiwa's savvy sense of strategy that his political protests went well beyond the devastation of his homeland. Although passionately centered in that cause, he came to situate it in a wider, global frame. He began to criticize corrosive international tendencies: above all, how, in Third World countries weakened by structural adjustment, unregulated transnational firms and the national soldiery are at liberty to vandalize the weakest minority communities.

Saro-Wiwa appreciated the improbability of converting an injustice against a small African people into an international cause. His strategic response was to scour the wider political milieu for possible points of connection. In the preface to *Genocide in Nigeria,* for instance, he takes heart from three contemporary developments: "the end of the Cold War, the increasing attention being paid to the global environment, and the insistence of the European Community that minority rights be respected, albeit in the successor states to the Soviet Union and in Yugoslavia." But, he worried, "It remains to be seen whether Europe and America will apply to Nigeria the same standards which they have applied to Eastern Europe" (Saro-Wiwa, *Genocide in Nigeria*, p. 7). His doubts have proved well founded.

A Month and a Day includes a record of his imaginative efforts to capitalize on these new forms of international attention. Initially, human rights groups and ecological ones proved equally unreceptive to the Ogoni cause. An African intellectual claiming ethnocide by environmental means? Saro-Wiwa seemed, at first, eccentric and unplaceable. At Boyd's prompting, he decided to contact Greenpeace, which replied, quite simply, that it did not work in Africa. Amnesty International, for its part, said it could only take up the Ogoni cause if the military were killing people or detaining them without trial, a process that had yet to begin. Saro-Wiwa responded with frustration: "The Ogoni people were being killed all right, but in an unconventional way" (Saro-Wiwa, *A Month and a Day*, p. 88). As he later elaborated:

> The Ogoni country has been completely destroyed by the search for oil. . . . Oil blow-outs, spillage, oil slicks, and general pollution accompany the search for oil. . . . Oil companies have flared gas in Nigeria for the past thirty-three years causing acid rain. . . . What used to be the bread basket of the delta has now become totally infertile. All one sees and feels around is death. Environmental degradation has been a lethal weapon in the war against the indigenous Ogoni people. (Saro-Wiwa, Interview, Channel 4 [UK], 15 November 1995)

Appeals to both minority and environmental rights have gained ground in the 1990s, but there was little precedent in Africa for their simultaneous invocation. Despite the early unresponsiveness of Greenpeace, Amnesty International, Friends of the Earth, and Survival International, Saro-Wiwa persisted in arguing that the Ogoni were victims of an "unconventional war" being prosecuted by ecological means. Undeterred, he sought to educate himself further through travel. An odyssey through the rupturing Soviet Union confirmed his sense of a growing international context for the articulation of minority claims. A visit to Colorado gave him access to an environmental group that had successfully salvaged a wilderness from corporate and governmental assaults (Saro-Wiwa, *A Month and a Day*, p. 79). These experiences persuaded Saro-Wiwa that his incipient Movement for the Survival of the Ogoni People (MOSOP) would be well served by linking minority rights to environmental rights. Through a young Dutch lawyer, Michael van Walt van der Praag, long active in the Tibetan cause, Saro-Wiwa made contact with the Unrepresented Nations and Peoples Organization (UNPO). This gave him access to the United Nations Working Group on Indigenous Populations, which he addressed in Geneva in 1992. (That same year, another Ogoni leader, Chief Harold Dappa-Biriye, spoke at the Rio Earth Summit on behalf of the delta peoples.) Saro-Wiwa discovered that "in virtually every nation-state there are several 'Ogonis'—despairing and disappearing peoples suffering the yoke of political marginalization, economic strangulation or environmental degradation, or a combination of these" (Saro-Wiwa, *A Month and a Day*, p. 183).

The parallel tracks of Saro-Wiwa's self-education had finally converged. From 1992 onward, the combined appeal to minority and environmental rights became fundamental to the MOSOP campaign. Human rights and ecological groups that had once found the Ogoni campaign enigmatic now became its most adamant international supporters. The Body Shop, Abroad, Friends of the Earth, Greenpeace, Amnesty International, Human Rights Watch/Africa, and International PEN all rallied to the cause.

These developments gave Saro-Wiwa's campaign a resonance it had previously lacked and challenged stereotypes about environmental activists: that they are inevitably white, young, and middle-class Europeans or Americans who can afford to hug trees because they have been spared more desperate battles. Saro-Wiwa's campaign for environmental self-determination may well prove historically critical to the development of a broader image of ecological activism. In the 1980s and 1990s, we have seen how the sometimes rarefied concerns of white feminists in the 1970s have given way to a more internationally diverse array of feminism, locally led and locally defined. So too, we are now seeing indigenous environmentalisms proliferate under pressure of local necessity. As the spectrum of what counts as environmental activism expands, it becomes harder to dismiss it as a sentimental or imperial discourse tied to European or North American interests. Nor does the case for this diversification any longer rest solely on Amazonian examples.

Saro-Wiwa understood that environmentalism needs to be reimagined through the experiences of the minorities who are barely visible on the global economic periphery, where transnationals in the extraction business—be it oil, mining, or timber—operate with maximum impunity. For him, environmental justice became an invaluable concept through which to focus the battle between subnational microethnicities and transnational macroeconomic powers. As an Ogoni suffering what he called Nigeria's "monstrous domestic colonialism" (Saro-Wiwa, *A Month and a Day*, p. 73), Saro-Wiwa was in no position to trust the nation-state as the unit of collective economic good. Instead, he advocated a measure of ethnic federalism in which environmental self-determination would be acknowledged as indispensable to cultural survival.

After the "judicial murder" of Saro-Wiwa and his eight codefendants, public outrage tended to divide into those who primarily condemned the Sani Abacha regime and those who went for Shell.[7] For Saro-Wiwa, however, the blame was indivisible. He consistently represented the Ogoni as casualties of joint occupying powers: the transnational oil corporations and a brutal, extortionate Nigerian regime. Shell, meanwhile, has sought to put a positive gloss on this relationship, with public relations primers like "Nigeria and Shell: Partners in Progress" (Saro-Wiwa, *A Month and a Day*, p. 165). But the regressive character of the relationship is more accurately portrayed by a leaked Nigerian government memo addressing protests in Ogoniland. Dated 5 December 1994, it reads: "Shell operations still impossible unless ruthless military operations are undertaken for smooth economic activities to commence" (*New York Times*, 26 January 1996).

This ruthless smoothing of Ogoniland was embarked on in a spirit of racism and ethnic hatred. Again, Saro-Wiwa resisted the temptation to reduce his people's suffering to either term.[8] Shell's racism is manifest: in Africa, the company waives onshore drilling standards that it routinely upholds elsewhere. Indeed, 40 percent of all Shell oil spills worldwide have occurred in Nigeria (Greenpeace, p. 9; see also Nixon, "The Oil Weapon"). When operating in the Northern Hemisphere—in the Shetland Islands, for instance—Shell pays lucrative rents to local councils; in the Niger Delta, village authorities receive no comparable compensation (Saro-Wiwa, *A Month and a Day*, p. 170). It is an irony not lost on the Ogoni that Shell has won awards in Europe for its environmentally sensitive conduct (Saro-Wiwa, *Genocide in Nigeria*, p. 82).

But Shell's racial double standard would be inoperable without brutal backing from a Nigerian regime whose record on minority rights verges on the ethnocidal. General Sani Abacha's dreaded Mobile Police Force has responded violently to peaceful protests by the Ogoni and their delta neighbors. After an anti-Shell rally in January 1993 drew several hundred thousand Ogoni, the police razed twenty-seven villages. Two thousand Ogoni were killed and 80,000 displaced (Rowell, p. 11). Saro-Wiwa has likened the fate of the Ogoni during the oil rush to their fate during the Nigerian Civil War of 1967–1970, when a conflict erupted between the nation's dominant ethnicities[9] (see Appendix 2). This battle over oil territory left the Ogoni flattened "like grass in the fight of the elephants" (Saro-Wiwa, *A Month and a Day*, p. 187). Ten percent of all Ogoni died in a war that was not of their making. The calamity drove home for Saro-Wiwa the distinction between minority and extreme minority status (Saro-Wiwa, *On a Darkling Plain*, p. 29; *Genocide in Nigeria*, pp. 87–88). A microminority was powerless to influence national events, particularly in a society run on the principles of kleptocratic militarism. The wealth that flowed beneath Ogoniland was wealth in name only: historically, it brought poverty, injustice, and death as outsiders stampeded for oil. A quarter of a century after the civil war, Saro-Wiwa's despair about Nigeria continued to deepen because the nation's rulers had "the hearts of stone and the brains of millipedes; because Shell is a multinational company with the ability to crush whomever it wishes; and because the petroleum resources of the Ogoni serve everyone's greed" (Saro-Wiwa, *Genocide in Nigeria,* p. 7).

The fact that the Ogoni have been casualties of racism and ethnic hatred may help, in a peculiar way, to explain the low-key U.S. response to the executions. The outcry in Britain, South Africa, and France was far more vocal and sustained. In the British case, this is understandable: Shell is an Anglo-Dutch conglomerate, and British coverage of Africa has traditionally been stronger than that of the United States because of the colonial ties. (For similar reasons, the reverse is true of Latin American news.) But there is more to the U.S. media's relative indifference to the executions than that. In U.S. political discourse, racial oppression and minority discrimination typically function as identical terms. This makes it difficult for liberal or minority Americans to condemn in a single breath an African regime for oppressing its own minorities and a European corporation for racism against Africans. Randall Robinson, director of TransAfrica, the African American foreign policy lobbying firm, has met with a ruptured response to his appeal for U.S. sanctions against Nigeria similar to those imposed on South Africa. Many black Americans—among them Louis Farrakhan, who recently visited Lagos and gave the Abacha regime his blessing—have argued that it is divisive to campaign against any African government (*The Guardian,* 26 March 1996).

But Saro-Wiwa never enjoyed the luxury of such long-distance communications. He insisted that the Ogoni were joint casualties of a brutal European racism and an equally brutal African ethnocentrism. He never hesitated to make such controversial connections. As he wrote in his prison diary,

> skin color is not strong enough to stop the oppression of one group by another. Sometimes it reinforces oppression because it makes it less obvious. White people oppressing blacks in South Africa draws instant condemnation because it is seen to be racism. But black upon black oppression merely makes people shrug and say, "Well, it's their business, isn't it?" (Saro-Wiwa, *A Month and a Day,* p. 188)

Saro-Wiwa called repeatedly for international measures—like those that had helped end apartheid—against a Nigerian regime that he deemed equally heinous.[10] The two countries rank as the powerhouses of the continent: South Africa boasts Africa's largest economy, and Nigeria the second largest, as well as being the continent's most populous nation. At the time of Saro-Wiwa's appeal for international intervention, the image of these two giants had undergone a sharp reversal. For over thirty years, Nigeria had stood as Africa's leader in the antiapartheid campaign. But as South Africa, under Nelson Mandela's leadership, finally moved beyond apartheid, Nigeria sank to its antidemocratic nadir.[11]

By the time the fifty-two-nation Commonwealth Summit met in Auckland, New Zealand, in November 1995, South Africa's and Nigeria's standing had largely been reversed. South Africa was present at a Commonwealth gathering for the first time in thirty-five years—and triumphantly so, in the magisterial form of Nelson Mandela. Previously the ritual object of Commonwealth condemnations, South Africa was now, by virtue of Mandela's moral gravitas, the de facto Commonwealth leader. Nigeria, by contrast, had become a potential new pariah. The Commonwealth, the United States, and the European Union were all goading Mandela to take the lead in Africa. Nigeria was to be his first major foreign policy test.

On arriving at the summit, Mandela voiced his opposition to isolating Nigeria, advocating instead quiet negotiations.[12] The Nigerian regime responded almost immediately by hanging Saro-Wiwa and the Ogoni eight. Mandela instantly became the target of outrage. Wole Soyinka charged him with appeasement, likening his "quiet diplomacy" toward the Nigerian junta to U.S. president Ronald Reagan and British prime minister Margaret Thatcher's notorious policy of "constructive engagement" toward the apartheid regime (*Mail and Guardian,* 11 November 1995). Kole Omotoso, one of the swelling ranks of Nigerian exiles who have found refuge in South Africa, agreed: "Those who know my country know how irrational and illogical the military regime is. There wasn't a chance that it would respond to what Mandela called 'softly-softly'" (*Mail and Guardian* 17 November 1995). Saro-Wiwa's lawyer protested angrily to Mandela that "[w]ere quiet diplomacy pursued in South Africa . . . I doubt you would be alive today" (*The Independent,* 21 November 1995).

Mandela's tragic misreading of the Abacha regime and the threat to Saro-Wiwa can best be understood in terms of the African National Congress's (ANC) historical sentimentality toward Nigeria. Many in South Africa's new political and cultural elite had found refuge in Nigeria in the 1960s, when it was emerging as a bulwark against apartheid and colonialism. Those exiles included such eminent people as the academic and writer Ezekiel Mphahlele and the South African deputy president Thabo Mbeki. It is no coincidence that Mbeki became South Africa's chief negotiator in the country's "softly-softly" response to the Abacha coup. He seemed to confuse South Africa's historical debt (and his own personal one) to the Nigerian people with a debt to Nigeria's rulers, even when they had deposed an elected government and enjoyed no popular mandate whatsoever. At the Commonwealth Summit, Nigerian human rights activist Innocent Chukwuma stressed the wrongheadedness of this confusion. Calling for an international ban on Nigerian oil, Chukwuma pointed out: "The proceeds from oil revenue are going into private accounts. They don't even get to the people" (*The Independent*, 13 November 1995). In 1994 alone, $12 billion worth of oil was missing from government accounts (*New Statesman and Society*, 17 November 1995).

The South African failure to provide international leadership against Abacha needs also to be understood in terms of the ANC's "fetish for compromise."[13] This fixation had enabled Mandela to maneuver the ANC into power and to avert the civil war that had looked menacingly imminent just before the South African elections. But he misjudged the Nigerian political climate: Abacha is more ruthless than F. W. De Klerk, and Nigeria lacks the matrix of civic bodies, trade unions, and other democratic organizations that exerted pressure on the apartheid regime while Mandela negotiated a compromise.

If Saro-Wiwa's execution triggered a national political scandal for Mandela's government, it also quickened the flow of Nigerian exiles and refugees into South Africa. These included intellectuals, journalists, and democratic activists. In perhaps the surest sign of the about-turn in Nigerian–South African relations, Johannesburg had become a prominent outpost of the Lagos-based Democratic Alternative, of the Saro-Wiwa support campaign, and of the international boycott of Shell. Where ANC activists once plotted against apartheid in Lagos and Kano, thirty years later Nigerian democrats were mobilizing in Johannesburg for the overthrow of the Abacha regime. Thus, the Ogoni "judicial murders" brought into focus both the critical vulnerability of Africa's microminorities and the shifting prospects for democracy on the continent.

Some years back the Philippine government placed an ad in *Fortune* magazine that read: "To attract companies like yours, we have felled mountains, razed jungles, filled swamps, moved rivers, relocated towns . . . all to make it easier for you and your business to do business here" (quoted in Korten, p. 159). The Philippines is just one of a succession of poor nations to have wooed transnationals in a manner inevitably catastrophic for the environment and microminorities. This process has been most acutely damaging in the world's equatorial belt, from Ecuador, Bolivia, and Brazil through Surinam and Guyana, on through Nigeria, Cameroon, the Central African Republic, Gabon, and Zaire, to the Philippines, Sarawak, and New Guinea. This strip contains a unique concentration of ethnic minorities for simple ecological reasons. Rich equatorial ecosystems encouraged the development of a higher concentration of self-sufficient cultural groups than was possible in less fertile regions. Today most of these ethnic groups exist as microminorities in undemocratic, destitute nation-states that register in the global economy principally as sites for the unregulated extraction of oil, minerals, and timber. It is thus no coincidence that indigenous environmentalism has burgeoned most dramatically in this zone, as microminorities battle for the survival of their land-dependent, subsistence cultures.

The plunder and terror suffered by the Ogoni are mirrored in other mineral-rich equatorial regions, West Papua and Ecuador among them. West Papua has an even higher concentration of minorities than the Niger Delta. And like the delta peoples, West Papuans have the curse of wealth—some of the world's richest deposits of copper and gold—beneath their land. They face a similar alliance between an occupying military power and an unscrupulous transnational corporation. The same Indonesian regime responsible for the second worst genocide of our century, in East Timor, has colonized West Papua with a brutality that has led to the killing of 43,000 indigenous people. Their accomplice in this endeavor has been the Louisiana-based mining transnational, Freeport McMoran. Since the arrival of Freeport in 1967, the indigenous people have endured detention without trial, torture, forced resettlement, disappearances, the plunder of their mineral wealth, and the uncompensated degradation of their environment.[14] Freeport's private security officers and the Indonesian military have, on occasion, combined to shoot and kill unarmed indigenous protesters. In an alliance even more devastating than that between the Abacha regime and Shell, the Indonesians and Freeport have pursued ethnocide as a condition of mandatory development. James Moffett, Freeport McMoran's chairman, himself seems confused as to whether such "progress" is a life-giving or death-dealing business. Freeport, in his proud words, "is thrusting a spear of development into the heart of West Papua" (*The Independent*, 17 January 1996: 16). In this deadly battle, the microminorities have fought back in a language that melds new modes of environmental defiance with a more traditional reverence for the land. As one Amungme leader put it, "Freeport is digging out our mother's brain. That is why we are resisting."[15]

Some of these acts of environmental defiance have begun to have results: for example, in the oil-rich Oriente region of Ecuador, where Texaco has devastated Indian territory in a manner similar to Shell's despoliation of Ogoniland. Oriente drinking water, fishing grounds, soil, and crops have all been polluted. According to the Rainforest Action Network, Texaco spilled 17 million gallons of crude oil in the Oriente, leaving a toxic legacy that has caused, as in Ogoniland, chronic health problems for the residents.[16] Here again, the seepage of oil-contaminated waste resulted from a jettisoning of procedures that are standard for onshore drilling in the Northern Hemisphere. The appeal of the Oriente and Ogoniland is precisely the prospect of profits without interference or limits. As one petroleum geologist working in the Oriente put it: "I want to stamp on the ground hard enough to make that oil come out. I want to skip legalities, permits, red tape, and other obstacles. I want to go immediately and straight to what matters: getting that oil" (Rick Bass, quoted in Kimerling, p. iv).

Ecuador's Acción Ecológica has led a successful national boycott of Texaco and has helped drive the corporation from the region. In addition, a coalition of indigenous federations, mestizos, grassroots environmentalists, and human rights groups has pursued an innovative avenue of redress, filing a $1.5 billion class action suit in New York against Texaco. The suit has earned the support of Ecuador's Confederation of Indigenous Nationalities, the country's largest Indian organization. Following the Ecuadorian example, a group of Ogoni villagers is suing Shell for $4 million for spillages that have robbed them of their livelihood.

The ravaging of West Papua New Guinea, the Oriente, and Ogoniland testifies to the growing abuse of subnational minorities by transnationals, which, in the 1990s, are enjoying enhanced mobility and experiencing fewer controls. Third World governments are often joint partners in the regional plunder or worse than useless at regulating transnationals that are more powerful than the states themselves. One result has been a reversion to concessionary economics, in which forested or mineral-rich areas are sold for a song. It is in this context that Saro-Wiwa's talk of recolonization and his invocation of André Gide's Congo journal begin to sound eerily apposite. When Shell can pump out $30 billion worth of oil, and the trade-off for the locals is disease, dispossession, military occupation, massacres, and an end to self-sustaining fishing and agriculture, the process seems more redolent of turn-of-the-century colonial buccaneering than the end-of-millennium international economics. But if the idea of the nation-state continues to lose any vestige of popular appeal through a failure to deliver local benefits, and if rulers lack the will or the resources to command a national polity, the continent's poorest countries will continue to fall prey to the 1990s version of nineteenth-century concessionary economics, unhampered by regulations or redress. The nation-state will become ever more marginal to deals negotiated between local chiefs and transnationals, an imbalance in bargaining power if ever there was one. A German diplomat recently foresaw as much: "In the twenty-first century German ambassadors and CEOs heading for Africa may again be authorized to sign treaties of cooperation with whatever coastal kings or leaders are able to assert some sort of control over the interior" (quoted in Kaplan, p. 63).

Under such circumstances, the kleptocrats and soldiery in the nominal capital will still demand their palm greasing, while locally, the chiefs will request their crude version of the same. Such practices are already widespread. Late last year, for example, a group of foreign explorers arrived by ship at the head of a marshy river near the Niger Delta village of Sangama. They sought to establish a station there. After lengthy bartering with a local chief, they settled on his cut: he would receive £1,000, twelve bottles of cognac, and twelve of gin. But as the foreigners pushed deeper into the hinterland, they found villagers blocking their river-route with a barricade of palm fronds and canoes. The explorers' leader felt bewildered and betrayed. He reported: "There were about a hundred people ahead of us. If we'd pressed ahead we would have risked killing them. So we took a boat and went back to get Chief Jumbo" (*The Independent,* 1 December 1995).

More bargaining, more demands. Another £300 changed hands, a further bottle of gin, an agreement to repair a building. The chief sacrificed a goat to the water gods; the barricade was lifted; the foreigners passed through. If they weren't pulling an oil rig in tow, this could have been an entry from Gidé's Congo journal or the opening scene of a lost Joseph Conrad novel.

Nearly a century has passed since Conrad immortalized in fiction the unregulated plunder that he witnessed in the Congo. In a gesture of imaginative cynicism, he christened the worst of these plunders the El Dorado Expedition. They were "sordid buccaneers: reckless without hardihood. . . . To tear treasures out of the bowels of the land was their desire, with no more moral purpose at the back of it than there is in burglars breaking into a safe" (Conrad, p. 99) Over great swathes of Africa and much of the former Third World, El Dorado Expeditions are rising from the dead. They are still the self-declared standard-bearers of progress and are still tearing at the bowels of the earth. Today one finds in their motley ranks a mix of international and indigenous colonialists, not least in Nigeria, of which Saro-Wiwa once remarked in exasperation, "there is no such country. There is only organized brigandage" (Saro-Wiwa, *Genocide in Nigeria,* p. 91).

We have witnessed in the past decade the accelerated extraction of African minerals, oil, and timber in many of the continent's least stable nations: Liberia, Gabon, Zaire, Central African Republic, Nigeria, Mali, Niger, Chad, Sierra Leone, Mauritania, and Angola among them. Newly legitimized South African mining corporations now compete on this terrain against European, U.S., Asian, and Australian outfits. However, in most of these shaky African nations, concessionary economics, kleptocratic rule, structural adjustment, and corporate deregulation mean that irreplaceable minerals and forests are being lost for little national gain and at considerable local ruin. It is in this climate that Saro-Wiwa's campaign against the destruction of microminorities through the devastation of their environment may prove to be a harbinger of a much broader discontent. He seemed to intuit as much at his trial, as he looked back on his life with an otherworldly eye: "I will tell you this, I may be dead, but my ideas will surely not die" (Saro-Wiwa quoted in *The Observer,* 12 November 1995).

The gospel cadences of Saro-Wiwa's prophecy are consistent with the passion play that the Nigerian junta inadvertently helped create. Saro-Wiwa was no messiah. He was a courageous man who stood outside the conventions of corruption but who could also be testy, inflexible, self-aggrandizing, and overweeningly ambitious. The junta took this very mortal and internationally obscure activist, gave him a show trial, and turned him through execution into a martyr. They thus amplified his cause and—as happens with martyrs—simplified it in his favor. Saro-Wiwa instantly became larger than life. The word flashed around Lagos and Port Harcourt that he had refused to die, that it had taken five hangings to kill him. As a final precaution against his posthumous revenge, the regime stationed armed guards at the cemetery with orders to shoot anyone seen approaching the grave to pay homage or claim relics.

Saro-Wiwa understood far better than his adversaries that you cannot crucify ideas, that there are some things that cannot be resolved by a show of force. Abacha and his sidekicks were exasperated by the unruliness of language, by its refusal to submit to military control. In countries like Nigeria where official brutality and paranoia feed off each other, unofficial writing begins to assume the status of latent insult. Thus, journalists, writers, and intellectuals are singled out for harassment, detention, torture, and execution often as much for what they represent as for anything they say. But Africa's musclemen who seek to shackle language and criminalize imaginings only flatter writers with their fears. Although Abacha was naive enough to believe that murdering Saro-Wiwa would silence him, another African autocrat, Kenyan president Daniel arap Moi, was simultaneously seeking to stamp out subversive fantasy. He had a journalist arrested for "the crime of imagining the death of the President" (*New York Times,* 29 October 1995). This is surely the high-water mark for the dictatorial tendency to equate fantasy, representation, and political advocacy.

Abacha clearly had no conception of the cost of creating a martyred writer, an image with considerable pulling power in the media—doubly so since the fatwa against Salman Rushdie. The threat of censorship typically raises the hackles of journalists and writers because they are professionally invested in freedom of speech. From this viewpoint, the execution of a writer on false charges is more than just another human injustice; it also becomes, as Harold Pinter observes, "the most brutal form of censorship" (*The Guardian* (London), 11 November 1995). It was predictable, therefore, that the image of Saro-Wiwa as writer-martyr would provoke intense journalistic outrage as well as the most vocal literary protest since the Rushdie affair. Pinter, Soyinka, Boyd, Chinua Achebe, Ben Okri, Fay Weldon, and Arthur Miller were just a few of the writers who spoke out publicly against Abacha and Shell. So in death, Saro-Wiwa extended—surely beyond his imaginings—the remarkable coalition of international interests that he had begun to forge while alive, an alliance that brought together environmentalists, minority rights advocates, antiracists, opponents of corporate deregulation, and defenders of freedom of speech. Whether his principles ultimately prevail will depend as much on the future of this coalition as on the timeliness of the ideas themselves.

NOTES

1. Saro-Wiwa repeatedly uses the terms "recolonization" and "indigenous colonialism" to describe relations between the Nigerian regimes that have favored the three major ethnic groups and violently suppressed the rights and claims of extreme minorities like the Ogoni. See, for example, *Genocide in Nigeria,* p. 20; and *Nigeria: The Brink of Disaster,* p. 71.

2. This cause referred to revenue generated by both mineral sales and mining rents. See *Genocide in Nigeria,* p. 21.

3. Most of the 1.5 percent has been unilaterally "borrowed" by the powerful states where the Yoruba, the Igbo, and the Hausa-Fulani are in the majority.

4. For the most authoritative account of the events leading up to these killings, see Human Rights Watch/Africa, "Nigeria: The Ogoni Crisis: A Case-Study of Military Repression in Southeastern Nigeria," *Human Rights Watch/ Africa* 7, no. 5 (1995), esp. pp. 7–25. See also *The Guardian,* 8 November 1995: 10–11; and *Village Voice,* 21 November 1995: 21–23.

5. Ken Saro-Wiwa, *Sozaboy: A Novel Written in Rotten English* (Port Harcourt, Nigeria; Saros, 1985). For a discussion of Saro-Wiwa's use of dialect, see Chantal Zabus's and Willfried F. Feuser's works listed in the section on "Critical Articles" in the Annotated Bibliography.

6. The traditions of socialism were never as prominent in anglophone West Africa as they were in Southern and East Africa, not least because West Africa was more shallowly colonized than Kenya, South Africa, Zimbabwe, Namibia, Mozambique, and Angola. West Africa was thus spared the ravaging liberatory wars in which the goals of decolonization and socialism typically converged.

7. The phrase "judicial murder" was coined by British prime minister John Major. See *Financial Times,* 13 November 1995.

8 See Saro-Wiwa, Interview, Channel 4 (UK), 15 November 1995; *Genocide in Nigeria:* 8, 82; and *A Month and a Day:* 18, 73, 186–188.

9. The Igbo dream of creating an independent secessionist nation called Biafra would not have been viable without the sea of oil beneath the Niger Delta, which they included in their projected Biafra. The prospect of losing that oil wealth intensified the ferocity of the Hausa-Fulani and Yoruba response to the secessionists.

10. See Saro-Wiwa, Interview, Channel 4 (UK), 15 November 1995, in which he called for economic sanctions and Nigeria's expulsion from the United Nations. He argued: "The military governments of Nigeria have sat on other Nigerians in a way that is just as evil as what was done in South Africa."

11. General Sani Abacha and his military regime annulled the democratic elections of November 1993 and imprisoned president-elect Moshood Abiola and other internal opposition leaders on trumped-up charges of treason. In July 1995, former president Olusegun Obasanjo and forty other opponents of the regime were convicted and sentenced to death. After an international outcry, these sentences were commuted to life in July 1995. Four months later, another of Abacha's kangaroo courts condemned Saro-Wiwa and the Ogoni eight to hang.

12. Mandela's stance echoed that of his first deputy, Thabo Mbeki, who had visited Nigeria in July 1995 and, failing to dissuade Abacha from his hard-line

course, had nonetheless concluded: "We need a more equal relationship. Western countries must accept the capacity of African countries to set an African agenda." Quoted in *The Economist,* 18 November 1995.

13. Peter Vale, quoted in *The Independent* (London), 21 November 1995.

14. *The Nation,* 31 July 1995; *Lingua Franca,* November-December 1995; *The Independent* (London), 17 January 1996.

15. Previous two quotes from *The Independent* (London), 17 January 1996.

16. See Judith Kimerling, *Amazon Crude* (San Francisco: National Resources Defense Council, 1991); Joe Kane, *Savages* (New York: Knopf, 1995).

WORKS CITED

Conrad, Joseph. *Heart of Darkness.* 1899. New York: Signet, 1978.

Greenpeace International. *Shell Shocked: The Environmental and Social Costs of Living with Shell in Nigeria.* Amsterdam: Greenpeace International, 1994.

Human Rights Watch/Africa. "Nigeria: The Ogoni Crisis: A Case-Study of Military Repression in Southeastern Nigeria." *Human Rights Watch/Africa* 7, no. 5 (1995): 7–25.

Kane, Joe. *Savages.* New York: Knopf, 1995.

Kaplan, Robert D. *The Ends of the Earth: A Journey at the Dawn of the 21st Century.* New York: Random House, 1996.

Kimerling, Judith. *Amazon Crude.* San Francisco: National Resources Defense Council, 1991.

Korten, David C. *When Corporations Rule the World.* London: Earthscan, 1995.

Mafika Gwala. "Writing as a Cultural Weapon." In *Momentum: On Recent South African Writing.* Ed. M. J. Daymond, J. U. Jacobs, and Margaret Lenta. Pietermaritzburg, South Africa: Natal University Press, 1984: 37–44.

Ngugi wa Thiongó. *Barrel of a Pen: Resistance to Repression in Neo-Colonial Kenya.* Trenton, N.J.: Africa World Press, 1983.

Nixon, Rob. "The Oil Weapon." *New York Times,* 17 November 1995.

Rowell, Andy. "Trouble Flares in the Delta of Death," in *The Guardidan,* 8 November 1995, p. 11.

Saro-Wiwa, Ken. *Genocide in Nigeria: The Ogoni Tragedy.* London: Saros International, 1992.

———. Interview, Channel 4 (UK), 15 November 1995.

———. *A Month and a Day: A Detention Diary.* Harmondsworth: Penguin, 1995.

———. *Nigeria: The Brink of Disaster.* London: Saros International, 1991.

———. *On a Darkling Plain: An Account of the Nigerian Civil War.* Lagos, Nigeria: Saros, 1989.

———. *Sozaboy: A Novel in Rotten English.* Port Harcourt, Nigeria: Saros International, 1985.

8

"Buried Beneath Six Feet of Crude Oil": State-Sponsored Death and the Absent Body of Ken Saro-Wiwa

Misty L. Bastian

As we speak, our dear beloved Ken and others have been submerged down into the crude oil rich land of his environment by the greed of Shell and Abacha, and you all must not let them get away with it. I'm appealing to all of you that yes, Nigerians are peace loving, but I don't know how long they will continue to be peaceful. I say that time only will tell. But I can assure everyone listening today that Shell will not get away with it, Abacha will not get away with it. Yes, Ken has gone to the greater beyond, and knowing him very well as I do, he has passed on, but has now passed on the fight. He is now invincible where he cannot be hanged again by Abacha, where he cannot be hanged again by Shell, where he can no more be submerged six feet under crude oil by Shell. He is now in a position to at his own time snatch away Abacha. I can only say, please, Ken don't snatch him away in a hurry 'cos we would like to take him apart piece by piece. Maybe, that'll serve as a good example for Shell. For Shell, if you don't get out of Nigeria today, we'll also take you apart piece by piece.
—Eddy Oparaoji, speaking in front of Royal Dutch Shell's corporate offices in Washington, D.C., 17 November 1995

"Saro-Wiwa's blood won't dry up," promises Morin Babalola, the Lagos businesswoman. "It will keep working."
—Wil Haygood, *Boston Globe,* 7 April 1996

In this chapter, I do two potentially disparate things. First, I give yet another interpretation of events during the mid-1990s in Nigeria, particularly relating to the execution and death of Ken Saro-Wiwa and eight other Ogoni activists. Even more specifically, I give an account of the discourses and practices that immediately began to grow up around the dead Ogoni activists—discourses and practices that I heard about from numerous sources, notably from individual Nigerians who reside in various locations in the West, Nigerian organizations at home and abroad, Nigerian immigrant electronic and print media, the international press, and governmental and nongovernmental agencies inside and outside the United States. Because of space constraints, I touch only briefly on each. Nonetheless, all were important in formulating discursive practice around the time of Ken Saro-Wiwa's execution, and all must be represented here in some manner.

Beyond basic reportage about how transnational Nigerians and global "others" perceived, discussed, and acted upon the latest aberration of the Nigerian state, however, I also discuss an old, paired theme of mine in relation to Nigeria—blood and petrol. This time, however, the pairing is being made more obviously by Nigerians and others in the international community and is not simply a stylistic conceit of my own, used to unpack the dense and symbolically encoded nature of the (southeastern) Nigerian state. The concatenation of blood and oil in Nigeria has been very much a part of local media representation—as well as part of Nigerian oral discourse—since at least the beginning of the Nigerian Civil War in the 1960s, when indigenous people (including Ken Saro-Wiwa himself) began to question more closely the reasons why violence was being visited on their communities in the name of nationalism, whether that nationalism was constructed as Biafran or federal.

To unpack the most recent connections between blood and petrol, in this chapter I analyze a major protest event (jointly sponsored by Nigerian immigrant groups and international "green" organizations) that I attended in Washington, D.C., during November 1995 as well as a host of data collected from various sources: personal conversations with immigrant Nigerians and interested others, materials published by international environmental and human rights agencies as well as by the U.S. government, both international and Nigerian news reports and opinion pieces, advertisements, and Internet discussions taken mostly from the Nigerian listserv originating from the Massachusetts Institute of Technology computer system. This last, an electronic "village" (as its "inhabitants" sometimes characterize it) with a shifting population of several hundred, is called Naijanet and is open to the most transnational and "high tech" of Nigerian immigrants. As will become clear below, Naijanet and its denizens were crucial to the international spread of information about the death of Ken Saro-Wiwa and central to the establishment of real-world public protests of Nigerian government and multinational collusion in the events leading up to the execution of the Ogoni nine.

DEATH, THE GENERAL, AND THE MEDIA

Judicial Murder

> To be at the mercy of buffoons is the ultimate insult. To find the instruments of state power reducing you to dust is the injury.
> —Saro-Wiwa, *A Month and a Day*

On 10 November 1995, the Nigerian military regime headed by Gen. Sani Abacha executed nine environmental and political activists. All of the activists were from the Ogoni minority group, and all had been involved with the Movement for the Survival of the Ogoni People (MOSOP).[1] Although all the executed men were well known in southeastern Nigeria, particularly in the Delta region, one of them was familiar to a more international audience—and his death at the hands of his own government drew global attention. This, of course, was Kenule (Ken) Saro-Wiwa, noted Nigerian novelist, sitcom writer/producer, satirist, general man of letters, and recently, public gadfly and emerging bane of the Nigerian federal military government as well as of Royal Dutch Shell Petroleum Development Corporation—the multinational responsible for most of the oil exploitation within Ogoni territory.

Saro-Wiwa and his colleagues in the MOSOP leadership had run afoul of the Nigerian government on many previous occasions, and they had all been detained, followed, and harassed by agents of the Nigerian state throughout the early 1990s. However, the state had found no reason to hold the activists, including Saro-Wiwa, until the events of 21 May 1994, when four older Ogoni leaders were killed by persons still unknown (and, as far as I know, unsought) while at a rally in Ogoni.[2] After the elders' deaths, a military tribunal charged the leadership of MOSOP's "youth wing," the National Youth Council of the Ogoni People (NYCOP), and especially Ken Saro-Wiwa with conspiracy to incite murder, claiming that Saro-Wiwa and others in NYCOP had, in November 1993, called the more conservative elders "vultures" and suggested that they be eliminated. A show trial was held, with some internal television and fairly extensive print media coverage, and nine of the defendants were declared guilty of all charges.

To the surprise of observers both inside and outside the country, the military state decided to use its most extreme sanction on the defendants— the death penalty. Both the verdict and the sentence were quickly reviewed and upheld by other military authorities and were never placed in the hands of Nigeria's civilian judiciary. Although it was widely suggested at the time that the Abacha regime was using the death penalty as a bargaining tool—or as an opportunity to show its clemency, along the lines of its decision not to execute a number of well-connected "coup plotters" (one of whom was former military ruler and retired Gen. Olusegun Obasanjo, elected in May 1999 as the new president of Nigeria a year after Abacha's death) just a short time before—the Ogoni activists were speedily sent to the gallows.

Like the trial, the executions were held under military auspices. According to the Port Harcourt military administrator who oversaw the execution, Col. Dauda Musa Komo, everything went along smoothly. The executions were videotaped, with the video supposedly sent along to General

Abacha himself, and the dead Ogoni "criminals" were "buried each one in a coffin in his own grave."[3] Accounts of the executions from outside official Nigerian military circles were rather more detailed and contradicted Colonel Komo's statements on several points. International news reports circulated suggesting that the gallows, which was constructed hurriedly and without plans, constantly malfunctioned. Saro-Wiwa's execution is said to have required five tries. At one point during his prolonged ordeal Saro-Wiwa was frustrated enough to quip—at least according to stories heard in the immigrant Nigerian community during November—"What a country! You can't even execute me properly!" Although that statement is very much in keeping with the character of the man I knew, Saro-Wiwa's official last words, when they finally did "execute him properly," were said to take the form of a rather nobler sentiment: "God take my soul, but the struggle continues."

It is surely a mark of the fluidity of popular reportage that even these official last words have come under dispute. The *Boston Globe* published a front-page report (dated 7 April 1996) by Wil Haygood, who said that Saro-Wiwa's last words were, "It is a black day for the black man." This appears to be a transposition from Saro-Wiwa's aborted, late October 1995 trial statement—portions of which were smuggled out of the country and widely circulated via Naijanet and various environmentalist computer discussion groups. Nonetheless, all of these "last words" seem credible to me since Saro-Wiwa was certainly self-possessed enough to imagine the importance of his final speech for (a Nigerian as well as an international) posterity. They also all have a certain manufactured quality that speaks to both popular and elite hagiographic processes. Unless the rumored execution tape surfaces, and we become video witnesses to the execution ourselves, however, we may never know which—if any—of the above statements was spoken by Saro-Wiwa as he faced his death.

Not only descriptions of the execution but Colonel Komo's account of the executed activists' burial were also hotly disputed by members of the Nigerian community abroad. A number of the Nigerians on Naijanet reported local rumors that the corpses were unceremoniously dumped into a garbage truck and carried, with police and military escort, to a Port Harcourt cemetery where they were unloaded (again without religious or any family intervention) into a single, hastily dug pit-grave. Some published news as well as Nigerian personal reports, again relying on witnesses or rumors from within the country, have suggested that acid or lime was then poured over the bodies. After covering the grave site with dirt and disguising its location as best they could, the military supposedly surrounded the cemetery with armored vehicles and denied access to all civilians, including the kin of the executed. As far as I am able to discover, the families of the deceased were still being kept from visiting the grave site, months after the execution—and it is unclear if anyone besides the military was allowed into the cemetery at all for some period of time. I return to the execution and irregular burial presently since they have become central to post–November 1995 representations of the Ogoni agony, but I wish, first, to turn briefly to the part played in the events of 1994–1995 by another corporate actor, Royal Dutch Shell, and more particularly to how its role was represented in the immediate postexecution discourse.

Abacha Killed, Shell Killed

Although the Nigerian military state had its supporters in the global arena after the November executions, its actions were roundly criticized by a majority of the world's nations and by many extragovernmental organizations. There was, however, a more mixed reaction to the purported participation of the multinational Royal Dutch Shell in contemporary Nigerian affairs. Environmental and human rights groups like Amnesty International, Human Rights Watch/Africa, Friends of the Earth, 50 Years Is Enough, and Greenpeace were very vocal in their condemnation of Shell's activities in Ogoniland and in Nigeria in general.

Human Rights Watch/Africa published a scathing exposé of Shell's exploitation of Ogoni resources as well as the most detailed, up-to-date report of military repression in the delta—before the execution of the Ogoni activists. This group continues to monitor human rights issues in Nigeria very carefully and to publish periodic reports on the state of Nigerian repression. Friends of the Earth, 50 Years Is Enough, and Greenpeace were extremely active on the Internet and worked to organize opposition to Shell "on the ground," also before the executions. Amnesty International made Saro-Wiwa and his fellow activists known as prisoners of conscience and, after the execution, mounted a major campaign to disseminate information about similar dissidents being held by both the Nigerian and Kenyan governments. As part of that late 1995 campaign, Amnesty International USA asked members and other interested parties to fax executive officers of Shell Oil, sending along a model fax saying, in part:

> Despite Shell's contention that it had nothing to do with human rights violations in Ogoniland, the fact remains that Ken Saro-Wiwa and his MOSOP organization were protesting environmental degradation due to Shell operations. In addition, the commander of the military unit that committed gross human rights violations in Ogoniland during May and August of 1994 boasted at a press conference that these actions were taken to protect Shell installations. (Amnesty International USA)

Most national governments around the world reserved their critical commentary for the safer target of General Abacha and maintained at least a partial silence regarding Shell. For example, during the 20 July 1995, hearing before the U.S. Senate's Subcommittee on African Affairs, the only witnesses to testify to Shell's pernicious influence in Nigeria came from outside "official" Washington—mostly from human rights groups or special interest groups like Randall Robinson's TransAfrica.[4] Although U.S. diplomats mentioned the importance of Nigeria's petroleum resources in the world economy, they very explicitly did not mention which multinational companies were engaged in exploiting those resources. A very few, lower-level governments made public statements and even supported an embargo of Shell products, but they were in a definite and quieted minority.

International print media split over their reportage of Shell's activities in relation to Ogoni activism, as well as the company's possible complicity in the executions of November 1995. Unsurprisingly, conservative, pro-business Western newspapers like the *Wall Street Journal* refused to denounce Shell's practices, although they seized upon the follies of the Abacha regime with alacrity as an example of what they wish to represent as the African continent's continuing slide into social/political/economic anarchy. *The Economist* actively defended Shell in its cover article in the edition of 18–24 November 1995. According to this magazine,

> Environmental and human-rights lobbyists have found a scapegoat in Shell, whose operations in Nigeria provide half the government's income. Shell is an easy target but it is the wrong one. Whatever it has done to despoil the Niger delta is now being put right. (Anon., p. 15)

This—as it turned out—overly positive evaluation of Shell's continuing operations in Nigeria was framed by a cover drawing of a silhouetted oil derrick exploding in a red stream, with a caption reading: "Nigeria foaming with blood." In this case, the blood that is "foaming" is certainly that of Saro-Wiwa and his compatriots—but the illustration also seems to represent *The Economist*'s belief in Nigeria's historically explosive propensities more than, as we saw above, in Shell's culpability in any potential explosion to come. Earlier in the same article, the anonymous writer notes that Nigeria has "blown" before, with disastrous results: "a civil war in which fighting and famine had claimed a million lives" (Anon., p. 15). This image of the frothing, bloody oil derrick was an important one—and not only for those who would put a conservative construction on Nigerian affairs. I return to it when we begin to reconsider the events surrounding the execution and its aftermath.

More liberal or left-leaning publications like the weekly *Manchester Guardian* (UK) and the *Village Voice* (United States) tended to cover the environmental and human rights issues involved in the Ogoni trial, reporting that Shell may have been closely involved in the allegations about, investigations into, and even in funding the harassment of Ogoni activists throughout the 1990s. (Later they would also cover the news of Shell's involvement in arms purchases for the federal military government, a story that more conservative publications buried.) The *Voice*'s first article on Nigeria after the execution, published on 21 November 1995, was called "Shell Shocked" and directly accused Royal Dutch Shell of collusion in Ken Saro-Wiwa's "judicial murder." According to *Voice* reporter Andy Rowell (p. 21), Shell not only refused to intervene on the Ogoni activists' behalf after their sentencing because "it couldn't get involved in the affairs of a sovereign state," but "[n]ew evidence . . . suggests that the real reason may be that Shell was already working with the military, not to save Saro-Wiwa, but to silence him." This was the strongest statement I read in the U.S. press, outside of Internet/grassroots socialist reportage like that of the Red Balloon Collective, which accused not only Shell but the International Monetary Fund (IMF) and the United States government of such collusion (see Cohen).

The visual rhetoric of the more leftist press immediately after the executions also explicitly made the connection between death and oil—but this time connected Shell explicitly to both. The *Voice* (Rowell, p. 22) published a photograph of a British Greenpeace volunteer hanging an effigy of an anonymous activist from a self-serve gasoline sign. Nearby we can see a hand-lettered banner that says "Shell Kills Ogoni" above a rendition of the Shell logo dripping blood. This modified corporate logo eventually gained very wide currency at other rallies around the world and could be seen as an illustration on several Web pages relating to Ogoni issues and the Shell boycott. The *Manchester Guardian Weekly* (see Bates and Bowcott) also featured a very striking illustration in its front-page coverage of the execution. In this line drawing, Saro-Wiwa is pictured with a noose around his neck—a noose that becomes a gasoline hose, attached to pumps marked "Shell." Saro-Wiwa stares directly at the reader in a compelling fashion, as the means of his death snakes away into the background. Looking at this image, the reader becomes aware of his or her possible complicity in what is not yet a finished act: the death of Saro-Wiwa (and, by extension, of the Ogoni themselves).

In the international iconography of Nigeria/Shell and Ogoni death, then, death is shown as technologically produced—even Shell's shell logo appears to be a knife, coated with blood. Oil, blood, and (unending) death become interchangeable signs in these highly condensed representations, which also allude to the efficiency and, indeed, modernity of the "product" being advertised. These technological representations have something very particular to do with the missing body of Saro-Wiwa, dispersed into the contemporary Nigerian landscape, as well as with a growing sense that the body/person of the dead was made even more potent because of its dispersal into a realm of imagination and advertising. Being absent in the body but present in image, as Saro-Wiwa knew before his death would fully transform him into an icon, affords both a sense of great power and a knowledge of powerlessness under conditions of late modernity.[5] In the next section of the chapter, I investigate this omnipresent absence more thoroughly in relation to Saro-Wiwa's hanging and its recurring representations.

BLOOD AND PETROL REVISITED

The Hanged Man

> And this superiority is not simply that of right, but that of the physical strength of the sovereign beating down upon the body of his adversary and mastering it: by breaking the law, the offender has touched the very person of the prince; and it is the prince—or at least those to whom he has delegated his force—who seizes upon the body of the condemned man and displays it marked, beaten, broken. The ceremony of punishment, then, is an exercise of "terror."
> —Michel Foucault, *Discipline and Punish*

When the regime of General Abacha decided to execute Ken Saro-Wiwa and his fellow activists, it was following both an escalating Nigerian public policy regarding state-sanctioned killing and a very personalized vengeance. The Nigerian federal military government (known as FMG within the country) has pursued the death penalty throughout its somewhat checkered history. In the 1970s, for example, alleged criminals and coup plotters were executed publicly by firing squad on Bar Beach in Lagos—a location otherwise known for its association with the leisure pastimes of Nigeria's elites. In the late 1980s, when I was doing fieldwork in the southeastern region of the country, the firing squad executions of several infamous "armed robbers" were front-page news in the Nigerian press. This came on the heels of the Babangida regime's declared intention (as we say in the United States) "to get tough on crime" by imposing the death penalty for any offense carried out with a handgun.[6]

More recently, the Abacha regime has applied the death penalty—in the form of the firing squad—with a heavy hand, sparing (as I noted above) only the most notable of supposed coup plotters or would-be presidents like General Obasanjo and Moshood Abiola. Some Nigerians have also suggested privately to me that not all of Abacha's death sentences have been carried out through official channels, pointing, as evidence, to late 1990s incidents like the botched "armed robbery" of one of the nation's premier journalists that resulted in no theft but left the victim near death, as well as to other, suspicious "armed robbery" deaths of prominent southerners, especially Alfred Rewane. These same Nigerians tend to recall the bombing death of journalist Dele Giwa in the late 1980s, during

Gen. Ibrahim Babangida's reign, as the beginning of this sort of ex officio death penalty practice.

Taking into account the fact that the death penalty is not only available but much availed of in Nigeria, one might think that Ken Saro-Wiwa's execution was simply business as usual. Although he did have powerful friends outside the country, he chose to stay inside and provoke the regime again and again—not only by his presence in the Ogoni area or his charismatic leadership of an activist organization that was targeting what is arguably the regime's biggest banker, but persuasively and in print.[7] It also appears that Saro-Wiwa, a member of the governmental and literary elite since the early 1970s and a former next-door neighbor of General Abacha, would not be bought off in relation to Ogoni rights. In interviews with both Saro-Wiwa's son, Ken Wiwa, and his relative Owens Wiwa, we are told that Saro-Wiwa was offered financial and personal incentives simply to be quiet or to leave Nigeria and act as a dissident in exile. (See, for example, the transcript of a late 1995 video interview made by Greenpeace and MOSOP expatriates with Owens Wiwa.)

This, in combination with his expressed determination to expose the regime both nationally and internationally in speeches and through publication, may have helped to seal the fate not only of Saro-Wiwa but of his fellow NYCOP organizers as well. Among the Nigerian ruling elite, where personal enrichment at public expense has become commonplace, a person who was once "their own" but who now refuses to participate in the expected rituals and confirmations of their community is a very frightening spectacle, indeed.[8] Wole Soyinka, who has a certain amount of experience being a Nigerian dissident as well as an elite insider, wrote about how he was unsurprised by the Abacha regime's decision to go forward with the executions:

> Ken Saro-Wiwa's fate had long been sealed. The decision to execute him was reached before the special tribunal was ordered to reconvene and pronounce a verdict that had been decided outside the charade of judicial proceeding. The meeting of the Provisional Ruling Council to consider that verdict was a macabre pretense, a prolongation of the cynicism that marked the trial proceedings from the outset.
>
> As the world knows, the executions were to have taken place immediately after the "ratification" session of the Military Council. Hence the sense of urgency, even panic with which we addressed our task in Auckland, at the summit of heads of Commonwealth nations, from the moment we learnt that Abacha had summoned his uniformed puppets to perform at his dance of death. A blatant unrepentant defiance of civilised norms, an atavistic psyche is what has characterized this regime from the beginning, so there should have been no cause for surprise. (Soyinka, p. 152)

Alongside the outrage Saro-Wiwa generated as a renegade against the political class of which he had long been a member, it now seems clear that he and his compatriots were seen as completely and necessarily expendable. They had spoken against multinational property rights in support of Ogoni human rights, and their followers may or may not have engaged in the sabotage of Shell pipelines in reaction to this speech. Royal Dutch Shell was known to be extremely concerned by Saro-Wiwa's international environmental connections and not to have his best interests strictly at heart. It was also rumored among Nigerians abroad that the Abacha regime was under heavy pressure from junior military officers to show some backbone after its earlier failure to enforce death sentences on former General Obasanjo and other politically well-connected prisoners. As Soyinka and others have suggested, the outcome appears to have been prearranged, and the manner of the execution, I argue, demonstrates exactly what sort of care and thought went into these particular state-sponsored deaths—as well as what lessons they were meant to teach the Nigerian public.

In the discussion of Nigerian state-ordered executions above, one salient fact should stand out: since independence, Nigeria has tended to execute its criminals (however they have been defined as such) by firing squad. This style of execution, of course, has its roots in the colonial period, but as far as I can determine it was used sparingly by the British administration. After searching rather extensively for sources on Nigerian executions, colonial or national, I have come up with very little. From what I can discover, however, the colonial administration tended to use the gallows as its ultimate sanction, making do with a death technology that could be locally and cheaply produced. The turn toward the firing squad on the part of subsequent Nigerian governments may well reflect a repugnance toward the methods of the colonizers as well as other indigenous repulsion toward hanging as a mode of extermination. Certainly for Igbo-speaking peoples of southeastern Nigeria, hanging is seen as the preferred method of suicide—a very shameful death. (This may also have been influenced by colonial practices. But recall the last scene of Achebe's *Things Fall Apart,* where the colonial official is asked to assist in taking down Okonkwo's hung body and is told his minions will be paid for performing the disturbing task.) Although not directly connected to Ogoni practices surrounding death, perhaps, Igbo (another southeastern Nigerian ethnic group) notions about death and hanging are nonetheless very suggestive in the context of the Abacha regime's decision to use this form of execution for the Ogoni nine.

Hanging, for Igbos, is an abominable death for several reasons, not the least of which is that it is associated with suicide—one of the worst of human offenses. Hanging is prohibited by the earth deity (Ala/Ani) partially because the corpse is not properly aligned with the earth's body—and hence, not properly dead. In a structuralist sense, the hung corpse is held vertical when its more appropriate posture should be a horizontal one, near the earth on the bed or the ground where the person died, then placed into the earth where Ala/Ani can reclaim her contribution to human bodi-liness, its form. The hanged, suicidal man is also offensive to the earth be-cause he is suspended over her and does not make proper human connec-tions with the ground. He cannot enter into the relations of the dead with the earth; he has taken himself out of this important site of spiritual and bodily exchange.

In addition, the improperly displayed Igbo corpse breaks down all the human social relations that should come into play at death. There is no room for mourners around the deathbed, and the funeral that is so depen-dent upon the laying out of the corpse and people's last visits with it, throughout the Nigerian southeast, cannot take place. In northern Igbo terms, at least, the hanging corpse is an object of terror that cannot be touched by its (former) relatives—and the spirits of people who die such abominable deaths are not allowed to enter the cycle of reincarnation or even to be buried with others who maintain their ties to the land and each other.

Although I do not want to maintain that what holds true for northern Igbo speakers I worked with also holds true for the rest of southern Nige-ria, I argue here that the sudden reinstatement of the gallows by General Abacha and his council for this special set of executions may speak to un-derlying, contemporary Nigerian notions of what constitutes a proper, as opposed to an improper, death. As Foucault (p. 33) notes, "Torture is a technique." It is well thought out and considered, never randomly per-formed; it is socially and historically based.

The regime did not simply want to kill Saro-Wiwa and the other Ogoni activists, it wanted to cause them both to suffer and to know who was vis-iting that suffering upon them—and then to visit a version of that suffer-ing/knowing upon their closest kin and associates by means of the ambigu-ous circumstances of the death. Hung betwixt and between, videotaped in their throes for the private viewing of the military "sovereign," and even kept on the edge of death but not quite pushed over it again and again, the unseen but well-known, tormented bodies of the Ogoni activists were meant as a chilling message to others challenging the Nigerian state's—and, perhaps, the multinational's—hold on power. The message was sim-ple and disciplinary: not that this *might* be the common Nigerian's fate, but that this already is his or her fate. Once a technology—whether the gallows, the firing squad, or mysterious, late-night "disappearances"—is available, its usage seems to become inevitable under conditions of modernity.

The state was not finished with the dead, even after placing them in this shameful and inappropriate posture (secretly, but still so much in view that I received the news of the execution not more than eight hours later on my computer screen). It did not turn the bodies over to their respective families or lineages for burial; it did not even officially notify the families that burial would be necessary.[9] Instead, adding insult to previous injury, the bodies were bundled away quickly—treated like garbage, according to indigenous accounts reported above—and placed anonymously into the ground of a cemetery outside Port Harcourt, whether in separate graves, as Colonel Komo tells us, or in a common pit. Once in these (semi-respectable) graves or in this (latrinelike) pit, however, the state continued to exercise its domination over the persons who were once its enemies. Officials almost certainly surrounded the cemetery with armed guards and refused entrance to those who should control and channel the energies lingering around the dead—the dead's relations and well-wishers.

Agents of the state may also have tried to eradicate all traces of these once living persons by destroying their corpses—dissolving them into a few, scattered, and forever anonymous fragments, making a symbolic gesture toward the power of the not-quite-gone dead or a more pragmatic gesture toward martyr management, hoping to keep relics out of the hands of eager acolytes. At the moment that the Nigerian state appears to have felt that it had its greatest control over its dissidents, it began to learn that it had, instead, lost all command over them. In this the state surely misread the power of the invisible in our global communications. Nothing could have better suited late modern media than a once-seen (and therefore objectified and forever fixed) but now vanished subject of "human interest." Ken Saro-Wiwa was about to be translated from a real person with an all-too-human history into that construct known as "celebrity," with repercussions that neither Nigeria nor Royal Dutch Shell seemed to anticipate.[10]

Blood in the Oil

Ironically, Saro-Wiwa himself used (and became) the visual trope of the unburied, tormented (Ogoni) body as a way to generate sympathy for his cause. First in a British Channel 4 film called *The Drilling Fields* and then after his death, in a Canadian repackaging called *Delta Force* that used some of the same amateur Ogoni video shown in the first documentary, Saro-Wiwa and other MOSOP activists helped make it possible for a global television audience to "see" the outrage of Ogoni dead, left limbless and without proper burial. His own corpse would be much less visible to global media and would gain, because of the lack of fixity that visibility offers, a certain power over death. Instead of photographs of the deceased, finished body of Saro-Wiwa in his coffin—or, indeed, even of a coffin being carried, like many other coffins we have grown accustomed to seeing in the evening news, on the shoulders of a mourning crowd—the world was treated on the evening of his death to pictures of him smiling confidently, to video of him cheering on his fellow activists at Ogoni Day a couple of years before, and to the sound of his (living) voice reciting poetry about the ruined Ogoni landscape. Saro-Wiwa dead and, perhaps, dissolving in a pit outside Port Harcourt suddenly became more present in the minds of an enormous international community than he had ever been before.

Within the Nigerian immigrant community who talk to one another in the "village square" of Naijanet, the news of the death and its possible ramifications for the country was met with what I can only describe as a stunned silence. Although Naijanet tends to be a very active listserv, sometimes sending out ten to twenty mails in an hour, all chatter ceased after the initial announcement. Desperate for news, I stayed on my computer for hours after the announcement, searching the Internet and Web for confirmation—or, more truthfully, for confirmation that this was yet another rumor. No Naijas entered the "square" to talk; maybe the rest were looking for the same confirmation. This eerie silence lasted almost all night. The next day, my screen exploded with mail, all of it about Saro-Wiwa and the meaning of his death for Nigeria. There were obituaries, poems, hastily scratched out but very heartfelt dirges, and a unity that I have never before seen in Naija: a unity that, although it technically lasted about a week, still has lingering effects to the present day.

After a week, this unity began to splinter along ethnic and political lines: suspicious Igbo speakers remembered Saro-Wiwa's defense of Rivers State people who took up Igbo "abandoned property" in Port Harcourt after the civil war; people from the North were afraid that the executions had become another excuse to blame their region for all of the country's ills. Even some months after the executions, however, the initials *KSW* or the word *Ogoni* in a post would garner more response than almost any other, most of it positive and directed toward the now fully established Ogoni martyrs. More than a year after the event, Saro-Wiwa was so firmly a part of the Naijanet virtual landscape that his name has taken on proverbial status: it is used almost as shorthand to signify either the afflictions of the nation or the nation's duping by outside influences, depending on the writer's political position. Activity remains consistent four years later, most likely due to the expectations and fears about the recent electoral campaign and a return to civilian adminstration.

Inside and outside Nigeria, the missing bodies garnered a great deal of sympathy for the very people who, I have argued, the military regime most wanted to torment. News of Saro-Wiwa's very aged parents being turned away from the putative grave site again and again was particularly pathetic. News of Saro-Wiwa's still-living relatives and associates fleeing the country spoke to the continuing danger of his all-too-present absence.

It became immediately obvious that rhetoric about the deaths was conflating the flow of oil out of Ogoniland with the flow of Saro-Wiwa and his compatriots' lifeblood. In the case of Nigerians talking about this bloody oil, it was as if, in dying and dissolving into the land without a proper, lineage-based burial, Saro-Wiwa and the other activists had taken on ancestral responsibilities for all of Nigeria. There were prayers addressed to them on Naijanet and ominous statements made about the efficacy of their martyred bodies; they were referred to as sacrifices and as powerful political medicines. Time and time again I noted that Nigerians cautioned each other (as well as interested foreigners) not to buy Shell gasoline, not just because a boycott had been called for by international environmental groups but because the gasoline could no longer be trusted as a substance. It was as if the body of Nigeria had been cut in Port Harcourt, and the wounds were bleeding a powerful mixture of the two fluids. Coming into contact with this hybrid substance was dangerous and polluting. Ken Saro-Wiwa's angry spirit seemed to have entered, in these characterizations, the world's gasoline pumps and would soon be credited with entering the engines of a private jet that carried General Abacha's son and his entourage to their deaths at the Kano airport.

In the final section of the chapter, I discuss how this blood/petrol conflation was represented at a protest event staged by Nigerian expatriates and international environmental activists in Washington, D.C., on 17 November 1995. Using this ethnographic material, I then make a few points in conclusion about missing bodies and what they can reveal about the state of the state at this juncture of history.

MOURNING NIGERIA: PROTESTING IN WASHINGTON, D.C.

The explosion of communication on Naijanet contained many different discourses. Some took the form of activist Nigerian immigrant plans for protest marches and prayer meetings to be held jointly on 17 November 1995 (a week after the executions) in the United States, United Kingdom, Canada, and other countries.[11] The two largest scheduled protests in the United States were set to take place in New York City and Washington, D.C., both around noon in order to make it possible for Nigerians who were employed to spend their lunch breaks at the protests. It happened that the American Anthropological Association annual meetings were taking place in Washington, D.C., on 17 November, so I decided to attend that march.[12]

Our anthropological party arrived just after noon at the front of the Nigerian Embassy, and the protest was already well under way. Approximately fifty or sixty marchers were carrying signs and circling, under the watchful eyes of Washington, D.C., police, the space directly in front of the embassy building. The majority of this group appeared to be Nigerian, although a number were obviously Euro-American students and older environmental activists. There were also several Afrocentric (at least in terms of dress) African Americans who were marching, and this number grew appreciably later as the march left the embassy and took to the streets on its way to the corporate offices of Shell.

When we arrived at the embassy, we were greeted by some Nigerian men who seemed to be in positions of authority—or to have constituted themselves as such—and who handed us locally produced leaflets, including a xerox portrait of Ken Saro-Wiwa under the title "Cry Tyranny in Nigeria." This leaflet informed us that Saro-Wiwa was "Hanged by the Military Govt.!! Nov. 9 [*sic*], 1995," gave us a quote from Saro-Wiwa that prefigured his death, and told us that the leaflet was published by New Nigeria Forum, London, but that it was now, in a handwritten annotation, being distributed in the United States and Canada "by the Nigerian Democratic Movement (NDM)." The quality of the printing of the photograph suggests that it had been copied frequently before or had, perhaps, been faxed. The transnational leaflet and its blurry but instantly recognizable image would be put to further creative use during the actual demonstration.

We were encouraged to read the leaflets and to join the circling marchers, who were being exhorted by a couple of activists to chant various slogans, notably: "Shell kills, Abacha kills!" and "No blood for oil!" While in this circle, I noted that some protesters carried homemade signs accusing the Nigerian government and Shell of complicity in the Ogoni nine's executions. Other signs were obviously printed by Greenpeace activists (they were professionally done and prominently displayed the Greenpeace logo) and addressed that organization's concerns with the executions and the continuing degradation of the Ogoni environment. Others among us decided to carry the portrait of Saro-Wiwa as a sign; we waved the portrait at passersby as we continued to walk.

After a short period of circular marching, I noted that the embassy—which was locked up and supposedly closed—was still inhabited. Although blinds were drawn on all the windows facing the street, it became clear that someone (or some people) was behind the blinds and was peering out. At first I took this to mean that curious embassy employees were watching the protest below them surreptitiously, but I (and others around me) began to notice that there was a strange regularity to the blinds' movements. I then understood that there was a camera operator behind the closed windows, busily taking photographs of the marchers on the street. Although this was of little concern to most African American and Euro-American marchers, it obviously distressed some of the Nigerians in the crowd. A couple of Nigerians put the Saro-Wiwa portrait up to the level of their faces and used it as a mask, directly pointing the portrait toward the invisible camera operator. Thus embodying the dead in a very Nigerian fashion—becoming, in effect, the kind of masquerade that makes its appearance at the final burial of a southeastern Nigerian person—we continued to march under the watchful eyes of still and video cameras.

After about twenty minutes of marching, we were asked to gather around a portable, central podium that was equipped with a microphone and speaker. Since the sound was not very good, I did not catch the names of the Nigerian gentlemen who addressed us, although I later learned from Ayodele Ayetigbo's column in *The U.S.-Nigerian Voice* that they were Dr. Gbadegesin, the president of the Egbe Isokan Yoruba (a local Yoruba-speakers' organization); the Rev. Joseph Ezeigbo, president of the Minister Council of Nigeria; and the Rev. Dr. Fred Ogunfiditimi, the supreme prelate of the International House of Prayer. Dr. Gbadegesin began the speeches by telling us:

> We are here to mourn, not just Ken and the eight others, but to mourn Nigeria. Nigeria is apparently dead, but with the commitment of good people, who are ready to lift up the voices of righteousness, people who are ready to commit themselves to furthering the struggle for freedom and democracy and human rights, it is our hope and prayer that Nigeria will survive. (quoted in Ayetigbo, "Saro-Wiwa," p. 5)

The other two speakers took this notion of mourning Nigeria very literally and led us all—including some very perplexed-looking, young Euro-American activists—in a series of lengthy prayers directed toward the need to resurrect the nation from its untimely grave. I also noted that a large, plywood coffin had appeared and was being displayed beside the speakers, making the event even more concretely into a funeral for the missing activists and for the nation itself.

The discourse in front of the embassy did not take on a directly confrontational tone, although it was extremely political in its invocation of the death of the state-entity "Nigeria." The march became the memorial service for the next half-hour; essentially an evangelical Christian prayer service, an activity that most southern Nigerians are familiar with here at the end of Christianity's second millennium. First the Rev. Ezeigbo prayed, and then the Rev. Dr. Ogunfiditimi took charge and gave a very elaborate prayer. (Again, it was difficult for some of us to understand what was being said because the loudspeaker was not powerful.) This prayer sounded fiery and received a very respectful chorus of "amen," "ise," and other Nigerian exclamations of the sort at its conclusion. The service ended with the singing of "Onward Christian Soldiers," and we were told to form a double line for our march to Shell.

I found it highly significant that Nigerians decided to have their memorial service in front of the embassy and to eschew any overt political rhetoric in that space. Knowing they were under the surveillance of Nigerian security agents and realizing how much in jeopardy they were placing not only themselves but their families, these courageous Nigerians took refuge in their religious practice. This practice is a subversive one that the Nigerian government tries to co-opt at every turn. Evangelical Christianity has become the currently fashionable religious practice of Nigeria's southern states. Television, music stars, military men, and some would-be southern politicians profess to be "born again" to their admiring publics.[13] Ordinary people, who increasingly feel the pressure of everyday survival in Nigeria's disastrous economy, turn to the various churches and prayer centers in hopes that prayer will heal their afflictions. (For examples from other parts of West Africa, see Meyer's and van Dijk's papers on how Ghanaian Christians use their churches to address the afflictions of modernity.) After Saro-Wiwa's death, the FMG attempted to "cash in" on evangelical Christianity's caché by requesting the immensely popular televangelist Benson Idahosa to speak out in favor of the regime's policies. Although I am sure that this was successful in some quarters, the Rev. Idahosa's spokesmanship was seen as a disappointment by many immigrant Nigerians.

Those immigrants expected their evangelical leaders to show the kind of skepticism and, indeed, animus toward the regime that was demonstrated by the Rev. Dr. Ogunfiditimi's participation in the 17 November march. Since many of these southern Nigerian immigrants see the Abacha regime as a northern, Muslim regime—however untrue this may objectively be—a militant Christian prayer meeting was also probably meant to signal that they would not accept the dominance of what some of my southern acquaintances do not scruple to call the "Hausa-Fulani jihadist conspiracy." The fact that "Onward Christian Soldiers" was chosen for our recessional hymn points toward evangelical militancy and offered a reminder to those listening within the embassy's walls that some Nigerians serve what they deem a much more legitimate (but still militarized) authority than the FMG.

John Comaroff and Jean Comaroff note, in a rather different context, that

> "organized protest" [is] easily recognizable as "political action" by western lights—[but that] much of what may be seen as the riposte of the colonized, as one or another form of (tacit, indirect) resistance, turns out to be a practical means of *producing* historical consciousness. (p. 259)

I suggest here that a prayer meeting or memorial service even in the context of a protest march can be used to insert a useful ambiguity into the category of "organized protest" and hence blur the boundaries between political action and religious experience that the Comaroffs have studied. The riposte of the immigrant oppressed must be no less circumscribed or occulted, particularly in the face of possible, late modern state surveillance.

The "political" nature of the march was thus made "plausibly deniable" in front of the embassy, where immigrant protesters stood to lose the most as individuals, but was made more explicit once outside the reach of their home government.

The group had, I estimated, grown to about seventy-five or eighty people by the time we were ready to move on to the Shell corporate offices. After singing "Onward Christian Soldiers" and lining up in twos, we were directed to cross the street and proceed along a set route in an orderly fashion, following the coffin as well as police directions and paying attention to traffic. After making sure we all were across the street, several activists took up positions along the line and began to exhort us again to chant. This chanting did draw quite a lot of attention toward the group, and I noted that several African American or African passersby stopped to ask people in the line the meaning of the demonstration. Some of these passersby joined in the line, usually next to the people they had conversed with. Some Euro-Americans were also drawn into the line along the way to I Street, but I noted that they were more likely to ask what the demonstration was about and then go about their business. In general, people on the street seemed less curious about our protest than I expected—although I suppose this could have something to do with the fact that the event was taking place in downtown Washington, D.C.—a city that sees more than the usual amount of street-level political action.

The I Street building that houses Shell's Washington corporate offices was unremarkable; a 1980s office building with large glass doors and no corporate logos on display. Security guards with walkie-talkies were stationed inside those doors, and some of the march organizers went up to these people—evidently to let them know our plans. Just as at the embassy, those plans consisted of a period of circular picketing, then another round of speeches. It appeared to me that more Euro-American environmental activists joined the protesters at the Shell location; certainly more Greenpeace and Friends of the Earth signs were in evidence there, and they seemed to take charge of the first round of picketing, whereas the Nigerian organizers were engaged in setting up an area for speeches. As it turned out, the Nigerians were also waiting for a rather dramatic addition to the demonstration.

While we continued to walk and chant, three taxis pulled up in front of the building and disgorged a number of Nigerian men dressed in the black hooded robes that symbolize death in the West. They also carried black and silver scythes constructed out of cardboard and plastic that were inscribed with slogans like "Nigeria Is Dying," some of which they passed out to members of the crowd and some of which they kept for themselves. They also began to unload a number of plywood coffins painted flat black; these were in contrast to the first coffin we had followed to I Street, which was larger than the others, marked on its lid with a prominent cross, and displayed with the narrow end of the coffin open. The coffins were carried in a solemn procession by the death figures to the space just in front of the building's doors and reverently placed in a line; the largest coffin was then propped up in the center. Unsurprisingly, there were nine of these coffins—one for each of the executed activists. The largest coffin in the center was used throughout the demonstration to stand in for Ken Saro-Wiwa, sometimes being addressed as if it actually held the Ogoni leader.

The arrival of death several times over, carrying scythes and coffins and emerging from taxi cabs on a busy Washington street, was, perhaps, the most dramatic moment of the event. Even some of the politics-hardened Washingtonians in neighboring buildings came out to take a look. As an anthropologist who first wrote about the poetic Nigerian association of public transport and death almost a decade ago, the sight was not as startling to me but was extremely poignant. I knew that many of Washington's taxicab drivers are Nigerians and that some (or all) of the representatives of death are likely to drive cabs for a living.[14]

Nigerian immigrants' ready and effective adoption of Western symbolic practice at an event like the Shell protest was not surprising, either. This immigrant population has embedded itself very firmly into the mainstream of North American culture in an extremely short time. They have been able to do this partly because urban elites in Nigeria have been comfortable with a transnational lifestyle since the 1930s and 1940s and have brought portable markers of transnationality, like books, clothing styles, music, and food preferences, back to Nigeria for other Nigerians to consider. They have also been able to do this because of the centuries-old engagement with European colonialism and the commodities and ideas that circulated along with the slave trade and colonial exploitation around the west coast of Africa.

This particular immigration has been, because of tightening U.S. immigration policies in the latter half of the twentieth century, largely one of the Western-educated and English-speaking incipient middle class as well. Indeed, it could be argued that Western immigration policies have so successfully screened for the African middle classes that they have also siphoned off a majority of those classes, making it difficult for their social reproduction at home. It should not be difficult to understand, then, why the various Nigerian regimes of recent years—not dependent on individual remittances as countries like Sudan and Egypt have become—look upon these overseas Nigerians with a slightly jaundiced eye. It should also be clear how overseas Nigerians might have the leisure and material wherewithal to construct elaborate and dramatic, Westernized symbolic displays for a protest march and why they would be extremely dissatisfied not only with the illegitimacy of military rule but with the bad press it generated about their country of origin.

The death/coffin display was highly photogenic, as were the attractive young Nigerian men chosen to impersonate the Grim Reaper. The only measure of immigrant Nigerian misreading of North American culture was that there was no one at the demonstration taking pictures or doing interviews for the *Washington Post.* Voice of America, however, with its active Africa radio service, was an obvious press presence.[15] The celebrity "Ken Saro-Wiwa" was front-page news, but Nigerian immigrant professionals protesting his death did not have enough clout to insert their own images into the international wire services. These images would become part of no less a transnational discursive structure, appearing in immigrant publications, faxed around the globe or sent by mail back into Nigeria, and discussed on radio for continental consumption, but they would not impinge directly on international consciousness because of local decisions about the event's "newsworthiness."

The arrival of the representatives of death and the activists' faux coffins signaled the next phase of our protest before Shell's corporate offices. Those who were engaged in picketing were now gathered around the front of the building, facing the doors and the death assemblage. Several speakers, including Eddy Oparaoji, then addressed us as well as Shell, which was not officially present at the gathering. While listening to the speeches, I was constantly aware of and confronted by the coffins before us. The open foot of Saro-Wiwa's coffin began to nag at me; why leave this, the center of the piece, unfinished? It seemed to have been a deliberate gesture.

It was clear to all onlookers that there was nothing in the coffin, and the speeches kept bringing up the point that there could be nothing in such a coffin. Saro-Wiwa had, for these speakers, escaped the bodily indignities of decomposition and had slipped into the very fabric of the Nigerian landscape itself—and possibly into the larger global landscape. His blood, along with that of his compatriots, was now circulating in our gas tanks as well as inside the tapped veins of Ogoni; his power as a spiritual force was unbounded and directed outward from his hidden grave; his coffin was an exit, not an enclosure. In its absence, Saro-Wiwa's person had become pervasive; it was felt by the Nigerians outside the country and even, through symbolic extension, by the Western environmental and human rights activists who visibly responded to the tenor of the speeches without fully comprehending why. They did understand that Shell was being threatened, and they applauded confrontation with the multinational, but the vaguely preternatural tone of the threats was not something they were familiar with.

Once the speeches were finished, the crowd picketed a bit more but was definitely in the mood for dispersal as it was just after the promised 2 P.M. deadline. Nigerians embraced and made plans for further meetings; the professional activists liaised and then disappeared rapidly; passersby who had been swept up into the event looked at their watches and moved away in every direction. Our anthropological party started back toward the Nigerian Embassy area, where we had parked, and met some of death's representatives, who had picked up the plywood coffins from the front of the Shell building and were carrying them through the streets and parks to the embassy. This was not a theatrical gesture, like the original arrival by taxi; clearly the young men had decided on their own (without the more cautious elders who staged the memorial service earlier) to take the tangible signs of the protest where they felt those signs belonged. A couple of now unhooded reapers waved cheerfully to us when they saw our captured scythe and clutched leaflets. As we turned away to go to our car, back to the shelter of DuPont Circle and the anthropology meetings, we noted these brave Nigerian men carefully placing the coffins all around the front door of the locked-up Nigerian Embassy, blocking that door with the largest and emptiest coffin of all.

CONCLUSION: THE EXCLUDED ELEMENT

> When it is repressed, death returns in an exotic language (that of a past, of ancient religions or distant traditions); it has to be invoked in foreign dialects; it is as difficult to speak about in one's own language as it is for someone to die "at home": these are the marks that define an excluded element, one that can return only in disguise. It is a paradoxical symptom of this death without words that a whole literature designates the point where relations with the meaningless are focused. Texts proliferate around this wound on reason. Once again, it supports itself on what cannot be mentioned. Death is the problem of the subject.
> —Michel de Certeau, *The Practice of Everyday Life*

Death *is* the problem of the subject, as de Certeau tells us—but who or what constitutes the subject in contemporary Nigeria? The discursive practices surrounding the executions of the Ogoni nine—whether in international media, among transnational environmentalist groups, or between immigrant Nigerians the world over—tended to focus first on the missing bodies of the activists, particularly that of Ken Saro-Wiwa, and then on the obliteration of human rights more generally within the country. In some sense, the lack of a corpse freed media and other participants in the global economy of communication to make poetic and powerfully charged connections between the martyred bodies and the very substance of the land— or the commodification of the land—that stood behind the tragic events of late 1995.

For print media, especially, popular connections between blood and oil made for intense pictorial images meant to translate, as cover or front-page art, into magazine and newspaper sales: derricks "foaming" with Ogoni blood, strangulation by gasoline pump, and hooded effigies hanging from

Shell signs. What particular newspapers or magazines did with their print interpretations of these images, however, was very much attendant upon prior editorial politics. Among environmentalists and human rights workers, the very name Ken Saro-Wiwa took on a talismanic quality, used to conjure up donations, focus attention on both multinational and state exploitation of indigenous peoples, and create at least a temporary climate of public outrage that could be directed against political and economic adversaries. Saro-Wiwa's photographs and interviews, for these groups, signified the ubiquity of corporate and state greed in a world populated by unsuspecting or helpless ordinary folk, no matter that Saro-Wiwa's pre-martyrdom biography would suggest a more ambiguous attachment to the very elites that activist groups in the West generally purport to despise.

For Nigerian immigrants, the executions stood as a profound example of the terror being generated by their government as well as an example of Western misunderstanding about and meddling in Nigerian politics. For instance, Igbo speakers on Naijanet and in personal conversations often countered images of spilled Ogoni blood with memories of the massacres that helped bring about the Nigerian Civil War, and the policy of "starvation as a weapon" instituted by the federal government during the war—a policy implicitly supported by the youthful, pro-federal Saro-Wiwa. Some Nigerians (of many different ethnicities, including Igbo) began to see Saro-Wiwa and his executed compatriots as something very like ancestors, in their disembodied power and scope. This new form of national ancestorhood offered immigrants both an appropriate mode of grief and a charter for action, as they tried to interpret what the deceased activists required from the Nigerians who have survived and therefore, in some sense, constitute the Ogoni nine's posterity. For them, the "wound against reason" that occurred in November 1995 could only be addressed in terms that brought together "traditional" notions of the afterlife with zealous, "modern" political rhetoric. The potency of this combination clearly reverberated throughout global representations of the simulacrum "Ken Saro-Wiwa," even if the source of this celebrity construct was never traced by the media who disseminated it.

For the FMG and particularly General Abacha, the celebrity "Ken Saro-Wiwa" became a most unexpected and unwelcome presence. Clearly under the mistaken impression that the dead would stay dead and that bodily dissolution was the ultimate sanction against political action, the state was shaken to learn that there could be international repercussions from "local matters" of hanged men and hidden graves. Itself more a facade for high-level expropriation than a functioning political organization, the FMG was not very apt in its dealings with passionate, human responses to its terrorizing order. The Nigerian government's reaction to the crisis precipitated by the global response to Saro-Wiwa's death was to engage in a strangely mixed campaign of sophisticated and clumsy advertising. If image was perceived to be the state's problem, then it would reconfigure its own image rather than reconsider or redress its practices.

The multinational Royal Dutch Shell also discovered that Saro-Wiwa's postmortem celebrity status had embroiled it in an image crisis. This crisis manifested itself not only in protest marches but also in a determined onslaught of activist-driven letters from the public; boycotts and threatened boycotts of their products; legislative resolutions; a renewed fervor on the part of old enemies; and even a desecration of its most cherished icon, the multinational's yellow shell logo. Its very corporate identity had been put at risk, and in a world where multinationals regularly pay millions of dollars for instantly recognizable and easily remembered corporate graphics, this last was hardly the least of Shell's worries. Such an assault on what Michael Hardt would call the "smooth surfaces" (p. 37) of late capitalism struck deeply at what is most currently *real* to such delocalized organizations: the multinational's virtual presence in the world, its place in the world's imaginary, and hence its (projected) profitability. A face—of a dead, and therefore dangerously untouchable, person—had been placed in opposition to the company's facelessness (literally and poetically its "shell"), thereby emphasizing one of the great contradictions and anxieties of capitalist practice: the lack of *corpus* in the corporation.

NOTES

1. The names of all executed on 10 November 1995 are Baribo Bera, Saturday Dobee, Nordu Eawo, Daniel Gbokoo, Barinem Kiobel, John Kpuinen, Paul Levura, Felix Nwate, and Kenule Saro-Wiwa.

2. All of the murdered elders were founding members of MOSOP, according to a controversial advertisement placed in the *New York Times* on 6 December 1995. Two of them were Saro-Wiwa's affines: Chief Samuel N. Orage and Chief Theophilus B. Orage. The other two murdered elders were Chief Edward Kobani and Albert T. Badey. The people who actually killed these men have never been satisfactorily identified.

3. Colonel Komo quoted in a Reuters news report dated 15 December 1995 that was widely circulated in the Nigerian immigrant community.

4. And, it should be noted, Randall Robinson never mentioned Shell by name. The strongest statement about the oil multinationals made during these hearings came from representatives of Human Rights Watch/Africa, who called upon the U.S. government to "encourage U.S.-based multinational oil companies operating in Nigeria, including Chevron and Mobil, to take constructive public steps to end egregious human rights violations" (U.S. Senate, p. 30).

5. Talking about a Port Harcourt policeman who was astonished to see the now-famous prisoner brought into custody, Saro-Wiwa (*A Month and a Day*, pp. 4–5) noted ruefully in his posthumously published memoirs of incarceration:

> He might have been star-struck. I had been very much in the news lately, and, as often happens to those who have that misfortune, was considered

more as a news item than as a living being with flesh and blood. Seeing me in the latter condition caused my friend's eternal surprise.

6. As I noted in my field journal at the time, this penalty just served to convince armed robbers to use their guns and silence any potential witnesses. Far from deterring gun-related crime in Nigeria, one constantly hears about the increasing dangers to anyone known to carry cash or to drive expensive cars. One Naijas (Sangoyomi 1996) recently gave a harrowing account of armed robbers invading his family's compound in Lagos just after his arrival from the United States. After bursting into the family home, they began shouting, "Where is the dollars? Where is the dollars?" Fortunately no one was actually shot, but everyone in the compound lost cash, other valuables, and even cars in the robbery.

7. The Abacha regime, as no military government before, has rigorously curbed the lively Nigerian press. It has done this by making a point of harassing newspaper and magazine publishers, even detaining those who refuse to write to the regime's specifications, and by shutting down those papers, such as the hitherto inviolate *Guardian*, which do not cooperate. The general, known to be a secretive person, seems unusually sensitive to public criticism, and many journalists besides Saro-Wiwa have run afoul of his sensitivities.

8. Karin Barber (1995), writing about Yoruba praises of the nineteenth century, shows that this association of the elite with the "chopping" of money is not merely a pathology of late modernity but has a longer history within (at least) southern Nigeria.

9. There were reports that Saro-Wiwa's wife realized that something was amiss when she attempted to take him some lunch and was turned away from the Port Harcourt prison where he was being held. Evidently she was told that the lunch would not be wanted. We know that the executions began sometime around 11 A.M.

10. See Soyinka's *Requiem for a Futurologist* (London: Rex Collings, 1985) for a satirical treatment of this issue.

11. The official invitation for Naijas "in the Baltimore/DC/Virginia area" was put on the listserv on Tuesday, 14 November 1995, by Mobolaji E. Aluko. Besides telling the location of the march—from the Nigerian Chancery at 1333 16th Street, N.W., to Shell's offices at 1401 I Street, N.W.—Aluko noted that people should march to tell the government and Shell that "Saro-Wiwa's blood now flows through their oil pipes!"

12. Julie A. Corsaro, Adeline Masquelier, and Brad Weiss agreed to attend with me. I want to acknowledge their participation not only for the sake of completeness, but because this was a very emotional period for me, and their presence made some of the difficult moments much more bearable.

13. Even Maj. Paul Okuntimo, who is credited with writing a memo in 1994 that suggested "wasting operations" against MOSOP activists and who has been charged by his own troops with rape during military operations in the delta, plans "a career in the evangelical Christian ministry when he retires from the army" (Hammer, p. 65).

14. It seemed very likely that the cabdrivers were part of the demonstration. After all, numerous popular sociological studies have shown how difficult it is for African American men to flag down a taxi in U.S. cities, even while dressed in a solidly middle-class manner. Compound this everyday problem by having six or so tall African men dressed in death robes and carrying scythes and coffins, and you see the likelihood of taxi driver complicity.

15. I would add here that several Nigerians expressed dissatisfaction with the fact that the *Washington Post* did not show up. Evidently they were called but did not consider the event newsworthy. The *Washington Post* was also remarkably slow to cover or editorialize about the Ogoni nine executions.

WORKS CITED

Aluko, Mobolaji E. "Memorial Service/Protest on Friday." Posting to naijanet@ mitvma.mit.edu, 14 November 1995.

Amnesty International USA. "Freedom in the Balance: Nigeria/Kenya" packet for African Studies Association members, 1995.

Anon. "Nigeria Foaming." *The Economist* 337 (18 November 1995): 15–16.

Ayetigbo, Ayodele. "Coffin to Abacha and Shell." *The U.S.-Nigeria Voice* 2, no. 17 (1995): 7–10.

———. "Saro-Wiwa on Our Minds." *The U.S.-Nigeria Voice* 2, no. 17 (1995): 5.

Barber, Karin. "Money, Self-Realization and the Person in Yoruba Texts." In *Money Matters: Instability, Values and Social Payments in the Modern History of West African Communities*. Ed. Jane I. Guyer. Portsmouth: Heinemann, 1995: 205–224.

Bates, Stephen, and Owen Bowcott. "Shell Undeterred by Nigeria Hangings." *Manchester Guardian Weekly* 153, no. 21 (19 November 1995): 1.

de Certeau, Michel. *The Practice of Everyday Life*. Berkeley: University of California Press, 1984.

Cohen, Mitchel. "Murder in Nigeria: Ordered by Shell and the IMF, Paid For by the U.S. Government." Red Balloon Collective broadside, distributed by the Brecht Forum. New York, 1996.

Comaroff, John, and Jean Comaroff. *Ethnography and the Historical Imagination*. Boulder, Colo.: Westview Press, 1992.

Foucault, Michel. *Discipline and Punish: The Birth of the Prison*. New York: Vintage Books, 1977.

Greenpeace/Movement for the Survival of the Ogoni People. "Transcript of 'A Testimony' by Dr. Owens Wiwa (Brother of Ken Saro-Wiwa)." Greenpeace Internet document, 1995.

Hammer, Joshua. "Nigeria Crude: A Hanged Man and an Oil-Fouled Landscape." *Harper's* 292, no. 1753 (1996): 58–70.

Hardt, Michael. "The Withering of Civil Society." *Social Text* 45 (1995): 27–44.

Haygood, Wil. 1996. "Nigeria on Trial." *Boston Globe,* 7 April 1996: 1.

Human Rights Watch/Africa. "Nigeria: The Ogoni Crisis: A Case-Study of Military Repression in Southeastern Nigeria." *Human Rights Watch/Africa* 7, no. 5 (1995): 7–25.

Meyer, Birgit. "African Pentacostal Churches, Satan and the Dissociation from Tradition." Paper presented at the American Anthropological Association Annual Meeting. Washington, D.C., 1995.

Rowell, Andy. "Shell Shocked." *Village Voice,* 21 November 1995: 21–23.

Sangoyomi, Taiye B. "Nigerian Visit (1)." Posting to naijanet@mitvma.mit.edu, 23 January 1996.

Saro-Wiwa, Ken. *A Month and a Day: A Detention Diary*. London: Penguin, 1995.

Soyinka, Wole. "Epilogue: Death of an Activist." In his *The Open Sore of a Continent*. New York: Oxford University Press, 1996.

U.S. Senate, Subcommittee on African Affairs, Committee on Foreign Relations. 20 July 1995. "The Situation in Nigeria." S. Hrg. 104–206. Washington, D.C.: U.S. Government Printing Office.

van Dijk, Rijk A. "From Camp to Encompassment: Discourses of Trans-subjectivity in the Ghanaian Pentacostal Diaspora." Paper presented at the Satterthwaite (UK) Colloquium on African Religion and Ritual, 1996.

9

Saro-Wiwa the Publisher

Laura Neame

EVOLUTION AS A PUBLISHER

Ken Saro-Wiwa returned to literary and intellectual pursuits after a long career as a businessman and trader. His growth and development as a publisher run parallel to his evolution as an author, a process Philip Altbach has commented on:

> The infrastructures of publishing are absolutely central to the growth of an intellectual culture. . . . Publishing is, in a sense, the intersection between intellectual life and commerce. It provides business experience to intellectuals and intellectual pursuits to those involved in business. (Altbach, "Perspectives on Publishing in Africa").

In 1977 Saro-Wiwa ran into his old friend Sam Amuka, who was at that time the editor of the newspaper *Punch*. Amuka was critical of the fact that Saro-Wiwa's activities had been limited to business and trading for the past ten years and encouraged him to begin writing again. The articles he wrote for Sam Amuka in *Punch* in the end formed the basis for *Prisoners of Jebs* (Wiwa, August 1997). He also wrote an occasional column for the *Sunday Times* called "Similia." Sam Amuka eventually went on to the *Vanguard*, and Saro-Wiwa moved his column there. It was at this time that he

> was in charge of the Directorate for Social Mobilisation, and that's when he wrote *Basi and Company,* so he was writing episodes of *Basi and Company* and he was writing his column "Similia," all under the aegis of this Directorate for Social Mobilisation. He began increasingly to criticise the government in his columns. (Wiwa, August 1997)

As a result, the column was eventually canceled. Similarly, his term as director for social mobilization lasted only a year.

It was in 1984 that Saro-Wiwa's interest in more substantive writing was renewed. An essay on the poetry of the civil war by Funsho Aiyejina had come to Saro-Wiwa's attention. No mention was made of early poems by Saro-Wiwa that had appeared in *Black Orpheus* and elsewhere (Saro-Wiwa, "Notes," p. 257). This was a blow, even though "having decided to go into business, I had placed all my writing on hold. In the ten years I spent in business, I only wrote the occasional newspaper essay or column and the long pidgin English poem, 'Dis Nigeria Sef' (Saro-Wiwa, "A Nigerian," n.p.). Saro-Wiwa saw the omission as "a reminder that I had to return to claim my place in Nigerian literature" (Saro-Wiwa, "A Nigerian"). He adds that at the same time, his business interests began to go awry in the difficult Nigerian economic climate. "Having earned enough money to take care of my responsibilities to my immediate family, I thought it was time to get a move on" (Saro-Wiwa, "A Nigerian"). Saro-Wiwa dug out his poems of the civil war and began to look for a publisher. He contacted Longman, which had published the Tambari books when he was minister of education in 1973. They were not interested in his poetry, so he sent the poems to a "critical friend," fellow Ogoni, Theo Vincent, a professor of English literature at the University of Lagos (Saro-Wiwa, "A Nigerian") for assessment. He then obtained an ISBN from the National Library and established Saros International Publishers (Saro-Wiwa, "Notes," p. 257). The decision to publish on his own had been made (see Appendix 1).

Preparing *Songs in a Time of War* for publication, Saro-Wiwa revived partially completed works written in the early 1970s. These included *Sozaboy*, some plays, short stories, and a diary of the civil war that was to become *On a Darkling Plain*. *Sozaboy* he sent to Longman for assessment. This took over a year; it proved to be another decisive step leading Saro-Wiwa to the decision to self-publish. "If I had to wait that long for reports and decisions, many of the manuscripts I had in my drawer might never see the light of day" (Saro-Wiwa, "Notes," p. 258). In so doing, Saro-Wiwa was building on a strong tradition of self-publishing in Nigeria.

Ken Wiwa, in an interview in 1997, describes his father's feelings about this decision:

> He agonised over a number of things. He didn't want to publish on his own obviously because it wasn't a money spinning venture. He would lose money, he knew that, but the publishers at that time were not interested in books that were purely set in Africa, or indeed with a very strong Africa message, they just weren't commercial. He felt that his message was so strong that it was worth publishing and be damned, and at his own cost as well. (Wiwa, October 1997)

In order to learn more about book publishing, Saro-Wiwa took courses at Book House Trust in London, organized for people in the publishing industry. "After three or four such courses, I knew enough to put me on the painful path of book publishing" (Saro-Wiwa, "Notes," p. 258). By the time he completed the last course in 1986, Longman had finally published *Sozaboy* and *A Forest of Flowers*. Saro-Wiwa's conclusion, after the delays he had experienced, was to continue with his plans to self-publish. "Publishing is largely a marketing operation, which a lover of books and culture with trading skills, money and bravado could undertake" (p. 258). While he was taking publishing courses, Saro-Wiwa met the Scottish novelist William Boyd, who was a speaker at a publishing course and became Saro-Wiwa's friend and eventual champion (see Boyd).

As a frequent visitor to Britain, it seemed simplest at the time to have his collection of poems *Songs in a Time of War,* which Longman had rejected, printed in London by Richard Clay rather than in Nigeria. His decision resulted in problems, however, because he then had to get the books to their primary market in Nigeria, which required an import license. Meanwhile, moving into the UK market proved difficult. Over the next five years, every UK distributor for both *Songs in a Time of War* and his other self-published works went out of business (Saro-Wiwa, "Notes," p. 258). In 1987, it finally became possible to ship books to Nigeria without an import license.

In 1988 Saro-Wiwa moved the printing and design part of his publishing operation back to Nigeria. He then went looking for Nigerian craftspeople: designers, illustrators, and proofreaders. Finding good proofreaders and printers was a problem; there was a shortage of skilled workers and of printing parts. By 1992 however, Saro-Wiwa was typesetting in-house, using freelance designers and illustrators, and buying paper, film, and plates (p. 258). His contacts as a businessman and his position as director of the Nigerian Newsprint Manufacturing Company from 1987 to 1992 (Saro-Wiwa, "Curriculum Vitae") almost certainly proved helpful in this process.

Within Nigeria, Saro-Wiwa encountered the predictable distribution problems of a small publisher. His distribution choices were university bookstores, chain stores such as Leventis, airport kiosks, and direct marketing to bookstores. In the end, distribution with such a small list (six titles at the time) proved impossible, and Saro-Wiwa fell back on the distribution experience of publishers within the trade. In 1992 Saro-Wiwa made an arrangement for distribution of his books within the country with Heinemann of Nigeria. At the same time,

> Another silver lining . . . presented itself in the African Books Collective (ABC)—thanks to the efforts of Hans Zell and his African Colleagues.

> ABC will now ensure that sales are made to libraries and others in Europe, America and to other African Countries. (Saro-Wiwa, "Notes," p. 258)

In fact, Saro-Wiwa could have taken advantage of this silver lining earlier, according to ABC manager Mary Jay. Saro-Wiwa had not been interested in becoming a founding member of ABC at its inception. He was not one of the original seventeen who put up money, displaying a more cautious attitude toward the venture and therefore remaining ineligible for a seat on the ABC board. The result was that he appeared to be unwilling to join in an effort to improve the status of African publishing through the African Books Collective until he was sure that he and his publishing company would benefit directly (Jay, August 1997).

Saro-Wiwa wanted to recoup his publishing investment and would have done so if he had been able to get his children's works and folktales adopted as part of the Nigerian school curriculum. He thought that they would be taken up by the West African Educational Council and put on the syllabi. This was one way, he hoped, whereby Saros International Publishers would become profitable (Wiwa, October 1997). However, Ken Wiwa feels that the lack of profitability of Saros International Publishers was only a secondary concern on his father's part:

> He [Ken's father] was somebody who worked hard and tried to maximize whatever he did. He worked hard at politics, he worked hard at his business, he worked hard at his books. He wasn't financially motivated, he could have made a lot more money if he wanted to; he published books at a loss not because, as they've tried to say, because he was vain, but simply because he wanted the germ of the ideas to remain forever. I think that's what irritated the Nigerian Government, because long after they are all gone, those books and the symbols will remain. (Wiwa, August 1997)

THE NIGERIAN PUBLISHING CONTEXT

The decline in book availability began in 1982, corresponding to Nigerian austerity measures. There was a shortage of paper, inks, and few binderies. The World Bank subsidy (which ended in 1996) was almost exclusively for the import of foreign titles. At $37 million, this represented significant lost revenue for Nigerian publishers and authors. The protective tariff policies of Nigeria during the 1970s and 1980s had a devastating effect on book publishing and purchase. As an example, in the years between 1979 and 1983, books purchased from overseas by the University of Port Harcourt Library dropped from 5,175 to zero.

Adding to Nigerian import policies intended to strengthen the Nigerian economy was the imposition of the Second-Tier Foreign Exchange

Market (SFEM), a government policy introduced in 1986 (Akobo, p. 87) that backfired badly. Before the imposition of SFEM policies, most library and bookstore purchases were from abroad, as there was not enough indigenous publishing to fill demand. However, the Nigerian government, affected by a decline in foreign exchange profits and hoping to improve the balance of payments, thought to boost the economy through a number of policy changes. The SFEM affected libraries and booksellers by making it difficult and expensive to buy books from abroad. One consequence was that it became impossible for libraries to make payment within the required ninety days due to government-initiated delays in receipt. This caused out-of-country book dealers to require payment before shipping. In addition, foreign exchange controls that were instituted in 1979 had already affected the import of journals. Periodicals ordered in 1982 were locked in customhouses and not released until 1984 or 1985. As a result, many titles were canceled altogether. The University of Port Harcourt Library was left with fifteen journals after these cancellations (Akobo, p. 88).

The Nigerian government may have thought that its policies would help the development of indigenous businesses, but as far as Nigerian publishing was concerned, they had the opposite effect. One of the outcomes of the Nigerian government SFEM and other Nigerian and World Bank strategies was to increase the price of imported books. While there was a greater market for indigenous publishers as a result, the price of imported paper and other products also rose. Publishers in Nigeria imported almost all their raw materials, equipment, and technology. Application of the SFEM made this prohibitively expensive. One ream of paper, which sold for 45 naira before SFEM, sold for 500 naira afterward. At the same time, inks, plates, and chemicals disappeared from the Nigerian market. Naturally, this caused the closure of a number of indigenous publishing houses (Akobo, p. 89).

The Nigerian federal government through its contracts with the World Bank and its agencies had created a "permanent dependent" (Thomas, p. 35) status. Millions of dollars were used to secure multiple copies of imported textbooks. If funding had been available from the government on a regular and consistent basis, this type of dependent loan program would have been unnecessary. Book buying within the country also decreased due to devaluation of the naira and rampant inflation. During the 1980s Africa's share of world book production dropped from 1.5 percent to 1.3 percent (Rathgeber, p. 78).

In the 1990s the physical quality of the Nigerian published book continued to decline. Newsprint largely replaced high-quality paper, and editorial and design efficiency deteriorated due to poor training. There were numerous production flaws, and the majority of Nigerian books did "not meet internationally accepted standards in physical and visual quality, or in the quality of content" (Ifaturoti, p. 13). Major Nigerian book publishers had print runs of only a few thousand, compared with tens of thousands in the two previous decades. Inadequate infrastructure remained the greatest obstacle to the development of publishing. There were constant power cuts, and not all areas of the country had electricity. Telephone lines could be dead for months. Ademdamola Ifaturoti describes the situation:

> Nigeria must continue to attempt to develop its print publishing industry. There is plenty of room for improvement, and desktop publishing should take care of a number of design and proof reading problems, as well as improving editing functions. Nigeria is not well placed for the electronic age, but it can and should take advantage of available computer technology for book production. (p. 13)

What responses have Nigerian publishers and writers made to the challenges of the unfriendly Nigerian environment? As described, half facetiously, by Victor Nwankwo, the choices are as follows: first, bread-and-butter publishing, that is, the production of core primary and secondary textbooks. This has traditionally been the preserve of local branches of multinational companies. The cost of "convincing" state government officials to adopt certain texts in the school systems makes this very costly (Nwankwo, "Nigeria: International," p. 412).

It was Saro-Wiwa's ambition to have his books adopted in the school curriculum, but without "the grease," and since he lacked influence within the appropriate ministry, success was unlikely. When he was minister of information and home affairs for Rivers State in 1973, things were different. Saro-Wiwa, at that time, had overall authority over the education ministry. As was customary for those in charge of education, he was able to have his books *Tambari* and *Tambari in Dukana* adopted as school texts (Mezu, p. 12). This guaranteed method of sales in the tens of thousands was not to occur for Saro-Wiwa again.

The second response to challenges facing the Nigerian publisher is the book launch (Nwankwo, "Nigeria: International," p. 412). At this event, it is expected that friends will attend and buy copies at astronomical prices and that the publicity will fuel sales. Saro-Wiwa promoted a number of book launches in Port Harcourt, Lagos, and London, often for the same titles. However, he opposed the "Nigerian-style" book launch. His launches were occasions "to present the book to the public, thank the media and talk book" (Obiagwu, p. 34). At the launch for *On a Darkling Plain*, he told guests, "A good book launch should be a meeting place for book lovers not those with money to throw about" (Ola, p. 3). His books were sold at launches for the published prices, not at the grossly inflated amounts common at these events. For Saro-Wiwa, these occasions were opportunities for contacts and for publicity and also allowed him to speak about the causes that were becoming essential to him (Saro-Wiwa, *A Month,* pp. 82–84).

Third, there is self-publishing.[2] Nwankwo attributes this emerging trend to the inability of existing publishers to meet publication demands, to high rejection rates by mainstream publishers due to poor quality, and to "the expectation by authors that they will be able to cream the publisher's expected return during the book launch. This is not usually successful, often due to inability to market effectively" (Nwankwo, "Nigeria: International," p. 411). Saro-Wiwa certainly found marketing and distribution his biggest barrier to sales. However, given the state of the publishing industry in Nigeria, self-publishing is the only way the majority of his works would have been published at all. Saro-Wiwa frequently spoke of the problems of publishing from the writer's perspective. In his address to the Ikoro Creative Association, he said to the neophyte author:

> [Y]ou have spent your last kobo on expensive pen and paper, or typewriter ribbon and carbon. Your manuscript has been considered publishable. You jump for joy, inform your friends, dance in the bathroom. Hold it. It will be another nine months before you get a proof. You read and re-read it. The typesetter has made a host of errors. You make a host of corrections. Perhaps you do not realize that every mistake you correct costs you money which will be deducted from your royalties. (Saro-Wiwa, "The Hazards")

Finally, Nwankwo concludes that "going out of business" ("Nigeria: International," p. 412) is the most common of all responses to the state of Nigerian publishing: a sure sign being the failure to publish a new title over a five-year period. Unfortunately, Saros International Publishers is one of these publishers, due not to the state of Nigerian publishing, but rather to the actions of the Nigerian state. Overall, in spite of the publishing problems in Nigeria, the hunger for books is overwhelming: "The publisher's handicap is funds, enough funds to produce print runs sufficient to meet demands as well as reduce unit costs" (p. 414). Titles adopted in some school systems sell over 100,000 copies in one season, and some well-established authors sell 10,000 copies a month. However, it is still the educational system that fuels large publishing runs in Nigeria, and this system is largely in the hands of the multinational publishing companies and their Nigerian branches. The well-established African author has either a European publisher or a place on a publishing list such as Heinemann's African Writers Series.

PUBLISHING IN POSTCOLONIAL NIGERIA

Saro-Wiwa was interested in recognition by the intellectual elite. He also wished for popular acclaim and recognition. He ultimately received both. His son, Ken Wiwa, expresses the ambivalence felt by his father:

> My father always used to lament that he could actually write a book that
> would be read in the literary circles of Europe, like Wole Soyinka does
> . . . but what he was interested in as a writer was reflecting the social
> conditions of Nigeria, for Nigerians. That's why he self-published, be-
> cause his stories were deemed not to have a market. . . . He was writing
> specifically for that market, and not for a worldwide market, or for peo-
> ple in literary circles. (Wiwa, August 1997)

This is not entirely true however. Saro-Wiwa was interested in a
worldwide audience in addition to Nigerian readers. He makes this point
when writing about his use of English as his written language, conveying
much the same sentiment as Chinua Achebe, in "In Defence of English: An
Open Letter to Tai Solarin" (1966):

> [T]he need to communicate with one another, and with the rest of the
> world, added to the fact of colonialism which is also real, has forced us
> to write in the language of the erstwhile colonial masters. I for one, do
> not feel guilty about this. Were I writing in Khana, I should be speaking
> to 100,000 people, most of whom do not read and write. Writing in Eng-
> lish as I do, I am able to reach, hypothetically speaking, 400 million peo-
> ple. That cannot be bad. (Saro-Wiwa, "The Language of African Litera-
> ture," n.p.)

Philip Altbach makes the same point from a broader perspective:
"Colonial languages have been used as a means of national unification in
a number of third world nations, particularly those in which no one indigenous language commands the loyalty of the entire population" (Altbach, "Literary Colonialism," p. 486). Language rather than nationality
seems to be the determining factor in the spread of multinational publishers to Third World countries. Multinational book publishers do not cross
the language barrier easily. Publishers are an integral part of this colonial
tradition, although it is an unconscious and profit-oriented policy rather
than a conscious neocolonial one: "they perceive that the largest market
for books is in English, and that, in fact, the only national market is for
such material" (p. 487). In Nigeria, with only a 52 percent literacy rate,
those who can read at all read English. Multinational publishers are no different than other multinationals and use the same techniques to maximize
profits, such as selling licensing and distribution rights to limited companies. These profits are not subsequently reinvested in the limited company
or even within the country (Gedin, p. 45). For example, Abiola Irele states
of the Nigerian branch of Oxford University Press in the 1960s: "There are
some half dozen publishing houses in Nigeria which are subsidiaries of
British based multinational companies. . . . Although they now undertake
some local publishing, this is still very limited . . . as manuscripts are often
sent to Britain for editing and production into books which are then

imported into Nigeria" (quoted in Gedin, p. 46). Irele gives Macmillan special mention as a company that has an agreement with Northern Nigerian Publishing Company but does its printing elsewhere. The multinationals stay in a Third World country only as long as there is a profit to be made.

Funding agencies will often give money to the large publishing companies while indigenous publishers are prevented from building an infrastructure in the country through lack of similar funding. These same multinationals will participate in the "dumping" of obsolete texts and use aid programs in order to rid themselves of old stock, which hurts the local bookseller and distribution system. Most important, the multinational publisher has no interest in encouraging new writers, thus hampering the emergence of a national literature (Gedin, p. 46). Although the multinational companies were already well established, for the most part, when the countries became independent, indigenous publishers have the unique challenge of building a book publishing industry from scratch. This is an "entirely post-colonial phenomenon," according to Gordon Graham, and Nigeria is an example of a postcolonial country that has built a substantial indigenous publishing industry (see Graham, "Multinationals and Third World Publishing").

Yet Nigeria's publishing record, when compared with that of other African countries, is poor. The African average of publications per capita is twenty-four, but in Nigeria in 1984 it was only eighteen. The growth of the education industry in the 1960s fueled the increase in the total number of indigenous publishers, as did the civil war literature of the 1970s. The number of Nigerian publishers listed as members of the Nigerian Publishers Association grew from ten in 1969 to about fifty in early 1985 (Ike, p. 177). Indigenous publishing was also helped by the "indigenisation policy" of 1973, which transferred 60 percent equity ownership of multinational subsidiaries to local hands (Nwankwo, "Publishing").

Indigenous publishing is not without its problems and issues. Criticisms can be made of the indigenous publishers and their business methods. Hans Zell speaks of the lack of professionalism often shown by African houses in publishing, printing, and marketing their indigenous authors. They are too often "notoriously unbusinesslike," with poor author relationships, faulty financial planning, and poorly trained and motivated staff. He criticizes both the quality of the books produced (layout, artwork, proofreading) and the marketing and publicity efforts: "there is finally, the dismal failure of many African publishers to bring their books to the attention of a worldwide buying public" (Zell, "African Publishing," p. 105).

In the end, it is still the multinationals that overwhelm the Nigerian market. Evans Brothers, Heinemann, Longman, Macmillan, Nelson Publishers, and Oxford University Press collectively produce 80 percent of the books in Nigeria. This is not just due to their intrinsic interest and quality but to the marketing and distribution advantage these larger companies have. Heinemann's African Writers Series showed annual sales for Nigerian authors in the hundreds in a 1986 sales report, and in the case of authors such as Chinua Achebe, the figures rank in the thousands. Authors such as Elechi Amadi and Cyprian Ekwensi average between 500 and 1,000 sales per title annually (see Table 9.1).

THE LANGUAGE OF INDIGENOUS PUBLISHING

Developing countries should not discourage publishing in a common language such as English, even if it is spoken and read by a minority, for it "provides a window on the world for the country, and, for its publishers, a basis of commercial cooperation" (Graham, p. 35). This view is one that Saro-Wiwa supported:

> I am aware of the points made by Ngugi wa Thiongó about decolonizing the mind and his determination to write in his native Kikuyu. He is welcome to the latter. . . . I am, I find, as Ogoni as ever. I am contributing to Ogoni life as fully, and possibly better than those Ogoni people who do not speak and write English. (Saro-Wiwa, "The Language of African Literature," n.p.)

Publishing plays a key role in cultural imperialism. The literate, educated products of postcolonial society identify with and reproduce the

Table 9.1 Heinemann: African Writers Series Sales Figures

Title, Year Published in AWS, Author	Total Sales Since Publication
Things Fall Apart, 1958, Achebe	901,954
Arrow of God, 1964, 1974, Achebe	433,048
No Longer at Ease, 1963, Achebe	1,153,502
Concubine, 1973, Amadi	83,716
Sunset in Biafra, 1973, Amadi	388,682
Burning Grass, 1962, Ekwensi	422,183
Efuru, 1966, Nwapa	61,898
Voice, 1970, Okara	49,098
Labyrinths, 1971, Okigbo	29,683

Source: Information gathered by the author, courtesy of Vicki Unwin, African and Caribbean publisher, Heinemann, 1986.

literary traditions of their former colonial masters (Graham, p. 32). In a list Saro-Wiwa provides of his favorite authors, only one, Chinua Achebe, is Nigerian or even African. The rest, all male, are in the traditional educated European tradition (Saro-Wiwa, "Curriculum Vitae"). He writes:

> The fact that I appreciate Shakespeare, Chaucer, Dickens, Tennyson et al., that I know something of European civilization, its history and philosophy, appreciate Mozart and Beethoven is a colonization of my mind? I cannot exactly complain about this.

He also says, in the same unpublished excerpt:

> In regard of English, I have heard it said that those who write in it should adopt a domesticated variety of it which would make it "African." I have to report that I have experimented in my writings with the three varieties of the language which are spoken and written in Nigeria: pidgin, "rotten" and standard [English] . . . my conclusion is that that which carries best and which is most favored is standard English, expressed simply and lucidly. (Saro-Wiwa, "The Language of African Literature," n.p.)

In *Cultural Pride: The Necessity of Indigenous Publishing,* Per Gedin quotes Achebe. When reading Joseph Conrad's *Heart of Darkness* in school, it suddenly occurred to Achebe that "I was not on Marlowe's boat steaming up the Congo. I was one of those strange beings jumping up and down on the river bank, making horrible faces" (Gedin, p. 43). This moment of self-knowledge is not a perception or point of view that seemed to have troubled Saro-Wiwa. He had a whole-hearted admiration for the British life. In 1954 at the age of thirteen, Saro-Wiwa went to Government College, Umuahia, where he was the only Ogoni (see Appendix 1). Use of his mother tongue was forbidden, and all work, reading, and conversation had to be in English. He was proud of the British public school tradition that permeated Government School. In his words, in a single generation, the school "produced Chinua Achebe, Gabriel Okara, Christopher Okigbo, Elechi Amadi, Vincent Ike and I. N. C. Aniebo" (Saro-Wiwa, "The Language of African Literature"). As his friend Anthony Daniels states, Saro-Wiwa was an "admirer of traditional British education and having made sufficient money to do so, he sent his sons to Eton" (Daniels, p. 51).

REACHING THE MASS MARKET

Indigenous Nigerian publishing houses began to develop after World War II. Tabansi of Onitsha published Cyprian Ekwensi's *Ikolo the Wrestler and Other Igbo Tales* in 1947. Ilesami Press began in 1955 and the largely Igbo Verity Press of Onitsha in 1957. Between 1958 and 1962, Onibonoje Press, the African University Press, the African Educational Press, and John West Publications were started. After the end of the civil war, some "more purposeful and committed" (Apeji, p. 211) publishing companies came into being, including Fourth Dimension, Spectrum Books, Flora Nwapa's Tana Press, and Ken Saro-Wiwa's Saros International.

The social status of writers in Nigeria is high. Literacy rates are low, so writers are not necessarily known outside of the educated classes, but within this group,

> [t]he writer enjoys considerable social standing; beyond it he gets nothing but passive recognition . . . he must get on to the popular bandwagon. One reason . . . market literature is more widely read than the polished English novels of the Heinemann series is precisely because the latter do not fully communicate. A writer must meet with his readers in a common environment. (Kotei, p. 483)

A look at the background of the growth of a popular postwar literature in Nigeria is important in understanding Saro-Wiwa's own publications, particularly those based on *Basi and Company*. Onitsha market literature of the 1950s is an example of remarkable success in popular communication. The Nigerian reading public devoured these titles: "It was a phenomenon of literary profusion without comparison anywhere in Africa, before or since" (Kotei, p. 481). Many of the entrepreneurs wrote romances and exam cram-books and also were self-publishers and distributors. There were an increasing number of literate Nigerian entrepreneurs with money in their pockets and a growing level of literacy in the general population.

> Among the most devoted readers of the pamphlet literature must be listed grammar and elementary school boys and girls, lower level office workers and journalists, primary school teachers, traders, mechanics, taxi-drivers, farmers and new literates who attend adult education classes and evening school. (Obiechena, p. 220)

To appeal to this group, the books were simply written, short, and cheap. The newly literate and the less educated were the consumers.

There is a tendency to discount or ridicule some of these productions, which make no pretension to literary merit. Titles such as *Money Hard to Get But Easy to Spend* and *Drunkards Believe Bar Is Heaven* are easy to mock, until the Western reader considers the prevalence of similar self-help books, particularly IDG Publishing's ubiquitous "Dummies" series. Newly literate readers, however, and those concerned with mobility in a competitive society are not as critical. The problems of reaching and teaching this group were dealt with admirably in this spontaneous eruption of publishing. Saro-Wiwa's *Mr. B.* series for children, taken directly from his television series, follows the format of these chapbooks. Their aims—

to entertain, instruct, and conclude with a suitable moral—would be familiar to all those Nigerians who had been exposed to Onitsha market literature. Saro-Wiwa was following a mass-market literary tradition and putting his own imprint on it. He was taking advantage of the exposure given to Basi and friends in his popular television show. It is little wonder that Saro-Wiwa's children's titles have consistently outsold his adult works. As a means of increasing reading and literacy levels within Nigeria, his works and his marketing methods are admirable.

THE PRODUCTION OF *BASI AND COMPANY*

Saro-Wiwa's entrepreneurial spirit and the great enthusiasm he brought to everything he undertook shows up clearly in his report of the development and production of the television show *Basi and Company*. In a chapter of his unpublished autobiography, written in 1990, Saro-Wiwa writes in detail about his involvement in television. In 1984, Victoria Ezeokoli, a friend from university days, asked Saro-Wiwa to produce a script she had written for the Nigerian Television Authority (NTA). At that same time, the PEC Repertory Theatre, J. P. Clark's (now, Clark-Bekederemo) new professional drama outfit, had just videotaped a production of *The Transistor Radio*. These two events inspired Saro-Wiwa to write five scripts with Basi as a central character. Saro-Wiwa had two meetings with British playwright Victor Pemberton for script advice and in April 1985 signed a contract with the NTA to produce a comedy series. Saro-Wiwa was enthusiastic and energetic, but the pace was demanding, even for him. He reports that

> the prospect of writing a script a week was not exciting; of the first fifty
> episodes, I wrote forty-six. After that, three young men associated with the
> series wrote sixty of the remaining one hundred episodes. I wrote eighty
> of the scripts myself and edited most of the others. To the end of the show,
> several young hopeful Nigerians sent in scripts which I considered carefully before accepting. (Saro-Wiwa, "A Nigerian Television Sitcom")

Zulu Adigwe wrote music for the show, later released as the album *Mr. B Hits the Million*. The show was recorded before a paid live audience: "To the very last, we were unable to make them laugh spontaneously. This was probably because they did not catch the humour in the English language easily" (Saro-Wiwa, "A Nigerian Television Sitcom").

Saro-Wiwa was, by necessity, heavily involved in coming up with money and sponsorship for the show. Nigerian banks would not loan for the purposes of television production, and Saros International Limited helped underwrite the show when it was without sponsors. Saro-Wiwa says that he lost more than one million naira as a result (Saro-Wiwa, "A

Nigerian Television Sitcom"). Marketing the show meant having an office and staff in Lagos. Because *Basi* was an independent production, Saro-Wiwa had to sell the show to an advertiser and buy air-time from the NTA. Several entities advertised for part of the show's run. These included Ibru Organization, a Nigerian business enterprise; Guinness Beer; the presidency; and the Directorate for Mass Mobilization, Social Justice, and Economic Recovery (the latter during the period that Ken Saro-Wiwa was the director of this government organization). In the end, a steep rise in the air-time charges of the NTA and a failing national economy drove away possible advertisers and meant the end of the show. Out of the television show came a number of children's novels, *Mr. B, Mr. B Again, Mr. B Is Dead* and for even younger readers, the Adventures of Mr. B Series. The first four episodes of the show came out in book form as *Basi and Company: Four Television Plays.*

AFTER *BASI AND COMPANY*

Basi and Company went off the air in October 1990, at the time when Saro-Wiwa was becoming more involved in environmental issues and political causes. Among other things, these issues caused him to reevaluate the purpose and value of literature in a developing country such as Nigeria. Previously, in 1989, he writes in response to Graham Hough's review of *A Forest of Flowers:*

> I have found that, basically, I write to tell a good story. And is that responsible enough? I think so. Because the moment we begin to speak of "the race" and of "informing the rest of the world about Africa," we, strictly speaking, move into the province of sociology and "the political history of a hundred tribes and a dozen emergent nations." And that, to my mind, is strictly not the responsibility of literature. Literature is a mirror held up to society; it is the direct expression of feelings (the writer's) overwhelming responsibility and the test of his ability is to validate his concerns for all time to different readers. (Saro-Wiwa, "The Writer")

By 1994 however, Saro-Wiwa's views had changed dramatically. In a filmed interview shortly before his second arrest, Saro-Wiwa says of writers in Western countries:

> [These] writers are not involved in what I am doing. [They] write to entertain. They raise the question of the angst of the individual. But for a writer in my position, you can't go into that. Literature has to be combative. . . . My writing has benefited by my perception of politics. My politics have benefited by the fact I am a writer. (*Ken Saro-Wiwa: An African Martyr*)

His son, Ken Wiwa, says that Ken Saro-Wiwa was more concerned with the message that his books contained than their literary qualities. He was concerned that he "might not be read by the people who should be reading his stories, so he didn't actually worry about the commercial aspects of the books. He self-published at a loss, and was quite happy to absorb the loss, just so long that the message was there for posterity" (Wiwa, August 1997).

SAROS INTERNATIONAL IN THE 1990s

In early 1993 the Nigerian "publishing industry went into almost a coma" (Nwankwo, "Nigeria: Publishing," p. 5). Between June and August, the naira's exchange rate dropped as much as 50 percent, which resulted in a shortage of book paper. Some paper, including newsprint, disappeared from the market. Distribution was affected because most booksellers had closed up shop. By October, the crisis was over, but prices had not come down: "Publishing in the situation of the Nigerian crisis faces the key problem of logistics: procurement problems, production schedules, hedging stock lists, reluctant transporters, and uncertain markets" (p. 5). Hans Zell also describes the 1990s as a time of worsening crisis. Factors include the economic recession, foreign exchange levels, government funding for textbooks and libraries, and the collapse of the Nigerian currency. In 1995 the Nigerian naira was worth thirty-eight times more against the U.S. dollar than it was in 1983 (Zell, "Publishing," p. 366).

African publishers have faced this reality in a number of creative ways, adopting pan-African and collective approaches to help cope. The African Publishers Network (APNET), formed in 1992, gives a unified voice to African publishers and is developing a training program. A general council of one representative from each participating country governs it. In addition to training and communication, its principal goal is lobbying, an example being efforts to persuade institutions such as the World Bank to move toward more support of indigenous publishing and private sector initiatives. The success of the Zimbabwe Book Fair is another sign of the growing strength of the still fragile publishing network. There is also the Noma Award for Publishing in Africa, established in 1979 and now Africa's premier book prize (Zell "Publishing," p. 370). There are now close to 300 indigenous publishers in Africa with sizable lists, as well as a number of smaller indigenous presses.

The African Books Collective plays a vital role in the growth and dissemination of African titles from African publishers, both in the West and within Africa. ABC carries more than 1,000 African titles, and the hard currency that has flowed back to African publishers and writers as a result has helped these publishers to survive (p. 371).

> [The] ABC initiative represents a significant reversal of historical trading
> directions. It is actively promoting and disseminating African scholar-
> ship, African writing, and African cultural identity, and also contributing
> towards a better understanding of the ethnic, cultural and religious diver-
> sity of Africa. (Jay, "The Role," n.p.).

Seventeen founding publishers own the African Books Collective. ABC, a
self-help initiative, the brainchild of Hans Zell, was established in 1990 to
help African publishers distribute their books outside Africa. ABC is non-
profit and remits 65 percent of net income to the member publishers. According to Mary Jay, the managing director of ABC's office in the Jam
Factory, a building close to Blackwell's in Oxford,

> One of the roles of ABC is rights facilitation. ABC initiates and facili-
> tates rights deals, and can offer advice and guidance on proposed con-
> tracts. ABC wishes to expand this aspect of its work, while stressing that
> there is not a lot of money to be made in rights facilitation. (Jay, "The
> Role," n.p.)

ABC is the distributor of those Saros titles for which foreign rights have
not been arranged. As Table 9.2 shows, Ken Saro-Wiwa's sales through
ABC were not high.

These sales figures represent a six-year period through December
1997 for Saro-Wiwa's books published by ABC only. It does not include
the Longman titles or the Penguin Books titles published posthumously.
Outside Nigeria, *Sozaboy, A Forest of Flowers, A Month and a Day,* and
Lemona's Tale are Saro-Wiwa's most successful adult titles. Unfortunately,
it has proved impossible to retrieve sales figures within Nigeria. Ken
Wiwa reports:

> Not many people want to be seen with his books. They still sell, but obvi-
> ously anyone caught selling these books are liable to be visited by security
> services. My father's businesses have been almost completely destroyed,
> for they wanted to destroy him financially as well as politically. The office
> is still running, but people are scared to go in, and it's a very restricted ser-
> vice. It is almost impossible to get information in and out of Nigeria and to
> contact the offices. Communication is terrible, you can spend days trying
> to get an international line to talk to someone. As well, there were raids,
> and many documents were seized and burned. (Wiwa, August 1997)

The Saros self-published books suffer in comparison with the Longman and Penguin titles, content aside. The quality of paper is low, the illustrations poor, and the binding of low quality. They lack the physical
polish and quality that would make them appealing to a Western market.
There is a dramatic difference in quality between editions of the same
work published in Port Harcourt and those published in Britain.

Table 9.2   Saro-Wiwa's Publishing Titles' Sales Through ABC

Title	Date Received	Total Stock	Sales to Dec. 1997
Adaku & Other Stories	Dec. 1991	320	239
Approaches to the African Novel			
(Charles E. Nnolim)	Sep. 1992	214	203
Basi and Company: Four Television Plays[a]	Apr. 1992	212	151
Basi and Company: A Modern African Folktale[a]		592	551
A Bride for Mr. B[a]	May 1994	200	146
Critical Essays on Ken Saro-Wiwa's Sozaboy			
(Charles E. Nnolim)	Sep. 1992	209	168
A Forest of Flowers	Dec. 1991	330	71
Four Farcical Plays	Dec. 1991	275	108
Genocide in Nigeria: The Ogoni Tragedy	Dec. 1992	199	199
A Letter to Linda & Other Poems			
(Funso Aiyejina)	Dec. 1991	180	86
A Message from the Madhouse			
(Maxwell Nwagboso)	Feb. 1992	202	171
Mr. B.[a]	Dec. 1991	379	379
Mr. B. Again[a]	Dec. 1991	509	363
Mr. B. Goes to Lagos[a]	Dec. 1991	381	366
Mr. B. Is Dead[a]	Dec. 1991	507	387
Mr. B.'s Mattress[a]	May 1994	100	97
Nigeria: The Brink of Disaster	Dec. 1991	200	200
On a Darkling Plain	Dec. 1991	272	106
Pita Dumbrok's Prison	Feb. 1992	360	272
Prisoners of Jebs	Dec. 1991	441	315
Segi Finds the Radio[a]	Dec. 1991	513	364
A Shipload of Rice[a]	Dec. 1991	416	416
Similia: Essays on an Anomic Nigeria	Dec. 1991	200	135
The Singing Anthill: Ogoni Folktales	Dec. 1991	697	540
Songs in a Time of War	Dec. 1991	596	423
Sozaboy: A Novel in Rotten English	Dec. 1991	582	94
The Transistor Radio[a]	Dec. 1991	300	300
Total Sales			
Fiction/poetry/drama	1,775		
Children's titles	3,220		
Political writings	1,227		
Through ABC of Saro-Wiwa's titles:	6,222		

Source: ABC. I wish to thank Ken Wiwa for giving permission for its release.
Note: a. Children's titles.

The children's books are written with a Nigerian audience in mind. The cover of *A Shipload of Rice* says "adapted . . . from the popular TV series *Basi and Company.*" At the end are questions for schoolchildren to answer: "Is the story of the tortoise interesting? Why or why not?" Clearly the concern is for sales within Nigeria and, as has been stated elsewhere by both Saro-Wiwa and his son, for adoption by the schools.

SARO-WIWA'S ESTATE AND HERITAGE

Saro-Wiwa's heirs sold the foreign rights for *Lemona's Tale* and *A Month and a Day* to Penguin. This was done through Ed Victor, a well-known literary agent. However, he was not interested in the remainder of the literary property, and Maggie Noach was hired as the new literary agent. Her experience with foreign rights is not large, and there have been no sales of rights (Wiwa, August 1997). In the summer of 1997, Penguin Books arranged translation rights for eleven countries for *A Month and a Day*.

Saros International Limited, the parent company of Saros Publishing, was involved in trading, book publishing, and TV production and had extensive properties in Nigeria. However, Ken Saro-Wiwa will not be remembered as a publisher or a businessman. As a businessman, he was successful but not famous, and his publishing efforts were a vehicle for his writings. Ken Saro-Wiwa wanted recognition and a place in the company of educated and literary men; he wished to be accepted as a man of letters and a man of influence. He put an enormous amount of energy toward these ends in the last ten years of his life. Before he discovered the power of environmental causes, he aimed for personal achievement in writing and television. And as always, these went hand-in-hand with self- and business interests. His first successful literary venture, *The Transistor Radio*, a radio play he had written in the early 1970s, became the jumping-off point many years later for the successful TV series *Basi and Company* Saro-Wiwa recycled Basi a third and even a fourth time, turning TV scripts into children's stories and published plays. Other than in his final role as representative, spokesperson, and finally martyr for the cause of the Ogoni people and the environment of the Niger Delta, it is through *Basi and Company* that Ken Saro-Wiwa is best known in Nigeria.

He was incredibly energetic and ambitious. A product of a British public school education, he identified strongly not only with that tradition but with his Khana background:

> We had in our school, [in] Bori, a lesson dubbed "vernacular." It was in reality a session of folktale narration and we looked forward to it eagerly. Boys from different villages retold the tales they had heard in the moonlight story-telling sessions which were a normal part of village life. . . . My holidays were spent in the dance groups of the village of Bani where we practised at night after the farm-work of the day was done. (Saro-Wiwa, "Notes of a New Writer")

Folktales, tradition, and an exotic background could be drawn on when he chose. He maintained two households, one in Nigeria and the other in Epsom, Surrey. The five children of his first wife, Maria, were raised in

Britain, and he also maintained a role in Nigeria as eldest son of the head of an extended family of over sixty individuals.

Joop Berkhout, editor of Spectrum Books in Nigeria, knew Saro-Wiwa as an author-publisher and speaks of him as "a colourful character, outspoken and forceful" (Berkhout, August 1997). Berkhout spoke at length of the corruption in Nigeria: a fee to the government to be allowed to get in line for watered-down fuel, World Bank funding that sent academics abroad who would never return, and the "brown envelopes" that smooth the way for everything, even to get into the country as a visitor. Berkhout was not optimistic about Nigeria's publishing future: "The deterioration of the education system (only 65 percent of primary age children are in school, down from 95 percent), and the closure of universities, as well as the disappearance of reading materials are all contributing to a loss of bright young writers" (Berkhout, August 1997).

Saro-Wiwa is now best known for his promotion of environmental issues as pertaining to Shell. He did a truly amazing job of raising international consciousness and forcing Shell and the Nigerian government to take actions they would rather not have taken. His detractors portrayed him as being completely self-interested, wanting to become the president of a new Nigerian government, wanting to benefit his own tribe at the expense of other Nigerians, and wanting to enrich himself and his close relatives. All these criticisms are stilled in the face of his death. He was vital, energetic, complex, and finally, in the words of his oldest son, Ken Wiwa:

> He was obsessed by his cause. . . . Anyone less driven would have given up a long, long time ago. He was that kind of person; an obsessive personality who would drive a horse and coaches through whatever obstacles were placed in his path, to get his message across, even when he knew that he would probably die. (Wiwa, August 1997)

NOTES

I would like to acknowledge the assistance of Joop Berkhout, Mary Jay, and Ken Wiwa, son of the late Ken Saro-Wiwa, for their time and permission to interview them for this project. I would also like to thank Ken Wiwa, who, acting on behalf of his father's literary estate, made Saro-Wiwa's unpublished material available and gave permission to quote from it.

1. The Scottish writer Duncan McLean refers to his early publishing efforts in similar terms in the introduction to *ahead of its time* (Clocktower Press, 1997): "mostly it was because I'd come to a realisation that this was what publishing was really all about: not a commercial, money-making venture, but a cultural intervention" (p. xi). The tradition includes Virginia Woolf's Hogarth Press and, closer to home, the Nigerian novelist Flora Nwapa, who left Heinemann to set up Tana Press.

WORKS CITED

ABC Newsline. *The Newsletter from African Books Collective Ltd.* May 1997.

Adesanoye, Festus Agboola. *The Book in Nigeria: Some Current Issues.* Ibadan, Nigeria: Sam Bookman Educational and Communication Services (Publishing Consultants), 1995.

African Books Collective. *Your Questions and Answers.* Pamphlet. Oxford: African Books Collective Ltd., June 1997.

Akobo, D. I. "Acquisition of Library Resources under SFEM." In *Proceedings of the National Seminar on Strategies for Survival by Nigerian Academic and Research Libraries During Austere Times.* Ed. S. M. Lawania. Ibadan: November 1987: 87–91.

Altbach, Philip G. "Literary Colonialism: Books in the Third World." In *The Post-Colonial Studies Reader.* Ed. Bill Ashcroft, Gareth Griffiths, and Helen Tiffin. New York: Routledge, 1995: 485–490.

———. "Perspectives on Publishing in Africa." In *Readings on Publishing in Africa and the Third World.* Bellagio Studies in Publishing no. 1. Buffalo: Bellagio Publishing Network, 1993.

———. "Publishing in the Third World: Issues and Trends for the 21st Century." In *Publishing and Development in the Third World.* Ed. Philip G. Altbach. Sevenoaks, Kent: Bowker-Saur, 1993: 1–28.

Apeji. E. A. "Book Production in Nigeria: An Historical Survey." *Information Development* 12, no. 4 (December 1996): 210–213.

Berkhout, Joop. Personal interview. Oxford, August 1997.

Boyd, William. "Death of a Writer." *The New Yorker* 71 (27 November 1995): 51–55.

Daniels, Anthony. "A Good Man in Africa." *National Review* 47, no. 13 (10 July 1995): 51–52.

Gedin, Per I. "Cultural Pride: The Necessity of Indigenous Publishing." In *Publishing and Development in the Third World.* Ed. Philip G. Altbach. Sevenoaks, Kent: Bowker-Saur, 1993: 41–52.

Graham, Gordon. "Multinationals and Third World Publishing: Publishing in the Third World: Issues and Trends for the 21st Century." In *Publishing and Development in the Third World.* Ed. Philip G. Altbach. Sevenoaks, Kent: Bowker-Saur, 1993: 29–41.

Ifaturoti, Ademdamola A. "The Information Age and African Publishing." *Bellagio Publishing Network Newsletter.* Oxford: Bellagio Publishing Network Secretariat no. 21 (December 1997): 12–14.

Ike, Chukwuemeka. *How to Become a Published Writer.* Ibadan: Heinemann Educational Books Nigeria PLC, 1991.

Jay, Mary. "African Books Collective: Its Contribution to African Publishing." In *Africa Bibliography 1992: Works on Africa Published During 1992.* Edinburgh: Edinburgh University Press, 1994.

———. Personal interview. Oxford, August 1997.

———. "The Role and Experience of African Books Collective in Facilitating Rights Sales and Coeditions of the African Books." Paper presented at the First African Rights Conference. Indaba, Harare, August 1994.

Ken Saro-Wiwa: An African Martyr. Films for the Humanities and Sciences. Princeton, N.J.: Millennium Movies Production, 1996.

Kotei, S. I. A. "The Book Today in Africa." In *The Post-Colonial Studies Reader.* Ed. Bill Ashcroft, Gareth Griffiths, and Helen Tiffin. New York: Routledge, 1995: 480–484.

Mezu, S. Okechukwu. *Ken Saro-Wiwa: The Life and Times.* Ed. S. Okechukwu Mezu. Randallstown, Md.: Black Academy Press, 1996.

Nwankwo, Victor. "Nigeria: International Book Publishing: An Encyclopedia." Ed. Philip G. Altbach and Edith S. Hoshino. *Garland Reference Library of the Humanities.* Vol. 1562. New York: Garland Publishing, 1995: 396–415.

———. "Nigeria: Publishing in a Situation of Crisis." *Bellagio Publishing Network Newsletter.* Oxford: Bellagio Publishing Network Secretariat no. 8 (December 1993).

———. "Publishing in Nigeria Today." In *Publishing and Development in the Third World.* Ed. Philip G. Altbach. Sevenoaks, England: Bowker-Saur, 1993: 151–168.

Obiagwu, Odilinye. "Let's Launch This Book." *Times International* (26 December 1988): 34.

Obiechena, Emmanuel. "Literature for the Masses: An Analytical Study of Popular Pamphleteering in Nigeria." Nwankwo-Ifejika and Co., 1971. Excerpted in *Twentieth Century Literary Criticism.* Vol. 30. Detroit: Gale, 1989: 219–227.

Ola, Boye. "At the Real Launch." *National Concord* (April 1990): 3.

Rathgeber, Eva M. "African Book Publishing: Lessons from the 1980s." In *Publishing and Development in the Third World.* Ed. Philip G. Altbach. Sevenoaks, Kent: Bowker-Saur, 1993: 77–99.

Saro-Wiwa, Ken. "Curriculum Vitae." From the unpublished manuscript, "Notes of a New Writer." 1994.

———. "The Hazards of Writing." Address delivered to the Ikoro Creative Association, Seat of Wisdom Seminary, Oworri, 1992.

———. "'The Language of African Literature': A Writer's Testimony." From the unpublished manuscript, "Notes of a New Writer." N.d.

———. *A Month and a Day: A Detention Diary.* London: Penguin Books, 1995.

———. "A Nigerian Television Sit-Com: Basi and Company." From the unpublished manuscript, "Notes of a New Writer." September 1990.

———. "Notes of a New Writer." Address delivered to the Creative Writing Class of Lagos State University, May 1988.

———. "Notes of a Reluctant Publisher." *The African Book Publishing Record* 22 (1996): 257–259.

———. "The Writer and His Audience." From the unpublished manuscript, "Notes of a New Writer." May 1989.

Saros International Publishers Titles. Original stock lists as supplied by the African Book Collective. Oxford, January 1998.

Thomas, E. Akin. "A Book Subsidy Scheme for Nigeria: The Way Forward." In *Making Books Affordable and Available.* Ed. Ezenwa-Ohaeto. Awka, Anambra State, Nigeria: Nigerian Book Foundation, 1995: 25–39.

Wiwa, Ken. Personal interview, London, August 1997.

———. Telephone interview, October 1997.

Zell, Hans M. "Africa: The Neglected Continent." In *Publishing and Development in the Third World.* Ed. Philip G. Altbach. Sevenoaks, Kent: Bowker-Saur, 1993: 65–75.

———. "African Publishing: Constraints and Challenges and the Experience of the African Books Collective." In *Publishing and Development in the Third World.* Ed. Philip G. Altbach. Sevenoaks, England: Bowker-Saur, 1993: 101–117.

———. "Publishing in Africa." In *International Book Publishing: An Encyclopedia.* Ed. Philip G. Altbach and Edith S. Hoshino. Garland Reference Library of the Humanities. Vol. 1562. New York: Garland Publishing, 1995: 366–373.

PART 4

Popular Media

10

The Children's Series

John LeBlanc

Children's literature in Africa is not merely a specialty genre but is integral to the productive development of the emerging African nations, so integral that Chinua Achebe "called on all serious African writers to write wholesome books for children" (Osa, p. xxiii). African children are not born into stable, fully developed societies but societies only beginning to define themselves in relation to those past, present, and future cultures that have had and will have an impact on their identity. In particular, African children face the "burden of African history" (p. xxvi), a history that has not always nurtured personal or social development. Hence, children's literature in Africa plays a key role not just in providing African children with reading material but in helping them to deal with the specific problems of identity formation generated by the African context. At the same time, African children's literature is not just about African children but also about African society as a whole. Consequently, this literature focuses not only on the children themselves but also on the wider society, for the fate of the children depends to a large extent on the development of a healthy society. In Africa today, writers of children's literature must deal with, to some extent at least, the social issues that will have a profound effect on children's lives. Therefore, African children's literature especially must not be marginalized but situated near the center of social debate.

The children's literature of Nigerian writer Ken Saro-Wiwa in particular exploits this nexus of children's literature and wider social issues. In doing so, Saro-Wiwa deals in interesting ways with the traditions of writing for children in Africa. Of all the emerging African nations, Saro-Wiwa's native Nigeria has been the most prolific in the production of children's literature, providing him with a rich literary background to draw from and to transform as he tackles the problems facing both Nigerian youth and Nigerian society as a whole. At the center of Nigerian writing for children stands Cyprian Ekwensi, who, although lamenting the passing of oral storytelling among Nigerian families, nevertheless called for "'books [to] be produced to replace the family gathering under the moonlit tree'" (quoted in Osa, p. 1). Saro-Wiwa has answered Ekwensi's call by producing a series of children's books focused on a character named Basi, but he has also gone a step further in integrating his children's books with the use of other, more contemporary media, such as television, to fulfill his purpose. This tactic has helped him not only to reach more children but also to develop a more integrated audience so that both young and old can participate together in the "reading" process. Hence, the stories focusing on Basi become a site where children's interests and those of the wider family and society can meet. At the same time, Saro-Wiwa has transformed the traditional storytelling situation around the moonlit tree into more contemporary configurations, such as around the television, without sacrificing the values of the older format.

Saro-Wiwa's revision of "children's" literature also deals in interesting ways with the genre's themes, forms, and techniques. Of particular importance is Saro-Wiwa's relation to the oral storytelling format that is typical of the writings of Ekwensi and others in the genre. Whereas other writers meticulously recreate the oral storytelling situation in their novels and stories, Saro-Wiwa relies on a more contemporary format of simply immersing the reader in the story itself, as in much of television narrative and modern fiction. He does not wish to abandon the older format, but rather to update it. He retains other, more crucial elements of oral storytelling but shapes his narrative according to current story forms. Instead of beginning by describing an oral storytelling situation, with children gathered around a storyteller, as Ekwensi often does, Saro-Wiwa merely strings together a series of incidents involving his characters, establishing an episodic structure that allows for flexibility in delivering his message, since the incidents are easily translated into other forms such as theater and television. Saro-Wiwa's aim is not to create a formally sophisticated modernist narrative but to employ narrative according to his didactic purpose. In fact, in taking this approach, Saro-Wiwa is only following the general tendency of African narrative to be "a far more public and socially and politically oriented literary form than its European counterpart" (Osa, p. xxvi).

Along with his innovative approach of transforming established children's narrative structures, Saro-Wiwa also reworks many of the traditional concerns present in African and Nigerian children's literature. For example, he does not concern himself with the actual lives of the children themselves and instead focuses on the key issues concerning children in Nigerian society. Instead of directly treating "the central theme of African children's and youth literature [which] is the rites of passage or initiation into adulthood" (Osa, p. xxvi), he focuses on adults almost exclusively, concerning himself with the world that the children will inherit more than the narrow world of the children themselves. Instead of writing traditional narratives of development (such as the bildungsroman), he focuses not on the individual but on society as a whole, suggesting that change must be initiated not so much within individuals as among them in a communal setting. Saro-Wiwa realizes that children will not have a chance to develop as healthy individuals unless a nurturing society is created around them.

Ultimately, then, Saro-Wiwa treats the same issues as other writers of African children's literature, but from a different perspective, that of the wider society. Like other writers of African children's literature, he concerns himself with "social malaise" and with "feud[ing] and vengeance" and like them he "extols the qualities of courage and loyalty" (Osa, p. 22). He also follows Ekwensi's tendency to "focus . . . on Nigerian society" (p. 22) and to replace the European novel's Dickensian tendency toward "solid chunks of description" with a more "functional description" (Ekwensi, quoted in Osa, p. 24). Other key elements in African children's literature that Saro-Wiwa reiterates include the "traditional African values" of "honesty, hard work, and integrity" in response to the disturbing increase in criminal activity among youth (Osa, p. 139). Yet Saro-Wiwa, cunningly, does not directly address children in relation to these problems. Instead of dramatizing youth crime and preaching at children, he shows these undesirable behaviors being practiced by foolish adults. Laughing at the adults, the children will reject these behaviors as beneath them.

In addition, the specific problem that Saro-Wiwa addresses in his children's literature is one he shares with other contemporary Nigerian writers, such as Buchi Emecheta—that of "the destructive power of the love of money and material possession" (Osa, p. 66). Like these other writers, he feels that behind this obsession with money lies "the structural weaknesses of African political and civil society" and a resulting "fear of impotence" in the African individual (Osa, pp. 66–67). Because Nigerian society is largely dysfunctional, Nigerians feel that they must situate themselves above society by making a lot of money. Tragically, this response only further weakens the social fabric by promoting rampant individualism. Saro-Wiwa tries to show the folly of this individualist approach by making fun of its practitioners and their methods. This mockery is situated in and around the figure of Basi, who appears in most of Saro-Wiwa's literature for children and who is usually at the center of the action. Throughout these works, Basi brings about this mockery in a manner similar to that of a trickster figure. Therefore, his character can best be understood as a manifestation of the trickster archetype, for the logic of the trickster lies at the heart of Saro-Wiwa's approach to literature for children in Africa.

The trickster figure can be found in many cultures throughout the world and primarily functions as an intermediary between various aspects of a culture, patrolling the borderlands where different identities and values intersect. Citing Victor Turner, Houston A. Baker Jr. describes the trickster as a figure of "'liminality'—that 'betwixt and between' phase of rites of passage when an individual has left one fixed social status but has not yet been incorporated into another" (Baker, p. 183). Consequently, tricksters are often associated with sites of transition (such as crossroads and entrances) (Pelton, p. 128), managing movements from one place to another as well as from one stage of human life to another. Given these attributes, the trickster is a very effective device for Saro-Wiwa's focus on the transitional nature of both Nigerian society and the identities of individuals who inhabit it. If, as in children, Nigerian society is undergoing a crucial stage in the development of its identity, then the presence of the trickster figure will not only highlight the transitional nature of that stage but will help to move it in a positive direction.

As a manager of transition, the trickster "oversees the movement from order to disorder to diagnosis to new order" (Pelton, p. 135), encompassing the seemingly opposed practices of destruction and creation (emphasized by his or her dual nature). The old order is broken down, and a new, more powerful one is put in its place, one that is "culturally benevolent" as well as an "amoral and nonlogical" expression of the "uncontrollable rhythms of nature" (Baker, p. 184). These aspects of the trickster are most evident in its tendency to cause trouble, seek vengeance, and take particular delight in "sowing confusion" (Pelton, pp. 130–131). Yet his vengeance is playful, exercised only to reconcile gods and humans so that divine knowledge might result in propitious action on earth (Pelton, p. 137). As troublemaker, he is an "instigator," but "more deeply, he is [a] revealer" (p. 140) who causes trouble only to show that this trouble already exists and needs to be exposed so it can be transformed. Hence, the trickster's role is mainly a social one, concerned less with individual growth (although this kind of growth may be a by-product) than with the wider concerns of race, gender, and class.

As intermediary, the trickster, while engaged in his destructive mischief making, ultimately attempts to integrate antagonistic forces in order to achieve a balance or harmony that will restore health to the community. By making Basi, the central character of his children's literature, a trickster figure, Saro-Wiwa has not only created a delightful version of this stock character often found in writing for children but has also employed a powerful force toward the reformation of Nigerian society. In order to achieve this gaol, Saro-Wiwa has modeled Basi on the Yoruba trickster Eshu, "the never-ending disturb[er] of social peace" (Pelton, p. 18), one of four prominent West African tricksters along with Anansi, the buffoon;

Legba, the libertine and cunning linguist; and Ogo-Yurugu, the solitary outsider. Ogoni by birth, Saro-Wiwa has chosen the trickster from the Yoruba pantheon as Basi's forbear because Yoruba mythology is more widely recognized in Nigeria, Africa, and the world beyond. Other writers, such as Hubert Ogunde and Wole Soyinka, have chosen Yoruba mythology for the same reason. When Soyinka speaks of the African world, he discusses it in Yoruban terms. Saro-Wiwa, like Soyinka, sees the more universally understood Yoruban mythology as ideal for addressing his broad concerns about Nigerian society that also reflect on Africa as a whole.

Eshu, the Yoruba trickster, is a suitable model for Basi also because his specific role is to transform society and expand it in a process that will "challenge, break open, and enlarge every possible structure and relationship" (Pelton, p. 161). Like Legba, he possesses phallic energy, yet his desire is not so much sexual but the more general "passion for what lies outside one's grasp which the Greeks saw in some sense as the sovereign mover of human life" (p. 161). Consequently, Eshu ultimately focuses less on the well-being of the individual and more on that of the society as a whole. In addition, this well-being is centered not so much on material wealth but on ideals of growth, progress, and enrichment realized by a spirit of inclusiveness and accommodation.

Eshu's work of transforming and expanding has as its home the marketplace, located near its obverse, the palace, where the "high seriousness" of the gods and the affairs of state are "humanized in the tension, excitement, caginess, and sheer fun" of communal activity (Pelton, p. 161). In such a place, potentially antagonistic aspects (the human and the divine, the individual and the social) can be mediated. Yoruba marketplaces often contain a shrine to Eshu, acknowledging his governance of this realm (pp. 158–159). The marketplace, with its emphasis on exchange, is the ideal site for Eshu's mediations, where he "brings to the surface hidden conflict" and unifies "together in true mutuality the relationships that forgetfulness, ignorance, passion, malice, or sheer routine have severed" (p. 138). Exchange also lies at the heart of the sacrifice principle so central to Eshu, for transformation requires the exchange of "the death of the victim for increased life for its offerer" (p. 146). Consequently, Eshu's milieu as well as his nature is well suited for Saro-Wiwa's project of social transformation.

Saro-Wiwa's Basi signals his status as an Eshu figure in many ways. His name suggests Obasin, a Yoruba god for whom Eshu acts as a messenger and who is associated with "terrifying disturbances in the sky" (Thompson, *Face,* p. 175), echoing the disturbances in the social framework instigated by Eshu. Traditionally, Eshu's colors are red and black (Murphy, p. 42), reflecting his dual characteristics of passion and mischief. Furthermore, the novel *Mr. B* (the first of the Basi stories for children to be published and the one that I treat as the ur-text for the Basi series as a whole) and other Basi narratives depict him in the cover picture as having a red singlet and black pants. He is also wearing a blue cap; blue suggests the sky and spirituality, evoking Eshu's connection, as messenger, to the gods and his emphasis on the need for humans to maintain contact with their spiritual guides. Blue also suggests water, whose coolness acts as a force for healing, reflecting Eshu's concern with restoring well-being. In the novel itself, Basi first appears wearing a blue jacket, covering a red singlet (Saro-Wiwa, *Mr. B,* p. 4), further emphasizing his healing function. In Africa, objects associated with Eshu, such as cone-shaped figures, are often anointed with medicine and indigo (Thompson, *Face,* p. 174).

The cover picture also depicts Basi among a group of children and pointing to the sky. The scene refers to an incident in the novel in which Basi urges the children to study hard for their examinations, after which he will accompany them to the moon. The sky, in much of African mythology, is known as God's home and the moon is sometimes considered as God's left eye (Mbiti, p. 68) or, more generally, as one of many manifestations of God (p. 72). As an Eshu figure, Basi, in this incident, is pointing out his connection with the gods (as their messenger) as well as his purpose of strengthening the connection between gods and human beings, a connection often plagued by disrepair and neglect in present-day Nigerian society. The moon is also associated with rituals asking God for prosperity, one of the main concerns of both Basi and Eshu. In addition, children themselves are often associated, in African mythology generally, with the notion of spirituality in that they ensure immortality (Mbiti, p. 157).

Furthermore, the cover picture's focus on learning points to Eshu's and Basi's roles as disseminators of the knowledge of the gods. New World versions of Eshu link him with St. Antony of Padua, a Catholic saint who, like Eshu, is a gifted speaker and messenger of God. In addition, the iconography of St. Antony usually depicts him reading a book. Basi reflects this emphasis on learning in his concern for the children's studies and in his general emphasis on knowledge itself. One of Eshu's major roles is to get people to educate themselves and, especially, to learn the knowledge that the gods make available to them. St. Antony, besides being the "greatest preacher of the middle ages and one of the finest orators of all time" (Duchet-Suchaux et al., p. 38), has also been adopted as a patron saint by the poor as well as an aid in the recovery of lost articles and the restoration of health. Basi and Eshu echo these concerns in their focus on prosperity and especially in their focus on progress from rags to riches.

Prosperity, in the more narrow sense of wealth and in the larger sense of well-being, is associated in the Eshu mythology with rain, seen in Yoruba culture as a positive sign and often associated with money, as in the "cowrie money-cape" known as "rain of money" that is placed on many of the symbols of Eshu (Thompson, *Face,* p. 178). Furthermore,

Eshu is sometimes nicknamed "money" because of his ability at tricking the rich into giving money to the poor. In *Mr. B*, Basi's central preoccupation is to experience a sudden windfall and become a millionaire. *Mr. B* opens during the rainy season with a heavy rainstorm, reinforcing the connection between Basi, Eshu, and Obasin, the god of fierce storms. Like water, so precious a commodity in African society, Basi can be identified as a life-giving force whose arrival signals a return to prosperity in every sense of the word, even if his methods for achieving that prosperity, given his identity as a trickster, are tortuous, to say the least.

As a figure of transition, Eshu lives on the margins of society (Murphy, p. 133). He is the typical outcast and wanderer, and Basi, a loner without family, mirrors these qualities. *Mr. B* opens with his journeys back and forth between Lagos and Ibadan, journeys that are not planned but result from Basi's taking refuge in the back of a truck during a rainstorm. Basi makes his home wherever he happens to find himself, and his situation and location can change abruptly. Waking up to find himself in Ibadan, Basi describes the sudden transformation as "magic" (Saro-Wiwa, *Mr. B*, p. 2), emphasizing not only Eshu's swiftness but also his fluidity, reinforcing again his connection with sudden and violent rainstorms. Like Eshu, Basi acts suddenly, unpredictably, and powerfully (Murphy, p. 72). As a wanderer, he is not aimless but merely someone who covers a lot of territory and entangles himself in many situations, quickly moving from one situation to the next as he carries out his transformative work.

As a figure of power and swiftness, Eshu is associated with strong and intricate rhythms and a piercing and lofty pitch (Murphy, pp. 94–95). An intense figure, he also possesses a voracious appetite for both sex and food. Essentially, he is characterized by orality: he swallows up all that surrounds him (Thompson, *Flash*, p. 32). Basi exhibits a prodigious appetite throughout his adventures, beginning in *Mr. B* with his tricking of Mama Badejo, the food seller (Saro-Wiwa, *Mr. B*, pp. 5–7). During this incident, his large appetite desires Western foods, such as cereals and eggs and wine. Truly, Basi's appetite knows no bounds and it is not limited to food alone, given his equally strong desire for wealth. On one level, such an appetite could be seen simply as selfish greed, but for an Eshu figure, such greed merely reflects a desire for growth and transformation on both the individual and social levels. For example, this appetite can be seen as the expression of Nigerian society's desire to go beyond colonial status and experience some of the riches of the wider world. In addition, his greed is balanced by generosity towards others (Thompson, *Flash*, p. 19). Significantly, Basi does not exhibit much sexual energy along with his appetite for food. That manifestation is usually left to Eshu's counterpart, Legba. Also, Eshu is supposed to channel his energy and, in particular, his love of feasting into praise for God rather than merely into triumph over others (p. 18). His intensity is also balanced by his propensity for calmness (suggested by his association with cool water through the color blue) and his ability to assuage anger and strife that can bring misfortune (Thompson, *Face,* p. 176). Basi shares Eshu's dual nature since Basi can be seen as a scoundrel who, in exhibiting some of the trickster's worst behaviors, mirrors some of the worst aspects of Nigerian society. Yet on a deeper level, Basi can be seen as a manifestation of Eshu's healing power. To what degree Saro-Wiwa exploits this more positive side of Eshu is the central question that must be confronted in a reading of *Mr. B* and the other Basi narratives.

Associated with children, Basi, like Eshu, often behaves in a childlike manner. At times, Eshu acts like an irresponsible little boy (Thompson, *Face,* p. 177; Murphy, pp. 46, 72). Yet he is also a source of wisdom and a warrior (Murphy, p. 46). This contradiction is typical of the trickster figure and culminates in the figure's purposeful mischievousness (Murphy, p. 14). Basi's mischief in *Mr. B* begins when he tricks the conductor into letting him ride the bus for free and Mama Badejo into giving him food without paying. Yet Eshu's mischief is supposed to be tempered by kindness toward others (Thompson, *Flash,* p. 19). Any kindness on Basi's part in *Mr. B,* such as his friendliness toward Alali, seems corrupted by Basi's own self-interest, but Basi has no desire to completely defeat and ruin others. He always seems to be bringing others together, if only to promote one of his schemes. *Mr. B* does not end with a positive transformation of its characters. It seems as if they will continue to exhibit their greedy tendencies. Yet Basi has made these tendencies more transparent, not only to the reader but also to Segi, the youngest and most vulnerable of the Adetola Street characters who is learning about the ways of the world. In any case, as a trickster figure, Basi can achieve good only indirectly through his disruptive mischief.

Paradoxically, it is the trickster's amorality that points to his concern with moral issues (Thompson, *Face,* p. 178) and his role of punishing those who behave immorally (Thompson, *Flash,* p. 18). He especially punishes those who forget to be humble and to acknowledge the gods and those who forget to temper their desires (Murphy, p. 19). One of Basi's most important functions in the novel is to humble greedy individuals such as Madam. However, this humbling activity is always accompanied by his own hunger for wealth. This contradiction can be understood in that, according to Eshu, both self-aggrandizement and self-denial must be tempered. For example, contemporary Nigeria must create wealth and refuse to accept a role as a colonial backwater. At the same time, the methods used to create the wealth must be moral and just. Basi's approach to becoming a millionaire is ridiculed in *Mr. B,* but his desire for prosperity is not.

Eshu's concern with health originates in his legendary defeat of small-pox (Thompson, *Face,* p. 174). Consequently, his shrines are doused with medicines in order to reinforce his promotion of a harmonious cycle of birth, growth, family, and individuality (Thompson, *Flash,* pp. 22, 27). In addition, in conjunction with his emphasis on morality, he assists those who have become immoderate (Murphy, p. 19), making him a protector of both spiritual and physical well-being. His protector role also appears in his ability to stand guard at entrances and foil intruders (Murphy, p. 46). In spite of his tendency to disrupt and make mischief, Eshu is ultimately a figure of order and balance, if only within the larger context of transformation and change. Basi's association with well-being is not obvious or frequent; however, he does help Alali avoid the extremes of poverty by taking him in, even though he does exploit Alali at times.

Eshu's insistence on change acts as a positive force in that his dynamism (Murphy, p. 133) encourages potentiality (Thompson, *Flash,* p. 19). His fondness for overturning order and upsetting complacency (Murphy, p. 46) has at its root the desire to reveal a higher, more expansive, more life-sustaining order (Murphy, p. 133). At the heart of his destabilizing/restabilizing process lies Eshu's emphasis on communication. Ultimately, his destabilizing activities are concerned with removing barriers, especially in the areas of finance and romance (Thompson, *Face,* p. 180) and generally to open blocked paths (Murphy, p. 42). As part of removing these blockages, he loosens people up (Murphy, p. 95) and allows the correct message to come through (Murphy, p. 68). His efforts foster generosity as well as highlight, for ridicule, absences in generosity (Thompson, *Face,* pp. 175, 178). Consequently, the ideal of generosity informs and tempers his concern with prosperity, for prosperity without generosity will wither. Nevertheless, the financial windfalls (Thompson, *Face,* p. 178) and luck (Murphy, p. 81) that Eshu brings must be accompanied by sacrifice to the gods, given that Eshu himself was the only one who sacrificed to the gods at a crucial moment in Yoruban mythic history (Thompson, *Face,* p. 178). Basi's espousal of generosity and expansiveness can be clearly seen in his preoccupation with great wealth. However, Basi does not seem to promote sacrificial practices.

As *Mr. B* opens, Basi displays optimism, energy, and quick thinking. He describes his arrival in Ibadan as fortunate, even magical. Returning to Lagos, he pursues his goal of becoming a millionaire wholeheartedly but relies more on positive thinking than a specific plan to achieve his goal. His mantra is "'To Be a Millionaire, Think Like a Millionaire'" (Saro-Wiwa, *Mr. B,* p. 4). Hence, his advice to the people of Lagos is not so much worldly as spiritual. At the same time, the advice can be read ironically as revealing the shortcomings of those who seek wealth but are unwilling to put in the effort to achieve it. Nevertheless, in spite of this ironic subtext, Basi emphasizes the potential for growth of the urban environ-ment of Lagos (p. 5). His emphasis on the positive, both within himself and in the surrounding environment, is reinforced by his energetic and in-genious methods of accomplishing his goals without the money to do so. For example, he defeats the bus conductor by claiming that he can't get the money out of his pocket (p. 3). In addition, he fools Mama Badejo (through the optimistic slogan on his T-shirt) into thinking that he is a wealthy man who will eventually pay her (p. 6). Yet as optimist, Basi him-self believes that he will eventually pay both her and the conductor (p. 8) and is determined to erase his debt. Miraculously, through his wily efforts, he is able to do just that.

Basi's optimism, nevertheless, does not negate the confusion that ex-ists both within himself and within the larger world of Adetola Street. In *Mr. B*, Adetola Street functions as a microcosm of contemporary Nigeria, which in itself mirrors the contemporary postcolonial world with its noisy and chaotic jumble of wealth and poverty, a site of possibility but also danger, a site of many signs but also one where communication is diffi-cult (pp. 8–9). As a messenger of the gods, Basi is to bring some order to this chaotic contemporary life so that Nigerians can successfully negoti-ate this confusion. Yet, ultimately, the confusion must not be denied: it is the unassailable reality of contemporary times. Basi himself exhibits this confusion when he unintentionally journeys from Lagos to Ibadan and then returns to Lagos again. Basi's indirect path acknowledges the vicissitudes of contemporary existence. However, he is also pleased to see that there is a church, a mosque, and a house of prayer on the street (p. 10), indicat-ing that the potential for a harmonizing spirituality still exists even though most of the signs on the street focus exclusively on money.

Having successfully dealt with the bus conductor and Mama Badejo, Basi is next challenged by Madam, who creates herself as a sign of wealth through her well-dressed appearance and expensive home, which has a room that Basi might rent. She, like Mama Badejo, is seduced by the opti-mistic slogan on Basi's T-shirt. This T-shirt, with its slogan of "To Be a Millionaire, Think Like a Millionaire," acts as a magnet for those like Madam whose love of money needs to be transformed so that its power can be focused in a more positive direction. At the beginning of the novel, when Basi first meets her, Madam is using this power to negatively fanta-size that the room she has for rent is a very nice room and therefore worth an exorbitant amount of money (p. 12). Yet her self-delusion and greed only encourage Basi to respond in kind as he accepts her outrageous price for the room and explains that he will have her money tomorrow after he goes to the bank (p. 13). It is not by rejecting Madam that he will trans-form her attitudes about wealth and success but by playing along with them and serving as a mirror for the flaws in her approach. It is not the trickster's job to criticize directly but to allow both character and reader to see for themselves what the problems might be. It is only in this way, through a realization of the old order's limitations, that a new order can evolve.

The next day, Basi continues to play up to Madam's vanity by calling his room a palace (p. 16) and by pointing out her wealth as he asks her for money for transportation to the bank. Ironically, the greedy Madam is the ideal person to ask for money because the request only emphasizes that she has money to throw away, which she frequently does on clothes and parties (p. 17). As a result, she overindulges Basi's request for transportation money and gives him 50 naira. Greedy for money, Madam, ironically, is unable to keep it and use it wisely in a productive manner. During this incident, the narrator suggests that Madam is typical of women in Lagos who

> earned money sometimes by trading, but mostly by doubtful means. And they showed off their wealth by holding noisy parties—birthday parties, wedding parties, burial parties, and house-warming parties. They dressed extravagantly to these parties and ate and drank and danced a lot. They formed a Club which they called "American Dollar Club." Only rich, vain women could be members of the Club. Madam was one of the first members of the Club. (p. 17)

In his depiction of Madam, Saro-Wiwa is satirizing an important class of individuals who, through their extravagant habits, are missing an opportunity to enrich the community. It is especially noted that their behavior is chaotic, in fact contradictory. They have lost the sense of purpose in their lives, a purpose formerly provided by the gods. Instead of channeling their energy in ways profitable for Nigerian society, they now look to the United States (and the U.S. dollar) for inspiration, when only chaos and aimlessness can be found there as well.

Having "tricked" the 50 naira from Madam, Basi's confidence soars: he can now pay back Mama Badejo and the bus conductor as well as obtain another breakfast (p. 17). On the way to the bank, the children stop him, and he performs his educative function by urging them to study for their examinations, to be prompt, and to take care while traveling on the roads (p. 18). They, in turn, refer to him as "Mister Bee," suggesting that he shares this insect's industrious nature. Leaving the children in a positive frame of mind, as they dream of traveling to the moon with him once they have successfully completed their examinations, Basi delights Mama Badejo by paying her for yesterday's breakfast. Then, he discovers the destitute Alali (Al), generously feeds him (p. 22), and offers him shelter in the room he rents from Madam (p. 23). Al, impoverished for the three months that he has lived in Lagos, views life in a brutally realistic manner; therefore, he has difficulty understanding Basi's more optimistic approach, which insists that a "millionaire-on-the-make" can also be a millionaire. Basi explains that this possibility exists because he has created it within his own personal dictionary. This notion of a "personal dictionary" demonstrates Basi's connection (like that of Eshu) with a new order, a new synthesis that goes beyond previous limitations. To accept the old order, as Al has done, is to accept poverty as undeniable fate, instead of transforming it as Basi is doing by transforming language.

As Al talks further with him, Basi reveals more of his philosophy, especially emphasizing that "you can make millions quickly without working" (p. 24). This tenet greatly disturbs Al because it goes against everything that Al has been brought up to believe in, that "'to earn money, we must work very hard'" (p. 24). Yet it is Basi's function, as a trickster figure along the lines of Eshu, to disturb and destabilize accepted notions. Hence, Basi's goal here is not so much a denial of the value of hard work but a transformation of the whole paradigm underlying conceptions of work and earning money. In contemporary society, the concept of work is being redefined. Hence, although Basi can be seen as a lazy rascal who does not want to work and whose behavior stands as an example of immorality, on another level his behavior invites us to consider a broader notion of work rather than to merely reject the idea of hard work.

Al's traditional outlook is further challenged when he points out that Basi's dirty, sparsely furnished, bug-infested room hardly deserves to be called a palace. In response, Basi reiterates his optimistic philosophy that in order "to be a millionaire think like a millionaire" (p. 29). Basi explains that "if you imagine that you are now living in a palace, if you dream that this is a palace, you will own a palace of your own in the near future" (pp. 29–30). Al is skeptical. Basi's logic seems faulty; it does not seem workable in the reality-based paradigm that dominates most contemporary thinking. Yet on another, higher level Basi's logic makes sense. Basi's philosophy has been practiced by other Africanist-thinking heroes, such as the boxer Muhammad Ali, as a means of countering negative portrayals of the black race through an enhanced self-esteem. Muhammad Ali's cry of "I am the greatest" was no mere hollow boast but a means of creating possibility amid depressing circumstances.

This emphasis on possibility lies at the heart of Basi's dream, which occurs in Chapter 3. Here, Basi dreams of flying first class and being treated with the utmost respect and deference, as if he were royalty. Both flying in a plane and being treated as if he were above the ordinary connect Basi, once again, with the sky and the gods. The suggestion is that Nigerians need not only to get in touch with their gods but also to take pride in themselves and remember their heritage as kings and queens. Once again, Saro-Wiwa goes beyond merely satirizing lofty pretensions to address a deeper need for self-esteem. When Basi's plane lands, he is taken to a palace located in an Edenic setting, a utopia where he ultimately ends up surrounded by gold and jewels. Although these details depict more of the greed that has corrupted contemporary Nigerian society, they also point backward to the ancient West African kingdoms, a past that needs to be relived so that it can help inform the present. In addition, the dream is also a vision of the future, a place beyond contemporary strife where that strife has become transformed. Thus, the dream is no mere fantasy but a powerful synthesis in which past and future act on the present to transform it. Significantly, this utopia contains a cornucopia of West African vegetation and foods, but more Western elements are also included. For Basi and Saro-Wiwa, the ideal Nigerian society of the future must be grounded in West African culture, history, and geography but not so insular as to exclude cosmopolitan influences. Nigerian society must embrace the world without neglecting its own considerable treasures.

Madam, demanding her money, awakens Basi from his dream, but he does not give in to her demands or to any sense of despair just because his dream is not yet reality. His optimism remains high, and both Al and the reader (one of Al's functions in the novel is to mirror the reader's developing relationship with Basi) continue to regard Basi quite favorably, appreciating his ability to tell "very entertaining stories" (p. 41) while still remaining suspicious of Basi's dislike of work. Basi's point that there are no jobs that can satisfy his desire for millions can be seen as a poor excuse, but it can also be seen as a trickster's disruption of the Protestant work ethic, showing its limitations from the point of view of the colonized, who are conveniently mired in low-paying jobs while the colonizers reap all the benefits. Basi's point is borne out by the fact that neither he nor Al can find work through traditional means. Still, Al can't believe that there are people "who have a lot of money although they do not work" (p. 44). Such people must be thieves. Here, Saro-Wiwa can point out the abuses of capitalism, allowing a chosen few to make huge profits from the hard work of many, but also show capitalism's potential in a world where more traditional approaches to labor have become outmoded. In both cases, the emphasis is on the need for transformation of existing attitudes toward work. Once again, it is the spirit of Eshu, the master of transformation, that is needed to move people beyond their limited and increasingly ineffective constructs.

Another hallowed precept that Al espouses is "that a good name is better than riches" (pp. 24–25). Once again, Basi insists that being a millionaire is better. Once again, he challenges Al's (and the reader's) preconceived notions about money and morality. Basi, as an Eshu figure, functions as a moral being but his morality exists within the context of his destabilizing mischievousness and on a higher, more expansive level than what is visible. Even more suspicious are Basi's plans for Al. Shockingly,

Basi's ultimate goal is to "do everything to stop Alali from getting a job" and to "make him [his] slave" (p. 26). It seems as if Basi only wants to use Al for his own ends and intends to thwart Al's freedom. Our suspicion is further aroused by the fact that Basi begins to order Al around as if he were a slave, insisting that Al call him "Mr. B," which points, ironically, to Basi's pretensions but also to Basi's elevated status as Eshu figure and messenger of the gods. Here, the complexity of the trickster's methodology is once again evident in that the reader is both reminded of key values such as freedom and taken beyond their sometimes confining and outmoded configurations. The trickster does not merely state what is right or wrong but forces readers to think about this question, to become moral individuals themselves by reinvigorating their moral faculties. At this point, early in the novel, Basi's contradictory behavior challenges readers' ability to judge character and their own beliefs about what qualifies as a moral act.

Questions of morality are much clearer when the focus shifts to the other characters in *Mr. B*, such as Madam. Yet here too there are complexities that must be sifted. For example, Madam's greed is not rejected in and of itself. Rather, the problem lies with her refusal to obey the law (p. 26). She deliberately ignores local laws by charging too much for Basi's room. This crime also points to a deeper sin against common decency: her ridiculous rents show that she has lost all sense of proportion and has become so greedy that she doesn't know "when to stop . . . she just goes on wanting more and more and more. In doing so, . . . she hurts other people without caring" (p. 26). Such a crime is more a crime against humanity and natural law than the breaking of a specific social code. It is a crime against the gods, and Basi, as messenger of the gods, is concerned with these types of crimes because they reveal the key difficulty faced by Nigerian society as it tries to establish its own identity—a lack of a clear moral purpose. Basi has arrived in Lagos to remind people like Madam, who is typical of the emerging Nigerian middle class, that their business efforts must be grounded in respect for the gods and their wisdom.

Basi disrupts Madam's greed (the first stage in the process of transforming it) by matching it, mirroring it, and egging it on. The possibility of getting 6,000 naira from Basi ultimately undoes Madam by putting her in a high state of excitement, and when Basi is late returning to the "palace" her agitation increases, suggesting that greedy individuals are forever lacking in harmony, balance, and contentment. Worry about her missing naira even disturbs her sleep (p. 30) as she is unable to detect Basi and Al's quiet return. In spite of her wealth, Madam has an approach to economics that is even more suspect than Basi's or Al's. Not only is she unproductively greedy and excessive, but she also deals with Basi ineffectively. Her vanity can be easily manipulated, and her tactics, such as her attempt to intimidate Basi with an empty beer bottle (p. 45) can be easily thwarted. Instead of being frightened by the beer bottle, Basi quickly transforms the situation by ordering Al to pretend to be sick to his stomach. This ruse throws Madam off temporarily; she is surprised to find this stranger she has never seen before in Basi's room, and even though she soon sees through the plan and gains the upper hand, her victory remains hollow.

Although Madam, with her money and social position, can claim the power that goes with being on the side of reality, and Basi and Al must be seen, in this situation, as liars, her reality seems cold and inhuman, perverted and false for all its appearance of truth. This sense of falseness is reinforced by the fact that Madam's wealth (in spite of its present reality) has its origins in morally suspect schemes. In addition, Madam, in spite of her seemingly absolute power, now needs Basi in that he owes her 50 naira (not to mention the 6,000 for five years' rent). Her power is contingent upon those she tries to dominate. One can even read Madam allegorically as representative of such agencies as the International Monetary Fund, and her behavior can be seen as an example of their stifling economic policies. These agencies also have power and seem aligned with what is true and right, but their treatment of their "customers" also undermines their exalted position.

An important foil for Madam in *Mr. B* is Dandy, another character who dreams of making a lot of money without doing any work. He owns a potentially profitable business, a bar, but he doesn't pay much attention to it. Instead, he hopes to make a big score elsewhere. Dandy's behavior obviously serves as a critique of an economics that eschews real productivity, that of building up a business, for morally, if not legally, suspect means of creating windfall profits. Dandy has been included in the novel to undercut any tendency to see the transformative powers of Eshu as supporting laziness. Instead, Dandy reminds us that Eshu's gift of a "sudden windfall" comes only from moral behavior aligned with the precepts of the gods. Paradoxically, sudden changes in wealth, ones that are permanent and satisfying, can only result from behavior that is diligent and humble. Like Madam, Dandy exhibits neither quality and instead lives up to his name by spending his money drinking and dancing.

In contrast to Dandy is Josco, who does not have Dandy's money and who lives under Eko Bridge with other down-and-out squatters (p. 50). Instead of owning a business, Josco lives mainly by thievery and has already spent time in prison. However, this contrast actually highlights how similar he is to Dandy by pointing out how disreputable Dandy's behavior really is. Both spend much of their time carousing. Dandy cultivates a relationship with Josco in order to capitalize on the inside information that Josco possesses as a member of the underworld. By associating Madam with Dandy and Dandy with Josco, Saro-Wiwa suggests that all are criminals, not just Josco, who is only the most obvious criminal of the lot. In reality, all share the same status, suggesting that the society itself has become criminal in character.

The kind of economic activity favored by these characters (and all too prevalent in Nigerian society, Saro-Wiwa suggests) is revealed in Chapter 4. Dandy and Josco take a radio left in their trust and use it in a scam. Dandy will award the radio as a prize, and Josco will take away the radio along with a 100 naira fine because the prizewinner will not have a radio license. This scam suggests that much of contemporary economics is merely a shell game where individuals are given something only to be forced to pay very dearly for it later on. There is no sense of true value, only the extremes of cheap and expensive, and no sense of morality, only a fixation on what can avoid detection and prosecution. It is into this immoral environment that Basi has arrived, both to mirror and transform it. When Dandy and Josco try to pull the radio scam on Basi, he thwarts them by accusing Josco of accepting a bribe when he takes both the radio and one naira away from Al. Basi mirrors Josco's false identity as a "licensing officer" by claiming to be "'Sergeant Basi of the Criminal Investigation Department, working under cover'" (p. 60). In the end, everything turns out to be fake, including the license and the one naira note that Josco returned because it was counterfeit. Even Basi is surprised at the amount of deception that is to be found in Lagos. During the incident, Basi seems to commit an evil, cowardly act when he insists that it is Al who owns the radio and thus is the one subject to the fine. However, this act is only part of his strategy of designating himself as the inspector in order to turn the tables on Josco.

Dandy deals with the owner of the lost radio (Segi) by telling her that Basi stole it and sending her to Basi's room to fetch it (p. 63). This visit precipitates a showdown between all involved parties at Basi's room. Meanwhile, Basi is able to use the radio incident to trick Madam, claiming that she owes him a favor because he saved her from a lot of trouble (pp. 68–69). Here, Basi employs Madam's own strategy by charging an outrageous fee of 1 million naira. The size of the fee helps Basi get what he really wants (some gin) since his reduction of the fee to a bottle of gin makes Madam think that she has gotten a bargain. When the others arrive, Basi ferrets out the truth, gives Segi her radio, makes Josco give Al a real one naira note, returns the empty beer bottle to Madam, and receives from her the bottle of gin in return. Such a scenario of giving and receiving constitutes a model of community that contrasts with the selfishness usually exhibited by the characters. Basi himself cannot resist an ironic comment on this contest between communal and individual tendencies by taking the gin, pouring himself alone a drink, and toasting the envious others (p. 72). More than pointing out his own greedy tendencies, he is mirroring the greediness of the others in order to teach them a lesson.

After the incident with the transistor radio, those involved (Basi, Al, Madam, Dandy, Josco, and Segi) form a community of friends who hang out together but remain jealous of one another and refuse to help each other (pp. 73–74). This situation suggests that community is the natural tendency among people and that, in Nigerian society, this natural tendency has been thwarted by an unnatural individualism. The shortcomings of the group become even more apparent when the focus shifts to Segi's point of view. In *Mr. B*, Segi, the youngest of the group, lacks the greediness of the others, although she is described as being "as vain as a peacock" (p. 92). Her difference from the others highlights their flaws. As for her own character, the reader wonders whether she will allow her vanity to be corrupted by the others and become caught up in their pursuit of riches. Saro-Wiwa does not allow Segi to become too entangled with the group and instead ties her to Professor, who continually points out the shortcomings in the others, including Basi. Significantly, Professor criticizes Basi's philosophy, dismissing him as a dreamer and insisting that wealth requires hard work over an extended period of time (p. 75). Furthermore, Professor insists that people should not focus on money as their ultimate goal but rather on knowledge, since it is with knowledge that "mankind can be made happier and human life better" (p. 77).

Professor's comments occur in the middle of the novel and seem to act as guidelines for the reader in assessing the behavior of the other characters and especially that of Basi. Professor himself seems to be leading a balanced and content life. The reader is told that he

> lived simply and kept his house very clean. There were beautiful flowers in the small garden in front of his house. The most notable part of his house was the library which was full of books. . . . Professor laughed a lot; and whenever he laughed in his boom voice, the sound echoed and re-echoed all over Adetola Street, spreading laughter all over as it made other people laugh as well. (p. 74)

These details link Professor with the admirable qualities of naturalness, knowledge, and perspective. He is in harmony not only with nature but with life in general, as his laughter shows. In addition, his laughter is contagious, making him a force for community. In contrast, as Segi begins to notice, the other members of the group feature grotesque idiosyncrasies that emphasize their absence of harmony. Basi "walk[s] with a jerk" (p. 77), Dandy, "rolling his weight from side to side" (p. 78), dances absurdly and smiles oddly "because one of his lower teeth [is] black" (p. 78). Al "yawn[s] hungrily," and Madam keeps saying "'It's a matter of cash!'" (p. 78). With the introduction of Professor, a moral center for *Mr. B* has been established, and Basi's complexity is deemphasized. Saro-Wiwa now focuses the novel mostly on the immorality of the greedy individuals and uses Basi as merely a mirror of that immoral greed. The many positives of

the trickster figure are left behind in the attempt to clearly pinpoint and
chastise immoral behavior. Yet the chastisement is not without its lighter
side, and Basi himself continues to be a figure of fun. The punishment for
wrongdoing is mostly confined to laughter, and consequently, the emphasis is more on healing than revenge since revenge only frustrates the development of community.

Immorality is clearly evident in all of the group in the incident involving the shipload of rice. Here, Basi obtains a letter making him the agent
for selling the rice. He promises to sell the rice to Madam for a 1-million-
naira fee and obtains from her a deposit of 1,000 naira (pp. 87–89). It seems
that Basi's strategy of thinking like a millionaire has worked. Yet the prosperity does not encompass everyone. Madam sells some of the rice to her
friends in the American Dollar Club but not to Dandy. Dandy, set on revenge, finds out that Segi has a similar letter of agreement to sell the rice.
Ultimately, it turns out that Josco has forged the letters. Basi is now in trouble with Madam for spending some of her deposit, and Dandy delights in
Basi's difficulties. The rice scheme reveals once again the desirability of
working together rather than as individuals as well as the pitfalls of specu-
lating to obtain extravagant profits. All of these behaviors go against Professor's values of hard work and naturalness.

At this point in *Mr B*, Basi is low indeed. Dandy and Josco are cele-
brating their defeat of Basi and Madam, but the two victors are intrigued
by Basi's unusual desire to have Madam's old pillow and mattress returned
to him (p. 101). Once again, the friends try to outdo each other, only to
bring more grief on themselves. Madam and Segi are also hooked in this
manner as Al, with a few well-placed lies, engages them in a struggle for
Basi's love. This struggle makes Segi determined to return the pillow and
mattress to Basi (p. 102). Meanwhile, Basi's innuendo about the value of
the mattress and pillow leads Dandy and Josco to speculate that they contain "several bars of gold" (p. 103). Once again, the economics of speculation leads to ruination. This speculation is so blinding that Dandy, absorbed
in his schemes, falls into a drain filled with dirty water (p. 106). In order
to make Basi give up the pillow and mattress, Dandy and Segi give Basi
money to leave Madam's "palace" (what Basi hoped they would do) and
proceed to inform Madam in order to claim the two objects. Basi frustrates
the others by taking the money and buying a new mattress and pillow,
claiming that Dandy and Segi were paying not for him to leave so much as
for the old mattress and pillow themselves, which they believed to be filled
with gold and love medicine. This incident, like others in the novel, combines a lesson with the healing power of laughter, including that of Professor, who laughs heartily at another defeat of the would-be millionaires.

In the contract incident in *Mr. B*, Saro-Wiwa continues to critique contemporary economics by comparing it to gambling. While Al is filling out

football coupons, Basi discovers a potential scheme in the newspaper having to do with a contract to supply spare parts to the government (pp. 112–113). The gambling connection becomes apparent when we learn that the individual who hopes to obtain the contract must endlessly fill out forms just like Al fills out his football coupons. Making money is less a matter of skill and work than a seemingly mindless process of doing paperwork. The paperwork itself can also be a mere illusion, given that Madam, in her attempt to win the contract, will use forged documents. Consequently, doing business is not a matter of possessing the relevant abilities and materials but of simply creating the impression that one is competent, of creating a convincing web of lies. The fact that the law is being broken does not seem to bother the participants. Once again, the importance of the law, religious as well as civic, is emphasized by Saro-Wiwa. A lack of reverence for the gods has spilled over into a lack of respect for social structures, and chaos is the result. This lack of respect is most evident in Madam's refusal to pay taxes. Furthermore, her refusal mirrors the tendency of large corporations to avoid or substantially reduce their taxes. Saro-Wiwa suggests that all sectors of the economy, not just a few greedy individuals, must be taken to task. The whole system has wandered away from what the gods have designated as just and good.

Madam further separates herself from social responsibility when she refuses to pay Al, Josco, and Dandy for the work they have done in acquiring and filling out forms until after the contract has been won (pp. 119–120). Basi, acting on behalf of the three, threatens Madam with reporting her to the police if she does not pay the others, but Basi is mainly concerned with receiving 1 million naira from Madam for not reporting her. In any event, Madam refuses to be blackmailed by Basi. Next, Segi, upon hearing about the situation, offers to write a letter to the government exposing Madam. Ironically, after Al writes and submits the letter and Madam's contract is canceled, it turns out that Madam was willing to pay them. Yet it is just as well that Al did submit the letter because Madam, with her greed, was only willing to pay them one naira each anyway. The end result of the confusion is that Madam ends up lonely, isolated, and facing prosecution, along with Josco and Dandy, for her crimes (pp. 127–128). They are saved from being convicted only by Professor, who points out that they are more "foolish" than "evil" (p. 128). This incident also reiterates the novel's emphasis on the law. People like Madam and the others only fear the police instead of respecting the law itself. They worry only about getting caught. Saro-Wiwa suggests that Nigerians must respect as well as obey the law in order to restore the communal order.

Typically, Basi, at this stage mostly mirroring the shortcomings of the others, vows not to reform his behavior but only to be more careful (p. 129). Also, he reasserts his dominance over Al (pp. 130–131) as the two begin to develop their next scheme, involving the creation of ghost-workers on the government payroll. Ironically, the very idea of ghost-workers or any kind of ghost scares Madam, suggesting that, ultimately, she relies more on superstition than rational thinking, another flaw that Saro-Wiwa finds in so-called modern society. Madam's susceptibility to Basi's suggestion about ghosts makes her an easy target for the others at Dandy's bar, and they quickly increase her fears. Dandy himself becomes caught up in the ghost phenomenon as Madam scares him into believing they exist (p. 136). Segi tries to allay Madam's fear about ghosts by explaining to her, as well as to Dandy and Josco, Basi's scam involving the ghost-workers. Here, Saro-Wiwa is able to point out a very specific problem with corruption in Nigerian society (adding nonexistent workers to the payroll) as well as make his more general point about the need to connect earning money with productive work. Unfortunately, each of the schemers ignores the lesson and concentrates instead on how to participate in Basi's scheme.

Madam involves herself in the scheme by using Basi's own tactic of threatening to inform the police; then, after she has frightened Basi, she successfully demands that he pay her 80 percent of his ghost-workers' wages (p. 142). Later, Dandy and Josco also place themselves on Basi's ghostly payroll. Segi voices a note of disapproval about the scam and later informs the conspirators that the government has closed the loophole by making workers "show a proper letter of appointment, a passport photograph and evidence of work done" (p. 147) in order to be paid. Defeated, Basi is nonetheless rescued by the sudden appearance of a ghost who scares away Segi and Madam, who was about to remove the door from Basi's room as punishment (p. 149). The ghost (Al in disguise) has ensured that Madam will not pester the two about rent for a while.

The final word in the novel about Basi and his scheming goes to Professor, the moral center of Saro-Wiwa's fictional Nigerian universe. Professor points out that Basi focuses on the wrong strategies in his attempt to earn money: Basi needs to reject his tricks and follow a more prudent plan. Yet Professor does not suggest that Segi (or the reader) reject Basi. Rather we should pay heed to the humorous lessons that he teaches us. We must not isolate ourselves from others in society but cooperate with them in order to promote healing and correction. Yet the lessons Professor speaks of are only beginning to be learned by people like Segi and the rest of the group. By the end of *Mr. B,* little transformation has occurred. Nevertheless, *Mr. B,* through its central character, the Eshu trickster Basi, has pointed the way toward a renewed sense of Nigerian community, one that, hopefully, the younger generation will internalize and develop.

Many of Ken Saro-Wiwa's other works of children's literature consist of expansions of the incidents featured in the novel *Mr. B,* the first of the works that focuses on the character Basi. Such is the case for short narratives such as *Mr. B Goes to Lagos* (1989), *The Transistor Radio* (1989), *Segi Finds the Radio* (1991), *A Shipload of Rice* (1991), and *Mr. B's Mattress* (1992). The incidents featured in these short narratives were first developed in the *Basi and Company* television series. Then the television treatments were adapted for children in the form of these short children's books. In these narratives, Basi is seen as intelligent and educated—"he had been to school and passed many examinations" (Saro-Wiwa, *Mr. B Goes to Lagos,* p. 3)—but also as lazy and greedy and even self-deluding at times. In these works, the audience distances itself from Basi immediately, although he does appear to be interesting and likable. As a result, Basi mainly functions as a mirror of ambitious people who try to become rich through suspect means. Yet he still retains his markers as an Eshu trickster figure, such as his red, black, and blue clothing and his ability to con others. Hence, the young audience will be critical of Basi but will laugh at him more than condemn him since the lessons learned from Basi's behavior are administered gently.

Other examples from these expanded incidents also make it clear that Basi's behavior should be frowned upon rather than embraced. For instance, the opening lines of *The Transistor Radio* emphasize Basi's dislike of work, avoidance of problems that must be dealt with, mounting debt, and fondness for "tricking others" (Saro-Wiwa, *The Transistor Radio,* p. 3). Yet the sequel, *Segi Finds the Radio,* ends much more positively than the corresponding version in *Mr. B,* in that the latter closes with Basi taunting the others by refusing to share an alcoholic drink while the former follows the taunt with Basi's announcement of a birthday party at Segi's, to which all are invited and at which all have a good time. This detail suggests that Basi, besides being a mirror of social ills, also functions as a communal force and, consequently, exhibits the traditional two-sided nature of the trickster.

In the novel *Basi and Company: A Modern African Folktale,* the adult version of *Mr. B,* Saro-Wiwa focuses the story on Adetola Street itself rather than on Basi. Instead, Basi becomes the epitome of the busy street's emphasis on "the possession of money, quick money" (Saro-Wiwa, *Basi and Company,* p. 14). Consequently, Basi represents the ambiguous tendencies of modern Nigeria, featuring both a productive energy and the debilitating problems that come with it. Here, the description of Basi suggests he is both an appealing figure, who arouses the curiosity of others and the admiration of children, and also a suspect one who has "secret designs on Madam's wealth" (p. 20). Much is made of his status in the community, where he is seen as possessing "courage" and "credibility" (p. 89) in engineering his schemes. Ultimately, in this work, he is not so much the mythic figure who drops from the skies in *Mr. B* but more of a typical businessman on the make who goes to greater and more practical lengths to achieve his goals than he does in the children's version. Also, he is less childlike and more determined to the point of being aggressive. Furthermore, there is no Professor to put Basi's actions into perspective, only a young narrator who is tricked into giving Basi money at one point (p. 115). Yet at the end of *Basi and Company*, this narrator rejects notions that Basi is of a piece with "'jokers,'" "clowns," and "childish idiots" (p. 201). Rather, he is evaluated in a more positive light:

> Basi was perhaps the most serious man on the Street. At least he took himself seriously and pursued his aims with a singlemindedness which was really quite uncharacteristic of the men of my acquaintance. I do not know how often I hoped that Basi would finally find the key, the missing link that would enable him to make his millions, just to show the residents of the Street that nothing was beyond our dreams. And perhaps I was not alone in wishing him well. Otherwise, why was he so popular on the Street? (p. 201)

Experiencing Basi and his schemes is associated with the narrator's passing from childhood to adulthood, with the process of developing an independent point of view that is so necessary to shaping the world in one's own image and achieving one's dreams.

Ultimately, Basi reminds the narrator of "the Tortoise, the hero of all the folktales of my childhood, an archetypal, the eternal trickster who, from story to story, was only temporarily bested, never defeated" (p. 201). More than simply mouthing the morals of hard work and fairness, experiencing Basi and Adetola Street can offer these morals in a human context that integrates them more deeply and profoundly. If, like *Mr. B*, *Basi and Company* does not end with transformation (the marriage of Basi and Madam disintegrates in confusion just like Basi's marriage schemes in *A Bride for Mr. B*), this adult version nevertheless confirms the trickster's dictum that transformation is an ongoing process and that it is this ongoing quality, this sense of potentiality, that makes possible the renewal. Life itself, then, according to Basi's trickster ethos, is about being alive rather than achieving a stable, unchanging state. Any corrective for society's ills must, as the trickster shows, go beyond mere condemnation and punishment of wrongs to embrace a more complex sense of aliveness that features a transforming, healing spirit. Such a spirit must be, like Basi's, an all-embracing, expansive one that knows no bounds and happily encompasses all kinds of contradictions.

Increasingly, children's literature is being recognized as the equal of adult literature in complexity and depth (Nikolajeva, quoted in Perrot, p. 210). Although Ken Saro-Wiwa's Basi narratives for children, on the surface, do not exhibit such postmodernist tendencies as metafiction, intertextuality, and avant-garde structures and styles, they nevertheless reflect, through their employment of both folktale and contemporary media forms, the complex cultural diversity favored by leading cultural critics such as Pierre Bourdieu (Perrot, p. 215). Saro-Wiwa's use of the trickster figure especially reinforces this approach, given this figure's propensity for doubleness and inclusiveness, characteristics that point toward a Nigerian society of the future in which all of its diverse elements can interact productively.

WORKS CITED

Baker, Houston A., Jr. *Blues, Ideology, and Afro-American Literature: A Vernacular Theory.* Chicago: University of Chicago Press, 1984.

Duchet-Suchaux, Gaston, ed. *The Bible and the Saints.* New York: Flammarion, 1994.

Mbiti, John S. *African Religions and Philosophy.* Garden City, N.Y.: Anchor, 1970.

Murphy, Joseph M. *Santeria: African Spirits in America.* Boston: Beacon Press, 1993.

Osa, Osayimwense. *African Children's and Youth Literature.* New York: Twayne, 1995.

Pelton, Robert D. *The Trickster in West Africa: A Study of Mythic Irony and Sacred Delight.* Berkeley: University of California Press, 1980.

Perrot, Jean. "Children's Literature Comes of Age." *ARIEL: A Review of International English Literature* 28, no. 1 (January 1997): 209–220.

Saro-Wiwa, Ken. *Basi and Company: A Modern African Folktale.* Port Harcourt, Nigeria: Saros International, 1987.

———. *A Bride for Mr. B.* Port Harcourt, Nigeria: Saros International, 1992.

———. *Mr. B.* Port Harcourt, Nigeria: Saros International, 1987.

———. *Mr. B Goes to Lagos.* Port Harcourt, Nigeria: Saros International, 1989.

———. *Mr. B's Mattress.* Port Harcourt, Nigeria: Saros International, 1992.

———. *Segi Finds the Radio.* Port Harcourt, Nigeria: Saros International, 1990.

———. *A Shiplord of Rice.* Port Harcourt, Nigeria: Saros International, 1991.

———. *The Transistor Radio.* Port Harcourt, Nigeria: Saros International, 1989.

Thompson, Robert Farris. *Face of the Gods: Art and Altars of Africa and the African Americas.* New York: Museum for African Art, 1993.

———. *Flash of the Spirit: African and Afro-American Art and Philosophy.* New York: Vintage, 1983.

11

Dream of Sologa, Eneka, and *The Supreme Commander:* The Theater of Ken Saro-Wiwa

Chris Dunton

> In the era of the World Wide Web, books and newspapers are often dismissed as waning powers. But across Africa the certainty persists that writing can make things happen.
> —Rob Nixon, review of *A Month and a Day*

Ken Saro-Wiwa's published plays are all one-act long, mostly collected in the two volumes *Four Farcical Plays* (1989) and *Basi and Company: Four Television Plays* (1988).[1] Common to both volumes is Saro-Wiwa's best-known play, *The Transistor Radio*, which began life as a review sketch performed at the University of Ibadan in 1964 and was later fleshed out and adapted into, successively, a 600-line stage play, a radio play (published in a Heinemann anthology in 1973), and then the television play that formed the kernel of the hugely successful *Basi and Company* comedy series. Comparison of the three versions throws light on Saro-Wiwa's intentions as a dramatist, on his working methods as a professional writer, and more generally, on questions having to do with the ideology of the text. Points of interest are the gradual abandonment of pidgin from stage to radio to television script; the softening of dialogue and the gradual removal of didactic elements; and the building up of dramatic elements useful for generating fresh situations in a sitcom (for example, the consolidation of "closed" characters, such as Basi's wit, and of recurrent

This chapter was first published in *Research in African Literatures* 29, no. 1 (Spring 1998): 153–162. The editors would like to express their thanks to Chris Dunton and Indiana University Press for their permission to reprint the article here.

dynamics, such as Dandy and Josco's plotting against Basi). Other Basi scripts gathered in *Basi and Company* include *Comrades All,* which is basically a direct spinoff from the plot of *The Transistor Radio,* and *The Mattress*: consistently in these plays, plot is generated from intrigue and counterintrigue, from the comic motif of "the swindler swindled." This is one of the most familiar—and most appreciated—motifs in Nigerian English-language theater, found in, to list just a few examples, Zulu Sofola's *The Wizard of Law*, Wale Ogunyemi's *Business Headache*, Charles Umeh's *Double Attack*, Femi Osofisan's *Who's Afraid of Solarin?* and—like the Osofisan, a play based on Gogol's *The Government Inspector*—Saro-Wiwa's unpublished *The Supreme Commander.*

Apart from the stage version of *The Transistor Radio*, the *Four Farcical Plays* volume contains *Bride by Return, The Wheel,* and *Madam No Go Quench Again. Bride by Return* is a slight piece (thematically, at least; here, as in *The Transistor Radio* and *The Wheel,* the dialogue is expertly written for effective comedy). The central dynamic depends on the audience's recognition of businessman Nubari's pretentiousness and its appreciation of his ludicrous lack of self-awareness. In performance it would be fascinating to try to gauge an audience's reaction to—and, in their own comments, interaction with—Nubari's constant enthusing about English culture and the English language. Interestingly, in the context of Saro-Wiwa's other work, although the dialogue touches on the fact that Nubari has made his fortune from winning a contract, the potential theme of corruption is not developed. The play's audience is left to construct a morally significant personal (and typifying) history for Nubari and to read him in that light or to enjoy what is simply given, the comic mechanism that distances them from him at a less significant level, that of his patent ridiculousness. As with many satirical plays in the Nigerian English-language theater, one wants to know how exactly an audience responds to the characterization of the (at one level or another) unlovely rich and undeservedly powerful.

This question arises again with *The Wheel,* a play whose plot deals explicitly with corruption and the way this is entrenched within an institution as—in chain reaction—successive applicants for preferment or employment succumb to the need to bribe to achieve their goal. This is perhaps the most theatrically effective of the short plays, and one that when adapted from the Nigerian context travels successfully (excerpts were performed to enthusiastic audiences in Lesotho and in Pietermaritzburg, South Africa, in November 1995). Saro-Wiwa's comic invention here is well-nigh irresistible, as he sustains the play's essential repetitive structure through ingenious parallelism, not only avoiding monotony but pointing the humor as each fresh change is rung, as each successive applicant bribes his way into power and (now an employer) compels the next applicant to bribe him in turn. The dialogue is expertly designed to show how each successive patron, each successive supplicant, strategizes corruption, to show their shifting emotional states of anxiety, expectation, and gratification. For its two actors the play is a gift, allowing them to establish its basic ground-plan and then to highlight variation: for example, by suggesting—as they swap, turn and turn around, from role as patron to role as supplicant—different species of arrogance, intelligence, voracity.

Again, though, some doubts arise about the nature of the impact of the play's satire: whether the verve with which the bribery is carried out, the comedy drawn from variation as the chain reaction proceeds, and the dramatic technique of self-exposure used as each applicant enthuses about his skill in corruption, do not seriously compromise the effectiveness of the play's exposé. Commenting on *The Transistor Radio,* Soyinka notes how Saro-Wiwa achieves the difficult task of "arousing condemnation and at the same time admiration for [individual characters]" (quoted in Saro-Wiwa, *The Transistor Radio,*" p. 88). Applied to *The Wheel,* this complex (satirical/empathetic) approach has more problematic implications.

The last two scenes of *The Wheel,* admittedly, add a slightly different dimension to the play. The final supplicant is unlike the others, impoverished, illiterate, and a pidgin speaker whose explicit references to his poverty and whose anger at having to bribe his way into a job appear to affect the audience through a slightly different combination of empathy and alienation from that provoked in the earlier scenes of the play. Even so, the character's pleas of poverty are part-comic empathetic.[2] To question the affective function of satire in performance and the political implications of this is, I suppose, something of a sociocritical cliché. But it is difficult not to pose such a question, in a situation in which satire is such a prominent medium. We tend to think of theater in performance in Nigeria as being dominated by historical epics such as Duro Ladipo's operas or a play like Soyinka's *Death and the King's Horseman.* Although this *is* an important strand in Nigerian theater practice, satire is another. The Nigerian satirical theater in the English-language medium includes plays such as Saro-Wiwa's *The Wheel,* Soyinka's *The Trials of Brother Jero* (satirizing religious charlatanism and the greed and gullibility of a congregation), Femi Osofisan's *Who's Afraid of Solarin?* (see below), and Ola Rotimi's as-yet-unpublished *Man Talk, Woman Talk* (a satirical debate on the relative ethical standing of Man and Woman, performed to capacity audiences in Ife in 1995). These plays attract large and appreciative audiences who vigorously enter into discussion of the truth-value of the satirical critique the plays offer of society. The question then arises as to how fully or cogently these plays develop a specific critique or to what extent they offset this through their use of "pure" comic elements, burlesque, or the development of empathetic characterization.

It is in the unpublished plays that one finds Saro-Wiwa working both on a more ambitious scale and with more searching, more disturbing subject matter. Below I describe three plays: *The Supreme Commander,* staged by Paul Okpokam in Calabar shortly after the Nigerian Civil War; *Dream of Sologa,* an adaptation of Gabriel Okara's *The Voice,* written in 1966 and, as far as I know, not performed to date; and *Eneka,* which was acted in Port Harcourt in 1971[?], with a cast that included Elechi Amadi and Okogbule Wonodi. *Eneka* was sufficiently provocative to lead the then military governor of Rivers State, A. P. Diete-Spiff, to disband the troupe who performed it, after attending the play as guest of honor.[3]

Biographical accounts of Saro-Wiwa's life and work record his activity in the theater in the 1960s, especially at the University of Ibadan (see, for example, Feuser; Ezenwa-Ohaeto). There is virtually no published information available, however, on the unpublished plays or the conditions under which they were performed. On their performance history, I have no information apart from the few details noted above. Mimeograph copies of *Dream of Sologa, Eneka,* and *The Supreme Commander* were very kindly given to me by Saro-Wiwa in 1991, when I was researching Nigerian English-language drama. The present chapter—in which I try to give a descriptive account of these—is just one of many tributes to Saro-Wiwa now appearing, as we attempt to gain a fuller understanding of the significance of his writing and of his work as a political activist. (I would like to draw attention here to a recent book that is, essentially, on Saro-Wiwa's work as an activist and on the history of the campaign against Shell but that also comments on his work as a writer: Manfred Loimeier's *Zum Beispiel: Ken Saro-Wiwa,* with contributions from, inter alia, Soyinka and Willfried Feuser. With all texts in German, this is a work that richly deserves translation.)

THE SUPREME COMMANDER

Saro-Wiwa's adaptation of Gogol's *The Government Inspector* comes in the form of a long one-act play (though the photocopied typescript from which I am working indicates a break in performance about halfway through, as the comedy of intrigue and exposure moves into its second stage). As in the Gogol and in Osofisan's adaptation, *Who's Afraid of Solarin?,* which was first staged six to seven years after Saro-Wiwa's play, *The Supreme Commander* combines different species of comedy: a notable difference between the Saro-Wiwa and the Osofisan is that the latter, while incorporating much caustic satire aimed at Nigeria's governing elite, contains much more extended elements of pure (and brilliantly executed) farce. Taken together, the Gogol, Saro-Wiwa, and Osofisan plays provide a case study in the construction of satire, its impact on its audience, and its relationship to other comic modes.

The Supreme Commander certainly opens in a way that suggests the comedy that follows will reflect uncompromisingly the brutality of the milieu it depicts. In the Gorilla Casino,[4] where wall posters read "No Wuru-wuru allowed" and "No Piss Careless," drunken customers blunder about and a soldier, Jide, abuses a slow waiter: "Why you no answer, bloody fucking silly idiot fool bastard ye-ye man God punish your mother. Bastard . . . can't you respect your Senior?" (p. 3). After a sycophantic praise-naming session with his mate, Jimba, Jide reels into memories of the Nigerian Civil War (just concluded when the play was first performed):

> my boys dey shit like no man business. I tell them don fear, God dey. Dem shit like mad. The one mortar shell come land inside the ship, break 'am into two. Jesus of England! My boys jump inside river. Some of dem sink one time, like lump of cassava. I laugh. . . . I say, dis na manpikin wey de time born 'an him mama and papa buy drink. Haba, life get no sense. Me too, I jump. (p. 5)

This is a long way away from the comedy of intrigue found in *The Transistor Radio* or the (relatively) genial satire of *The Wheel:* much closer to the rawness of Saro-Wiwa's civil war novel *Sozaboy.*

This harshness is sustained through the second episode of the play, when the two bar waiters (Sahvees) complain bitterly about the corruption and extortion they see all around them (and that they have to negotiate to survive). Their dialogue is in pidgin, but Saro-Wiwa's depiction of their alienation is far removed from the comic/sympathetic pidgin-speaking stereotype found in, for example, the character Patrick in Wale Ogunyemi's *The Divorce* or (though comic characterization here stands at a bizarre and intriguing angle to the stereotype) in the servant Polycarp in *Who's Afraid of Solarin?* At the same time, Saro-Wiwa's extension of the boundaries of comedy here has its limits. In the end the Sahvees are beneficiaries of the identity-error on which the plot revolves. Boasting about his neatness to the soldier Jide, mistaken as the Supreme Commander, one of them comments:

> Sahvees 2: Na me dey wash him pant self. I wash de pant of de
>   Supreme Commander!
> Sahvees 1: True?
> Sahvees 2: Believe me yours sincerely.
> Sahvees 1: Give me your hand. You don try. (p. 30)

As with the Security Guard in *The Wheel,* despite their clearheadedness and their acerbic commentaries on power and exploitation, the Sahvees are not shown to find any way to survive other than to jump on (the tail end of) the wagon of corruption.

When it comes to the play's core material, the elite's exposure of its own corruption, like Gogol and Osofisan, Saro-Wiwa has this prompted by fear of a powerful outsider's imminent investigation and by the lack of solidarity among the elite, who squabble about each other's degree of venality. The third quarter of Saro-Wiwa's play has individual members of the elite approaching the Supreme Commander in turn to put their case and to undermine that of their colleagues.

Three elements here sustain a harshness that is distinct to the Saro-Wiwa play. First, Saro-Wiwa includes in his circle of administrators a young man, Ledogo, who speaks out against their corruption. This is in a context in which, according to the administrator called Bribe (pronounced, he insists, Bribé): "[there is an] enemy in our midst. . . . Subverts, activists, rabble-rousers. All the young men . . . are communists" (p. 27). (Bribe goes on to claim he'd like to hang them at the first opportunity.) Ledogo joins a group of Saro-Wiwa characters—young men who resist/ contest oppression—to which belongs also Okolo in *Dream of Sologa* and the hero of *Eneka.* Like them, he is warned off by his elders, who tell him he is still young and who order him to obey traditional rules of respectful conduct (p. 7). In *Dream of Sologa* and *Eneka,* however, Ledogo's counterparts are far more foregrounded from the outset, as is their quarrel with the powerful, the corrupt, and (a very prominent concern of Saro-Wiwa's) the citizens who collaborate with these. In the end, Ledogo has no place in the comic scheme of *The Supreme Commander* and drops out of the play.

More striking is the fact that the administrators whose corruption the play exposes are appointees of a military regime; the friction between civilian and military elites is emphasized throughout the play. This relationship represented a major issue of concern at the time of the play's first performance, and Saro-Wiwa's treatment of the problem is quite raw. Near the beginning of the play, a distinction emerges between those who accept that they are beholden to the military and those who resent the relationship (protesting, "if they want our support they should pay for it" [p. 11]). Later Saro-Wiwa shows the civilians humiliated as the soldier Jide—mistaken by them as military top brass—forces them to perform a parade-ground routine (p. 19). The episode cuts both ways, pointing the ugliness of both sides in the military/civilian "coalition."

Perhaps, though, the element in *The Supreme Commander* that has the harshest impact is its ending, when the civilian council decides it can protect its own interests only by political secession, by declaring its local government area an independent state. As comedy, the play here suddenly shifts ground, careering into wild burlesque, as the military arrive (the real top brass, not the army deserter Jide) and the civilians declare independence. This, in a play that was staged just at the end of the civil war, during which Saro-Wiwa supported the federal side. *The Supreme Commander* draws to a close with Bribe reading the civilian declaration of independence. I do not wish to quote this because the typescript version has (apparent) errors that make it in places difficult to pinpoint the exact target of Saro-Wiwa's satire. But beyond Saro-Wiwa's parody of pompous speech making, there is what must have been taken by the play's audience as a scathing attack on Biafran secession, closing the play on a note that was perhaps more painfully topical than any issue addressed in the Gogol or Osofisan plays.

DREAM OF SOLOGA

Saro-Wiwa's dramatization of Okara's *The Voice* is in three short acts, corresponding to the novel's triple setting: village, city, and return to village. With a total running time of about seventy minutes, the play offers a highly succinct dramatization of the key scenes of the novel, the most substantial omission being the boat journey that takes the hero, Okolo, from his village to Sologa (the capital city, Sologa being an anagram for Lagos-o).

Saro-Wiwa makes no attempt to repeat Okara's experiment in translingualism yet generally sticks closely to the substance of the novel's dialogue. Apart from some significant passages written for Okolo, there is little "invented" material: a handful of characteristic touches of humor (when Okolo claims the city of Sologa stinks—morally—the police Superintendent replies, "we can stand the stench. Plenty of Izal in the shops" (p. 24); in the city restaurant scene, Saro-Wiwa intensifies Okara's portrayal of the population's moral cynicism by having them sing "Mammy water go bury we / If we die tomorrow," a song that is later repeated—in an effective linking of the village Amuta to Sologa—by one of the village tyrant's messengers (pp. 18, 25).

The main loss in Saro-Wiwa's objectification of the action is the powerful sense of interiority achieved in the highly subjective narration. There is a severely reduced sense of Okolo's personal anguish and of Tuere's spiritual power. In the novel, for example, Tuere's stigmatization and her ideological kinship with Okolo are "realized"—through a third-person narration that is saturated with a sense of Okolo's apprehension—as Okolo seeks refuge in her hut; in the play Saro-Wiwa employs the conventional device of having Tuere named and placed, prior to this, in the first conversation of the two messengers. In the dramatized version, the facts are made clear, but the *frisson* is missing.

What one might have expected is for Saro-Wiwa to move away from Okara's parabolic approach (and his intense evocation of Okolo's consciousness) toward a more specific political critique. *The Voice,* after all, was written at the point of Nigeria's independence, while Saro-Wiwa's play was written several significant years later, some months after Chinua Achebe's archetypal novel of postcolonial disillusionment, *A Man of the People,* and shortly after the 1966 coup, as Nigeria moved toward civil war. To some extent, Saro-Wiwa does make the material more immediate in terms of its political impact. In places (even though not very extensively), the play's corrupt leaders sound more specifically, idiomatically, Nigerian than do the novel's: during, for example, Abadi's speech, which Saro-Wiwa rewrites with references to the village's "august and memorable leadership," and Abadi's condemnation of "irresponsible elements" subverting state security (p. 7) (nowadays usually put down, with intimidating indefiniteness, as "certain" irresponsible elements). Two points stand out more sharply and with obvious and poignant resonance vis-à-vis Saro-Wiwa's work as political and human rights activist. First, there is a strong emphasis from the very opening lines on the role of the complacent, the collaborators with a dictatorial regime, who warn each other "don't think," who "dance as the drum dictates" (p. 2). This, of course, is a major theme of the novel, but more than any other motif this one is foregrounded in Saro-Wiwa's severe condensation of the original. Second, there is Saro-Wiwa's reworking of the novel's ending. Like Okara, Saro-Wiwa has Okolo and Tuere die, but in a move that draws the material closer to another work on the theme of the visionary dissident Soyinka's *The Strong Breed,* he emphasizes the posthumous effectiveness of the outcasts' message, having (in Ukule's account) Chief Izongo lose his authority over the village, calling meetings and wandering from market to market, trying to convince a now-alienated population to speak to him, and finally committing suicide in Tuere's hut. Before this, Saro-Wiwa has written for Okolo a speech—to the people of the village—that does not appear in the novel and that includes these lines:

> I have returned to ask you to join me in questioning, in asking whether we do not have a right to choose what sort of life we want to live; whether we do not have a right to think and speak and act without the big ears of Izongo listening and driving us from our town. (p. 35)

ENEKA

The opening and expository scene of *Eneka* has elderly villagers discussing their deepening poverty under the corrupt and exploitative rule of the provincial chief, Ezomo. In a phrase that recalls Bertolt Brecht[5]—and that anticipates recognitions such as those on which Osofisan's *Once upon Four Robbers* is built—they complain "the man whose goat is stolen becomes the thief, the man who stole the goat the judge" (p. 3). As the play develops, there is an emphasis on the leadership's wastage of the land's resources: "did you never ask yourself whether [the district of] Uzebu has done nothing worthwhile since Ezomo became chief?" (p. 31). There is, too, a powerful emphasis on the corruption of political and ethical discourse under this leadership, on the failure of civil society (a failure that is sponsored by the ruling elite). In the words of the enlightened village elder, Okogun:

> these are the marks of the times. For the accused have turned to be judges, honesty has been dethroned, truth expunged from amongst us. Cowards have become heroes, the ignorant are clever, the broadminded foolish; fools have become philosophers, the narrow-minded are sages, and seekers after the truth are called malcontents. (pp. 50–51)

Thematically, much of the interest the play offers derives from the same kind of triple conflict found in *Dream of Sologa:* here, between Ezomo and his court; the progressive forces led by Eneka; and those complacent villagers (at first in the majority) who recognize Ezomo's corruption but find it safer and easiest not to resist this.

Throughout the play's first half (roughly fifty minutes of playing time), there are two basic dramatic foci: the interlinked plotting for power and advantage at Ezomo's court and at the court of the Oba of Benin (under whose jurisdiction Uzeba falls) and the campaign by Eneka to persuade Uzeba to rise against Ezomo.

In the absence of firsthand information such as personal interviews, it is not possible to say for certain what caused such offense to the authorities when the play was first performed. Perhaps it was, though, the emphasis Saro-Wiwa places on the relationship between the center and the provinces. In the first half of the play he shows the Oba—the highest authority, manipulated by his Prime Minister, who is himself actively exploiting the wealth of the provinces through placing pressure on their local rules to extort taxes from the people and to suppress dissent. Saro-Wiwa exonerates the Oba himself from any charge of corruption. He is allowed the recognition: "what misery, if the instrument of government instead of being used to the benefit of the citizen is turned against him?" (p. 13). In what must have been a woundingly embarrassing moment for the dignitaries at the play's first performance(s), when Eneka directly confronts Ezomo by seizing his ceremonial sword from him in public, the Oba bursts out laughing (p. 30). Having established the point, however, Saro-Wiwa does not press it: despite the Oba's prominence in the first part of the play, he is not seen again, and the action from here on focuses entirely on the conflict within the village.

That the village's complacency in the face of extortion is in the end self-defeating is very strongly emphasized, especially in a series of speeches by Eneka at the beginning of the play:

[speaking of his father, who was arrested and executed for resisting corruption] My father was marked out because he spoke against them. But when they've broken all the men who can resist, they will turn on you and wolf you up. . . .

so long as you gaze and gawp at them, so long will they tyrannise over you. . . .

A people who don't know their rights; who don't do anything to alter their fate for the better. They complain of poverty, but won't accept proposals for the slightest change. (pp. 6–8)

The last section of this quotation represents a line of argument that reemerges in Saro-Wiwa's writing during the years of his work as campaigner for the Ogoni people. In his detention diary, *A Month and a Day*, for example, he records his perception of the Ogoni people's potential at the outset of the Movement for the Survival of the Ogoni People (MOSOP) campaign:

They had been sleepwalking their way towards extinction, not knowing what internal colonialism had done and was doing to them. It had fallen to me to wake them up from the sleep of the century and I had accepted in full the responsibility for doing so. Would they be able to stand up to the rigours of the struggle? (Saro-Wiwa, *A Month*, p. 18)

During the second half of the play, the emphasis is on Eneka's growing strength as the village comes to accept his moral authority. The point about the self-destructiveness of compliance with injustice is reiterated. Wura, Eneka's fiancée and a young militant, proclaims: "alas for a people who dare not speak for truth and wholesomeness . . . our lethargy reeks to the Heavens" (p. 52). During the play's melodramatic final action, Eneka is executed by Ezomo. But Ezomo himself is displaced (and killed) by a village now in open rebellion, and the play ends—more optimistically than *Dream of Sologa*—by defining a new order.

Earlier, despite the play's foregrounding of his individual strength and heroism (as with that of Okolo in *Dream*), Eneka comments on his personal expendability, demanding that his comrades "swear you'll continue the struggle whether I'm there or not" (p. 33). Saro-Wiwa's last words before his execution were "Lord take my soul but the struggle continues." In his closing statement to the military appointed tribunal, Port Harcourt, he stated:

I predict that the scene here will be played and replayed by generations yet unborn. Some have already cast themselves in the role of villains, some are tragic victims, some still have a chance to redeem themselves. The choice is for each individual. (Saro-Wiwa, "Closing Statement," p. 4)

NOTES

1. In this chapter, I focus chiefly on three of Saro-Wiwa's unpublished stage plays, preceded by a brief discussion of the published plays (for stage, radio, and television). A more detailed account of the published plays and bibliographical references to commentaries on these can be found in Chris Dunton, *Nigerian Theatre in English: A Critical Bibliography.*

2. Something of the same tension is maintained in *Madam No Go Quench Again,* the last piece in the *Four Farcical Plays* volume, a play written entirely in pidgin and in which the emphasis is on closely delineated realistic characterization. Here elaborate dramatic action emerges only in the play's final moments, with the device Saro-Wiwa refers to as "a treatment of the classical story of the phoenix" (Saro-Wiwa, *Four Farcical Plays,* p. 7). What Saro-Wiwa in fact offers here is a dramatized version of an ancient story, one retold in many literatures (including, according to J. P. Sullivan [p. 197], Chinese). The best-known version of this story in the West is usually referred to as "The Widow of Ephesus." As R. Bracht Branham and Daniel Kinney explain, this is a Milesian tale, "a variety of bawdy short [story] first attested in the 1st century BC" (Branham and Kinney, p. 107). Appearing in Greek versions, later in Latin, "The Widow of Ephesus" makes a celebrated reappearance in Petronius's novel *Satyricon.* Saro-Wiwa's reference to "the classical story of the phoenix" may be a pointer to another twentieth-century theatrical reworking of the Widow of Ephesus story, Christopher Fry's *A Phoenix Too Frequent.*

3. Personal communication, Saro-Wiwa to Chris Dunton, 21 January 1991.

4. In the typescript, written cancellations show the bar renamed "Ocean" and the [male] manager, Akue, transformed into "Madam." As with other changes in the script, I do not know when these were made or whether they were made by/sanctioned by Saro-Wiwa.

5. Introducing a court scene during which justice is deftly evaded in the interests of the merchant class, the actors' chorus comments in *The Exception and the Rule:*

> the law courts will give the vultures food-a-plenty
> Thither fly the killers. The tormentors
> Will be safe there. And there
> The thieves hide the loot they call profit, wrapped up neatly
> In paper with a law written on it. (Brecht, p. 52)

WORKS CITED

Brecht, Bertolt. *The Measures Taken and Other Lehrstücke.* London: Eyre Methuen, 1977.

Branham, R. Bracht, and Daniel Kinney, eds. *Satyrica* (Petronius). London: J. M. Dent, 1996.

Ezenwa-Ohaeto. "Ken Saro-Wiwa." In *Twentieth Century Caribbean and Black African Writers.* Ed. Bernth Lindfors and Reinhard Sander. *Dictionary of Literary Biography* 157: 3rd series. Detroit: Gale Research, 1996: 331–339.

Feuser, Willfried. "The Voice from Dukana: Ken Saro-Wiwa." *The Literary Half-Yearly* 29, no. 1 (1988): 11–25. Also in *Matatu* 2 (1987): 52–66.

Loimeier, Manfred. *Zum Beispiel: Ken Saro-Wiwa*. Göttingen: Lamuv Verlag, 1996.

Nixon, Rob. "Pipe Dreams." Review of *A Month and a Day* by Saro-Wiwa. *London Review of Books,* 4 April 1996: 18–19.

Saro-Wiwa, Ken. *Basi and Company: Four Television Plays.* Port Harcourt: Saros, 1988.

———. "Closing Statement to the Military Appointed Tribunal, Port Harcourt, Rivers State, Nigeria." *ALA Bulletin* 21, no. 4 (1995): 3–4.

———. *Four Farcical Plays.* London: Saros, 1989.

———. *A Month and a Day: A Detention Diary.* Harmondsworth: Penguin, 1995.

———. *The Transistor Radio.* In *African Theater; Eight Prize-Winning Plays for Radio.* Ed. Gwyneth Henderson. London: Heinemann, 1973.

Sullivan, J. P., ed. *Satyricon.* By Petronius. Harmondsworth: Penguin, 1986.

PART 5

Epilogue

12

"From This Hurt to the Unquestioning World": Seven Poems from *Delta Blues*

Tanure Ojaide, with an Introduction by John Lent

> Inside the drum hides a spirit
> that wants me to succeed beyond myself.

I have excerpted these two lines from Tanure Ojaide's poem "My Drum Beats Itself" because they capture something of the essence in his suite of poems, *Delta Blues*, that is hard for writers like myself to comprehend in some ways. What I mean is that, as Ojaide enters into the violence that is his subject here—the death of Ken Saro-Wiwa and the others hanged with him—he must try to force his poetry beyond the personal, the political, so it transcends these things in order to acquire the power of a public voice that might heal as it speaks. I do not believe this is an easy task for poetry these days. In fact, it would be tempting for anyone removed from the political complexity and violence of the delta in Nigeria to suspect the rhetoric in some of these poems or feel uneasy about the way some of them flirt with political absolutes. But I do not live in the delta of Nigeria, and I have not been exiled from my country like Ojaide. And when I think of my distance from his landscape and the brutal events taking place in it, I feel humbled by Ojaide's voice and eye. That humility, in time, allows me to open up more to the poems themselves and to admire both what Ojaide is trying to capture in them and the poetics he employs to achieve them. In the same poem, he goes on to say: "I say this because there's another music / that fills the air but cannot be heard without effort." It is this music we cannot hear and the effort required to reach it that makes these poems difficult but strong, demanding but full of dignity in the end, and successful artistically.

As Ojaide walks a fine line between directness and metaphor, between the abstractions of the politics that surround him and his people and the nature of the concrete landscape that has produced them, he achieves something strong and enduring. In the title poem, "Delta Blues," for example, he captures both a concrete sense of the delta's beauty and the abstract vulnerability built into that beauty that has made it so tempting to exploit:

> The rivers are dark-veined,
> a course of perennial draughts.
> This home of salt and fish
> stilted in mangroves, market of barter,
> always welcomes others—
> hosts and guests flourished
> on palmoil, yams and garri.
> This home of plants and birds
> least expected a stampede;
> there's no refuge east or west,
> north or south of this paradise.

In another poem, "Sleeping in a Makeshift Grave," however, Ojaide shifts from the lyrical to the political, allowing image to sustain the shift and to temper the rhetoric:

> If Nigeria wakes from the grave after the murders,
> let the people cast general, staff, and cap
> into a marble grave in their born-again memory.
> There's no other way to live free here than kill
> or be killed. You can tell from our stone country.

And Ojaide's vision does not flinch from the more complex ironies and betrayals built into these political events. In "The Chieftain and His Tribe," he explores and exposes the complicity he sees around him: "If you accuse the chieftain of being an evil idol, / don't spare his tribe of willing worshippers; / they share the same monstrous faith."

I have made these selections from *Delta Blues* because they achieve two things: they honor Ken Saro-Wiwa, and they honor him especially by their complexity, courage, and subtlety.

—John Lent

* * *

My Drum Beats Itself

Now that my drum beats itself,
I know that my dead mentor's hand's at work.
This sound I lipsing and others think is mine
could only come from beyond this world—
the little from there makes abundance in my hands.
Inside the drum hides a spirit
that wants me to succeed beyond myself.
I forsee a thunderstorm breaking out in my head—
I wonder how I can contain the gift in lines
that I must chant to earn my griot's name.
I bow to the master who never forgot my service.

If I can wait and listen
Iye iye
Brothers and sisters, if my ears will open wide
Iye iye
If I will sleep awake every season
Iye iye
My people, if I keep my ears primed
Iye iye
I say this because there's another music
that fills the air but cannot be heard without effort
Iye iye
The deer knows why it only comes out
when the whole world's withdrawn to bed
Iye iye

The air ripples with birdsong,
the tapster's gourd brims with fresh wine,
and the hunter's god blesses him with a bristling game.
The little from beyond will make abundance in my hands.
My drum beats itself
& I await the carnival the drum divines.
Sing with me
Iye iye iye iye
Iye iye iye iye
Iye iye iye iye
Iye iye iye iye.

Delta Blues

This share of paradise, the delta of my birth,
reels from an immeasurable wound.
Barrels of alchemical draughts flow
from this hurt to the unquestioning world
that lights up its life in a blind trust.
The inheritance I sat on for centuries
now crushes my body and soul.

The rivers are dark-veined,
a course of perennial draughts.
This home of salt and fish
stilted in mangroves, market of barter,
always welcomes others—
hosts and guests flourished
on palmoil, yams and garri.
This home of plants and birds
least expected a stampede;
there's no refuge east or west,
north or south of this paradise.

Did others not envy my evergreen,
which no reason or season could steal
but only brighten with desire?
Did others not envy the waters
that covered me from sunstroke,
scourge of others the year round?

My nativity gives immortal pain
masked in barrels of oil—
I stew in the womb of fortune.
I live in the deathbed
prepared by a cabal of brokers
breaking the peace of centuries
& tainting not only a thousand rivers,
my lifeblood from the beginning,
but scorching the air and soil.
How many aborigines have been killed
as their sacred soil was debauched
by prospectors, money-mongers?

My birds take flight to the sea,
the animals grope in the burning bush;
head blindly to the hinterland
where the cow's enthroned.
The sky singes my evergreen leaves
and baldness robs me of youthful years.
These are the constitutional rewards
of plenitude, a small fish in the Niger!

Now we are called to banquets
of baron robbers where space's belatedly
created for us to pray over bounties,
the time to say goodbye to our birth
right, now a boon cake for others.

With what eyes will *Olokun*
look at her beneficiaries,
dead or still living in the rack
of uniformed dogs barking
and biting protesters
brandishing green shrubs?
The standard-bearer's betrayed
in the house by thieves, relatives,
& the reapers of the delta crop
could care less for minority rights!

And I am assaulted by visions of
the foreign hangman on a hot Friday noon,
the administrator witnessing failed snaps,
the cries in the garden streets of the port
and the silence in homes that speak loud
in grief that deluged the land's memory.
Those nine mounds woke
into another world, ghostly kings
scornful of their murderers.

Nobody can go further than those mounds
in the fight to right chronic habits
of greed and every wrong of power.
The inheritance I have been blessed with
now crushes my body and soul.

(2 December 1995)

Sleeping in a Makeshift Grave

Nigeria sleeps in a makeshift grave.
If she wakes with stars as her eyes,
the next world will be brighter for me and my compatriots.
A gunful of children broke the tetrarch's legs
& the elephant that once pulled the forest along for a path has fallen—
can she get up before she's covered for dead?
If the game's quartered, the delta will be swallowed whole—
the hunters know they only came together for this prize.
You cannot measure the size of the overfilled pits
that trail the boots of strong men that come and go
trampling and thrashing in their ironed uniform.
The hanged men are thrusting their fists from beyond.
The gunners strip their mother before the world,
their undertaker presides over the land with a swaggerstick.
If Nigeria wakes from the grave after the murders,
let the people cast general, staff, and cap
into a marble grave in their born-again memory.
There's no other way to live free here than kill
or be killed. You can tell from our stone country.

                              (Chicago, 30 December 1995)

Elegy for Nine Warriors[1]

1
Those I remember in my song
will outlive this ghoulish season,
dawn will outlive the long night.
I hear voices stifled by the hangman,
an old cockroach in the groins of Aso Rock.[2]
Those I remember with these notes
walk back erect from the stake.

The hangman has made his case,
delivered nine heads through the sunpost
and sored his eyes from sleepless nights.
The nine start their life after death
as the street takes over their standard.

The forest of flowers[3] mock
the thief, commander of roaches;
there are some heads like the hangman's
that will never have a vision of right.
What does a crow know of flowers?

When ghosts sit down the executioner,
let him plead for neither mercy nor pity;
the General will meet the Master Sergeant
and share the naked dance to the dark hole.

I hear voices from the dead assault
the head cultist daubed with blood—
he runs from demons of his high command.
The cockroach will not live through the sun
but those I remember in my song—
nine marchers who died carrying
our destiny on their broad chests—
will surely outlive the blood-laden season.

2
The sun's blinded by a hideous spectacle.
And the boat of the dead drifts mistward.
They will embrace the Keeper of *Urhoro* Gate
even as the soil that covered their bodies
despite guards rises into a national shrine.
Birds that fly past click their beaks in deference,
the community of stars makes space for the newborn;
they will always light the horizon with hope
& those in the wake who raise grieving songs
will look up to the promise of unfettered dawn,
hope against the rope of the barbarian chief.

3
The butcher of Abuja
dances with skulls,
Ogiso's[4] grandchild by incest
digs his macabre steps
in the womb of Aso Rock.
To get to his castle,
you would stumble over skulls,
stumble over jawbones.
With his ordnance of guns,
a trail of mounds; bodies broken
to arrest the inevitable fall.
Flies buzz round him,
throned amidst flukes of courtiers.
Is the prisoner who presides
over cells and cemeteries
not slave of his own slaves?

4

In these days of mourning
some of my fellow singers laugh.
O Muse, reject their claim on you!

These children who laugh at their naked mother
incur the wrath of their creator-goddess.
They forfeit their kinship, these bastards.

Those whose tribal cackles break loose
as the house's torn with grief
draw on themselves the fate of vultures.

They even ride on the dead
with "Tragedy provokes laughter."
Laughter of the flock of vultures!

They smite the upright ones cut down
in full glare of the noon sun.
Earth and Sky dismayed by the apostasy.

From their corners, they laugh
before somber faces reeling from pain
& mourners can only spit at their noses.

In this suffocating gloom
I turn from my own grief
to weep for fellow singers without a heart.

Only a fool fails to reflect his lot
when an age-mate dies,
& I didn't know there were so many in the trade.

Let no accomplices in the murder
of the Muse's favorite son
think they can fool the divine one.

5

The sorcerer to my shame still lives
as I drown in tears over my brother
he sent away at noon from this world.
The cobra to my shame still lives
as I run from home looking for a big
and long enough stick to smash the demon,
or leave it to suffocate itself with bones.
The world sees the sorcerer's harangues
covering himself with a council of diviners
outnodding their heads in complicity.
He has brought down the eagle
and now plucks feathers off the totem bird!
Does he not know of forbidden acts
that he dismembers the nine eaglets?
He forgets he has left Ken's name behind
& the communal chant of the singerbird's name
rising along the dark waters of the Delta
will stir the karmic bonfire
that will consume his blind dominion.
Surely, that name will be the rod by which
the cobra will meet its slaughter.
The sorcerer to my shame still lives,
but day will surely break over the long night.

6
We'll surely find a way in the dark
that covers and cuts us from those waiting
to raise the white-and-green flag to the sky.
The eagle nests in the nursery of advancing days.
We'll find a way to reach there
where the chorus rehearses a celebratory chant.
We'll make our way in the dark
but would have lost the fear in our hearts—
the dark will not close eyes
to knowledge of stars, dawn and sun;
nor can it smother the message
of good neighbors, lovers and another country.
No ambush will douse the high spirit
that drives us in the course.
We shall get there
through decades of dark years,
we know we'll have to cross
holes of ambush of hangmen
who do not commit their eyes
to sleep, love and things of beauty.
With the sort of luck we have had
with generals, vultures, and presidents,
we'll find a way to reach there in the dark
without government roads and light
but with the rage of being held back
from what we could grasp, stretching ourselves
to the point of exhaustion or death.
None of the survivors will then be
ashamed of being afraid.

I Will Save My Enemy

If I can, I will save my enemy from shame.
It's just not proper to subject them to the un-
speakable torture that mocked my manhood.
Day will always break to end the bewitching night.
A butcher gave up his executioner's knife
after a cow tied to a stake looked him in the eye—
whatever he saw there made him think of his life.
Imagine if every safari hunter were hounded
by the herd they decimate for sport!
I will use my life to save my enemy from shame—
I have travelled that shameful territory, stripped
and danced helplessly to laughing drums
to the satisfaction of local chieftains.
I will not defile my scars and the memory of
marching daily to the gallows for a surprise end—
inflicting shame on a defeated enemy
does not fit the battle-cry for human rights.
I will always try to save my enemy from shame
so that I will not be an accomplice of torturers.
In mufti or uniform, Johnson and Doe[5] were murderers.
This said, only the remnant barbarian of the century
will build a scaffold of dishonor that with his orders
dangle the poet's body at noon for the world to see.
Osonobrughwe,[6] give me a full cup of courage
so that I will not shame my worst enemy in death.

(4 January 1996)

The Chieftain and His Tribe

A chieftain boasts of herding a far-flung tribe.
His people cannot live without bribes.
He spits at them; still they follow him;
they have given up on where he's going.
Each person has something to trade:
money, sex and power are there to die for;
extortion's the thriving national business.
The men lie on their commodities of women,
who still praise them to revive their courage.
Bearing grudges propels their history—
"Because your Papa shot down my dog,
I will not accept the genius of his grandchild!"
The chief chokes his gods with human offerings;
cavalries of greed crush whoever stands in their way.
The grumbling men are ashamed and turn to their wives,
the abused women give out sex with left and right hands—
none is anymore intimidated by guns pointed at them,
these can be silenced by instantly prepared charms.
The tortoise-brained people invent praise-songs
to get to the leftovers of the chief
who throws confettis of *naira* at them—
he knows no dog will bark with its mouth full.
Do you wonder why the Lord of the Rock
still possesses millions of worshippers
despite the bloodstained soil on which they kneel?
The lord has hired a crop of fortune-tellers,
the gifted children of his victims, to counsel
that more human offerings need to be made
to ensure that he lives and rules forever.
If you accuse the chieftain of being an evil idol,
don't spare his tribe of willing worshippers;
they share the same monstrous faith.

(7 January 1996)

A General Sickness

One sick man can bury a country with his boots,
though he may lack the sense to cover the mass grave.

From the kind of groans the earth has witnessed,
from the faces that have disappeared,
from the blood that has soaked the flag

an evil djinn torments the federation.
Death is a halfblind general lost in politics—
nobody knows all his hands that fan out
to clear the way and dig holes.

He does not like the looks of freedom.
Nor of prosperity and peace & so throws
them into his voluptuous slaughterhouse.

No innocence, no beauty, young or old
moves in his circle of existence—
is it sweat, tears, or acid rain falling
from the brows of subjects?

Birds lose their way in the skies,
on land I return home with a map.
At the intersection of power and greed,
covered by a rock lives the beast.

The head has choked us with poisons
& the land rebounds with insufferable groans.
                                        (Charlotte, 1 June 1996)

NOTES

1. They are Baribo Bera; Saturday Dobee; Nordu Eawo; Daniel Gbokoo; Dr. Barinem Kiobel; John Kupuinen; Paul Levura; Felix Nwate; Kenule Saro-Wiwa.

2. The current home of Nigeria's head of state.

3. The title of Saro-Wiwa's first volume of short fiction.

4. Ogiso was a legendary tyrant in Urhobo and Edo folklore.

5. Prince Johnson was a factional warlord who ambushed, captured, and tortured to death Master Sergeant Doe of Liberia.

6. *Osonobrughwe:* the Urhobo for the Supreme God.

Appendixes

Appendix 1

Chronology of
Ken Saro-Wiwa's Life

Laura Neame

Much of the following information has been gleaned from the pages of
Ken Saro-Wiwa's two published memoirs: *On a Darkling Plain* and *A
Month and a Day*. I have also made authorized use of an unpublished autobiography, which I obtained from the executors of Saro-Wiwa's estate,
and interviews with Ken Wiwa. That said, the information tends toward
the subjective remembrance. Hence the gaps, question marks, and omis-
sions, particularly in relation to his family life.

Name: Kenule Beeson Saro-Wiwa. "Saro" is an honorific name
meaning "eldest son."
Birth: 10 October 1941, in Bori, Ogoni (then in eastern Nigeria, now
Rivers State). His father, Chief J. B. Wiwa, was born in 1904, trained as a
forest ranger, and earned his living as a businessman. His mother, Widu (b.
1920), was a trader and farmer.
Family: Two marriages in Nigeria, one to Hauwa Wiwa, with whom
he had children before their separation. One child by a third wife (uniden-
tified). The children are currently in Uganda and Nigeria.

CHRONOLOGY

1947–1954 (Primary Schooling)   Saro-Wiwa's mother tongue is Khana,
and his first few years of schooling at the Native Authority School in Bori
are in that language.
1954–1961 (Secondary Schooling)   Saro-Wiwa attends Government
College in Umuhaia, initially on a school scholarship. This is one of Nigeria's
foremost schools, run on the English public school model. The students are
about 90 percent Igbo, and Saro-Wiwa is the only Ogoni student. In his

final year he is college prefect and house captain as well as a member of the First Eleventh Cricket Team. He earns his Higher School Certificate in 1961.

1956   At Government College, Saro-Wiwa first becomes ill with a heart ailment.

1962–1966 (University Schooling)   He attends the University of Ibadan, graduating with honors in English. He is a member of the University Cricket Eleventh, chairman of Mellanby Hall for one year, and president of the Dramatic Society. While there, he edits two college newspapers: *Mellanbite* (1963–1964) and *Horizon* (1964–1965). He graduates with a B.A. (Honors) in English, with a B+ grade average, in 1965.

1965   Teaches at Stella Maris College, Port Harcourt, from June to December.

1966   Teaches for one term at Government College in Umuhaia.

1967   Serves as graduate assistant at the University of Nigeria at Nsukka. At this time, Eastern Nigeria declares independence as the Republic of Biafra. Saro-Wiwa leaves Nsukka in order to avoid involvement in the war and travels to Lagos via Bori.

1967   Appointed administrator of Bonny Province after Bonny was freed from Biafran control. He is a member of the Interim Advisory Council, Rivers State.

1967–1973   Serves as assistant lecturer at the University of Lagos.

December 1968–June 1969   Serves as Rivers State commissioner for works, land, and transport.

1968–1973   Appointed Rivers State commissioner and member, Executive Council, from December 1968 to March 1973.

1968(?)   Marries Maria when she is seventeen. Ken Wiwa, their eldest son, is born in 1968. There are five children from this marriage, the youngest being born in 1978, after Maria and her children move to England.

1969–1971   Serves as Rivers State commissioner for the Ministry of Education.

1970   Gian Wiwa is born to Ken and Maria.

1972–1973   Appointed commissioner for the Ministry of Information and Home Affairs. Ken Saro-Wiwa's first two books are published and adopted for the school curriculum at this time.

1973   Removed from his position as commissioner, he moves into business and property development, setting up Saros International Limited.

1973–1985   During this period, Saro-Wiwa engages in a number of business ventures. Among other things, he sets up an "anti-inflation" grocery store called Gold Coast Stores and a wholesale trading company, the Market Masters.

1976   Twin daughters Zina and Noo are born to Ken and Maria Saro-Wiwa.

1977 Writes columns for the Nigerian newspaper *The Punch.*

1978 In January, the family moves to England. Tedum is born shortly thereafter.

1985–1986 Moves his column to *Vanguard* after his friend from *The Punch,* Sam Amuka, launches the newspaper.

1985 Establishes Saros International Publishers at the same Port Harcourt address as Saros International Limited.

Self-publishes his first two Saros titles.

Writes and produces the situation comedy *Basi and Company,* which runs through 1990.

1987–1988 Serves as executive director of the National Directorate of Social Mobilisation (MAMSER). The directorate is a public relations arm of the Nigerian government.

1987–1992 Serves as director of the Nigerian Newsprint Manufacturing Company, an appointment by the federal military government of Nigeria.

1987 *Sozaboy* wins honorable mention in the Noma Award for Publishing in Africa, and *A Forest of Flowers* is short-listed for the Commonwealth Writers Prize.

1988 Meets the writer William Boyd at a British Council Seminar in Cambridge and begins a friendship that persists until Saro-Wiwa's death.

1988–1990(?) Writes the column "Similia" for the government-owned *Sunday Times.*

1989–1993 Elected president of the Ogoni Central Union.

1990 Loses the first draft of *Lemona,* either through theft or after leaving his briefcase in a taxi. This discourages him from writing until his 1993 imprisonment.

1990–1993 Elected president of the Association of Nigerian Authors.

1992–1995 Serves as president, Ethnic Minority Rights Organization of Africa (EMIROAF).

1992 Saros International Publishers becomes a member of the Oxford-based African Books Collective.

His youngest son by his first marriage, Tedum, dies of a hereditary heart ailment at the age of fourteen.

1993–1995 Serves as president of the Movement for the Survival of the Ogoni People (MOSOP).

1993 Appointed vice chairman of the Unrepresented Nations and Peoples Organization, The Hague.

Imprisoned. Adopted by Amnesty International as a prisoner of conscience.

1994 Wins the Fonlon-Nichols Prize. Arrested for incitement to violence in May.

1995 Tried for murder on 2 November. Saro-Wiwa is executed by the military government of Gen. Sani Abacha on 10 November.

Appendix 2
Chronology of the Nigerian Civil War

Ross Tyner

The Nigerian Civil War began on 30 May 1967, with the declaration of a sovereign Biafra by Lt. Col. Chukwuemeka Odumegwu Ojukwu, military governor of Eastern Nigeria, and ended with Biafra's surrender on 15 January 1970. The following chronology lists the significant events of the war. In order to put those events in context, the chronology also includes events dating from Nigeria's independence from Great Britain in October 1960 up to February 1999. Given the importance of the military coup of 15 January 1966, and the events that followed it in contributing to the war's outbreak, the period between the coup and the beginning of the war is described in particular detail. As much as possible, the chronology takes the perspective of the Ogoni, hence the emphasis on Saro-Wiwa's experience during the war.

The chronology was compiled using a variety of sources, including such standard reference tools as chronologies, yearbooks, and almanacs as well as several monographs, journal articles, and Websites. Interestingly, many discrepancies exist between various sources, with regard not only to dates but also to the events themselves. For example, one source reported that Mid-Western Nigeria declared itself independent as the Republic of Benin on 20 September 1967, the day before the Nigerian army liberated Benin City from the Biafrans. In fact, the "Republic of Benin" was a hoax perpetrated by the Biafrans. The speech declaring its existence, dutifully reported by some media—and dutifully transcribed by at least one chronology—had been recorded several weeks prior to its public release (Saro-Wiwa, *On a Darkling Plain*, pp. 118–122). In the case of such discrepancies, accounts of the war written by participants or eyewitnesses—Saro-Wiwa's *On a Darkling Plain*, N. U. Akpan's *The Struggle for Secession,*

1966–1970, and John De St. Jorre's *The Nigerian Civil War*—were most useful in distinguishing facts from the direct transcription of news headlines, many of which were based on war propaganda from either the Nigerians or the Biafrans. If nothing else, these discrepancies illustrate the power of propaganda during the civil war.

CHRONOLOGY OF EVENTS

1960

October 1   Independence from British colonial rule.

1963   Nnamdi Azikiwe becomes the first president of the Federal Republic of Nigeria; he will remain president until the 1966 coup.

1966

January 15   Prime Minister Alhaji Abubakar Tafawa Balewa, three government ministers, and several army officers are assassinated in a military coup.

Maj. Gen. John Aguiyi-Ironsi, commander of the Nigerian Army, heads the new military administration.

January 19   Lt. Col. Chukwuemeka Odumegwu Ojukwu assumes his position as military governor for Eastern Nigeria.

January 25   Ojukwu abolishes provincial assemblies in Eastern Nigeria and removes power from most politicians and bureaucrats, handing much of the power to the military and police.

February   Isaac Boro declares Eastern Nigeria the "Niger Delta Republic"; he is quickly captured and sentenced to death; he will be released in August 1967 but will be shot dead on 17 May 1968, while fighting for the federal side.

May 24   Aguiyi-Ironsi proclaims Decree no. 34, which ends the federation of regions and replaces regions with four "Groups of Provinces," headed by military governors; all civil services are to be administered from Lagos.

May 29   Several hundred civilians, mainly Igbos, are killed during riots in the Northern Region.

July 29   Countercoup: Ironsi is kidnapped and executed by northern Nigerian members of the Nigerian Army; his death will not be officially announced until January 1967.

Lt. Col. Adekunle Fajuyi, military governor of the Western Region, is also kidnapped and executed.

Ironsi's chief of staff, Lt. Col. Yakubu Gowon, comes to power and forms the second military government of the year.

August 1   Gowon announces he has assumed the positions of supreme commander and head of the military government of Nigeria.

August 8   Gowon announces the impending repeal of Decree no. 34.

August 9   Gowon orders all soldiers back to "their respective Regions of origin."

September   Attacks are renewed on Igbos in the North, with 8,000 to 10,000 killed; more than 1 million Igbos return to the Eastern Region; in retaliation, some northerners are massacred in Port Harcourt and other eastern cities.

Saro-Wiwa participates in the Rivers Leaders of Thought Conference in Port Harcourt, which, at its conclusion on 14 September calls for the creation of Rivers State within Eastern Nigeria.

September 26   Members of non-Igbo minorities in the East send a petition to Ojukwu, expressing their fear of attacks against them by the Igbos.

September–November   In an ad hoc constitutional conference in Lagos, four regions attempt to negotiate a return to civilian government; efforts fail, in part due to nonparticipation of official Eastern Region representatives.

October   Ojukwu orders the expulsion of all noneasterners from his region; Igbos from the Mid-West are exempt from the order.

1967

January 4–5   The Supreme Military Council holds a "peace summit" in Ghana, resulting in the Aburi Agreement (or Accord). Among other things, it restores some power to the regions.

January 14   The first official announcement of Ironsi's assassination is made.

January 26   Gowon publicly reneges on certain parts of the Aburi Agreement, significantly, the creation of new states.

February 25   Ojukwu announces he will take whatever measures are necessary to give effect to the Aburi Agreement by the end of March.

February 28   Gowon asserts his willingness to use force to "maintain the integrity of the nation."

March   As many as 1.5 million refugees inhabit the Eastern Region; most have returned from other regions.

March 10   The Supreme Military Council meets, without Ojukwu, to try to implement the Aburi Agreement; resulting Decree no. 8 delegates more powers to the regions but also authorizes the Supreme Military Council to declare a state of emergency anywhere in the country with the consent of three out of four regional governors.

March 31   Ojukwu announces the Eastern Region will take over all federal departments and services, effective 1 April and withhold all federal taxes and revenue collected in the region from the federal government.

April 4   The Nigerian government suspends flights by Nigerian airways to Eastern Nigeria.

April 20   The Supreme Military Council meets in Lagos, without Ojukwu, to decide on measures to deal with eastern rebellion.

April 24   Gowon announces that he will create a Calabar/Ogoja/Rivers (COR) State as a means of protecting the minorities of Eastern Nigeria if Ojukwu persists in his secessionist bid.

April 29   The Nigerian government suspends postal and money order transactions between Eastern Nigeria and the rest of the country.

May 1   Chief Obafemi ("Awo") Awolowo, leader of the Yorubas, declares that if the Eastern Region is allowed to secede then the Western Region should do the same.

May 3   Chief Harold Dappa-Biriye issues a statement to the press rejecting Gowon's proposal for a COR state and calling instead for the creation of a Rivers State.

May 6   Northern leaders declare their support for the federation and urge Gowon to create between eleven and thirteen states.

May 23   Gowon lifts the economic and communications blockade against the East.

May 26   The Eastern Region Consultative Assembly votes to secede from Nigeria.

Saro-Wiwa returns home from the university in Nsukka to Bori.

May 27   Gowon proclaims a state of emergency, reimposes economic sanctions against Eastern Nigeria, and unveils a plan for the abolition of regions and redivision of Nigeria into twelve states, one of which will be Rivers State.

May 30   The sovereignty and independence of the Republic of Biafra is proclaimed by Ojukwu.

June   Awolowo is appointed by Gowon to the federal cabinet.

Early June   Saro-Wiwa returns to the university in Nsukka.

June 28   With word of federal troops advancing on Biafra, Saro-Wiwa returns to Bori.

July 6   Federal troops cross the Biafran border; first fighting between federal and Biafran forces occurs; federal troops overrun Ogoja within a few days.

July 7   Federal army units attempting to advance into Biafra at Nsukka are initially stopped by rebel troops; the town will be in Nigerian control by 15 July.

Mid-July   Fearing hostility against minorities from Igbos in Bori, Saro-Wiwa and his family move to Bane.

July 25   Nigerian troops capture Bonny, Nigeria's main oil export port.

Late July   Biafran propaganda falsely alleges several military victories against federal forces, increasing the confidence of Biafran supporters.

Economic sanctions cause suffering of civilians in Biafran-controlled areas.

August 9   Biafran troops invade Mid-Western Nigeria and capture its capital, Benin.

August 17 Biafran troops cross the Ofusu River into the Western Region/Nigeria, heading for Lagos and Ibadan; they are eventually repelled by Nigerian forces and retreat by the end of August.

September 21 Federal troops recapture Benin.

September 23 Lt. Col. Victor Banjo, who had led the Biafran offensive into the Mid-West, Col. Emmanuel Ifeajuna, and other Biafran military officers are condemned to death by Ojukwu for allegedly collaborating with Gowon to plot Ojukwu's overthrow.

September 24–October 2 Saro-Wiwa and his family move from Bane to Lagos.

September 26 Biafrans launch an attack on Bonny.

October 4 Nigerian troops take the Biafran capital, Enugu. Ojukwu blames the fall of Enugu on Biafran traitors; indiscriminate detention of suspected "saboteurs" begins.

Mid-October Saro-Wiwa takes a post with the Rivers State Interim Advisory Council.

October 18 Nigerian troops take Calabar.

November 11 Saro-Wiwa begins his appointment as administrator for Bonny, although he will not return to Bonny until three months later.

November 22–23 The Organization of African Unity (OAU) sends its consultative mission to Nigeria; the OAU perceives the war as an internal matter to be resolved by Nigeria and calls for the "territorial integrity, unity and peace of Nigeria" (Stremlau, *The International Politics*).

December Biafra launches a massive attack on Bonny.

The Vatican sends two emissaries to Lagos and Biafra to urge a negotiated settlement.

1968

February Saro-Wiwa makes his first visit to Bonny in his capacity as administrator; after a brief return to Lagos, he will spend the following six months in Bonny.

April 13 Tanzania recognizes Biafra as a sovereign state.

April 24 A Nigerian detachment of troops lands in the Ogoni village of Bane, en route to Port Harcourt; most Ogoni begin to evacuate their towns and villages.

April 28 Nigerian troops arrive in Bori.

May–August Four thousand Ogonis are killed by forced relocation and Igbo attacks.

May 8 Gabon recognizes Biafra.

May 14 Côte d'Ivoire recognizes Biafra.

May 16 Most civilians have abandoned Port Harcourt in the face of advancing Nigerian troops.

May 17 Isaac Boro is shot dead.

Federal troops capture Port Harcourt.

May 20   Zambia recognizes Biafra.

May 23–31   Peace talks between Nigeria and Biafra in Kampala, Uganda, fail to end war or to bring sides closer together.

June 11   The body of Nigerian peace negotiator Johnson Banjo is found in Kampala; there is evidence that he was murdered.

July 3   British director of famine relief Leslie Kirkley reports that approximately 400 children are dying every day of starvation in Biafra.

July 5   Nigeria warns relief agencies that unauthorized flights over its territory will be shot down.

July 20–26   The OAU initiates peace talks between Biafra and Nigeria; the agenda is set for talks in Addis Ababa.

July 29   Nigerian troops capture the Biafran divisional headquarters of Ahoada.

July 31   France announces it supports the "self-determination" of the Biafran people and begins to sell arms to Biafra, routing them through Côte d'Ivoire and Gabon.

August   Saro-Wiwa publishes a pamphlet, *The Ogoni Nation Today and Tomorrow.*

August 5–?   The Addis Ababa talks fail to bring peace.

August 10   The International Red Cross suspends emergency relief flights to Biafra because of recent antiaircraft fire by the Nigerian military.

August 15   The Nigerian government rejects a Red Cross plan to continue emergency airlifts of food to the Biafrans; since July, 6,000 Igbos a day have died from malnutrition.

August 16   UNICEF, the World Council of Churches, and other international agencies claim that the war is the biggest emergency since World War II.

September 1   Nigeria establishes a military government for Rivers State, based in Port Harcourt.

September 4   Aba is captured by Nigerian troops.

September 6   Owerri is captured by Nigerian troops.

September 27   The International Red Cross estimates that 8,000 to 10,000 people are starving to death every day in Biafra.

End of September   Saro-Wiwa ends his position as administrator for Bonny and leaves Bonny for Lagos, where he will remain until the end of 1968.

1969

January 2   UNICEF reports that approximately 2 million people have starved to death during the war.

Saro-Wiwa is sworn in as commissioner and member of the Executive Council of Rivers State in Port Harcourt.

April Nigerian troops take Umuahia.

The Biafrans retake Owerri.

May–June The Biafrans launch air attacks on Nigerian-controlled airports and power stations in the former Eastern and Mid-Western Regions.

June 1 In the Ahiara Declaration, Ojukwu refers to the war as the "Biafran Revolution" and outlines the ideals and principles of the revolution.

1970

January 2 Nigerian troops divide Biafra into three sections; a federal military government is appointed for each section.

January 6–10 Owerri falls; the Biafran resistance collapses.

January 11 Ojukwu flies into exile to Côte d'Ivoire.

January 12 The Biafran chief of staff, Brig. Gen. Philip Effiong, capitulates.

January 15 Nigeria accepts the unconditional surrender of Biafra; the Republic of Biafra ceases to exist.

War's end An estimated 1 to 3 million people are dead in the Eastern Region as a result of the civil war; 3 to 5 million refugees have crowded into a 2,500-square-kilometer area.

March Saro-Wiwa holds a thanksgiving service in Bori for the safe return of a fair number of the Ogoni from the rebel area; in his address, he draws attention to the past and continued exploitation of the Ogoni and other minorities by the Nigerian government.

April 1 Gowon seizes for the federal government a large portion of the oil revenue that had formerly belonged to the Mid-Western and Rivers States.

1975 Gowon is overthrown by Gen. Murtala Mohammed.

1976 Mohammed is assassinated in an attempted coup; Gen. Olusegun Obasanjo assumes power.

1979 Alhaji Shehu Shagari is elected president.

1983 Shagari's civilian government is overthrown; Gen. Mohammadu Buhari assumes power.

1985 Buhari is overthrown in a bloodless coup; he is replaced by Gen. Ibrahim Babangida.

1993 Babangida annuls the results of presidential elections, believed to have been won by Moshood Abiola; Babangida resigns and is replaced first by Ernest Shonekan's interim government and then by Gen. Sani Abacha on 17 November.

1994   Abiola is imprisoned after proclaiming himself president.

1995
March   Obasanjo is imprisoned.
November 10   Saro-Wiwa and other Ogoni activists are executed.
November 11   Nigeria is suspended from the Commonwealth.

1997   Parties supporting Abacha receive strong support in local elections.

1998
June 8   Abacha dies; the cause of his death is announced as a "heart ailment."
June 9   Gen. Abdulsalam Abubakar, a career military officer, becomes Nigeria's ninth military ruler since independence.
July 7   Abiola dies.
December 5   Local elections are held.

1999
January 9   State elections are held; the People's Democratic Party wins the governorship of twenty out of thirty-six states and 528 assembly seats.
February 20   Parliamentary elections are scheduled.
February 27   The presidential election is held.
February 28   Retired general Olusegun Obasanjo is elected the nation's third civilian president. Olu Falae, the Alliance for Democracy, will contest the election result because of "irregularities."

Appendix 3
An Annotated Bibliography

Craig W. McLuckie and James Gibbs

The following annotated bibliography is an attempt to place all print and electronic sources by and about Ken Saro-Wiwa before the scholar of African literature and politics. In this endeavor, we are appreciative of the assistance of librarians at Okanagan University College, the University of Victoria, the University of Washington, the University of Calgary, and the University of Alberta; as well as the Africa Book Publishing Collective; the pioneering work in Africana bibliography undertaken by Bernth Lindfors, particularly his *Black African Literature in English, 1987–1991* (London: Hans Zell Publishers, 1995); the *MLA Bibliographies;* the *ALA Bulletin* bibliographic updates; and all of those interested in Saro-Wiwa who responded to our call for information through the *ALA Bulletin* and on the Internet.

The aim is for comprehensiveness and accessibility, so that new, fresh, and invigorating perspectives on the issues that concerned Ken Saro-Wiwa may be produced. A review of the available material shows a lack of sustained engagement with Saro-Wiwa's aesthetic and, not surprisingly, an overengagement with the political. Annotations are provided for material directly related to Ken Saro-Wiwa's life and writing; however, issues of related interest and newspaper reports, unless they add significant material, are not annotated—their titles will provide readers with a useful description of the content. We have been unable to access all of Saro-Wiwa's occasional writing, so annotations are incomplete in this area.

CONTENTS

Memoirs *246*
Politics/Environment *246*
Short Stories *247*
Children's Books *247*
Drama *248*
Novels *248*
Poetry *249*
Nonfiction *249*
Serializations *250*
Anthologized Works *250*
Essays/Speeches *250*

Newspapers *251*
Television *252*
Interviews *253*
Juvenilia *255*
Online Resources *256*
Biographical Sources *257*
Critical Articles *261*
Dissertations/Theses *272*
Reviews of Books *272*
Bibliographies *275*
Works of Related Interest *275*

MEMOIRS

Saro-Wiwa, Ken. *A Month and a Day: A Detention Diary.* "Introduction" by William Boyd. Harmondsworth: Penguin, 1995.
[ISBN 014025868X; ISBN 0140259147 (U.S.)]
———. "Curriculum Vitae." From the unpublished manuscript, "Notes of a New Writer." 1994
———. "A Nigerian Television Sit-Com: *Basi and Company.*" From the unpublished manuscript, "Notes of a New Writer." September 1990.
———. "The Writer and His Audience." From the unpublished manuscript, "Notes of a New Writer." May 1989.
———. "Notes of a New Writer." Address delivered to the Creative Writing Class of Lagos State University. May 1988.
———. *On a Darkling Plain: An Account of the Nigerian Civil War.* Saros Star Series 10. Lagos, Nigeria: Saros International, 1989.
[ISBN 97-2460-12; 268 pages.]
———. "'The Language of African Literature': A Writer's Testimony." From the unpublished manuscript, "Notes of a New Writer." N.d.

POLITICS/ENVIRONMENT

MOSOP (Movement for the Survival of the Ogoni People). [Saro-Wiwa, Ken] *Ogoni Bill of Rights: Presented to the Government and People of Nigeria October 1990.* Port Harcourt, Nigeria: Saros International Publishers, 1992.
———. *Nigeria: The Brink of Disaster.* Saros Star Series 12. London, England, and Lagos, Nigeria: Saros International Publishers, 1991.
[ISBN 1870716167; 131 pages.]
———. *Similia: Essays on Anomic Nigeria.* Saros Star Series 16. Port Harcourt, Nigeria: Saros International Publishers, 1991; Nigeria: Spectrum Books, 1996.
[ISBN 9782460206; 200 pages.]
———. *Letter to Ogoni Youth.* Port Harcourt, Nigeria: Saros International Publishers, 1983.
[22 pages.]
———. *The Ogoni Nation Today and Tomorrow.* Port Harcourt, Nigeria: Saros International Publishers, 1968.

Saro-Wiwa, Ken. *Flames of Hell: Nigeria and Shell: The Dirty War Against the Ogoni.* Reinbeck, Germany: Rowohlt, Schleswig, proposed book.

——. *Genocide in Nigeria: The Ogoni Tragedy.* Saros Star Series 18. London, England, and Port Harcourt, Nigeria: Saros International Publishers, 1992.
[ISBN 9782460222; 103 pages.]

——. *Ogoni Moment of Truth.* Port Harcourt, Nigeria: Saros International Publishers, 1994.

——. *Second Letter to Ogoni Youth.* Port Harcourt, Nigeria: Saros International Publishers, 1993.

SHORT STORIES

Saro-Wiwa, Ken. *Adaku and Other Stories.* Saros Star Series 8. Port Harcourt, Nigeria: Saros International Publishers, 1989.
[ISBN 9782460095 (Nigeria); 1870716108 (UK); 174 pages.]

——. *A Forest of Flowers: Short Stories.* Saros Star Series 3. Port Harcourt, Nigeria: Saros International Publishers, 1986; London: Addison-Wesley Longman, 1995.
[Includes "Home Sweet Home," "The Inspector Calls," "The Overhaul," "A Family Affair," "The Bonfire," "A Share of Profit," "The Divorcee," "A Death in Town," "High Life," "Case No. 100," "Acapulco Motel," "The Stars Below," "Robert and the Dog," "Night Ride," "Garga," "Love Song of a Housewife," "A Caring Man," "The Shopkeeper and the Beggar," "A Legend on Our Street." Winner of the Commonwealth Writers Prize, 1987. ISBN 9782460044 (paper); ISBN 9782460036 (hardcover); ISBN 058227320X (UK, paper); 150 pages.]

——. "Dial-a-Tribe." Story read at Ola Rotimi Symposium.

Tsaro-Wiwa, Kay. "Case No. 100." *The Horizon* (Students' Magazine for the Department of English, University of Ibadan) 3, no. 4 (May 1966).
[An earlier version of the story published in *A Forest of Flowers.*]

CHILDREN'S BOOKS

(*Indicates that the book is based on the text of a *Basi and Company* script.)

*Saro-Wiwa, Ken. *A Bride for Mr. B.* Saros Junior Series 4. Illus. by Peregrino Brimah. Port Harcourt, Nigeria: Saros International Publishers, 1992.
[ISBN 1870716264; 96 pages. Dedicated to "my beloved son Tedum, who died at Eton College, on the ides of March 1993."]

*——. *Mr. B.* Saros Junior Series 1. Illus. by Peregrino Brimah. Port Harcourt, Nigeria: Saros International Publishers, 1987.
[ISBN 1870716019; 154 pages.]

*——. *Mr. B Again.* Saros Junior Series 2. Illus. by Peregrino Brimah. Port Harcourt, Nigeria: Saros International Publishers, 1989.
[ISBN 1870716086; 143 pages.]

*——. *Mr. B Goes to Lagos.* Adventures of Mr. B Series 1. Illus. by Peregrino Brimah. Port Harcourt, Nigeria: Saros International Publishers, 1989.
[ISBN 1870716051; 48 pages.]

*——. *Mr. B Goes to the Moon.* Port Harcourt, Nigeria: Saros International Publishers, 1992.

*————. *Mr. B. Is Dead.* Saros Junior Series 3. Illus. by Peregrino Brimah. Port Harcourt, Nigeria: Saros International Publishers, 1991.
[ISBN 1870716140; 144 pages.]
*————. *Mr. B's Mattress.* Illus. by Peregrino Brimah. Port Harcourt, Nigeria: Saros International Publishers, 1992.
[ISBN 1870716248; 55 pages.]
*————. *Segi Finds the Radio.* Adventures of Mr. B Series 3. Port Harcourt, Nigeria: Saros International Publishers, 1990.
[ISBN 1870716124; 56 pages.]
*————. *A Shipload of Rice.* Port Harcourt, Nigeria: Saros International Publishers, 1991.
[ISBN 1870716132; 56 pages.]
*————. *The Transistor Radio.* The Adventures of Mr. B. Series 2. Port Harcourt, Nigeria: Saros International Publishers, 1989.
[ISBN 9782460060; ISBN 187071606X; 48 pages.]
Tsaro-Wiwa, Ken. *Tambari.* Lagos: Longman, 1973.
————. *Tambari in Dukana.* Lagos: Longman, 1973.

DRAMA

Saro-Wiwa, Ken. *Basi and Company: Four Television Plays.* Saros Star Series 6. Port Harcourt, Nigeria: Saros International Publishers, 1988.
[ISBN 1870716035; 82 pages.]
————. *Bride by Return.* British Broadcasting Corporation, 1973.
[For radio.]
————. *Dream of Sologa.* 1966.
[An adaptation of Gabriel Okara's *The Voice.*]
————. *Eneka.* Performed at Port Harcourt ca. 1969.
————. *Four Farcical Plays.* Saros Star Series 9. Port Harcourt, Nigeria: Saros International Publishers, 1989.
[The plays are *The Transistor Radio, Bride by Return* (broadcast by the BBC in 1973), *The Wheel* (earlier version performed in 1964; produced by Paul Worika at Ibadan 1984), and *Madam No Go Quench Again* (written in 1977). Drama Prize, Association of Nigerian Authors, 1990.
[ISBN 1870716094; 95 pages.]
————. *The Supreme Commander.* Performed at Calabar ca. 1969.
Tsaro-Wiwa, Ken. *The Transistor Radio.* In *African Theatre: Eight Prize-Winning Plays for Radio.* Ed. Gwyneth Henderson. London: Heinemann, 1973: 87–107.
[Heinemann; ISBN 0435901346. For radio. Joint Fourth Place Winner, African Theatre Prize, BBC. Broadcast: British Broadcasting Corporation, 1972. The plays were judged by Wole Soyinka, Martin Esslin, and Lewis Nkosi. A review sketch version was presented at Trenchard Hall in October 1964.]

NOVELS

Saro-Wiwa, Ken. *Basi and Company: A Modern African Folktale.* Saros Star Series 4. Port Harcourt, Nigeria: Saros International, 1987.

[ISBN 1870716035; ISBN 1870716000 (Blackwell's listing); 216 pages.]
————. *Lemona's Tale.* Harmondsworth: Penguin, 1996.
[ISBN 0140260862; 144 pages.]
————. *Pita Dumbrok's Prison.* Saros Star Series 15. Port Harcourt, Nigeria: Saros International Publishers, 1991.
[ISBN 9782460192; 1870716191; 280 pages.]
————. *Prisoners of Jebs.* Saros Star Series 5. Port Harcourt, Nigeria: Saros International Publishers, 1988.
[ISBN 1870716078; 180 pages.]
————. *Sozaboy: A Novel in Rotten English.* Saros Star Series 2. Port Harcourt, Nigeria: Saros International Publishers, 1985. "Introduction" by William Boyd. London: Addison-Wesley Longman, 1994; White Plains, N.Y.: Longman, 1994.
[ISBN 9782460028 (paperback); ISBN 978246001X (hardcover); ISBN 0582236991 (Longman); 186 pages. NOMA Award for publishing in Africa, 1987: Honorable Mention.]
————. *Sozaboy.* (Pétit minitaire). Arles-le-Méjear: Actes Sud, 1998.
[ISBN 2742716602.]

POETRY

Saro-Wiwa, Ken. "Corpses Have Grown." *African Literature Association Bulletin* 20, no. 3 (Summer 1994): 22–23.
[Poem taken from *Songs in a Time of War*; editorial note regarding Saro-Wiwa's last detention.]
————. "The Nigerians! The Nigerians!" In *Elechi Amadi at 55: Poems, Short Stories, and Papers.* Ed. by Willfried Feuser and Ebele Eko. Ibadan: Heinemann (Nigeria), 1994: 10–12.
————. *Songs in a Time of War.* "Introduction" by Theo Vincent. Port Harcourt, Nigeria, and Epsom, UK: Saros International Publishers, 1985.
[Nigerian Authors' Prize, runner-up for poetry. Twenty poems. ISBN 9782460001; 44 pages. "Dedicated to the officers and men / Of the Third Marine Commando Division / Of the Nigerian Army."]
Tsaro-Wiwa, Ken. "Poems Prophesying War." *Black Orpheus* 2, no. 1 (February 1968): n.p.
[Emotional and personal poems on the war by Saro-Wiwa were published alongside Christopher Okigbo's "Path of Thunder."]

NONFICTION

Saro-Wiwa, Ken. "Notes of a Reluctant Publisher." *The African Book Publishing Record* 22 (1996).
————. *The Singing Anthill: Ogoni Folk Tales.* Saros Star Series 11. Port Harcourt, Nigeria: Saros International Publishers, 1991.
[ISBN 1870716159 (UK); 978246015X (Nigeria); 144 pages. Contains "Author's Note," "The Promise," "Crime and Punishment," "The Man Behind the Door," "Kuru Goes Hungry Again," "The Mischevious Bird," "The Coward," "The Creditor," "The Scoundrel," "The Wives' Revolt," "Revenge," "A Mother in

the Sky," "The Singing Anthill," "The Voice," "A Final Home Coming," "Lelewa Sira Kuru," "Sira Mene and the Deformed Healer," "The Childless Woman," "The Poor Wise Man," "A Servant's Vengeance," "Medicine for Love," "The Python's Eggs," "The Power of Truth," "The Tale Bearer," "Okuguru," "The Spirit Maiden," "The Vain Belle," "The Market Husband," and "Madola." Dedicated to "The Ogoni People."]

SERIALIZATIONS

Saro-Wiwa, Ken. *Prisoners of Jebs.* In *The Vanguard* (Nigeria), 1985–1986.

ANTHOLOGIZED WORKS

Saro-Wiwa, Ken. "Africa Kills Her Sun." *Africa Rhapsody.* Ed. Nadezda Obradovic. New York: Doubleday, 1995.
———. "High Life." *Africa in Prose.* Ed. O. R. Dathorne and Willfried Feuser. Penguin African Library. Harmondsworth: Penguin, 1969: 183–188.
[The story ends differently than in *A Forest of Flowers.*]
———. "The New Beggars." *Index on Censorship* 25, no. 6 (1996): 79–86.

ESSAYS/SPEECHES

Saro-Wiwa, Ken. "Acceptance Speech by Ken Saro-Wiwa: 1994 Fonlon-Nichols Laureate." *African Literature Association Bulletin* 20, no. 2 (Spring 1994): 17–21.
———. "Before the Curtain Falls."
[Speech focusing on political stability and the political future of Nigeria.]
———. *A Comedy of Terrors: The Making of a Nigerian Television Series.*
[Described as forthcoming in ca. 1986. An unpublished manuscript.]
———. "The Constitutional Conference and National Cohesion." *The Sunday Magazine,* 27 February 1994: 22–25.
———. "Death Cannot Stop Our Ultimate Victory." *Dateline,* 23 November 1995: 10.
———. "Editorial." *The Horizon* (University of Ibadan) 3, no. 3 (December 1965): 6.
———. "For Budding Writers, Some Advice." *Daily Times,* 21 October 1989: 12.
———. "Ken Saro-Wiwa." In *My UI.* Ed. Bunmi Salako. Ibadan: Bookcraft, 1990: 149–155.
[Statement on his time as a student at university.]
———. "The Language of African Literature: A Writer's Testimony." *Research in African Literatures* 23, no. 1 (Spring 1992): 153–157.
[On his education as it relates to exposure to languages. Summary of his fight against "the oppression and bad faith of majority ethnic groups . . . in Nigeria." Holds a position similar to Chinua Achebe's regarding the use of English: attaining the largest possible audience. On Ngugi wa Thiongó's decision, Saro-Wiwa "detects some posturing." He concludes: "That which carries best

and which is most popular is Standard English, expressed simply and lucidly."]

———. "Letter." *The Mail and Guardian* (Johannesburg), 11 November 1995. [Reproduced at the following Website: http://www.mg.co.za/mg/news/nov17-kenletter.html. Deals with South Africa's response. Cross-reference to Soyinka's call to Mandela to act, and so on.]

———. "Letter from Ken Saro-Wiwa (from prison, to a French colleague)." *African Literature Association Bulletin* 21, no. 3 (Summer 1995): 21.

———. "Lord Take My Soul but the Struggle Continues: Ken Saro-Wiwa's Last Words." *ALA Bulletin* 21, no. 4 (Fall 1995): 3–4.

———. *Newsweek,* 20 September 1993.

———. "Ogoni as Metaphor." *The News* (Lagos), 19 December 1994: 7. [Part of his acceptance "speech" for the Right Livelihood Award.]

———. "Planting Creative Writing in Schools." *Vanguard,* 7 January 1988: 8–9.

———. "The Presidential Address: It's Many Happy ANA Returns." *Association of Nigerian Authors Review* 6, no. 8 (1991): 1, 20–21.

———. "A Television Drama in Nigeria: A Personal Experience." A paper read at the African Literature Association Conference in Pittsburgh, April 1988. [A brief historical overview that stresses the artistic and economic difficulties faced by all artisans involved. "Nigerian television drama can be said not to have outgrown its 'novitiate period.'" Very brief discussion of his involvement. Refers to "the souvenir magazine published on the occasion of the shooting of the fiftieth episode of (*Basi and Company*) in 1987."]

———. "We All Stand Before History." *New Solutions: A Journal of Enviro* (Spring 1996).

———. "A Classic" and "A Company Is Born," in *Everything About Basi and Co., the Most Hilarious Comedy on TV!* Lagos: Saros International, 1986: 3, 4–7.

———. "Ken Saro-Wiwa Final Address to Military Appointed Tribunal." http://www.earthisland.org/ei/journal/w95-25b.html. [Declaration of innocence.]

———. "Stand by Me and the Ogoni People. . . . " *Earth Island Journal* 10, no. 3 (Summer 1995): 35ff. [Letter from Saro-Wiwa, smuggled out of prison. Acceptance speech for the Goldman Environmental Prize. Reproduced at http://www.earthisland.org/ei/journal/ogoni.html.]

———. "Pen Voice: Ken Saro-Wiwa." *Daily Times* (Lagos),15 November 1989: 26; 22 November 1989: 22.

Saro-Wiwa, Ken, and Abiola Irele. "The Nigerian Review: A Journal of Contemporary Culture." *Association of Nigerian Authors Review* 3, no. 3 (1987): 23. [Announcement of forthcoming journal.]

Tsaro-Wiwa, 'Kay. "The Travelling Theatre on Tour in 1963." *The Beacon* (University of Ibadan) 1, no. 9 (May 1963): 40.

NEWSPAPERS

(Saro-Wiwa wrote occasionally for *The Sunday Times* (Lagos) in 1967 and from 1977 for *The Punch*.)

Saro-Wiwa, Ken. "Crux of *The Trouble*." *The Guardian* (Nigeria), 22 January 1984: B6.

[On Achebe's pamphlet, *The Trouble with Nigeria.* See section on "Works of Related Interest."]

———. "Democracy and the Nigerian Army." *A. M. News,* 19 November 1995.

[Report from *The Guardian,* 22 September 1994.]

———. "Detainee's Diary." *The Guardian* (London), 29 July 1995.

———. "The Environment Is Man's First Right." *A. M. News,* 8 October 1995: 6.

———. "The Evil at the Heart of Nigeria." *The Independent* (London), 14 November 1995.

[Also used in "Without Walls: The Hanged Man—Nigeria's Shame." Channel 4, 14 November 1995.]

———. "I Bow and Tremble." *A. M. News,* 26 November 1995: 6.

[First published in September 1993.]

———. "Last Diary of a Poet Crusader." *Observer Review* (London), 3 December 1995: 1–2.

———. "Let Us Confront History." *Tell,* 19 December 1994: 34.

———. "Letter from Saro-Wiwa." *Prime People* (Lagos), 6 July 1990: 19.

[Response to Onyeka Owenu's article in the same publication on 27 April 1990, on "Igbo-bashing" in *On a Darkling Plain.*]

———. "Missive from a Prison Bed." *The Guardian,* 18 May 1995.

[Written in Port Harcourt Hospital.]

———. "Musing." Included in "Just Before the Blackout" by Sola Olorunyomi. *Glendora Review* (Lagos) 1, no. 3 (1996): 22–23.

[A dialogue with a cockroach, written while in jail in 1995.]

———. "My Testimony." *Sunday Vanguard* (Kirikiri, Lagos), 19 January 1992: 15.

———. "The Odd, the Odious and Our Very Odia." *Guardian,* 5 January 1989: 10.

[Reprinted in the *Association of Nigerian Authors Review* 4, no. 6 (1989): 31. Argues that the typical Nigerian book launch has become a display of wealth.]

———. "Odia and the Politics of Book Launching." *Guardian,* 7 February 1989: 8.

[Reply to Odia Ofeimun's article, "Saro's Sour Logic."]

———. "Of Books and Bookmen." *Sunday Times,* 27 May 1990: 7.

———. "Open Letter." *The News* (Nigeria), 8 August 1994.

———. "Open Letter to Wole Soyinka." *Nigeria* (1991): 86–88.

[This is a reprint of a letter dated 24 October 1989. Reprinted in *Nigeria: The Brink of Disaster.* Saros Star Series 12. London, England, and Lagos, Nigeria: Saros International Publishers, 1991, 86–88.]

———. "Saro-Wiwa Speaks." *New African* (January 1996): 13–14.

[Extract from the prison diary.]

———. "Similia," column in *The Sunday Times* (Nigeria), October 1989–1991.

TELEVISION

Amina. January 1987.

[Pilot episode for a soap opera.]

Basi and Company.

[Rob Nixon notes that Saro-Wiwa wrote some one "hundred and fifty episodes of *Basi,* a robust satire with a moralistic edge" (see citation for Nixon 1996, p. 43, under "Critical Articles"). Reviews of the television series appeared in the *New York Times, South, West Africa.*]

The Drilling Fields, London: Catma Film Production for Channel 4, 1994.

[Includes an interview/profile of Saro-Wiwa. Repackaged in Canada as *Delta Force.*]

The Heat of the Moment, Channel 4 (UK), October 1992. Glen Ellis, director. [Documentary film on the Ogoni.]
Ken Saro-Wiwa [videorecording]: An African Martyr. Produced by Nathan Sheppard; a Millennium Movies Production. Princeton, N.J.: Films for the Humanities and Sciences, ca. 1996. VIDEO 4174.
[One videocassette (23 minutes): col., sd.; 1/2 inch. Performers: narrator, Leon Herber. Credits: director, Mark Johnston; production manager, Elaine Sheppard; production assistant, Mary Lucas; researcher, Christina Barchi; camera, Nathan Sheppard. VHS. Ken Saro-Wiwa, the Ogoni writer and political activist, was hanged in November 1995 by the Nigerian military dictatorship. Saro-Wiwa had been campaigning for the rights of Nigeria's Ogoni people, who have suffered from decades of resource exploitation by foreign oil companies and oppression by the Nigerian military government. This program tells Saro-Wiwa's story through his own words and those of his wife. Personal author: Mark Johnston. Corporate author: Millennium Movies; Films for the Humanities. Personal subject: Interviews with Maria Saro-Wiwa.

INTERVIEWS

Adinuba, C. Don. "To Cheer and Challenge." *African Concord,* 27 February 1989: 32.
Ajibade, Kunle. "Kick Nigeria out of UNO: Conversation with Ken Saro-Wiwa." *Weekend Concord,* 21 July 1990: 7, 18.
———. "A Pen Merchant." *African Concord,* 5 March 1990: 52.
———. "Tempestuous Ken." *African Concord,* 30 July 1990: 57.
Akindoyo, Dele. "Be Warned." *Classique,* 30 September 1991: 24–25.
[Saro-Wiwa saying he will take Ogoni case to the United Nations.]
Akinpelu, Mayor. "The Untold Story of *Basi and Company* Palaver." *Prime People,* 8 January 1988: 14–15, 23.
[Saro-Wiwa disputes ownership of *Basi and Company* with Albert Egbe.]
Akinsola, 'Biyi, Sola Osofisan, and Kayode Ogunfeyetimi. "Ken Saro-Wiwa." *Crown Prince,* October 1991: 26–30, 44, 51, 58.
Anikwe, Ogbuagu. "Behind Ken Saro-Wiwa's Humour." *Guardian,* 8 April 1990: 9.
Anim, Etim. "Prose of an Underdog." *Newswatch,* 9 April 1990: 43–54.
[Biography, interview, and excerpts from *On a Darkling Plain.*]
Anon. "*Basi and Company* Goes International." *Sunday Times,* 18 October 1987: 20; 25 October 1987: 20; 1 November 1987: 20.
Anon. "Saro-Wiwa Was a Saboteur, Says Abacha." *A. M. News,* 19 November 1995: 1–2.
Anon. "Why Ojukwu Hates Saro-Wiwa." *Tempo,* 9 February 1996: 16.
Bello, Remi. "Why I Wrote *Prisoners of Jebs.*" *Vanguard,* 14 December 1988: 8–9.
Channel 4 (UK), 15 November 1995.
Edafioka, Veronica, Abiola Oloke, and Sam Smith. "Newsliners." *Newswatch,* 28 November 1988: 38.
[*Basi and Company* and *Prisoners of Jebs.* A Brief overview of each book, highlighting Saro-Wiwa's range.]
Egbe, Nkanu. "Our Country is Anti-Art—Ken Saro-Wiwa." *Top News,* 11 January 1989: 12–14.
Ezenwa-Ohaeto. "Interview: Ken Saro-Wiwa." *Daily Times,* 29 July 1989: 20; 12 August 1989: 9.

[On *Sozaboy*.]
Ezugha, Dili. "Biafra Was a Heroic Necessity: Interview with Ben Obumselu." *Quality*, 6 September 1990: 32–39.
Fiofori, Tam. "Conversation with Saro-Wiwa." *Vanguard,* 5 April 1990: 8–9.
[About *On a Darkling Plain*.]
Ikandu, Hakeem. "Enter New Mr. B: Soldier Go, Soldier Come, Says Creator Ken Saro-Wiwa." *Vanguard,* 2 September 1987: 7.
[On *Basi and Company*.]
Ike, Osita. "A Chat with Ken Saro-Wiwa." *National Concord,* 17 December 1987: 5.
Iloegbunam, Chuks. "The Death of a Writer." *The Guardian,* 11 November 1995: 30.
[A valuable summary. Secession for the Ogoni from Nigeria is not an option.]
The Independent (London), 11 November 1995.
Iserhime, Emu Dorcas. "Nigerians Are Vulgar, Says Ken Saro-Wiwa." *Prime People,* 3 April 1987: 16.
[On the fiftieth anniversary party for *Basi and Company*.]
Ivens, Martin. "The Misery of Black Gold." *The Times* (London), 11 December 1993.
[Interview about his time in detention.]
Johnson, Daniel. "Literary Giant with a Common Touch." *Times,* 11 November 1995.
Jukwey, James. "Struggle for an Ogoni Homeland Spawns Accusations of Genocide." *Times,* 11 November 1995.
Lawal, Sola. "Writers Also Speak." *Hotline,* July 1991: 34–36.
Mofe-Damijo, Richard, Prince Emeka Obasi, and Dozie Arinze. "A Voice for the Minority." *Classique,* 23 April 1990: 27–28, 31–33.
The News Editors. "They Are Killing My People: Interview with Ken Saro-Wiwa." *The News,* 17 May 1993: 22–27.
[An abridged reprint of the original appears in Na'allah (1998, pp. 329–342). See section on "Critical Articles." Deals with the Ogoni struggles, MOSOP, Saro-Wiwa's expressed desire for a "confederal" Nigeria, his opposition to secession, and his view that Nigeria as it currently exists should be dismantled.]
Nigerian High Commission, London. "The Conviction of Ken Saro-Wiwa." *Independent,* 6 December 1995: 15.
Nnoru, Joe. "Interview with Ken Saro-Wiwa." *Guardian,* 21 December 1988: 15.
[On the Association of Nigerian Authors (ANA).]
Nwagboso, Maxwell. [Published under pseudonym "Matchet."] "So Long Kenule . . . " *West Africa* 4075 (20–26 November 1995): 1790.
[Recalls Saro-Wiwa's visit to London in May, refers to his humor and courage, and comments on his attitude toward Biafra.]
Nwakanma, Obi, et al. "There Was No Other Thing to Do but Say No: Interview with Ken Saro-Wiwa." *Sunday Vanguard,* 12 November 1995: 4.
Obaigbo, Aoiri. "How Saro-Wiwa Made the Million Naira That Got *Basi and Co.* to the Screen." *Vintage People,* 8 December 1989: 18, 22.
[About his successes in business.]
Obasi, [Prince] Emeka. "*Basi and Co.* has caught the Imagination of Nigerians." *Guardian,* 5 November 1988: 9.
Obi, Ben Charles, and Joseph Ohen. "I Betrayed Ojukwu and Biafra: Interview with Ken Saro-Wiwa." *City News,* 8 May 1992: 6–7.

Ogbuanoh, Jossey. "The People's Entire Mentality Should Change." *Probe,* 29 December 1988: 50–52.
[Includes comments on his writing.]
Ojo, Damilola. "Saro-Wiwa, a Sad and Funny Guy, Talks of Nigeria's Vulgar Book Culture." *Daily Times,* 3 December 1988: 12.
Okoh, Sunday. "Saro-Wiwa Deserved Death: Diete Spiff." *Abuja Mirror,* 6–12 December 1995: 1.
Okome, Onookome. "Saro-Wiwa: 'Not Right to Judge Yet.'" *Daily Times,* 28 August 1991: 26; 4 September 1991: 22.
[On the Association of Nigerian Authors (ANA).]
Okonedo, Tony, Ola Boye, and Debo Fatiregun. "Saro-Wiwa Comes Back Smoking." *Vanguard,* 6 May 1988: 8.
[On difficulties with Nigeria's television authorities.]
Okonta, Ike, Bolaji Adebiyi, Aluko Akinyele, Nkechi Attoh, Samson Ojo, and Clifford Amadi. "Ken Saro-Wiwa: Create Ethnic States." *Citizen,* 12 August 1991: 16–21.
Ola, Boye. "How I Write—Saro-Wiwa." *Sunday Concord,* 1 July 1990: 14.
Omoifo, Isi. "Humour as a Mask." *African Guardian,* 19 December 1988: 36.
Onuorah, Madu, and Kehinde Latunde-Dada. "Literary Novels Give Only Fame." *Thisweek,* 30 January 1989: 31.
Osewele, Nat Beifoh. "Ken Saro-Wiwa, a Baby at 50." *National Concord,* 10 October 1991: 5.
Oshuntokun, Bisola. "Ken Saro-Wiwa Writes Children's Books on Late Papa Awo." *Aura* (Ibadan), 22 July 1991: 19–21, 37–39.
Tell Editors. "We Will Defend Our Oil with Our Blood." *Tell,* 8 February 1993.
[An abridged reprint of the original appears in Na'allah (1998, pp. 343–359). See section on "Critical Articles." Covers the Ogoni mass protests over "the despoliation of their land through oil-producing activities." Saro-Wiwa draws the parallel between the Ogoni of Rivers State and the Isoko of Delta State. Saro-Wiwa responds to Chief Anthony Enahoro's call for eight federations within Nigeria with his own position: "It's what I call erectism; ethnic autonomy, resolve and environmental control."]
Tella, Yinka. "People." *Citizen,* 17 June 1991: 51.
Tetteh-Lartey, Alex. "Interview with Ken Saro-Wiwa About His Poetry and Plays." *BBC Arts and Africa* 602 (1985): 1–5.
———. "Interview with Ken Saro-Wiwa About *Sozaboy* and His Television Series *Basi and Company.*" *BBC Arts and Africa* 602 (1986): 1–5.
Udenwa, Onuora, and Chinwude Onuwuanyi. "Q Interview with Ken Saro-Wiwa." *Quality,* 15 December 1988: 36–38, 41–44.
Yakubu, Ikhazs. "Ken Saro-Wiwa: 'Not Right to Judge Yet.'" *Daily Times,* 28 August 1991: 26.
[On Saro-Wiwa as president of the Association of Nigerian Authors.]

JUVENILIA

Saro-Wiwa, Ken. "Editorial." *The Horizon* (students' magazine for the Department of English, University of Ibadan) 3, no. 3 (December 1965): 6.
[Saro-Wiwa on the need for a Nigerian literary language; he astutely observes that it is a problem "which will continue to plague our literature for some time."]

Tsaro-Wiwa, Kay, 1st Year Honors English Student. "The Travelling Theatre on Tour in 1963." *The Beacon* (Official organ of the Students' Union, University of Ibadan) 1, no. 9 (May 1963): 40.

ONLINE RESOURCES

Aluko, Mobolaji E. "Memorial Service/Protest on Friday." Posting to naijanet@mitvma.mit.edu, 14 November 1995.

Amnesty International. http://www.derechos.org/amnesty/nigeria/response.txt.
[A refutation of Desmond Orage's Website—see citation later in this section.]

Anon. "Major Writings." http://www.derechos.org/nigeria/sarowiwa/saro-writings.txt.
[A one-page bibliography; publishers are not listed.]

Anon. "Nigeria: Kein Blut für Öl." http://www.weltmusik.de/iwalewa/nigeria.htm.
[Photographs, illustrations, and brief commentary on the crisis.]

Anon. "The Ogoni Nine Judgement." http://www.derechos.org/nigeria/sarowiwa/judgement.txt.
[A fifty-eight-page transcript of "In the Ogoni Civil Disturbance (Special) Tribunal Holden [*sic*] at Port Harcourt, Rivers State on Tuesday the 31st Day of October, 1995." It is difficult to determine the veracity of the material, in part because the transcriber's identity is unknown.]

Anon. "Quick Bibliography of Recent Books and Articles on Ogoni People." 19 November 1995. http://www.prairienet.org/acas/ogonibib.html.
[A three-page list, including some annotated entries and several works on Saro-Wiwa.]

Catma Films. "The Drilling Fields." http://193.128.6.150/owbt/drilling_video.html.
[Catma Films's homepage on the documentary. 11 pages. Includes quotations from Saro-Wiwa and General Ibrahim Babangida.]

Domoto, Akiko. "Ken Saro-Wiwa, President of the Movement for the Survival of the Ogoni People (MOSOP), The Gallows, 10 November 1995." http://www.globeint.org/html/press-releases/nigeria.html.
[The president of Global Legislators Organization for a Balanced Environment (GLOBE), Japan summarizes the case, emphasizes that "environmental rights are human rights," and notes that "Diana Wiwa and her husband, younger brother of Ken . . . were smuggled out of Nigeria with the aid of the Body Shop. They are now travelling . . . to promote the plight of the Ogoni people."]

Greenpeace and Movement for the Survival of the Ogoni People. "Transcript of 'A Testimony' by Dr. Owens Wiwa (Brother of Ken Saro-Wiwa)." Greenpeace Internet document, 1995.

Olanyin, Tejumola. "Nigerian Casefile 2: The Ken Saro-Wiwa Ogoni Handbook." http://envirolink.org/homepp/eric/nigeria2.html.
[11 pages, including "The World Bank and Us," "The Death of a Writer," "Farewell, Ken Saro-Wiwa," "The Writings of Ken Saro-Wiwa: A Bibliography," "Action Against the Nigerian Junta and Its Leaders," "Why the General Killed." The last piece is by Wole Soyinka.]

Orage, Desmond. "An Open Letter to All Interested in the Ogoni Situation in Nigeria." http://www.derechos.org/nigeria/sarowiwa/ad.txt.
[Saro-Wiwa's nephew, Desmond Orage, the son of murdered Chief Samuel N. Orage, gives his perspective on the Ogoni Nine Trial. The Website reproduces an advertisement financed by Desmond Orage in the *New York Times*. Includes refutation by Amnesty International.]

Sangoyomi, Taiye B. "Nigerian Visit (1)." Posting to naijanet@mitvma.mit.edu, 23 January 1996.

BIOGRAPHICAL SOURCES

Abu, Bala Dan. "'Saro-Wiwa Is No Friend of the Igbos'—Chief Ahanonu." *Quality,* 16 August 1990: 13, 15.
[On Saro-Wiwa's businesses and an interview regarding his response to *On a Darkling Plain.* The primary resentment against Saro-Wiwa has to do with the civil war period issue of "abandoned property"—whether or not the writer's estate business was made up of Igbo property—and discrimination against Igbo students by the Ministry of Education, of which Saro-Wiwa was minister.]
Abuah, Valerie. "At Ken Saro-Wiwa's Launch, It Was Book, Talk and Art." *Vintage People,* 25 October 1991: 15.
Agbor, Ajan, Soji Olaitan, and Stella Oyibo. "A Giant at 50." *Tell,* 28 October 1991: 38.
Agbor, Alphonsus, et al. "Ken Saro-Wiwa: Soldiers Won't Quit Cemetery." *Sunday Punch,* 25 February 1996: 1–2.
Akanni, Tunde. "Ken Saro-Wiwa at 50." *Mid-Week Concord,* 17 October 1991: ii.
Alibi, Idang. "Ken Saro-Wiwa." *Daily Times,* 29 May 1990: 13; 5 June 1990: 13.
[On minority issues.]
———. "Saro-Wiwa: A Short Giant." *Sunday Times,* 25 June 1989: 20.
Anon. "After the Hangings." *The Economist* 337 (18 November 1995): 41.
Anon. "Executions Outrage World." *Okanagan Saturday* (11 November 1995): A13.
[Associated Press/Canadian Press story.]
Anon. "The First Right." *Amicus Journal* 18 (Spring 1996): 11.
Anon. "The Human Spirit." *World Watch* 8 (September/October 1995): 40.
Anon. "Ken Saro-Wiwa: In Memoriam." *Research in African Literatures* 27, no. 1 (Spring 1996).
[Obituary.]
Anon. "Martyrdom of Saro-Wiwa." *New African* (December 1995): 19.
[Reports that Fawehimni withdrew because video evidence of Colonel Komo's press conference was not produced. Reports that the judge said Saro-Wiwa's refusal to make a statement weighed heavily against him.]
Anon. "Nigeria Faces Criticism After Execution of Writer." *UN Chronicle* 33 (Spring 1996): 80–82.
Anon. "Nigeria Foaming." *The Economist* 337 (18 November 1995): 15–16.
Anon. "Nigeria: Saro-Wiwa as a Columnist." *West Africa* 75 (1992).
Anon. *Ogoni Crisis: The Untold Story.* n.d. (1996?)
[A federal apologist makes a number of important points and a number of allegations, for example, that Saro-Wiwa wanted to be addressed as "Your Excellency" and that he abandoned his wife after she bore him twins. Several documents, including letters are included in the booklet.]
Anon. "Saro-Wiwa's Peril." *The Economist* 337 (4 November 1995): 46ff.
[On the death sentence.]
Arnold, Stephen. "Ken Saro-Wiwa Update." *African Literature Association Bulletin* 19, no. 3 (Summer 1993): 15.
[Report on Saro-Wiwa being released on bail.]
Ayetigbo, Ayodele. "Coffin to Abacha and Shell." *The U.S.-Nigeria Voice* 2, no. 17 (1995): 7–10.

―――. "Saro-Wiwa on Our Minds." *The U.S.-Nigeria Voice* 2, no. 17 (1995): 5.

Bacon, David. "Oil Politics Rule in Nigeria." *Earth Island Journal* 10, no. 3 (Winter 1995).

Birnbaum, Michael. "Judicial Travesty Whose Verdict Was Preordained." *The Times,* 13 November 1995.

[A brisk summary of findings.]

―――. "Letter." *The Independent* (London), 8 December 1995.

[Response to Nigerian High Commission statement.]

―――. *Nigeria, Fundamental Rights Denied: Report of the Trial of Ken Saro-Wiwa and Others.* London: Article 19 in association with the Bar Human Rights Committee of England and Wales and the Law Society of England and Wales, 1995.

[80 pages.]

Boyd, William. "Introduction" to Saro-Wiwa's *A Month and a Day.* Harmondsworth: Penguin, 1995: vii–xv.

[Previously published in *The New Yorker,* 27 November 1995, pp. 51–55, as "Death of a Writer." A personal account of getting to know Saro-Wiwa, with a brief commentary on his work. Covers ecological and political involvement and the charges, trial, and death. Reprinted in Na'allah (1998, pp. 49–55). See section on "Critical Articles" and Emeka Nwabueze's response, also in that section.]

Bright, Chris. "Eco-Justice in Nigeria." *World Watch* 9 (July-August 1996): 9.

Contemporary Authors, vol. 150. Detroit: Gale Research: 391.

[Obituary notice.]

Damu, Jean, et al. "Oil Rules Nigeria." *The Black Scholar* 26 (Winter/Spring 1996): 51–54.

Daniels, Anthony. "A Good Man in Africa." *National Review* 47, no. 13 (10 July 1995): 51–52.

Darah, G. G. "Dying for the Niger Delta." *The Guardian,* 19 November 1995: B1–2.

Emereole, Olisaemeka. "Ken Saro-Wiwa's Literary Harvest." *Guardian,* 14 October 1991: 33.

[Launch of eight books at once.]

Ette, Mercy, and Josephine Akarue. "Newsliners." *Newswatch,* 28 October 1991: 43.

Fashomi, Dele. "Ken Saro-Wiwa and the National Polity." *National Concord,* 3 October 1991: 7.

[Ogoni campaign.]

Fiofori, Tam. "Saro-Wiwa's Words and Music." *Vanguard,* 18 January 1990: 8–9.

Gberenen, Adewole. "A Day with Ken Saro-Wiwa." *Daily Times,* 19 September 1992: 11.

Gberenen, Ledisi. "Like Jesus, Like Ken." *A. M. News,* 17 December 1995: 9.

Igwe, Dimgba. "The Day Professor Osofisan, a Socialist, Was Happy in the Company of Capitalists." *Sunday Concord,* 5 April 1987: 17.

[Fiftieth episode of *Basi and Company.*]

―――. "Saro-Wiwa: 120 Minutes of Critical X-ray." *Sunday Concord,* 15 January 1989: 8, 13.

[Launch of *Prisoners of Jebs.*]

Ilagha, Nengi. "Seven Up for Saro-Wiwa." *Eko,* 12 October 1991: 15.

[Launch of the seventh book.]

Ilesanmi, Obefemi. "An Agenda for Saro-Wiwa." *Daily Times,* 29 December 1990: 11.

[Speech as Association of Nigerian Authors president.]

Ivbijaro, Monica. "Why *Basi and Co.* Is in the Cooler." *Vanguard,* 4 May 1988: 12–13.

Knox, Paul. "Nigerian Was Voice of Ogoni." *The Globe and Mail* (Toronto), 11 November 1995: A9.

———. "Saro-Wiwa's Execution Sparks Global Outrage." *The Globe and Mail* (Toronto), 11 November 1995: A1.

Kobani, Kenneth. "Saro-Wiwa Hijacked a Peaceful Organization." *Panafrica* (London), November 1996: 26.

[Kobani and Saro-Wiwa fell out over an election in Ogoniland in 1977. This article is Kobani's negative reaction to *A Month and a Day* and its claims regarding the founding of MOSOP.]

Kogbara, Donu. "Ken Saro-Wiwa Was Never a Saint." *Independent,* 12 November 1996.

[Claims that Saro-Wiwa profited from the civil war. She makes a number of claims about human rights abuses within Ogoniland and MOSOP.]

Lewis, Paul. "Nigeria Group Defends the Execution of 9 Nigerian Activists." *New York Times,* 7 December 1995: A15.

Maier, Karl. "Steel-Willed Playwright Defies the Generals." *The Independent,* 2 November 1995.

[Effective quotes from Saro-Wiwa on Nigerian greed, ethnocentricity, and on the relationship with the federal state. Good biographical portrait.]

Meier, Didi. "The Man Inside Mr. Basi." *New African* (October 1988): 41.

Momoh, Siaka. "The Return of *Basi and Company.*" *Vanguard,* 9 July 1988: 9.

———. "Saros' Unique Launch." *Vanguard,* 30 November 1989: 9.

[A recording produced by Saro-Wiwa and books.]

North, Richard D. "Can You Be Sure of Saro-Wiwa?" *The Independent,* 8 November 1996: 18.

[Provocative article about his posh speech in his large house in Surrey and claims that he "feathered his nest" when working in Bonny. Suggests Ogoni movement started "with an element of a scam." Writes approvingly of Shell's activities in the Delta.]

Nwabueze, Goddy. "Ken's National Project: The Guilty Tribes." In *Ken Saro-Wiwa: The Life and Times.* Ed. S. Okechukwu Mezu. Randallstown, Md.: Black Academy Press, 1996: 153–157.

[Reprinted from *Sunday Times* (Lagos), 25 November 1990. Another attack on Saro-Wiwa for his "ego trip."]

Nwangbu, Chido. "Ken Saro-Wiwa's Wars." *National Concord,* 10 May 1990: 7.

[About his anti-Igbo sentiment.]

Nwiadoh, Deebi. "Saro-Wiwa at 50." *Daily Times,* 21 September 1991: 17.

[Eight Saro-Wiwa books.]

———. "Saro-Wiwa Is Not a Tribalist." *Daily Times,* 13 July 1990: 13.

[A response to Chinedu Offoaro.]

Obi, Chioma. "*Basi and Co.* May Go Off the Screen." *Vintage People,* 20 July 1990: 23.

Obiagwu, Kodilinye. "Let's Launch this Book." *Times International,* 26 December 1988: 34.

[Discussion of a reading of *Prisoners of Jebs.*]

Obiagwu, Kodilinye, and Dapo Olasebikan. "Popular TV Comic-serio Series." *Times International,* 16 November 1987: 33.

Ofeimun, Odia. "Steak for *Prisoners of Jebs.*" *Guardian,* 14 December 1988: 13; *Association of Nigerian Authors Review* 4, 6 (1989): 23.

[Saro-Wiwa will not use book launch for fund-raising.]

Offoaro, Chinedu. "Saro-Wiwa, Alibi and Tribalism." *Daily Times,* 14 June 1990: 13.

[Response to Idang Alibi and Odia Ofeimun.]

Ogundipe, Taiwo. "Beyond Our Ken Saro-Wiwa: A Drama of Life." *This Day,* 19 November 1995: 5.

Okediran, Wale. "Ken Saro-Wiwa at 50." *Guardian,* 19 October 1991: 11.

Okonta, Ike. "A Writer's Vision." *Citizen,* 21 October 1991: 46.

[Fiftieth birthday launch of seven books.]

Oladeinde, Sina. "Saro-Wiwa Wins Award in Detention." *Nigerian Tribune,* 18 October 1994.

Orji, Udenna. "Saro-Wiwa, Eight Others Hanged." *The Guardian,* 11 November 1995: 1–2.

Saesun, Segun, and Simi Awosika. "Saro-Wiwa's Vision." *African Guardian,* 4 November 1991: 37.

[Launch of eight books.]

Saro-Wiwa, Ken, Jr. [See also Ken Wiwa.] "A Chill Wind Blows at the Summit." *The Guardian* (London), 28 October 1997.

[Sees Edinburgh meeting of the Commonwealth heads of state as "a disappointment and a missed opportunity." Disappointed by the extra year given to Gen. Sani Abacha and the general display of temerity.]

———. Introduction to "The Nigerian Gulag." *The Guardian,* 29 July 1995.

———. "Quotes of the Week." *Independent on Sunday,* 19 November 1995.

———. "Silencing the Voice." *The Guardian,* 4 January 1995: 2–3.

[Includes quotations from recent letters.]

———. "Speakeasy." *Weekly Journal* (London), 23 November 1995.

———. "There's Only One Ken Saro-Wiwa, and It's Not Me." *The Guardian,* 17 November 1995.

Saro-Wiwa, Maria. "Relative Values." *Sunday Times,* 24 March 1996: 12.

[Describes marriage, Ken Jr.'s birth, her return to college, annual trips to Nigeria (1984–1985), and her husband's coming and going.]

———. "Ken Was Never a Problem." *Panafrica* (London), November 1996: 24–25.

Saro-Wiwa, Owens. [See also Owens Wiwa.] *The Guardian Weekend,* 30 March 1996: 8.

Shepherd, Rose. "Relative Values: Interviews with Maria Saro-Wiwa and Ken Jr." *Sunday Times Magazine,* 24 March 1996: 11–12.

[Provides information about family life: Saro-Wiwa married Maria when she was seventeen and at school; she had Ken Jr. in 1968; he walked at seven months as his father did; Gian was born in 1970, then Maria went back to teacher training college for three and a half years; twin daughters, Zina and Noo, were born in 1976. Went to England in January 1978 and Tedum was born shortly after. Ken and Gian were sent to boarding school in Derbyshire. Ken went on to Tonbridge and to London University, now engaged to Olivia Burnett. Clearly, Saro-Wiwa had neglected his children and, in his teens, Ken Jr. turned "negative energy" against his mother. The family had been shattered by Tedum's death while playing rugby; Saro-Wiwa "barely stopped over for the funeral." Ken Jr. had the same heart defect as Tedum, so he had a pacemaker fitted. Ken Jr. wrote to his father in jail. He describes hearing of his father's death and gives an account of his subsequent movements. He also indicates that his mother had received support from one of the men killed by MOSOP. He says his father "let her sink or swim." Ken Jr. is not prepared to take on his father's political legacy at the expense of his children. Mother describes herself as "pushy."]

Uzoatu, Theo. "A Celebration of Talent." *Timesweek,* 28 October 1991: 40.
[A brief overview of his career on the occasion of Saro-Wiwa's fiftieth birthday.]

Wheeler, David. "Blood on British Business Hands." *New Statesman and Society* 8 (17 November 1995): 14–15.

Wiwa, Ken. "The Return." In *No Refuge.* London: The Guardian and Amnesty International, 1997.
[Account of the conviction and execution of his father.]

———. "Why I Cannot Agree with this Tainted Account of My Father's Life." *The Independent,* 9 November 1996: 5.
[Response to the article by Richard D. North, cited earlier in this section; points out that, for example, his father did not buy a house until 1977. Challenges other elements of North's piece.]

Wiwa, Owens. "Interview by Pini Jason." *New African,* November 1996: 32–33.
[Describes flight from Nigeria in November 1995 and help in Ghana provided by The Body Shop. Owens flew back through Kano but was not taken off the plane. Ken Saro-Wiwa did not expect to die: "he was relying on the cabinet of Abacha." Many were his friends.]

———. "The Spirit of Saro-Wiwa." *Guardian Weekly,* 30 March 1996: 8.
[A reaction to Chris McGreal's 1996 article in *The Guardian Review,* particularly to comments about the Spirit of Ogoni—a code of courage, defiance, and unity. Also covers National Youth Council of the Ogoni People (NYCOP), a democratic organization that was not formed by Saro-Wiwa and did not have vigilante ends. See section on "Works of Related Interest."]

CRITICAL ARTICLES

Adagboyin, Asomwan. "The Language of Ken Saro-Wiwa's *Sozaboy.*" In *Critical Essays on Ken Saro-Wiwa's Sozaboy: A Novel in Rotten English.* Ed. Charles Nnolim. Saros Star Series 17. Port Harcourt, Nigeria: Saros International Publishers, 1992: 30–38.
[An examination of the "peculiarities" of Saro-Wiwa's language to prove that it is the creation of "an Africanized English." Perceptively notes that "Saro-Wiwa perhaps tries too often to drag himself into the linguistic consciousness of the hero. . . . These are glaring instances of when the experiment with language is pushed too far."]

Adekeye, Muyiwa, et al. "Will the Ogonis Leave Nigeria?" *The News,* 17 May 1993: 16–21.

Adepitan, Titi. "The Man They Should Have Named Moses." *A. M. News,* 3 December 1995: 9.

Adera, Taddesse. Chair. "Ken Saro-Wiwa: Writing, Culture, Resistance, and Politics." Modern Languages Association Division on African Literature.
[Participants were: Ernest N. Emenyonu, "Of Martyrs and Scaffolds: Fatalism in Ken Saro-Wiwa's Fiction"; Robert Ness, "To Wither into the Truth: Language and Politics in Saro-Wiwa's *Sozaboy*"; Mary Harvan, "Ken Saro-Wiwa, Resistance Literatures, and the Problems of Authorship." Cited in *PMLA* 112, no. 6 (November 1997): 1296.]

Afejuku, Tony. "*Sozaboy* and the Reader." In *Critical Essays on Ken Saro-Wiwa's* Sozaboy: A Novel in Rotten English. Ed. Charles Nnolim. Saros Star Series 17. Port Harcourt, Nigeria: Saros International Publishers, 1992: 108–116.
[Introduces the novel enthusiastically as doing most things for most readers and then settles down to an examination of "The Pleasure of the Text": "its setting and episodes," the comic and the erotic, point-of-view, and the "distinctness and unusualness of this novel which can be likened to Ngugi's *A Grain of Wheat* in which there are uncertainties of style and tone connected with the attempt to find the right images and idioms for African experience."]
Ajayi, Sesan. "Saro-Wiwa and the National Question." *Guardian,* 24 November 1991: B4; 8 December 1991: B7; 22 December 1991: B5; 29 December 1991: B7.
Akaraogun, Olu. "A Lone Voice Crying in the Delta Region." *Sunday Times,* 6 October 1991: 9.
Akekue, Doris. "Mind Style in *Sozaboy:* A Functional Approach to Language." In *Critical Essays on Ken Saro-Wiwa's* Sozaboy: A Novel in Rotten English. Ed. Charles Nnolim. Saros Star Series 17. Port Harcourt, Nigeria: Saros International Publishers, 1992: 16–29.
[Employs the British linguist M. A. K. Halliday's ideational function of language as a model for the "study of mindstyle in *Sozaboy*." Repetition, lexical repetition, structural repetition, lexical features of mindstyle, syllabic content, morphemic content, the mixture of lexical varieties, adulteration of words, nouns, adjectives, coordination, sentence fragments, code mixing and switching lead Akekue to conclude that the novel's protagonist has a "dislocated consciousness." Less specifically, "the linguistic choice is made at a functional level, and it reveals a particular strand of meaning to the literary interpretation of the text."]
Akpederi, Joni. "An Impressive Sitcom." *African Guardian,* 23 April 1987: 26.
———. "Reaching Out." *African Guardian,* 29 October 1987: 22.
[Regarding the international reception of *Basi and Company.*]
Alabi, Adetayo. "Saro-Wiwa and the Politics of Language in African Literature." In *Ogoni's Agonies: Ken Saro-Wiwa and the Crisis in Nigeria.* Ed. Abdul Rasheed Na'allah. Trenton, N.J.: Africa World Press, 1998: 307–318.
[Stresses the importance of *Sozaboy* to Saro-Wiwa's experimentation with the English language, and notes that the writer, in an Ngugi-like turn, was writing a novel in Khana—to reach literates within his own community—at the time of his death.]
Alem, K. "Et si Ken Saro-Wiwa n'etait pas innocent apres tout?" *L'Autre Afrique* (February 1998): 31.
Anon. "Persecution of Ken Saro-Wiwa." *New African* 330 (1 May 1995): 18.
[Summary of international protests, Saro-Wiwa's position, the realities behind the case, and the changing testimony of Charles Danwi.]
Apter, Andrew. "Death and the King's Henchmen: Ken Saro-Wiwa and the Political Ecology of Citizenship in Nigeria." In *Ogoni's Agonies: Ken Saro-Wiwa and the Crisis in Nigeria.* Ed. Abdul Rasheed Na'allah. Trenton, N.J.: Africa World Press, 1998: 307–318, 121–160.
[Apter sums up his point of view this way:

(W)e will examine how the plight of the Ogoni people came to represent the contradictions of oil-capitalism in Nigeria at large. We will see how the pollution of natural ecosystems and environments provided the language for opposing historically specific forms of economic alienation and political dispossession throughout the nation, as rentier-capitalism and prebendal politics privatized the state and undermined the public sphere. Only then can we appreciate how Ken Saro-Wiwa's demand for Ogoni autonomy escalated into a struggle for universal citizenship in Nigeria, and why, as the world waited to see what would happen, he was hanged.]

Awosika, Olawole. "Narrative Style in *Sozaboy*." In *Critical Essays on Ken Saro-Wiwa's* Sozaboy: A Novel in Rotten English. Ed. Charles Nnolim. Saros Star Series 17. Port Harcourt, Nigeria: Saros International Publishers, 1992: 64–72.
[An examination of Mene as direct narrator, structure, Mene as limited commentator, Mene as mature commentator, Mene as physical guide, aesthetic distance, and multiple alienation lead Awosika to affirm that "the narrative style of *Sozaboy* indeed produces an elaborate aesthetic structure."]
Birnbaum, Michael. *Nigeria, Fundamentalist Rights Denied: Report of the Trial of Ken Saro-Wiwa and Others.*
[Listed at Amazon.com as out of print; no other information available.]
Bolawole, Bola. "'Oh No, Ken Saro-Wiwa.'" In *Ken Saro-Wiwa: The Life and Times.* Ed. S. Okechukwu Mezu. Randallstown, Md.: Black Academy Press, 1996: 139–141.
[Reprinted from *The Punch,* 10 August 1990. Anecdotal piece on Saro-Wiwa and his writing.]
Breitinger, Eckhard. "Ken Saro-Wiwa: Writer and Cultural Manager." In *Ogoni's Agonies: Ken Saro-Wiwa and the Crisis in Nigeria.* Ed. Abdul Rasheed Na'allah. Trenton, N.J.: Africa World Press, 1998: 241–253.
[An examination of Saro-Wiwa's language and his attempts to reach a large, diverse audience, between the positions of Ngugi (African languages) and those of West Africans (Africanized European languages).]
Brooke, James. "30 Million Nigerians Are Laughing at Themselves." *New York Times,* 24 July 1987: 1, 4.
[On *Basi and Company.*]
Cayford, Steven. "The Ogoni Uprising: Oil, Human Rights, and a Democratic Alternative." *Africa Today* 43 (April-June 1996): 183–197.
Chukwuma, Helen. "Characterization and Meaning in *Sozaboy*." In *Critical Essays on Ken Saro-Wiwa's* Sozaboy: A Novel in Rotten English. Ed. Charles Nnolim. Saros Star Series 17. Port Harcourt, Nigeria: Saros International Publishers, 1992: 39–52.
[Through "the internal and external features of character . . . meaning is realized." Mene is "an internalizing character" who changes, though "the traumatic process of such a change is neither desirable nor pleasurable" as Saro-Wiwa indicates.]
Cooly, Glen. "Shell's Secret Dealings: Did Shell Promise to Intervene for Ken Saro-Wiwa in Return for His Silence?" *Now* (Toronto), 7–13 December 1995: 18–20.
Contemporary Authors, vol. 142. Detroit: Gale Research: 389–390.
[Personal information: addresses; career; memberships; awards, honors; writings; sidelights; periodicals by him and about him.]
Dunton, Chris. "Sologa, Eneka, and The Supreme Commander: The Theater of Ken Saro-Wiwa." *Research in African Literatures* 29, no. 1 (Spring 1998): 153–162.
[The most comprehensive and authoritative discussion of the plays to date.]
Ehling, Holger. "Ken Saro-Wiwa (Nigeria)." *Literaturnacrichten* (Frankfurt) 17 (1988): 15–16.

Essiet, Jimmy. "Writers Keep Saro-Wiwa Alive." *A. M. News*, 3 February 1996: 13.

Ezenwa-Ohaeto. "Bridges of Orality: Nigerian Pidgin Poetry." *World Literature Today* (Winter 1995): 69–77.

————. "The Cultural Imperative in Modern Nigerian Drama: A Consolidation in the Plays of Saro-Wiwa, Nwabueze, and Irobi." *Neohelicon: Acta Comparationis Litterarum Universarum* 21, no. 2 (1994): 207–220.

[Deals with the *Four Farcical Plays,* where "the struggle to acquire wealth and its subsequent effect when it is acquired is the major cultural issue" explored. Notes the use of "contemporary issues as the raw material for his artistic statements." Language ("slangy" and pidgin) is used to capture "the cultural (and) educational background" of the characters. Ezenwa-Ohaeto argues against Michael Etherton's sense of African drama. Notes "varying degrees of creative competence" without delineating them fully.]

————. "Ken Saro-Wiwa." *Twentieth Century Caribbean and Black African Writers.* Ed. Bernth Lindfors and Reinhard Sander. The Dictionary of Literary Biography 157: 3rd series. Detroit: Gale Research, 1996: 331–339.

[A comprehensive and balanced overview of Saro-Wiwa's career. He "compels serious critical attention because of his innovative use of language, his utilization of the oral traditions of his culture, and his sensitive exploration of contemporary society."]

————. "A Web of Ironies: The Artistic Realization of War in Ken Saro-Wiwa's *Sozaboy.*" In *Critical Essays on Ken Saro-Wiwa's* Sozaboy: A Novel in Rotten English. Ed. Charles Nnolim. Saros Star Series 17. Port Harcourt, Nigeria: Saros International Publishers, 1992: 53–63.

[A more sophisticated, less linguistics-centered analysis than many of those collected in Nnolim's volume. Ezenwa-Ohaeto examines the "thematically interwoven and artistically contrived" ironies in the text. These ironies are "intended to correct undesirable habits, attitudes and even beliefs, associated with violent situations."]

Feuser, Willfried. "The Voice from Dukana: Ken Saro-Wiwa." *Matatu* 1, no. 2 (1987): 52–66; reprinted in *Literary Half-Yearly* 29, no. 1 (1988): 11–25.

[On *Songs in a Time of War, A Forest of Flowers, Sozaboy*, and language. Feuser notes that "a look at his own prose style reveals the almost total absence of what Femi Osofisan has derogatorily called 'proverbalization.'" Compares *Sozaboy*, sketchily, to *Simplicius Simplicissimus* (a 1669 novel by Hans Jacob Christoph von Grimmelshausen—a classic of German literature, set during the Thrity Years' War [1616–1648]); asserts that *Sozaboy* "is a mighty single heart-beat in the body of Nigerian literary history, which will resound forever along the corridor leading towards an authentic national history."]

Garner, Jason. "No Minor Matter." *Index on Censorship* 23, nos. 4–5 (September-October 1994): 218ff.

[A description of events leading to Saro-Wiwa's death sentence and an outline of MOSOP activities. Includes quotations from a speech by Saro-Wiwa and a poem titled "Ogoni! Ogoni!"]

Garuba, Harry. "Ken Saro-Wiwa's *Sozaboy* and the Logic of Minority Discourse." In *Ogoni's Agonies: Ken Saro-Wiwa and the Crisis in Nigeria.* Ed. Abdul Rasheed Na'allah.Trenton, N.J.: Africa World Press, 1998: 229–239.

[Uses the story of Sozaboy as an archetype for the story of "suppressed minorities."]

George, Karibi T. "Myth and History in Ken Saro-Wiwa's *Basi and Company: A Modern African Folktale.*" In *African Literature and African Historical*

Experiences. Calabar Studies in African Literature no. 6. Ed. Chidi Ikonné, Emelia Oko, and Peter Onwudinjo. Ibadan: Heinemann, 1991: 107–115.

Gibbs, James. "Ola Rotimi and Ken Saro-Wiwa: Nigerian Popular Playwrights." In *Signs and Signals: Popular Culture in Africa.* Ed. Raoul Granqvist. Umea, Sweden: University of Umea Press, 1990.

[Gibbs opens with an overview of developments in Nigerian theater, concentrating on the work of Wole Soyinka. A description and an analysis of recent work by Ola Rotimi and Ken Saro-Wiwa follows, leading to the conclusion that

(t)he decline in quality from *Transistor Radio* to *A Shipload of Rice* might be explained in terms of the toll taken by the need to keep fuelling the (television) series or by the failure to recognize that situation comedy does not easily lend itself to tackling serious economic problems. Undoubtedly popular, *A Shipload of Rice* does not "skewer" any "national foibles" or lampoon Nigerian attitudes. It provides a distracting, escapist half-hour in genial company.]

———. "One Act Play—1." *Newsletter of the School of Performing Arts* (Legon) 2 (April-June 1994): 11–13.

[On "The Wheel."]

Hammer, Joshua. "Nigerian Crude: A Hanged Man and an Oil-Fouled Landscape." *Harper's* 292, no. 1753 (1996): 58–70.

Harvan, M. "'Its Eventual Victory Is Not in Doubt': An Introduction to the Literature of Ken Saro-Wiwa." *Alif: Journal of Comparative Poetics* 17 (1997): 161–182.

[Harvan says:

Often drawing on his extensive journalistic production, his literary work scrutinizes Nigerian politics and culture and dissects problems common to postcolonial African nations. Much of his work, especially his most recent, addresses the political, economic, and ecological injustices the Ogoni have suffered at the hands of transnational oil companies.

Divided into: "Redeploying the Folktale," "Developing a Social Critique," and "Co-authoring Ogoni Resistance."]

Idambue, Barika. "Ken Saro-Wiwa at 50." *African Literature Association Bulletin* 18, no. 1 (Winter 1992): 32–34.

[Summary of various Nigerian newspaper and magazine comments on Saro-Wiwa's contribution to literary and cultural life, as well as oral reviews of his work at a seven-book launch in the same year. Includes Saro-Wiwa's statement of purpose.]

Inyama, N. F. "Ken Saro-Wiwa: Maverick Iconoclast of the Nigerian Literary Scene." *African Literature Today* 20 (1996): 35–49.

[Focuses on the novels and short stories. Brief commentary on self-publishing, his prolific nature, and substantive coverage in the Nigerian press. Lucid summaries and critical discussion of the texts. Notes "certain faults and weaknesses" in the books. In *Sozaboy,* "(c)ertain expressions are rather obscure, and even as slang, they appear to belong to the generation of slang more current in the early sixties than in the seventies or eighties." According to Inyama, the book is successful linguistically but not in point of view. *Prisoners of Jebs* is a success as a satire, including the satire of Saro-Wiwa and his reviewers. Saro-Wiwa "refuses to promote a false optimism about a future that will correct itself without a reformed, penitent populace." In the same vein, "the satire in *Pita Dumbrok's Prison* arouses . . . a strong sense of social tragedy." Saro-Wiwa will also need "to abandon certain clichés and stylistic habits," and avoid repetitiousness and tense shifts.]

———. "Point of View in Saro-Wiwa's *Sozaboy.*" In *Critical Essays on Ken Saro-Wiwa's* Sozaboy: A Novel in Rotten English. Ed. Charles Nnolim. Saros Star Series 17. Port Harcourt, Nigeria: Saros International Publishers, 1992: 102–107.
[Another examination of point of view, reliant here on Wayne C. Booth's early study, *The Rhetoric of Fiction.*]

Irele, Abiola. "The Fiction of Saro-Wiwa." *The Guardian* (Lagos), 17 January 1987: 13; 24 January 1987: 13.
[Reprinted as "Ken Saro-Wiwa." In *Perspectives on Nigerian Literature: 1700 to the Present.* Vol. 2. Ed. Yemi Ogunbiyi. Lagos: Guardian Books Nigeria Limited, 1988: 333–344. Also reprinted in *Ogoni's Agonies: Ken Saro-Wiwa and the Crisis in Nigeria.* Ed. Abdul Rasheed Na'allah. Trenton, N.J.: Africa World Press, 1998: 255–267. An analysis of *Sozaboy* and *A Forest of Flowers* in light of other civil war literature and the historical period itself leads Irele to conclude:

Saro-Wiwa's stories represent an advanced stage in the movement towards a new realism in African literature. In the Nigerian context, his fiction has come as a singular expression of a process of *transvaluation* through an expansion of the writer's consciousness beyond its ethnic horizons and ideological conditioning.]

Joseph, P. A. Curtis. "Fall Outs from *On a Darkling Plain.*" *Guardian,* 29 June 1990: 11.
[Contends that commentators are getting historical facts wrong.]

Kassim, Omololu. "The Story of *Basi and Co.*" *National Concord,* 17 December 1987: 5.

King, Bruce. "Saro-Wiwa, Ken." In *Encyclopedia of Post-Colonial Literatures in English.* Ed. Eugene Benson and L. W. Connolly. London: Routledge, 1994: 1415–1416.

King-Aribisala, K. "*Basi and Co.* and *WAI.*" In *Everything About Basi and Co., the Most Hilarious Comedy on TV!* Ed. Ken Saro-Wiwa. Lagos: Saros International, 1986: 8.

Koroye, Seiyifa. "*Sozaboy:* First Person Narration and Mene's 'Very Bad Dream.'" In *Critical Essays on Ken Saro-Wiwa's* Sozaboy: A Novel in Rotten English. Ed. Charles Nnolim. Saros Star Series 17. Port Harcourt, Nigeria: Saros International Publishers, 1992: 82–101.
[An examination of how Mene tells his story. Overly reliant on Robert B. Paltrow's examination of point of view in Dickens.]

Lewis, Paul. "In Nigeria's Oil Wars, Shell Denies It Had a Role," *New York Times,* 13 February 1996.

Lindfors, Bernth. "De-ciphering the Canon." Paper presented at the African Literature Association Conference, Rutgers University, New Jersey, 1995.

———. "Ken Saro-Wiwa—in Short, a Giant." *African Literature Association Bulletin* 20, no. 2 (Spring 1994): 15–16.
[Lindfors, a jurist for the prize, pays tribute to the 1994 Fonlon-Nichols Prize winner. Reprinted in *Ogoni's Agonies: Ken Saro-Wiwa and the Crisis in Nigeria.* Ed. Abdul Rasheed Na'allah. Trenton, N.J.: Africa World Press, 1998: 195–197.]

Loimeier, Manfred, ed. *Zum Bespiel Ken Saro-Wiwa.* Grottingen: Lamuv, 1996.
[Includes contributions by Holger Ehling, Wole Soyinka, Bob Drogin, Willfried
Feuser, and a bibliography.]

Macdominic, Nkpemenyie. "Saro-Wiwa as a Black Prophet." *Vanguard,* 5 September 1996: 7.

Mair, Christian. "The New Englishes as a Basis for Stylistic Innovation in the New
English Literatures: Ken Saro-Wiwa's *Sozaboy: A Novel in Rotten English.*" A
paper read at the 1990 European Branch of the Association for Common-
wealth Literature and Language Studies (EACLALS), Conference in Lecce,
Italy.
[Unable to obtain a copy.]

Maja-Pearce, Adewale. *A Mask Dancing: Nigerian Novelists of the Eighties.* London: Hans Zell, 1992.

———. "The Murderers in Our Midst." *Index on Censorship* 1 (1996): 57–60.
[Provides an account of the last statement and last hours of Saro-Wiwa. Summarizes the reaction of Gen. Sani Abacha and of government spokespersons to
South African president Nelson Mandela's interventions. Ademola Adeshina
had, apparently, implied that Mandela was insane. Indicates that Abacha had
subsequently attempted to eat his words. A postscript entitled "Image Makers"
(p. 60) describes the position adopted by government media organs and the
confusion they are in.]

———. "Whatever Happened to Ken?" *Index on Censorship* 6 (1996): 180–181.
[Nigeria's situation on the anniversary of the execution.]

Martini, Jürgen. "Experiments with the English Language in Contemporary Nigerian Literature: Pidgin and Rotten English." A paper read at the 1989 European Branch of the Association for Commonwealth Literature and Language
Studies (EACLALS), Conference in Canterbury, England. [Unable to obtain
a copy.]

Mezu, S. Okechukwu, ed. *Ken Saro-Wiwa: The Life and Times.* Randallstown,
Md.: Black Academy Press, 1996.
[ISBN 0878311653; 157 pages. Examines the life, offers a literary overview, and
describes Saro-Wiwa's relations with the military, the trial, and the execution.
Attention is also paid to Saro-Wiwa's poetry and nonfiction. Includes three
poems, letters, and a bibliography.]

———. "The Life and Times of Ken Saro-Wiwa." In *Ken Saro-Wiwa: The Life and
Times.* Ed. S. Okechukwu Mezu. Randallstown, Md.: Black Academy Press,
1996: 5–60.
[A historical overview of minority relations in Nigeria, particularly in the east,
leading to the creation of Rivers State. Rather choppily written. Useful biographical information: under the "Abandoned Property Edict," "Ken Saro-
Wiwa personally acquired several (Igbo) properties" in Rivers State (p. 11).
Mezu also argues that Saro-Wiwa "blossomed as a writer" as a direct result
of his position as minister of education because his "books were adopted as
required texts for elementary and secondary schools" (p. 12). On *Basi and
Company,* Mezu concludes "that the tales are neither edifying nor instructive"
(p. 12).

Saro-Wiwa is an OUT-standing writer. He stands out for his controver-
sies, his contradictions, conflicting sentiments and sometimes even internal contradictions of time and space, character and plausibility even

within a single short story. His language . . . is OUT-standing for its cru-
dity, unorthodoxy and unconventionality. (p. 13)

On politics: "From 1967 to 1979 when he was in power and in a position
to change the lot of his people—he did little for them or for the wasting
environment" (p. 26). "He appeared to want a little empire he could control and manage. . . ." (p. 31). Mezu's piece is informative and critically
assesses Saro-Wiwa's various contributions, but its tone and its invective
are an ongoing testament to intertribal conflict in Nigeria.]

Mezu, Rose Ure. "Ken Saro-Wiwa and *A Forest of Flowers.*" In *Ken Saro-Wiwa:
The Life and Times.* Ed. S. Okechukwu Mezu. Randallstown, Md.: Black
Academy Press, 1996: 91–114.
[Positive review of the writing: "But as a writer, there is no doubt about it—he is an
accomplished one. His writing style is expressively elegant, with well-crafted
texts, swift changes of tone laced with direct realism" (p. 92). Uses *A Forest of
Flowers* to illustrate this argument and Saro-Wiwa's "sardonic humour."]
Na'allah, Abdul Rasheed. "Introduction." In *Ogoni's Agonies: Ken Saro-Wiwa and
the Crisis in Nigeria.* Ed. Abdul Rasheed Na'allah. Trenton, N.J.: Africa
World Press, 1998: 3–29.
[Offers Na'allah's sense of the edited collection and what its various pieces offer
to the whole. Rhetorically emphatic:

There is nothing wrong with Shell or any international company, from
India, Nigeria, Finland, Canada or anywhere, doing business in any part
of the world. But when such business is being done as a game of re-en-
slavement, conscientious peoples of the world, as their brothers' and sisters' keepers must ask questions and insist on answers. That is precisely
what this collection of writers in *Ogoni's Agonies* has achieved.]

Na'allah, Abdul Rasheed, ed. *Ogoni's Agonies: Ken Saro-Wiwa and the Crisis in
Nigeria.* With a preface by Kwame Anthony Appiah and a foreword by Biodun
Jeyifo. Trenton, N.J.: Africa World Press, 1998.
[388 pages, primarily of reprinted articles, interviews, and memorabilia; a sub-
stantive portion of the text is given over to poetry honoring Saro-Wiwa. Con-
cludes with a brief bibliography. See individual entries.]
Nixon, Rob. "Pipe Dreams: Ken Saro-Wiwa, Environmental Justice and Micro-Mi-
nority Rights." *Black Renaissance/Renaissance Noire* 1, no. 1 (Fall 1996):
39–55.
[Originally published in *London Review of Books* (April 1996).]
Nnolim, Charles, ed. *Critical Essays on Ken Saro-Wiwa's* Sozaboy: A Novel in
Rotten English. Saros Star Series 17. Port Harcourt, Nigeria: Saros Interna-
tional Publishers, 1992.
[ISBN 1870716213; 128 pages.]
———. "Saro-Wiwa's World and His Craft in *Sozaboy.*" In *Critical Essays on Ken
Saro-Wiwa's* Sozaboy: A Novel in Rotten English. Ed. Charles Nnolim. Saros
Star Series 17. Port Harcourt, Nigeria: Saros International Publishers, 1992:
73–81.
[Reprinted in In *Ken Saro-Wiwa: The Life and Times.* Ed. S. Okechukwu Mezu.
Randallstown, Md.: Black Academy Press, 1996: 122–133. Nnolim argues that
the world of *Sozaboy* is "topsy-turvy" and that "events go higgledy-piggledy."]

Nwabueze, Emeka. "Death of a Writer: A Reply to William Boyd." *A.L.A. Bulletin* 23, no. 1 (Winter 1997): 11–14.
[Describes Boyd's article as "romantic lachrymose." See Boyd's 1995 article in "Works of Related Interest."]

Nwabueze, Goddy. "Ken's National Project: The Guilty Tribes." *Sunday Times*, 25 November 1990: 7.
[Critical of Saro-Wiwa's ethnic views.]

Nwachukwu-Agbada. "The Poetry of Saro-Wiwa." In *Ken Saro-Wiwa: The Life and Times*. Ed. S. Okechukwu Mezu. Randallstown, Md.: Black Academy Press, 1996: 79–90.
[Positive, contextual assessment of the poetry: "(I)t was probably in poetry that he handled his emotions with utmost effective control probably because of the intervening distance of twenty years" (p. 80).]

Nweke, Mrs. Therese. "Sentiments Vs Saro-Wiwa." In *Ken Saro-Wiwa: The Life and Times*. Ed. S. Okechukwu Mezu. Randallstown, Md.: Black Academy Press, 1996: 61–65.
[Reprint from *The Guardian on Sunday*, 26 November 1995: A11. His business and political involvement "so severely affected the quality and thrust of his literary output that the promise . . . was never actualized" (p. 61).]

Odugbemi, Sina. "Saro-Wiwa Threatens Your Ribcage." *Vanguard*, 10 December 1987: 9.

Oduwole, Yinka. "Armed Forces Behind Abacha." *This Day*, 2 December 1995: 1–2.

Ofeimun, Odia. "Come Down to Earth, Writer." *Guardian*, 15 February 1989: 13.
[Information on book launchings.]

——. "Come to Our Book Launching." *Guardian*, 23 November 1988: 13.
[Reprinted in *ANAR* 4, no. 6 (1989): 30–31. Defends cash contributions at book launchings.]

——. "Saro's Sour Logic." *Guardian*, 11 January 1989: 11.
[Reply to Saro-Wiwa.]

Ogbowei, G. Ebinyoo, and Ibiere Bell Gam. "*Sozaboy:* Language and a Disoriented World." *English Studies in Africa* 38, no. 1 (1995): 1–18.
[Predominantly a linguistic study, the article views the novel as a depiction of Ogoni concerns during the civil war and analyzes "the extent to which language has been manipulated by the author to simulate a disordered world." The authors claim that the language "is socio-culturally conditioned and intelligible only to those steeped in its history."]

Ogbuji, F. N. "Saro-Wiwa and the National Census." In *Ken Saro-Wiwa: The Life and Times*. Ed. S. Okechukwu Mezu. Randallstown, Md.: Black Academy Press, 1996: 136–138.
[Reprint of article in *Nigerian Tribune*, 6 July 1990. Accuses Saro-Wiwa of writing "without considering previous researches" (p. 136) and of having a predetermined point of view and relates these traits to Saro-Wiwa's "Similia" column on the census.]

Ogu, Julius. "Variations on the Use of English in Fiction: A Look at Four Nigerian Novelists." In *The Use of English in Communication*. Ed. Solomon Unoh. Ibadan, Nigeria: Spectrum Books, 1986.

Okere, Augustine. "Patterns of Linguistic Deviation in Ken Saro-Wiwa's *Sozaboy*." In *Critical Essays on Ken Saro-Wiwa's* Sozaboy: A Novel in Rotten English. Ed. Charles Nnolim. Saros Star Series 17. Port Harcourt, Nigeria: Saros International Publishers, 1992: 9–15.

[Assesses the novel on "whether the morphology and syntax of (its) English
. . . are totally deviant and whether the deviant segments manifest any discernible
pattern." Okere discovers "a basic framework of grammaticality from which the
narrator deviates occasionally for aesthetic and communicative purposes."]

Okome, Onookome, ed. *Before I Am Hanged: Ken Saro-Wiwa—Literature, Politics, and Dissent.*
[In production. Due September 1999, Africa World Press. ISBN 0865437459.]

Okpewho, Jerome. "Content and Style in Ken Saro-Wiwa's Works." *Muse* 20 (August 1990): 40–43.

———. "Psychological and Social Perspectives in Ken Saro-Wiwa's *Sozaboy.*" In
Critical Essays on Ken Saro-Wiwa's Sozaboy: A Novel in Rotten English. Ed.
Charles Nnolim. Saros Star Series 17. Port Harcourt, Nigeria: Saros International Publishers, 1992: 117–128.

[According to Okpewho, "*Sozaboy* is an 'elastic novel,' in the sense that it leaves
room for extensive discussion . . . on diverse psychological and social issues."
The psychological issues are the application of the "learning-process phenomenon" to the characters. The social issues are "the female factor in the novel."]

Olafioye, Tayo. "Ken Saro-Wiwa Echo." In *Ogoni's Agonies: Ken Saro-Wiwa and
the Crisis in Nigeria.* Ed. Abdul Rasheed Na'allah. Trenton, N.J.: Africa
World Press, 1998: 179–186.

[An examination of his own and Tanure Ojaide's unpublished poetry, *An Anthology
of Agonies* and *Delta Blues* respectively, for references to Saro-Wiwa and minority causes. A badly written and self-serving piece.]

Oloruntoba-Oju, Taiwo. "The Writer and the Junta." In *Ogoni's Agonies: Ken Saro-Wiwa and the Crisis in Nigeria.* Ed. Abdul Rasheed Na'allah. Trenton, N.J.:
Africa World Press, 1998: 187–194.

[The author says: "Nigerian writers have constantly functioned as the voice of vision in their society," and "(t)he writer, constantly calling for renewed consciousness, clashes inevitably with the junta." Poorly written and clichéd.]

Olukoya, Sam. "The Ogoni Agony." In *Ken Saro-Wiwa: The Life and Times.* Ed. S.
Okechukwu Mezu. Randallstown, Md.: Black Academy Press, 1996: 66–78.

[Reprint of article in *Newswatch*, 26 September 1994: 21–26. Summarizes military
activity in Ogoniland—either to stamp out unrest or to put down MOSOP.
Lengthy discussion of intra-Ogoni fighting.]

Oluwajuyitan, Jide. "Saro-Wiwa's Misplaced Aggression." *Guardian*, 28 August
1990: 11.
[On his defense of the Ogoni.]

[Onwenu], Onyeka. "Letters from Saro-Wiwa." *Prime People*, 6 July 1990: 19.
[Response to Saro-Wiwa.]

———. "Remembering Papa." *Prime People*, 27 April 1990: 19.
[Against anti-Igbo sentiment in *On a Darkling Plain.*]

Opara, Chioma. "Magical Effect in Magic Land: The Pain of the Game in Ken
Saro-Wiwa's *Prisoners of Jebs.*" *Review of English and Literary Studies* 7, no.
1 (1990): 11–17.

Orage, Desmond. "The Ogoni Question and the Role of the International Community in Nigeria." In *Ogoni's Agonies: Ken Saro-Wiwa and the Crisis in Nigeria.*
Ed. Abdul Rasheed Na'allah. Trenton, N.J.: Africa World Press, 1998: 41–48.

[A paper delivered at Duke University in February 1996. A variation of the Website, http://www.derechos.org/nigeria/sarowiwa/ad.txt, and its attack on Saro-Wiwa, MOSOP, and Amnesty International.]

Oriaku, R. O. "Ken Saro-Wiwa's War Songs." *Review of English and Literary
Studies* 2, no. 1 (1985): 57–64.

[On the poetry.]

Osundare, Niyi. "The Longest Day." *A.L.A. Bulletin* 23, no. 1 (Winter 1997): 7–10. [A tribute to the writer.]

———. "Not an Internal Affair." In *Ogoni's Agonies: Ken Saro-Wiwa and the Crisis in Nigeria.* Ed. Abdul Rasheed Na'allah. Trenton, N.J.: Africa World Press, 1998: 105–108. [The poet's personalized and anecdotal plea for consideration by all of what is occurring in Nigeria.]

Oti, Sonny. "Good Theatre for the Screen and Stage." In Saro-Wiwa, ed., *Everything About Basi and Company,* 1986: 9.

Quayson, Ato. "For Ken Saro-Wiwa: African Post-Colonial Relations Through a Prism of Tragedy." *Salt* 9 (1996): 157–176. [Reprinted in Na'allah (1998, pp. 57–80). See citation in this section. A highminded consideration of Saro-Wiwa's role that fails to problematize his complicity in the circumstances and context of Nigeria.]

Sachs, Aaron. "Dying for Oil." *World Watch* 9 (May-June 1996): 10–21.

Saint-Andre Utujian, Elaine. "13 Ghana and Nigeria." *Post-Colonial English Drama: Commonwealth Drama Since 1960.* Ed. Bruce King. London: Macmillan, 1992: 197–198.

———. "Ken Saro-Wiwa's Stifled Voices." *Commonwealth* 19, no. 1 (1996): 3–15. [Examines published plays and *Sozaboy.*]

Schipper, Mineke. *Theatre and Society in Africa.* Johannesburg: Ravan Press, 1982.

Schmied, Josef J. *English in Africa: An Introduction.* London and New York: Longman, 1991.

Schulze-Engler, Frank. "Civil Critiques: Satire and the Politics of Democratic Transition in Ken Saro-Wiwa's Novels." In *Ogoni's Agonies: Ken Saro-Wiwa and the Crisis in Nigeria.* Ed. Abdul Rasheed Na'allah. Trenton, N.J.: Africa World Press, 1998: 285–306. [Along with N. F. Inyama's 1996 essay (see citation in this section), one of the more thorough treatments of the prose writings:

Given the evidence of Saro-Wiwa's own writing which explored the effectiveness of a popular satirical genre with great success as well as his long-standing commitment to a decidedly literary culture as a vehicle of democratization and civil change, one cannot help noticing a certain tension between this somewhat populist emphasis on "interventionism" and "orature" and his own earlier literary theory and practice.]

Soyinka, Wole. "Epilogue: Death of an Activist." In his *The Open Sore of a Continent: A Personal Narrative of the Nigerian Crisis.* New York: Oxford University Press, 1996: 145–153. [On the tribunals and events leading up to Saro-Wiwa's hanging, including notes from international observers at the tribunal and rhetorical pieces in support of Saro-Wiwa by Soyinka.]

———. "A Frankenstein in Lagos." *New Perspectives Quarterly* 1 (Winter 1996): 64–65. [An interview with Soyinka following the execution of Saro-Wiwa and other Ogoni leaders. Soyinka argues that "(t)he Ogoni region is the testing ground for Gen. Sani Abacha's blueprint for ethnic cleansing among all national groups in Nigeria that are resolutely opposed to his rule." Calls for international sanctions against Nigeria, which has "ethnic minority rule just as in South Africa." To General Abacha, Soyinka suggests the following international response: "'if

you don't want to be hunted down for the rest of your whole (*sic*) life like a
war criminal, tidy your desk, steal what you can, get amnesty and get out now
so the democratic process you disrupted can resume.'"]
Vidal, John. "Black Gold Claims a Higher Price." *Manchester Guardian Weekly*,
15 January 1995.
Zabus, Chantal. *The African Palimpsest: Indigenization of Language in the West
African Europhone Novel.* Amsterdam and Atlanta: Rodopi, 1991.
——. "Ken Saro-Wiwa." In *Post-war Literatures in English: A Lexicon of Con-
temporary Authors.* Vol. 14. Ed. Hans Bertens, Theo D'haen, Joris
Duytschaever, and Richard Todd. Houten: Bohn Stafleu Van Loghum; Gronin-
gen: Wolters-Noordhoff, 1988–1991: 1–5, A1–A2, B1–B5.
——. "Mending the Schizo-Text: Pidgin in the Nigerian Novel." *Kunapipi* 14,
no. 1 (1992): 119–127.
[On language, in the work of Joyce Cary, Cyprian Ekwensi, and Ken Saro-Wiwa.
Discusses the novel "as the potential vehicle for multilingual and cross-cul-
tural hybridized poetics." *Sozaboy* "is thus far the most conscious and sustained linguistic experiment with non-standard speech in the West African
first-person narrative to emerge from the tiny corpus of writing in Pidgin."]
——. "Under the Palimpest and Beyond: 'The Original' in the West African European Novel." In *Crisis and Creativity in the New Literatures in English.* Ed.
Davis and Maes-Jelinek. Antwerp: Rodopi, 1990: 103–121.

DISSERTATIONS/THESES

Abu, M. A. I. "A Stylistic Analysis of Ken Saro-Wiwa's *Sozaboy*." Master's thesis,
University of Lagos, 1990.
Klein, Alex. [On *Basi and Company*.] Ph.D. diss., University of London, 1988.
Ngene, Charles Emeka. "A Critical Study of the Language of Ken Saro-Wiwa's
Songs in a Time of War." Master's thesis, University of Lagos, 1991.

REVIEWS OF BOOKS

Basi and Company

Contemporary Review 252 (January 1988): 48.
Gibbs, James. "Nigerian Sit-com." *West Africa*, 13 July–6 August 1989: 1253.
Lawrence, Bisi. *Vanguard* (Lagos), 27 October 1985.
Omotoso, Kole. "In the Company of Basi and Company." *West Africa* (28 Septem-
ber 1987): 1919.
School Librarian 36 (May 1988): 77.

A Forest of Flowers: Short Stories

Akst, Florence. "Arts in Africa." *BBC Africa Service.*
Awoyinfa, Michael. *The Sunday Concord* (Nigeria).

Hough, Graham. "Afro-Fictions." Review of *A Forest of Flowers* by Ken Saro-Wiwa. *London Review of Books,* 3 July 1986: 22–23.
Maja-Pearce, Adewale. *The New Statesman* 112 (11 July 1986): 32.
Odugbemi, Sina. "The Tales of Saro-Wiwa." *Vanguard,* 5 March 1987: 9.
Times Educational Supplement, 21 August 1987: 15.

Four Farcical Plays

Gibbs, James. "Laughter No Get Enemi." *West Africa,* 11–17 June 1990: 968.

Genocide in Nigeria

Naanen, Ben. "*Genocide in Nigeria*: The Ogoni Tragedy." *The Journal of Modern African Studies* 32, no. 3 (Spring 1994): 536–539.
[Notes repetition of material used in *On a Darkling Plain* for Chapter 4 of *Genocide in Nigeria*. The book "is clearly a work of propaganda, not least because its exaggerations and occasional vitriolic language are deliberately designed to both shock and provoke."]

Lemona's Tale

Babayode, Fola. *New African,* June 1997.

A Month and a Day

Ankomah, Baffour. "Saro-Wiwa Speaks." *New African* (London), January 1996: 13–14.
Bloomsbury Review 16 (March 1996): 30.
Book World 26 (11 February 1996): 12.
Kirk-Greene, A. H. M. *African Affairs* 95, no. 379 (April 1996): 294–295.
[It "is . . . less of a diary and more of an Ogoni declaration."]
London Review of Books (14 April 1996): 18.
New Statesman and Society (12 January 1996): 37.

Mr. B

Contemporary Review 252 (January 1988): 48.

Mr. B Is Dead

Aji, Aron. *Africa Book Publishing Record* 19, no. 3 (1993): 161.

On a Darkling Plain

Fiofori, Ferdinand O. "The Underpinnings of Nigeria's Civil War: The Quest of Minorities for Egalitarian Independence." *Africa Today* 38, no. 1 (1991): 79–80.

[Notes some lapses and disjointed prose but fails to review the book on its artistic merits.]
Ola, Boye. "At the Real Launch." *Sunday Concord*, 1 April 1990: 3.
Olugbile, Femi. "The Writer as a Protagonist." *Vanguard*, 7 June 1990: 9.

Pita Dumbrok's Prison

Vincent, Theo. "The Rehabilitation of Pita Dumbrok." *The Daily Times* (Lagos), 8 January 1992: 187.
World Literature Today 66 (Autumn 1992): 762.

Prisoners of Jebs

Contemporary Review 253 (October 1988): 220.
Fiofori, Ferdinand O. "Saro-Wiwa Satirized Africa's Malaise." *Africa Today* 39, no. 2 (1992): 24–25.
[Positive review: "Considering its origins as a series of more-or-less self-contained newspaper columns, the book reads surprisingly well as a novel. . . . (Saro-Wiwa uses) satire as a weapon of political and economic criticism."]
New Statesman and Society, 28–29 July 1988: 44.
Observer, 10 July 1988: 42.
Ojo, Damilola. "Mirror of Our Time." *Daily Times*, 16 December 1988: 7.
Times Literary Supplement, 5 August 1988: 857.
Vincent, Theo. "The Mirror of Our Times." *Daily Times*, 23 December 1988: 13.
World Literature Today 63 (Summer 1989): 524.

Similia: Essays on Anomic Nigeria

Boyd, William. "Saro-Wiwa: Smile on the Face of the Niger." *Times* (London), 15 December 1990; *Daily Times*, 23 March 1991: 12.
Ofeimun, Odia. "Saro-Wiwa as a Columnist." *West Africa* 3895 (11 May 1992): 793.
[Ofeimun says: "The general intent is to arouse common sentiments in people through a constant harping on issues and national problems that will not go away." A minor negative point is the maintenance of chronological rather than thematic ordering of the material. Relates the book to Chinua Achebe's intervention, *The Trouble with Nigeria* (see section on "Works of Related Interest"): both evaluate "Nigerian history and society through the vexed problems of ethnicity, the national question and the injustices of Nigerian federalism." More critically, Ofeimun notes: "It is as if he means to prop up the rightist tradition among Nigerian intellectuals who would rather give fire a try before re-establishing that it burns." Similarly, Saro-Wiwa's emphasis on his Khana people inhibits links to other microminorities "or to an agenda that covers the whole country." Saro-Wiwa, then, is a separatist, who has had the freedom of using a large-circulation newspaper to promulgate his views—a not entirely despairing situation.]

Sozaboy: A Novel in Rotten English
Africa (London) 176 (April 1986): 63.

Birch, Helen. *City Limits* (London).
Nation (Iowa) 262 (27 May 1996): 31.
Omotoso, Kole. "Ken Saro-Wiwa—Writer Extraordinaire." *West Africa,* 19–25 March 1990: 454.
Times Literary Supplement, 24 June 1994: 23.
Wordsworth, Christopher. *The Guardian* (London).
World and I (August 1995): 281.

BIBLIOGRAPHIES

See previous section on "Online Resources."
Lindfors, Bernth. *Black African Literature in English, 1987–1991.* London: Hans Zell Publishers, 1995: 477a–483b.
[Authoritative, particularly for African-based resources.]
Na'allah, Abdul-Rasheed. "Ken Saro-Wiwa: A Bio-Bibliography." In *Ogoni's Agonies: Ken Saro-Wiwa and the Crisis in Nigeria.* Ed. Na'allah.Trenton, N.J.: Africa World Press, 1998: 363–377.
[A useful, if incomplete (e.g., *Lemona's Tale* is uncited), oddly structured (e.g., essays, books, and interviews are grouped together), and unannotated bibliography of primary and secondary sources drawn from Lindfors's 1995 compilation (see previous entry). Includes a three-and-a-half-page biography and a list of awards and honors bestowed on Saro-Wiwa.]

WORKS OF RELATED INTEREST

Achebe, Chinua. *The Trouble with Nigeria.* London: Heinemann, 1983.
———. "The Role of the Writer in a New Nation." *Nigeria Magazine,* 18 June 1964.
———. *Things Fall Apart.* London: Heinemann, 1958.
Adekeye, Muyiwa. "Tried: From the Diary of a Judicial Reporter." *Glendora Review* (Lagos) 1, no. 3 (1996): 25–28.
Aiyejina, Funso. *A Letter to Lynda and Other Poems.* Saros Star Series 7. Port Harcourt, Nigeria: Saros International, 1988.
[ISBN 1870716043; 35 pages.]
Akwei, Adotei. "And Justice for All? The Two Faces of Nigeria." In *Ogoni's Agonies: Ken Saro-Wiwa and the Crisis in Nigeria.* Ed. Na'allah.Trenton, N.J.: Africa World Press, 1998: 33–40.
[An important essay on the nature of law and resistance in Nigeria.]
Alagoa, E. J., and Tekena N. Tamuno, eds. *Land and Peoples of Nigeria Rivers State.* Port Harcourt: Riverside Communications, 1989.
[Includes chapters on language, the creative arts, and social development. Reports that excavations funded by Tsaro-Wiwa were undertaken at Derefaka during March 1985. An invaluable sourcebook.]
Altbach, Philip G. "Literary Colonialism: Books in the Third World." In *The Post-Colonial Studies Reader.* Ed. Bill Ashcroft, Gareth Griffiths, and Helen Tiffin. New York: Routledge, 1995.
Amnesty International USA. "Freedom in the Balance: Nigeria/Kenya." Packet for African Studies Association members, 1995.
Anderson, Janet. "Champion Who Sought a Fair Deal." *Daily Telegraph,* 11 November 1995.

[Refers to Saro-Wiwa's job in newsprint manufacturing and cites the words that weighed with the tribunal: In reference to Shell, he said, "get the vultures." He offered no defense. Under the tribunal's terms, a defendant could be convicted of murder if it is satisfied that there have been disturbances that led to deaths and that a person's beliefs and membership in an organization may have contributed to the disturbances.]

———. "Ken Saro-Iwa [*sic*]: A Playwright and Revolutionary, but a Man with Trading Instinct." *Daily Telegraph,* 13 November 1995.

[Valuable firsthand account by a BBC producer and correspondent who took Saro-Wiwa's claims with a grain of salt.]

Ankomah, Baffour. "How Can We Forget?" *New African* (January 1996): 31.

[Reports Cyril Ramaphosa's African National Congress (ANC) description of Gen. Sani Abacha as a "dictator" and his threats to Shell if the gas scheme went ahead. Quotes in full the powerful text from the International Parliament of Writers.]

Ankomah, Janet. "Does Nigeria Make You Sick?" *New African* (June 1995): 8.

[Refers to *Delta Force,* a Canadian modification of *The Drilling Fields* material.]

Anon. "Nigeria Foaming." *Economist* (18–24 November 1995): 15–16.

Anon. "Shell Purges Top Staff in Nigeria." *Sunday Times* (London), 17 December 1995: 26.

Anon. "Shell Shocked." *The Times,* 23 November 1996.

[Leading article on Shell's shift.]

Anon. "UN Fact-Finding Mission Visits Nigeria." *The Nigerian News* (London), 15 April 1996: 3.

Anon. (special correspondent). "Under the Spotlight." *West Africa* (20–26 November 1995): 1797–1798.

[Account of events at the Auckland Commonwealth Summit.]

Ayetigbo, Ayodele. "Coffin to Abacha and Shell." *The U.S.-Nigeria Voice* 2, no. 17 (1995): 7–10.

———. "Saro-Wiwa on Our Minds." *The U.S.-Nigeria Voice* 2, no. 17 (1995): 5.

Bakhtin, M. M. "Epic and Novel." In *The Dialogic Imagination.* Ed. M. Holquist and C. Emerson. Austin: University of Texas Press, 1981.

Bates, Stephen, and Owen Bowcott. "Shell Undeterred by Nigeria Hangings." *Manchester Guardian Weekly* 153, no. 21 (19 November 1995): 1.

[Shell (24 percent) and its partners—the Nigerian Government (49 percent), Agip (10 percent), Elf (15 percent)—in Nigerian Liquefied Natural Gas will proceed with multibillion dollar gas and oil project, in spite of the executions and environmental concerns. The International Finance Corporation (World Bank subsidiary) "will not take up its former 2% interest in the plant."]

Bernstein, Dennis, and Leslie Kean. "War Crime: Rape of Ethnic Women Just Another Strategy for Burmese Army." *The Globe and Mail* (Toronto), 4 July 1998: D4.

Birnbaum, Michael. "New Victims of Nigerian 'Justice.'" *The Independent,* 21 November 1996.

[Reaction to Richard D. North's controversial 1996 article (see section on "Biographical Sources").

Black, Ian, Owen Bowcott, and John Vidal. "Nigeria Defies World with Writer's 'Judicial Murder.'" *The Guardian* (London), 11 November 1995.

Black, Ian, Peter Hillmore, and Adrian Hamilton. "Nigeria's Well-Oiled Machinery of Death." *The Observer,* 12 November 1995.

[Coverage of the Auckland Commonwealth conference and reaction to Saro-Wiwa's execution. Includes sidebars: "Abacha: The Idi Amin of West Africa" by Cameron Daodu and David Harrison, and "Bruised Mandela Says Too Little, Too Late" by Ian Black and Peter Beaumont.]

Bourne, Richard, et al. "Letters." *The Independent,* 11 November 1996.
[Reactions to Richard D. North's 1996 article (see section on "Biographical Resources").]

Boustany, Nina. "His Country Right or Wrong." *Washington Post,* 16 November 1995: D1, D2.
[Revealing account of the problems facing the Nigerian ambassador to the United States.]

Boyd, William. "Look What They Have Done to My Friend." *The Sunday Telegraph,* 15 November 1995.
[Describes how news came through of the trial; very critical of Mandela.]

Brutus, Dennis. "Poem for Ken Saro-Wiwa." *African Literature Association Bulletin* 22, no. 2 (Spring 1996): 35.

Burrell, Ian. "Vigils in Memory of Executed Dissident." *The Independent,* 9 November 1996: 5.
[Reports on the furor caused by Richard D. North's 1996 article (see section on "Biographical Resources").]

Clover, Charles. "Shell Backs 2.5bn Nigeria Deal." *Daily Telegraph,* 15 November 1995.

Clwyd, Ann. Letter to the Editor, *The Guardian,* 16 January 1995.
[Letter in support of Saro-Wiwa.]

Cohen, Mitchel. "Murder in Nigeria: Ordered by Shell and the IMF, Paid For by the U.S. Government." Red Balloon Collective broadside. New York: distributed by the Brecht Forum.

Cowe, Roger. "Shell Reports Show Its Green Side." *Guardian,* 22 May 1998: 25.
[Chris Fay, chairman and chief executive officer of Shell UK, acknowledged that "responsibilities to the environment, to the health, safety and welfare of our staff, and to a wider society will form an integral part of the way in which we do business."]

Drayton, Arthur D. "Good Morning, World." *ALA Bulletin* 22, no. 2 (Spring 1996): 5.
[Poem for Saro-Wiwa.]

Duodu, Cameron. "'Dance the Guns' Urges the Smuggled Message." *Gemini* (1995). Ref. GN34302.
[News service report, circulated to, for example, The Commonwealth Institute.]

———. "Hanged Activists Were Starved." *Observer,* 19 November 1995.
[A day-by-day account of the period from sentencing to execution.]

———. "Jailed Nigerian Writer Pledges Victory." *Observer,* 8 January 1995.
[Quotes extensively from a letter from prison, written in January 1995.]

———. "Mandela Vows to 'Explode the Volcano' Under Abacha." *Observer,* 26 November 1995.
[An account of an exclusive interview in which Mandela makes his case and outlines his action.]

ECCR (Ecumenical Committee for Corporate Responsibility). Document on Nigeria prepared 28 March 1996.
[Partly a report on a meeting with Mark Moody-Stuart, managing director of Shell, 22 March 1996.]

The Economist, 18 November 1995.

Enyinnaya, Innocent C. K. "Tribute to Ken Saro-Wiwa (1941–1995)" and "For Ken Saro-Wiwa." In *Ken Saro-Wiwa: The Life and Times.* Ed. S. Okechukwu Mezu. Randallstown, Md.: Black Academy Press, 1996: 115–118.

[Poems.]
Etete, Dan L. "Nigeria: The Untold Ogoni Story." *West Africa* (London), 27 November 1995: 1835–1836.
Everett-Green, Robert. "Dance of the Dialect." *The Globe and Mail* (Toronto), 29 October 1996: A12.
[On language, including references to *Sozaboy* and issues of the relationship between language and power.]
Ezenwa-Ohaeto. "Ken Saro-Wiwa: A Death Not in Our Stars." *African Literature Association Bulletin* 22, no. 1 (Winter 1996): 2.
Feuser, Willfried. "Report from the International Janheinz Jahn Symposium on Popular Culture in Africa." *African Literature Association Bulletin* 21, no. 4 (Fall 1995): 19–24.
Gates, Henry Louis, Jr. "Is There a Spark of Hope in Nigeria's Darkest Hour?" *Globe and Mail,* 16 December 1995: D4.
Graf, William D. *The Nigerian State: Political Economy, State Class and Political System in the Post-Colonial Era.* London: James Currey, 1988.
Greenpeace International. *Shell Shocked: The Environmental and Social Costs of Living with Shell in Nigeria.* Amsterdam: Greenpeace International, 1994.
The Guardian, 8 November 1995: 10–11.
Hadwen, Alden. "Morn [Morning] for Ken Saro-Wiwa." *Queen's Quarterly* 104, no. 4 (Winter 1997): 752.
[Two-stanza, nineteen-line poem.]
Hammer, Joshua. "Nigeria Crude: A Hanged Man and an Oil-Fouled Landscape." *Harper's* 292, no. 1753 (1996): 58–70.
Haygood, Wil. "Nigeria on Trial." *Boston Globe* , 7 April 1996: 1.
Hepple, George. "Poker Game with Death in Fragmenting Nigeria." *Sunday Times,* 5 November 1995.
[Good background material on Saro-Wiwa, oil in Nigeria, and the political scene. Anticipates a poker game that did not get going.]
Hirschman, Jack. "Poetry in Honor of Saro-Wiwa." *Social Justice* (Winter 1996).
Human Rights Watch/Africa. "Nigeria: The Ogoni Crisis: A Case Study of Military Oppression in Southeastern Nigeria." *Human Rights Watch/Africa* 7, no. 5 (1995): 1–44.
Hutchful, Eboe. *Political Economy of Nigeria.* London: Longman, 1985.
[Chapter 7 offers a substantive contribution: "Oil Companies and Environmental Pollution in Nigeria."]
Iloegbunam, Chuks. "The Death of a Writer." *The Guardian,* 11 November 1995: 30.
[A valuable summary, with a useful quote on secession—that it is not a viable option.]
———. "Obituary: Courageous Campaign of a Writer—Ken Saro-Wiwa." *The Guardian Weekly* 153, no. 21 (19 November 1995): 5.
[Biographical summary, with a bitingly ironic eulogy: "Somebody wanted to know the meaning of Saro-Wiwa's death. Simple. It means that nothing has changed."]
Jennings, John. "Chairman's Foreword." "The 'Shell' Transport and Trading Company, plc., Annual Report 1995." 1996: 1–3.
Johnson, Daniel. "Literary Giant with Common Touch." *Times,* 11 November 1995.
Jukewey, James. "Struggle for the Ogoni Homeland Spawns Accusations of Genocide." *Times,* 11 November 1995.

Kane, Joe. *Savages.* New York: Knopf, 1995.

Katz, Ian. "Press Adverts by Ogoni Chiefs' Sons Stirs Up Row." *The Guardian,* 8 December 1995.

[Reports that $136,000 had been paid for a two-page advertisement in the *New York Times* in support of the judgment on Saro-Wiwa. The letter was from a Philadelphia-based foundation of "family and friends" of the executed Chief Orage. Pro-Nigeria advertisements had appeared in newspapers in South Africa, Zimbabwe, and Ghana.]

Kiley, Sam. "Writer's Death on Gallows Marks Death of a Dark Age." *Times,* 11 November 1995.

Kimerling, Judith. *Amazon Crude.* San Francisco: National Resources Defense Council, 1991.

Kinnock, Glenys. "Nigeria Visa Protest." *The Times,* 23 November 1996.

[On the issuing of a visa to Tom Ikimi to visit the Netherlands.]

Kogbara, Donu. "Ken Saro-Wiwa Was Never a Saint." *The Independent,* 12 November 1996.

[Alleges she has suffered because of opposition to Saro-Wiwa's "canonization."]

———. "Persecuted Hero or Pet Prisoner of the Chattering Classes?" *Sunday Times,* 22 January 1995.

[See also her article in *Evening Standard,* 14 November 1995.]

———. "To Hell with Abacha and His Tinpot Dictatorship." *Sunday Times,* 12 November 1995.

Leavitt, Page. "Nigerian Lecturer Addresses Human Rights Abuses." *The Daily Texan,* 31 October 1996.

[Report on address to University of Texas students by Owens Wiwa.]

Leuzinga, Elay. *The Art of Black Africa.* London: Studio Vista, 1972.

[Quoted in *The Singing Anthill* on the abstraction of Ogoni masks.]

Lewis, Paul. "Nigerian Group Defends the Execution of 9 Nigerian Activists." *New York Times,* 7 December 1995: A15.

Makinde, Akin. "Transition to Martyrdom." *A. M. News,* 26 November 1995: 8.

McGreal, Chris. "Nigeria Aims for Facelift with PRO Video." *The Guardian,* 30 November 1995.

[Refers to "two hours of murky pictures and wobbly sound."]

———. "Nigerian Hangman Defends His Country's Honour." *The Guardian,* 27 November 1995.

[An interview with Dauda Muakomo, military governor of Rivers State. He directed the executions.]

———. "Spilt Oil Brews Up a Political Storm." *The Guardian* (London), 11 August 1993.

[As Vice President Admiral Augustus Aikhomu threatened imposition of a state of emergency, McGreal visited Ogoniland, spoke to Saro-Wiwa, and reported on pollution.]

———. "A Tainted Hero." *The Guardian Review,* 23 March 1996: 25–28.

[An article in which Saro-Wiwa is held responsible for creating the atmosphere in which the four Ogoni leaders were murdered. McGreal draws on a variety of sources and traces the development of divisions within Ogoni protest movements. On 30 March, letters appeared challenging various aspects of the article from Owens Saro-Wiwa, Roger Diski, Richard Boele, and Samuel Olorunsola Adenekan.]

———. "Why the Generals Feared Saro-Wiwa." *The Guardian Weekly* 153, no. 21 (13 November 1995): 4.

[Because the army could not quell Ogoni resistance, the army lost revenues. McGreal raises the question of whether Saro-Wiwa created a "climate of violence" against "vultures" and whether NYCOP was out of control. Notes that Saro-Wiwa's "pursuit of Ogoni interests sometimes at the expense of the quest for broader democratic change in Nigeria deprived him of more active backing beyond his own people."]

Mustafa, Abdul Raufu. "Tribute to Ken Saro-Wiwa." *Review of Political Economy* 66 (1995): 4762–4763.

Na'allah, Abdul-Rasheed, ed. *Ogoni's Agonies: Ken Saro-Wiwa and the Crisis in Nigeria.* With a preface by Kwame Anthony Appiah and a foreword by Biodun Jeyifo. Trenton, N.J.: Africa World Press, 1998: 81–101; 161–175; 199–226; 269–282; 319–326.

[Poems of varying quality, divided into five groups, on and about Saro-Wiwa and the Nigerian crisis. The sections are "Tribute and Condemnation"; "Inside/Out"; "Lament, Struggle"; "Works"; and "Politics, Satire." The poets and their respective poems are Tanure Ojaide, "Elegy for Nine Warriors"; Niyi Osundare, "The Man Who Asked Tall Questions"; Tayo Olafioye, "Ken Saro-Wiwa"; Jonathan Hart, "Remembrance of a Certain Death in Nigeria"; Felix W. J. Mnthali, "Farewell, Ken Saro-Wiwa!"; Doris Hambuch, "At Ken's"; Ezenwa-Ohaeto, "A Village Owns the Voice of the Cock"; Jacqueline Onyejiaka, "Tom-toms"; Kofi Mensah, "For Ken Saro-Wiwa"; Tayo Olafioye, "Ogoni People, the Oil Wells of Nigeria"; Abdul-Rasheed Na'allah, "Ogoni, the Eagle Birds' Agony in the Delta Woods"; Jacqueline Onyejiaka, "Ken's Blues"; Tanure Ojaide, "Delta Blues"; Marcielle Brandler, "Upon Receiving an Invitation to a Memorial for Ken Saro-Wiwa"; Haba G. Musengezi, "Thunder from the Mountains"; Jonathan Hart, "The Lie"; Oluwatoyin A. Asojo, "Why?"; Abdul-Rasheed Na'allah, "Daga ni sai kai"; Lisa Mahoney, "I Will Keep You in My Heart"; Abdul-Rasheed Na'allah, "Good Morning Nigeria"; Tanure Ojaide, "Wails"; Wumi Raji, "On Seeing a Dead Body at Oshodi"; Abdul-Rasheed Na'allah, "The Scorching Sun"; Jacqueline Onyejiaka, "Delta"; Andre Karl, "Slick Shells"; Ikhide R. Ikheloa, "Heavy Curtains"; Ronke Luke Boone, "But the Dream Was Stolen"; Jonathan Hart, "Tyrants"; Pius Adesanmi, "Siege"; Jacqueline Onyejiaka, "Not for Long"; Felix W. J. Mnthali, "Liberation in Our Time"; Olu Obafemi, "Towards the Light"; Abdul-Rasheed Na'allah, "Zani Fada—I Shall Fight!"; Sonia Atwal, "Fists That Can Move the Universe"; Olu Obafemi, "Sewing a Path from the Tatters"; Joseph Ushie, "Song of the Season"; Charles Burmeister, "My Red Beret"; Jacqueline Onyejiaka, "Crossroads"; Femi Dunmade, "Confession from a Sex Clinic"; Jonathan Hart, "The Sea"; Abdul-Rasheed Na'allah, "When Rain Falls"; Olu Obafemi, "Song of Hope"; Wumi Raji, "The Mosquito and the Ear"; Abdul-Rasheed Na'allah, "The Nigerian Cockroaches"; Tayo Olafioye, "The Million Naira March"; Abdul-Rasheed Na'allah, "Zomo and Bshiya in the Nigerian Forest"; Eze chi Chiazo, "Made in Nigeria."]

Nalley, Paul. *The Adventures of Kuru.* Port Harcourt, Nigeria: Saros International Publishers, 1992.

[56 pages; of interest because it is a Saros title not by Ken Saro-Wiwa and offers a sense of him as a publisher.]

The New Statesman and Society, 17 November 1995.

The New York Times, 26 January 1996.

Ngugi wa Thiongó. "Interview." *ALA Bulletin* 22, no. 2 (Spring 1996): 21–25.

[Includes a reference to Saro-Wiwa's death as part of a condemnation of the African human rights record.]

Niboro, Ima. "Shell's Racism in the Delta." *Tell* (Lagos), 18 August 1997: 28–31.
[Remembering the Ogoni struggle in 1994. People and events in Shell's operations are discussed.]

Nigerian Government. *Nigeria: The Ogoni Crisis: The Truth of the Matter.* Lagos: The Federal Ministry of Information and Culture, n.d.
[The government's perspective, with appendixes: Saro-Wiwa letter to T. Garrick on "The Ogoni Bill of Rights"; Ralph Egbu's "The Ogoniland Massacre," *The Sentinel*, no. 15, 6 June 1994.]

Nigerian High Commission, London. "The Conviction of Ken Saro-Wiwa." *The Independent,* 6 December 1995: 15.

Nixon, Rob. "The Oil Weapon." *New York Times,* 17 November 1995.

Nnadozie, Emmanuel U. *Oil and Socio-economic Crisis in Nigeria.* Lewiston: Edwin Mellen Press, 1995.

Nnolim, Charles. "To Ken Saro-Wiwa and Ogoni Irredenta (a Poetic Tribute in Macaronic)." *ALA Bulletin* 21, no. 4 (Fall 1995): 9–10.
[A poem, republished in *Ken Saro-Wiwa: The Life and Times.* Ed. S. Okechukwu Mezu. Randallstown, Md.: Black Academy Press, 1996: 119–121.]

Nwagboso, Maxwell. *A Message from the Madhouse.* Saros Star Series 13. Port Harcourt, Nigeria: Saros International Publishers, 1991.
[ISBN 9782460176; 136 pages; of interest because it is a Saros title not by Ken Saro-Wiwa and offers a sense of him as a publisher.]

Nwakanma, Obi. "Ken Saro-Wiwa: The Heart of a God." *Sunday Vanguard,* 30 October 1994: 7, 11.

———. "Ken Saro-Wiwa: Time and the Man." *Sunday Vanguard,* 5 November 1995: 3.

Nwoko, Chinedu Munir. "Why Sanctions Against Nigeria Are Not the Answer." *Caribbean Times,* 16 December 1995: 5.
[Quotes from *Nigerian Tide,* 23 May 1994, on perambulation of Edward Kobani's head around shrines. Refers to Donu Kogbara's November article (see citation earlier in this section). Provides a version of what happened in Gokana in May 1994—Saro-Wiwa was stopped because he was campaigning outside his constituency: "Infuriated at the refusal of the security forces to allow him to proceed, he incited his men against the people at the reception as being responsible for the situation." Nwoko argues for the tribunal and for Gen. Sani Abacha's confirmation of the sentence. Makes excuses for Abacha. The final paragraph indicates a concern for image.]

Obasanjo, Olusegun. *My Command: An Account of the Nigerian Civil War.* London: Heinemann, 1981.

'Obe, Ab'obe. "Sanctions for Sanity." *The Guardian,* 13 November 1995.

Obijiofor, Levi. "Writers Against Writers." *Guardian,* 14 January 1989: 11.
[Book launch debate.]

Obituaries. *The Daily Telegraph,* 11 November 1995.
[Reports that *Basi and Company* had been seen on cable in the UK and that Saro-Wiwa was a graduate assistant at Negerioa (*sic*) University. Quotes from what seem to be the tribunal's findings: "it was established beyond all doubt that he set up the machinery that consumed the four Ogoni leaders."]

Obiwu [Obi Iwuanyanwu]. "What Ken Saro-Wiwa Told Me." *The Legend,* 31 December 1995: 6–7.

Oculi, Okello. "Saro-Wiwa: A Revolutionary's Mistake." *The Guardian,* 19 November 1995: A12.

Ofuoko, Mudiaga. "Divided by Money." *Newswatch* (Lagos), 18 August 1997: 25–27.

[Examines the situation in Eruemukohwoarien, in Ughelli North. Shell is accused of colluding with corrupt elders.]

Ojaide, Tanure. "We Are Many" and "Ughelli" in his collection *Labyrinths of the Delta.* Greenfield Center, N.Y.: Greenfield Review Press, 1986: 72, 74.

[Poems on the despoliation of the Delta region.]

Ojo, Eddie Ayo. "Ken Saro-Wiwa's 'Yorubaphobia.'" In *Ken Saro-Wiwa: The Life and Times.* Ed. S. Okechukwu Mezu. Randallstown, Md.: Black Academy Press, 1996: 146–148.

[Reprint from *Sunday Times* (Lagos), 9 September 1990. Poorly written condemnation of Saro-Wiwa's tribal politics.]

Okafor, Obiora Chinedu. "In Spite of the Crucifix? International Law, Human Rights, and the Allegory of the Ogoni Question." African Studies Association Conference, Hyatt Embarcadero Center, San Francisco, 23 November 1996.

Oke, Sola. "On the Question of Minorities." In *Ken Saro-Wiwa: The Life and Times.* Ed. S. Okechukwu Mezu. Randallstown, Md.: Black Academy Press, 1996: 142–145.

[Reprinted from *Sunday Times* (Lagos), 9 September 1990. Addressed to Sir Kay; attacks the perceived elitism that is found within all ethnic groups; calls for engagement with substantive issues, not "shadows" (p. 145).]

Olatunbosun, Tokunbo. "Right on National Question, Ogoni Issue, Wrong on 'Yorubaphobia.'" In *Ken Saro-Wiwa: The Life and Times.* Ed. S. Okechukwu Mezu. Randallstown, Md.: Black Academy Press, 1996: 149–152.

[Reprinted from *Sunday Times* (Lagos), 14 October 1990.]

Olojede, Dele. "Human Rights: Licensed to Crush." *The Guardian,* 14 June 1995: 27.

[Reports that Capt. Tunde Odina admitted that the Internal Security Task Force had been given orders to destroy five Ogoni villages.]

Olorunyomi, Sola. "Just Before the Blackout." *Glendora Review* (Lagos) 1, no. 3 (1996): 22–23.

[A dialogue with a cockroach, written while in jail during 1995.]

Olowo, Bola. "The Furor over Saro-Wiwa." *West Africa,* 27 November–3 December 1995: 1833–1834.

[Covers responses in South Africa; Nigeria; Auckland, New Zealand; and Washington, D.C. David Atta, press secretary to Gen. Sani Abacha, called Saro-Wiwa a mass murderer.]

———. "Out on Themselves." *West Africa,* 13–19 November 1995: 1757.

[On splits within the Ogoni protest movement.]

———. "Saro-Wiwa Convicted." *West Africa,* 13–19 November 1995: 1756–1757.

———. "The Shell Factor." *West Africa,* 27 November–3 December 1995: 1834.

[Brief history of oil extraction in the Delta; compares figures on costs and gains of exploration.]

Onyeama, Dillibe. *A Nigger at Eton.* London: Leslie Frewin, 1972.

[Background on Nigerians at Eton.]

Orr, David. "Generals Move to the Offensive." *The Independent,* 25 November 1995.

[On Gen. Sani Abacha's actions following the outcry over the executions.]

———. "How Shell Won over a Village with Cash and Cigarettes." *Tempo,* 14 December 1995: 12.

[See also, "Shell Wins over Village with Cash and Liquor." *Independent,* 1 December 1995. Account of events at Sangama village when Shell wanted to move in with a rig.]

Osaghae-Eghosa, E. "The Ogoni Uprising: Oil Politics, Minority Agitation and the Future of the Nigerian State." *African Affairs* 376 (July 1995): 325–344.

[Includes analysis of Saro-Wiwa's leadership role.]

Osondu, E. C., ed. *For Ken, for Nigeria.* Lagos: Service International, 1996.

[An anthology of poetry by Nigerians, in support of Saro-Wiwa.]

Owouwari, Simon. "'Smoking Is Really Not Good, Ken.'" In *Ken Saro-Wiwa: The Life and Times.* Ed. S. Okechukwu Mezu. Randallstown, Md.: Black Academy Press, 1996: 134–135.

[Reprinted from *Sunday Times* (Lagos), 3 June 1990. Owouwari says that as a public figure, Saro-Wiwa should set a healthy example.]

Oyatomi, Kunle. "Different Strokes: Ken Saro-Wiwa Looks Death in the Face." *Sunday Vanguard,* 5 November 1995: 20.

Pallister, David. "Archbishop Changes Tune in Nigerian Charm Offensive." *The Guardian,* 16 December 1995.

[On bizarre behavior by emissaries from Gen. Sani Abacha to UK and United States.]

———. "Nigerian Tribe Puts Environment on Election Agenda." *The Guardian* (London), 17 May 1993.

[On the disturbances by Ogonis that might delay 12 June election; quotes from Saro-Wiwa.]

Panter-Brick, Keith, ed. *Soldiers and Oil: The Political Transformation of Nigeria.* London: Cass, 1978.

Povey, John F. "The Nigerian War: The Writer's Eye." *Journal of African Studies* (Fall 1974) 1.

Purvis, Andrew. "*Time* Man of the Year: Africa, Ken Saro-Wiwa." *Tell,* 1 January 1996: 33.

Raji, Wumi. "Oil Resources: Hegemonic Politics and the Struggle for Re-inventing Post-colonial Nigeria." In *Ogoni's Agonies: Ken Saro-Wiwa and the Crisis in Nigeria.* Ed. Abdul Rasheed Na'allah. Trenton, N.J.: Africa World Press, 1998: 109–120.

[An analysis of the complicity between Shell and the Nigerian government, as well as an indication of change: "We all stand at the door-post of history."]

Rake, Alan. "Hit Abacha Where It Hurts." *New African* (London), January 1996: 11–12.

[On the need for concerted action, with some background on corruption in Nigeria and its relationship to oil income.]

———. "Nigeria's Life Blood Up for Sale." *New African* (London), February 1997: 30.

[The Nigerian government announces plans to privatize the oil industry with the backing of the International Monetary Fund and the International Bank for Reconstruction and Development. Indicates that the sale would benefit the oil companies and those in power in Abuja.]

———. "Saro-Wiwa." *New African* (London), January 1996: 8–10.

[Quotes Komo and Okuntimo in the course of an impassioned statement about the injustice that Saro-Wiwa experienced.]

Riemenschneider, Dieter. "Biafra War in Nigerian Literature." In *Jaw Bones and Umbilical Cords.* Ed. Ulla Schild. Berlin: D. Reimer Verlag, 1984.

Roddick, Anita. "Shell Must Heed the Danger." *Guardian,* 28 November 1995.

[Challenges Shell employees to search their consciences.]

———. "Shell Should Speak Out to Help the Ogoni." *Financial Times,* 1 November 1995.

[Draws on Michael Birnbaum (see section on "Biographical Resources").]

———. "Shell Should Wash Its Dirty Hands." *New Statesman* (London) 125 (8 November 1996): 10.

Rowell, Andy. "Shell Shocked." *Village Voice,* 21 November 1995: 21–23.

Rowohlt Publishers. "Shell Blocks Saro-Wiwa's Book." *Sunday Vanguard,* 11 February 1996: 1–2.

Russell, Alex. "Fear and Intimidation in Ogoni Heartland." *The Sunday Telegraph,* 12 November 1995: 29.

[Reports on a visit to Ogoniland "last month"—a cowed people, victims of military; notes excesses of young people in MOSOP.]

———. "Mandela Urges Oil Embargo on Nigerian Regime." *This Day,* 19 November 1995: 17.

[Excerpted from *Daily Telegraph,* 16 November 1995.]

Sekoni, Ropo. *Folk Poetics: A Sociosemiotic Study of Yoruba Trickster Tales.* Westport, Conn.: Greenwood, 1994: 117–120.

[Includes a section on "The Trickster in Contemporary Tele-Fiction."]

Shell Briefing Notes. "Developments in Nigeria," March 1995.

———. "The Ogoni Issue," January 1995.

———. "Operations in Nigeria," May 1994.

———. "Statement of General Business Practices."

Shiner, Cindy. "Nigerian Writer Awaits Verdict." *The Guardian,* 31 October 1995.

Soyinka, Wole. "The Writer in a Modern African State." In *The Writer in Modern Africa.* Ed. Per Wastberg. New York: Africana Publishing Corp., 1969.

———. "The Failure of the Writer in Africa." In *The Africa Reader: Independent Africa.* Ed. Wilfred Cartey and Martin Kilson. New York: Random House, 1970.

Stremlau, John J. *The International Politics of the Nigerian Civil War, 1967–1970.* Princeton: Princeton University Press, 1977.

Thompson, Bature. "Killings Reveal Divided Nigeria." *The Independent,* 18 November 1995.

U.S. Senate, Subcommittee on African Affairs, Committee on Foreign Relations. 20 July 1995. "The Situation in Nigeria." S. Hrg. 104–206. Washington, D.C.: U.S. Government Printing Office.

Vidal, John. "EcoSoundings." *The Guardian,* 20 September 1994: 24.

[Asserted that £2 million given by Shell did not reach the Ogoni. Says the company should apologize for misleading the public.]

The Village Voice, 21 November 1995: 21–23.

Wachuku, Ugonna. "Still No Salvation in Ogoniland." *New African* (London), February 1997: 31.

[Refers to European Community sanctions following execution of Saro-Wiwa and creation of Dayelsa State—a sop to the Ogonis with capital at Gokana. It has no budget, and the army remains in control.]

Wambu, Onyekachi. "Ken Saro-Wiwa—a Lamb to the Slaughter." *Voice,* 21 November 1995: 21.

Weaver, Martin, and Philip Johnston. "Outrage in Nigeria. . . ." *Daily Telegraph,* 11 November 1995: 1, 2.

[Quotes Prime Minister John Major, U.S. secretary of state Madeline Albright, and Saro-Wiwa. Refers to the writer as an "old Etonian."]

Welch, Claude E., Jr. "The Ogoni and Self-determination Increasing Violence in Nigeria." *Journal of Modern African Studies* 33, no. 4 (December 1995): 635–649.

Withers, Kate. "Zina's Way." *International Women's Festival Programme,* Bristol (Spring 1996): 5.

[Profile on Zina Saro-Wiwa, a nineteen-year-old student at Bristol University, who has ambivalent feelings about Nigeria.]

The Contributors

Misty L. Bastian is an assistant professor in the Department of Anthropology, Franklin and Marshall College (United States). She is coeditor of *Great Ideas for Teaching About Africa.*

Chris Dunton teaches in the Department of English at the University of the North West (South Africa). He has taught at universities in Nigeria, Libya, and Lesotho. Among his publications are *Wole Soyinka's Three Short Plays* (Longman), *Make Man Talk True: Nigerian Drama in English Since 1970* (Hans Zell), and *Nigerian Theatre: A Critical Bibliography.*

Maureen N. Eke is a professor of comparative literature at Central Michigan University (United States).

James Gibbs is a professor in the Department of English at the University of the West of England (UK). He has also taught at the Universities of Ghana, Malawi, Nigeria, Bristol, and Liège and has directed and acted in Ghana, Malawi, and Nigeria. He has published extensively on the work of Wole Soyinka, most recently *Research on Wole Soyinka*, coedited with Bernth Lindfors.

John LeBlanc is a professor of English at Okanagan University College (Canada). His research is in the area of Caribbean studies, as well as popular culture: music and film.

John Lent is a Canadian poet and short story writer. His collected works include *A Rock Solid, Wood Lake Music, Frieze, The Face in the Garden,* and *Monet's Garden.* He is currently at work on a novel and a new collection of short stories.

Charles Lock is a professor at the University of Copenhagen (Denmark).

Joseph McLaren is a professor of comparative literature at Hofstra University (United States).

Craig W. McLuckie is a professor of English at Okanagan University College's Kalamalka Campus (Canada). His work on African literatures has appeared in *Black American Literature Forum, Twentieth Century Literature,* and *Research in African Literatures.*

Aubrey McPhail is a lecturer at the College of the Rockies (Canada). He is a contributor to *The 1890s: An Encyclopedia of British Literature, Art, and Culture.*

Laura Neame is a librarian at Okanagan University College (Canada). Founder and former editor of the quarterly journal *CD-ROM News,* she has presented and published in a number of forums and received the 1992 Micromedia Canada award for contributions to libraries.

Rob Nixon is an associate professor of English at Columbia University (United States). His books include *London Calling: V.S. Naipaul, Post-Colonial Mandarin* and *Homelands, Harlem, and Hollywood: South African Culture and the World Beyond* as well as a memoir, *Dreambirds.*

Tanure Ojaide, a Nigerian poet, has published seven collections of poetry and two books of literary essays. A professor at the University of North Carolina (United States), he has won major national and international poetry awards, including the Commonwealth Poetry Prize for the Africa Region (1987), the BBC Arts and Africa Poetry Award (1988), the All-Africa Okigbo Prize for Poetry (1988), and twice the Association of Nigerian Authors' Poetry Prize (1988 and 1994). His memoir, *Great Boys: An African Childhood,* was published in 1998.

Ross Tyner, librarian, farmer, and community activist, is currently conducting research on the life and works of Kenneth Arthur Nortje.

Index

Abacha, Gen. Sani, 5, 12, 14, 46, 64,
    110, 116, 118–120, 122, 123,
    124n11, 127, 129, 131, 134–137,
    140, 148, 150n7, 236, 244, 276
ABC. *See* African Books Collective
Abiola, Moshood, 134, 243, 244
Aburi Agreement, 239
Achebe, Chinua, 3, 32, 54, 59–60, 63,
    66, 88, 103, 123, 136, 160, 162–163,
    177, 207
African Books Collective (ABC),
    155–156, 167–168
African National Congress (ANC),
    118–119
African Publishers Network (APNET),
    167
Aguiyi-Ironsi, Gen., 35, 40, 42, 56, 238
Ahiara Declaration, 243
Akpan, N. U., 237
Ala/Ani. *See* Earth deity
Amadi, Elechi, 50; *Estrangement,* 35;
    Ethics in Nigerian Culture, 35, 39;
    Sunset in Biafra, 35–39, 41
Amnesty International, 114, 115, 131
Amuka, Sam, 153
Awolowo, Chief Obafemi, 240
Azikiwe, Nnamdi, 238

Babangida, Gen. Ibrahim, 23, 47, 135,
    243
Bakhtin, M. M., 7, 8, 85n4, 86

Balewa, Alhaji Abubakar, 35, 238
Banjo, Lt. Col. Victor, 32, 56, 241
Biafra, resistance to, 43
Boro, Isaac, 56, 238
Boyd, William, 88, 103, 104, 110, 114,
    123, 155
Brecht, Bertolt, 208, 211n5
Brutus, Dennis, 24–25
Buhari, Gen. Mohammadu, 23, 243

Christianity, 142–143, 189
Chukwuma, Innocent, 118–119
Clark-Bekederemo, J. P., 54, 56, 59,
    60, 63, 66, 165
Commonwealth Summit (Aukland), 5,
    118, 135, 276, 282
Conrad, Joseph, 122, 163

De Certeau, Michel, 147
De Klerk, F. W., 119
Democratic Alternative, 119
De St. Jorre, John, 237
Dialogue, use of, 202–203
Diary, genre of, 46, 48–49

Earth deity (Ala/Ani), 131, 136–137
Ekwensi, Cyprian, 178
Eliot, T. S., 7, 62
Emecheta, Buchi, 179
Environmentalism, 115, 120–122
Esu/Eshu, 100, 105n1, 179–183, 185

Ethnicity, 110, 111, 115–116
Ethnocentrism, 117
Eyi-Acquah, Kobena, 54
Ezenwa-Ohaeto, 40, 45

Fajuyi, Lt. Col. Adekunle, 32, 33
Fanon, Frantz, 88, 92–95
Feuser, Willfried, 75
Foucault, Michel, 134, 137

Gide, André, 110, 121
Gogol, N., 204–205
Gowon, Lt. Col. Yakubu, 36, 37, 40,
    42, 50, 51n4, 55, 238, 239, 240, 243
Greenpeace, 4, 5, 6, 18, 115, 131
Gwala, Mafika, 113

Hanging, and Ibo beliefs, 136
Heinemann African Writers Series, 155,
    159, 162
Human Rights Watch, 18, 131

Indigenous colonization, 47, 50
International Monetary Fund (IMF), 24,
    133, 283
Inyama, N. F., 70, 74
Irele, Abiola, 85, 160

Kazantzakis, Nikos, 78
Kobani, Chief Edward: murder of, 46,
    279, 281
Komo, Col. Dauda Musa: administrator
    of execution, 129–130, 138

Lent, John, 215–216
Liminality, 180. *See also* Turner, Victor
Lindfors, Bernth, 245
Literacy, 163–165

Macmillan Publishers, 161
Mandela, Nelson, 5, 118–119, 124n12
Marginalization, 54, 65, 88
Mbeki, Thabo, 118
McIlvanney, William, 29, 31
Memoirs, as genre, 29–31
Mezu, Rose Ure, 69, 85n1, 85n2, 86n5,
    86n6
Minorities, 17–25, 35–45, 47, 50, 54,
    65, 110
Mohammed, Gen. Murtala, 243
Movement for the Survival of the
    Ogoni People (MOSOP), 4, 19, 46,

47, 65, 105, 114–115, 129, 131, 135,
    138, 149n2, 210
Mphahlele, Ezekiel, 88, 118
Mythology, African, 180–185

Naijanet, 139–140
National Youth Council of the Ogoni
    People (NYCOP), 129
Ngugi wa Thiongó, 48, 51n7, 103, 113
Nigerian Civil War, 10, 11, 20–21,
    31–45, 87, 237–244
Nigerian Newsprint Manufacturing
    Company, 155
Nigerian publishing, 156–162;
    language in, 162–163; mass market,
    163–165
Nigerian Television Authority (NTA),
    165
Nzeogwu, Maj. Chukwuma Kaduna,
    36, 90

Obasanjo, Gen. Olusegun, 32, 45, 129,
    134, 243, 244
Ogoni, 4–6, 18–26, 109–116, 127,
    130–132; activism and discourse,
    127–149; Igbo relations, 20. *See also*
    Movement for the Survival of the
    Ogoni People; National Youth
    Council of the Ogoni People
Ogoni Central Union, 20
Ogoni State Representative Assembly
    (OSRA), 20
Ogunde, Hubert, 181
Ojaide, Tanure: "The Chieftain and His
    Tribe," 227; "Delta Blues," 218–219;
    "Elegy for Nine Warriors," 221–225;
    "A General Sickness," 228; "I Will
    Save My Enemy," 226; "My Drum
    Beats Itself," 217; "Sleeping in a
    Makeshift Grave," 220; "Ughelli," 55
Ojukwu, Lt. Col. Chukwuemeka
    Odumegwu, 11, 32, 36, 37, 43, 51n4,
    55, 237–243
Okara, Gabriel: *The Voice,* 207–208
Omotoso, Kole, 118
Organization of African Unity (OAU),
    241

Pascal, R., 30
Postcolonial theory, 88, 104, 161

Rape, 44–45

Rivers State, 38, 42, 56, 234, 239–242

Said, Edward, 48
Saro-Wiwa, Ken, general: activism,
109–115, 122–123, 127–128, 131,
132, 136; administrator, 44–45;
aesthetic, 160, 163–167, 177–179,
245; alienation, 54, 57; children's
literature, 177–200; Commonwealth
Writers Prize, 69; corruption, 13;
drama, 201–214; environmental
rights, 6; estate, 170–171; execution
of, 4, 49, 116, 128–140, 148,
151n15; Hauwa (wife), 233; Ken
(son), 135, 154, 156, 159–160, 167,
171; language, 6–8, 15; literature,
9–10; Maria (wife), 58, 62, 234;
memoirs, 29–52; metaphor use, 41;
nonfiction, 3–16; Noo (daughter),
235; novels, 87–108; Owens
(brother), 5, 135; politics and the
environment, 17–28, 109–126; Saros
International Publishing, 153–156,
158–165, 168, 235; short-fiction,
69–86; style, 40; as symbol,
134–138; Tedum (son), 235; trial of,
5; Washington, D.C., demonstration,
140–147; wealth and society, 10–13;
women, 84
Saro-Wiwa, Ken, works: "Acapulco
Motel," 80–81; *Adaku and Other
Stories,* 83–85; *Basi and Company,*
9, 10, 12, 42, 53, 93, 113, 153,
164–166, 197, 201, 281; "The
Bonfire," 75–76; "Case No. 100,"
80; "Corpses Have Grown," 58; "Dis
Nigeria Sef," 56, 64, 65, 154; "The
Divorcee," 76–77; *Dream of Sologa,*
207–210; "The Drilling Fields," 4;
"The Empire Builders," 83; *Eneka,*
208–210; "Epitaph for Biafra,"
63–64; "A Family Affair," 73–75; *A
Forest of Flowers,* 53, 69–83, 155,
166, 168; *Genocide in Nigeria,*
17–26, 110, 113–114, 116–117, 122;
"High Life," 8, 79–80; "Home,
Sweet Home," 71–72; "The
Inspector Calls," 72–73; "A Legend
on Our Streets," 78–79; *Lemona's
Tale,* 168, 170; "A Message from
Adama," 84; *A Month and a Day,* 11,
46–49, 51n6, 95, 109, 110, 112,
114–117, 128, 168, 170, 233, 246;
Mr. B, 164, 166, 181–199; "Near the
Front," 60; *Nigeria: The Brink of
Disaster,* 110, 113; "Night
Encounter," 59; "Ogale—An
Evacuated Town," 58–59; the *Ogoni
Bill of Rights,* 24; *The Ogoni Nation
Today and Tomorrow,* 17, 96;
"Ogoni! Ogoni!" 3–4; *On a Darkling
Plain,* 11, 21, 39–45, 55, 56, 57, 64,
116, 154, 158, 233; "Papa," 82–83;
"Prayer on a Moonlight Night," 60;
Prisoners of Jebs, 153; "Robert and
the Dog," 81–82; *Segi Finds the
Radio,* 197; *Songs in a Time of War,*
53–67, 154–155; *Sozaboy,* 7–8,
14–15, 50, 53, 70, 79, 85n3, 88–104,
112, 154, 168; *The Supreme
Commander,* 204–207; *Tambari in
Dukana,* 158; "Thoughts in Time of
War," 64; "To Saroguna, Rain
Maker," 61; *The Transistor Radio,*
165, 170, 197, 201, 203; "Voices,"
57; "War Games," 57; *The Wheel,*
202–203, 205–207; "Yoor Zaansin
Ogoni", 48
Second-Tier Foreign Exchange Market
(SFEM), 156–157
Shell Petroleum, 3, 5, 13–14, 17,
21–23, 53–61, 109–113, 116–117,
119–121, 127, 129, 131–134, 149,
171, 275–279, 282–284
Soyinka, Wole: 24, 25n1, 37, 50, 54,
63, 66, 103, 123, 135, 150n10, 181,
203–204; *The Man Died,* 31–34, 35,
42, 53, 57; *The Open Sore of a
Continent,* 46, 49, 50; *A Shuttle in
the Crypt,* 32–33, 53, 61–62

Texaco, 120–121
Trickster. *See* Esu/Eshu
Turner, Victor, 180

Unrepresented Nations and Peoples
Organization (UNPO), 25, 114–115

Vincent, Theo, 54, 65, 154

Webb, Hugh, 39
World Bank, 156, 157

Zell, Hans, 155, 161

About the Book

The shocking execution of Ken Saro-Wiwa at the hands of the Nigerian government in 1995 stirred new interest in the many facets of his life—as novelist and short story writer, radio and television personality, publisher and entrepreneur, political and environmental activist. This interdisciplinary collection critically assesses Saro-Wiwa's exceptional life and work from a range of fresh perspectives.

The authors examine Saro-Wiwa's literary output both in terms of literary criticism and within a political framework. They give equal attention to his more public roles, including public reaction within Nigeria to his work. A comprehensive, annotated bibliography of print and electronic resources on Saro-Wiwa is an indispensable feature of the book.

Craig W. McLuckie is professor of English at Okanagan University College in British Columbia. He is author of *Nigerian Civil War Literature* and coeditor of *Critical Perspectives on Dennis Brutus*. **Aubrey McPhail** is in the English Department at the College of the Rockies.

DATE DUE